Trust: Interdisciplinary Perspectives

Volume 3

More information about this series at http://www.springer.com/series/15199

Takashi Inoguchi • Lien Thi Quynh Le

The Development of Global Legislative Politics

Rousseau and Locke Writ Global

Springer

Takashi Inoguchi
Institute of Asian Cultures
J.F. Oberlin University
Tokyo, Japan

Lien Thi Quynh Le
College of Economics
Hue University
Hue, Vietnam

ISSN 2509-7679 ISSN 2509-7903 (electronic)
Trust: Interdisciplinary Perspectives
ISBN 978-981-32-9388-5 ISBN 978-981-32-9389-2 (eBook)
https://doi.org/10.1007/978-981-32-9389-2

This Springer imprint is published by the registered company Springer Nature Singapore Pte Ltd.
The registered company address is: 152 Beach Road, #21-01/04 Gateway East, Singapore 189721, Singapore

Endorsements

Profs. Inoguchi and Le's book is not only innovative, informative and path-breaking, but they are also addressing the need for a world government – an issue that is gaining traction by the day. Very wisely, the authors anchor their propositions in the theories of Rousseau and Locke. From that start point, they check to what extent the conditions that were present when they developed their ideas, are somehow evolving today in a similar manner.

—Miguel E Basáñez, Professor of Values, Cultures and Development, the Fletcher School, Tufts University

The surging revolutions of digitalization and globalization over the past three decades have led to the fundamental transformation of global politics. Takashi Inoguichi and Lien T.Q. Le develop a new theoretical paradigm of global politics that links shifts in citizens' value preferences to those in their states' participation in multilateral treaties. Their highly innovative qualitative and quantitative analyses of multinational polls and multilateral treaties offer invaluable contributions to the study of global politics. Anyone who is concerned about the future of increasingly contentious global politics should read this brisk volume.

—Doh Chull Shin, Jack W. Peltason Scholar in Residence, Center for the Study of Democracy, University of California, Irvine

Inoguchi and Le have developed a genuinely original perspective on world politics, one that opens up a new research agenda for thinking about state and global actors simultaneously. Global problem-solving in the 21st century may well require global legislative processes without global government.

—Anne-Marie Slaughter, Bert G. Kerstetter '66 University Professor Emerita of Politics and International Affairs, Princeton University

Few books touch the intellectual and spiritual life of people as much as does "Trust– Interdisciplinary Perspectives." This is a remarkably rich book which warrants a broad range of highly critical readers. This is one of those books that warrants a global readership given its emphasis on the implied trust that we invest in public institutions as viewed from an interdisciplinary perspective. This is an issue of critical assessment for all of us in leadership positions of promoting high levels of trust at all levels of social, political, economic, and social organization. This book belongs on the shelves of every serious thinker.

—Richard J. Estes, Professor of Social Policy & Practice, University of Pennsylvania, Philadelphia, Pennsylvania

The Inoguchi and Le book is innovative and distinctive in carving out a new way to look at "global legislative politics." I do not know of anything that compares in this interesting and novel niche of international relations analysis.

—William R. Thompson, Distinguished Professor and Rogers Chair of Political Science Emeritus, Indiana University

Inoguchi and Le offer a fresh answer to the puzzle of what some have called the 'increasing normativization' of the international system since World War II, a process which has accelerated since the 1970s. While some have attributed this growth of international normative commitments among states to ideological change among elites or to the needs of globalization, the authors instead link the proliferation of international treaties to broad changes in the values adhered to by global publics. This is an original and stimulating hypothesis, which they support with a range of ingenious empirical tests.

—Andrew J. Nathan, Class of 1919 Professor of Political Science, Columbia University

Preface

The theory of global legislative politics is an attempt to carry out a "perspective revolution" (Zakaria 1997, cited in Funabashi 2019, p.227) in the study of global politics. Not only does it look at global politics from an unusual angle but also generate an entirely new bundle of data and analyze it with an empirical and scientific spirit. The orthodox Westphalian theory of international relations is constructed by its primordial actors, i.e., sovereign states, and two major sources of power, i.e., might and wealth. The Cold War theory of international relations has added ideology as the third major source as the Cold War period was characterized by the division between capitalist democracy and communist dictatorship. After the Cold War, two new ideologies claimed as the only game in town: democracy (Fukuyama 1992) and civilization (Huntington 1997), as key sources of power of sovereign states. During the thirty years of crisis (1989–2019), these two kinds of claimants receded to some extent as digitalized globalization has transformed the configuration of the world map in terms of might and wealth, while the third ideological sources of power have been inadvertently dizzied and muzzled with democracy being contaminated by the rise of illiberal democracy and with civilization being conflated by ethnic and religious factors. Here, the newcomer called global legislative politics can be claimed as a new "perspective revolutionary" of a sort in that rather than thinking about the power sources of sovereign states, this theory formulates state interactions as a bundle of global quasi-social contracts while it analyzes state participation in multilateral treaties as the outcomes of the global quasi-legislative behavior of sovereign states. This fresh and unusual perspective sheds new lights on post-Cold War global politics, focusing on speed, angle, and strategy adopted by sovereign states' decision on joining or not joining multilateral treaties to reveal varying types of engagement, both internal and external, of sovereign states.

This study is the first systematic and scientific study of global quasi-legislation with a global scope, taking into account individual values and opinions. In the seventeenth to eighteenth centuries, an era of preindustrial revolution, neither Jean-Jacques Rousseau nor John Locke could have anticipated digitalized globalization. Yet this key feature of the twenty-first century (especially the Internet and transnational organizations) illustrates how relevant Rousseau's and Locke's social contract theories are in the realm of global politics. Considering public opinion and multilateral agreements as the international equivalent to national elections and passing laws on the national scale and extending nation-state concepts to a global society, we analyze citizens' preferences, as measured in the 2005–2009 World Values Survey of 93 states, alongside states' willingness to enter into 120 multilateral treaties. By finding some links between these two data sets, in Part I, we take the first step toward conceptualizing quasi-legislative global politics as a bundle of global quasi-social contracts. In Part II, we examine how each of the 193 states manifests its quasi-legislative behavior by factor-analyzing six instrumental variables including the treaty participation index and six policy domains of multilateral treaties, i.e., (a) peace and disarmament; (b) trade, commerce, and communication; (c) human rights; (d) intellectual property; (e) environment; and (f) labor, health, and safety, and modified Welzel world regional groups. The yielded dimensions of behavior relate to a sovereign state's speed, angle, and strategy. Global quasi-legislative behavior differs from country to country. Thus, a study on participation in multilateral treaties is conceptualized from a combined consideration of the joiner's foreign policy and transnational policy. In Part III, we deal with the characterization of global politics during the 30-year period (crisis of 1989–2019) from which the following three theories of global politics were born: theory of power transition, theory of civilizational clash, and theory of global legislative politics. After conducting conceptual and empirical examinations to rethink the three theories, this study concludes that the theory of global legislative politics is politics on the basis of an awareness that this world constitutes the global common goods in which the entire world could aspire to and abide by safely with mutual gains and losses.

This book introduces the perspective revolution in empirical international relations research, asking the question whether those ideas of social contract of Jean-Jacques Rousseau's and John Locke's can be writ global. To answer the question, three tasks are carried out. First, Chaps. 2, 3, 4, and 5 deploy the concept of global quasi-social contracts and produce the good results of conceptualizing global social contract as a bundle of global quasi-legislative behavior by sovereign states and verifying the rough convergence between global citizens' preference about value orientation and sovereign states' orientation in participating in multilateral treaties. The limitation of citizens' preference data and the problem of matching data on citizens' value orientation and states' treaty orientation on top of the insufficient articulations of social contract by the two philosophers at times of preindustrial revolution and pre-digitalized globalization make the results less than definitive. Thus, this book begins as a metaphor and ends as one strident step forward in empirical analysis but short of empirical verification. Much remains to be explored in the study of complex systems (Hidalgo 2016). Second, Chaps. 6, 7, and 8 deploy the concept of global quasi-legislative behavior and produce an innovative typology of sovereign states' participation in multilateral treaties on the basis of multilateral treaties since 1945 up to 2014. The modes of and attributes to sovereign states' joining multilateral treaties, i.e., six instrumental variables (year of membership, year of deposit, number of current members, treaty participation index, modified Welzel regional group, policy domain), are factor-analyzed, yielding three dimensions of speed, angle, and strategy. On the basis of eight combinations of the three dimensions, eight types of sovereign states' quasi-legislative behavior are mapped, first, globally, and, second, regionally, focusing on 27 Asian states; in Chap. 8, joining or not joining multilateral treaties represents sovereign states' calculi of global politics or global statecraft. Third, in order to show this volume is a product of perspective revolution in the context of post-Cold War global politics, Chaps. 10, 11, 12, and 13 compare and contrast three theories of post-Cold War global politics: the theories of power transition, of civilizational conflict, and of global legislative politics. The theory of power transition as represented by Robert Gilpin (1983) with a focus on hegemonic leadership in relation to war is critiqued in reference to Inoguchi (2010) with emphasis on vulnerability in relation to power exercise. The theory of civilizational conflict as represented by Samuel Huntington (1997) is critiqued in reference to Collet/Inoguchi (2012), focusing on Huntington's four hypotheses empirically tested using the Asia Barometer Survey data. The theory of global legislative politics comes out of our perspective revolution in empirical international relations research in which might, wealth, and ideology are most likely to be key three factors of state's power sources. The theory of global legislative politics differs from most others in a most pronounced way as far as empirical international research is concerned. The theory of power transition focuses on power sources without adequate attention to vulnerability in association with exercise of power. The theory of civilizational conflict emphasizes civilizational differences in adversarial manifestations without adequately placing civilizational clash in complex contexts. The theory of global legislative politics takes up what has been hithertofore rarely taken up for empirical, systematic, and scientific examinations. In this theory, global statecraft is focused, and agreement is the key concept.

Summarizing, this book sheds fresh light on the transformative nature of multilateral treaties as a bundle of global quasi-social contracts not only for researchers and students of political philosophy, international law, and international relations but also for practitioners of all walks of life.

Keywords Global social contract, Global legislative politics, Global quasi-legislative behavior, A bundle of global quasi-social contracts, Jean-Jacques Rousseau, John Locke, Direct democracy, Representative democracy, Theory of power transition, Theory of civilizational conflict, Theory of global legislative politics

Tokyo, Japan Takashi Inoguchi
Hue, Vietnam Lien Thi Quynh Le

References

Collet, C., & Inoguchi, T. (2012). Is globalization undermining civilizational identities? A test of Huntington's core state assumptions among the publics of Greater Asia and the Pacific. *Japanese Journal of Political Science*, *13*(4), 553–585.

Fukuyama, F. (1992). *The end of history and the last man.* London: Penguin.

Funabashi, Y. (2019) *Think Tank towa nanika-Seisakukigyouryoku no jidai* [What is think tank? – The era of policy entrepreneurship]. Tokyo: Chuokoronshinsha.

Gilpin, R. (1983). *War and change in world politics*. Princeton: Princeton University Press.

Hidalgo, C. (2016). *Why information grows: The evolution of order; From atoms to economies*. New York: Penguin.

Huntington, S. (1997). *The clash of civilizations and the remaking of world order.* New York: Simon and Schuster.

Inoguchi, T. (2010). World order debates in the twentieth century: Through the eyes of the two-level game and second image (reversed). *Chinese Journal of International Politics*, *3*(2), 155–188.

Zakaria, F. (1997). The rise of illiberal democracy. *Foreign Affairs*, *76*(6), 22–47.

Acknowledgements

The completion of this book has been made possible by many generous helping hands extended to both authors. Two large data sets that we analyze here are the World Values Survey and Multilateral Treaties Survey. With respect to the former, we are most indebted to Christian Welzel (Leuphart University, Germany) for warmly sharing the factor analysis results reported in his magnum opus, *Freedom Rising* (Cambridge University Press). Welzel has most kindly allowed us to use the latest data from the factor analysis results (2013), for which we are most grateful. Without his help, our analysis would have taken much more time. No less important is the magnanimous advice and help from Miguel Basáñez Ebergenyi (Tufts University), whose magnum opus, *A World of Three Cultures: Honor, Achievement and Joy* (Oxford University Press), has given us important insight into sovereign states' willingness to join in multilateral treaties. With respect to the latter, Vice President Yoshiki Mikami of Nagaoka University of Technology must be singled out: he has been courageous enough to nominate Takashi Inoguchi as one member of the dissertation committee for Lien T. Q. Le, specializing in applied information science. Since then, rare cooperative work was completed between the fields of political philosophy and information science.

Regarding the efforts required to produce this book, we are indebted to Yoshinobu Yamamoto (University of Niigata Prefecture) and Keisuke Iida (University of Tokyo) who offered invaluable comments on earlier drafts. Similarly, we are appreciative of those who participated in the first Pacific Empirical International Relations Research Conference at Doshisha University, Kyoto—Eric Gartzke (University of California, San Diego), Takeshi Iida (Doshisha University), Benjamin Goldsmith (Australian National University), and Koji Kagotani (Osaka University of Economics). These researchers invited Inoguchi to be a keynote speaker and provided indispensable comments on our work. William Thompson (Indiana University, Bloomington), whose research testing of a few major hypotheses of world hegemonic leadership and cycles inspired Inoguchi to model such global dynamics, has invited Inoguchi to contribute a chapter focusing on the theoretical underpinnings of this book to his edited book *The Oxford Encyclopedia of Empirical International*

Relations Theory (Oxford University Press). Inoguchi is grateful to Christian Collet (International Christian University, Tokyo) no less because of his gracious permission to use the article we coauthored (Collet and Inoguchi 2011).

We must also thank two individuals—David Held and Peter Katzenstein, whom Inoguchi have been lucky to call friends for nearly half a century—for providing us timely encouragements and serendipitous advice on our collective endeavor during the later stages of the production of this book. Held (University of Durham) provided opportunities for Inoguchi to learn about multilateral treaties from his and his colleagues' work on *Gridlock* (2013, Polity Press) and *Beyond Gridlock* (2017, Polity Press) when he presented them at the University of Tokyo late in 2017. In early 2018, while presenting a half-a-dozen lectures on *Protean Power* (2018, coedited with Lucia A. Seybert, from Cambridge University Press), Katzenstein (Cornell University) found time in his busy schedule to discuss my book. Based on their encouragement and advice, I decided to add a section to more broadly focus the subject of this book. To our great shock and grief, David suddenly passed away in early 2019, embraced by his beloved wife, Eva. Our deepest condolence.

We are also indebted to the constructive critical comments from participants when we presented our earlier papers at the annual meetings of the Behaviormetric Society (September 2018), the Federated Statisticians (September 2018), and the Japan Politics-Law Studies Association (June 2018), *AJCP*'s (*Asian Journal of Comparative Politics*, Sage Publications) two international conferences (March 2017 and March 2018), J.F. Oberlin University (Tokyo)-Peking University symposium (March 2019), and J.F. Oberlin University monthly forum (June 2017) and in my commemorative speech on the 30th anniversary of Ritsumeikan University's School of International Relations (2016). We are most grateful to them, especially to Atsuko Abe (J.F. Oberlin University, Tokyo), Chu Xiaobo (Peking University), Mitsuo Ezaki (Nagoya University), Baogang He (Deakin University), Liang Yunxiang (Peking University), Nozomu Matsubara (University of Tokyo), Siripan Nogsuan Sawasdee (Chulalongkorn University), and Satoru Miyamoto (Seigakuin University).

The reviewers have impacted our draft manuscript in a most significant way. William R. Thompson, one of the most knowledgeable persons about theoretical-empirical international relations works, has forthrightly pointed out several series of theoretical, conceptual, explanatory, interpretative, organizational, and other issues in our final manuscript, leading us to revise it similarly. Miguel Basanez, a person who wears the three hats of professor, ambassador, and entrepreneur, has indicated a number of places that need to be more clearly accentuated from the reader's perspective. Doh Chull Shin (University of California, Irvine) has prompted us to clarify our key concepts (a bundle of global quasi-social contracts and global quasi-legislative behavior) and our analytical schemes (based on our interpretation of Rousseauesque and Lockean social contract ideas writ global) to the maximum extent possible. To them, we express our heartfelt gratitude.

Our work colleagues [from the University of Niigata Prefecture (until 2017) and then J. F. Oberlin University (Tokyo) for Takashi Inoguchi and at Nagaoka University of Technology (until 2015) and then the College of Economics (Hue University, Viet

Nam) for Lien T. Q. Le] have been wonderful in helping us facilitate our analysis and produce this book. At the University of Niigata Prefecture, Seiji Fujii must be singled out for his help at times of muddling in data analysis. At J.F. Oberlin University, Tokyo, Yoko Kiriishi and Masae Toyoizumi most professionally and efficiently helped Inoguchi with grace out of the last phase of this book-making. Takashi Inoguchi expresses his heartfelt gratitude to Chancellor Toyoshi Sato of J. F. Oberlin University, Tokyo, for providing an ideal setting for completing this book.

At Springer Nature in Tokyo, Chino Hasebe, executive editor, has been encouraging and tenacious in pushing us to write it up while she accumulates the list of probable authors of various academic disciplines under her domains like an Arctic anthropologist, a biological physicist, disaster-mitigating engineers, sociologists of marriage, and an evolutionary biologist. Her boss, Antoine Bocquet, gives Inoguchi a big smile in Springer Nature's annual sakura party at Happoen (Shirokanedai). At Springer Nature in Beijing, Leana Li, editorial director of Humanities and Social Sciences and regional director in China, has recently succeeded Chino Hasebe and takes care of Springer's book series Interdisciplinary Perspectives on Trust. Her clarity and efficiency have been most helpful in the last stage of making this book come out safely in time within 2019. Fiona Wu, editorial assistant at Springer Nature in Beijing, is most dexterous in coming up with unique selling points of our book.

Finally, we acknowledge the unflinching encouragement and support for our workaholic attitude from Kuniko Inoguchi, an academic turned parliamentarian, and Dzung Quoc Ho, a fellow engineering academic. This book is dedicated to them.

The Japan Society for the Promotion of Science has enabled Takashi Inoguchi to work on multiple democracies with its grant for the period between 2014 and 2018 [JSPS KAKENHI Grant Number: JP26285029].

Introduction

In the midst of World War I, in which Russia—under the leadership of Alexander Kerensky—fought against Germany, Leon Trotsky called for "neither war nor peace," meaning that the first priority should not be to fight against Germany but rather to fight against Kerensky's pro-war continuation policy. Throughout most of the twentieth century, international politics focused on the question of war and peace. Once disputes between nations proved unresolvable through negotiations, this question semiautomatically arose. It seemed that only by resorting to war can one hope to settle disputes among nations. Today, 100 years after Leon Trotsky uttered his famous call for revolution against pro-war policy continuation, wars among sovereign states have dramatically decreased. Glancing at the number of war-related deaths among soldiers, barring civilians, per annum for the World War II period, the Cold War period, and the post-Cold War period, this statistic has dropped by 5 million (each year between 1938 and 1945), 100,000 (each year between 1945 and 1989), and 10,000 (each year between 1989 and 2018). This significant decline shows how war as a human activity has become rara avis (Pinker 2018, Ch 4, note 17, Pinker 2011; Mueller 1989, 2004; Levy and Thompson 2011; Goldstein 2011).

Immediately after the end of the Cold War, Francis Fukuyama published *The End of History and the Last Man* (1992) in which he argued that once ideological confrontation between democracy and communism ended in favor of democracy, one had to be on the lookout for many kinds of fundamentalism, such as international terrorism, that could jeopardize the long-term survival of democracy. A year later, Jean-Marie Guéhenno published *La fin de la democratie* (1993) in which he argued that the growing tide of globalization—constructed on the shoulders of the nation-state—could jeopardize democracy's survival and that *la democratie sans frontiers* may not be easily sustained. Both authors predicted a changed democracy in that beyond the mostly nationally nurtured democratic theory and practice, there could emerge transnational forces and structures that could metamorphose democratic institutions in one way or another (Cf. Held and Maffettone 2019).

Indeed, after the Cold War, the number of democracies increased dramatically to 120 out of 193 United Nations (UN) member states. In a large number of UN member states, the legislative branch now functions to channel citizen preferences into government public policy. One may argue that only in democracies can one talk about how public opinion can transform into legislative action and that many other social forces than public opinion exert influence on legislation. We consider the simplified focus on public opinion and legislation: public opinion is perceived as an input from those governed to those governing, whereas legislation is viewed as the set of decisions of those governing. Such states are the evolutionary variants of representative democracy that John Locke envisaged in 1689 (Locke 1993). By the end of the twentieth century, representative democracy's variants had spread all over the world. Similarly, after the invention of the World Wide Web in 1991, the galloping tide of digitalization has changed global citizens' lives and institutions by leaps and bounds, resulting in the worldwide growth of the direct democracy envisioned by Jean-Jacques Rousseau in 1762 (Rousseau 1968). Public opinion polls have been so frequently and so densely conducted all over the world that global citizens' preferences are widely and instantaneously known in the world. What Rousseau thought was the sphere of his envisioned world only went as far as Poland and Corsica. Now, the entire globe is instantaneously connected. Ergo, the fertile ground for direct democracy is more or less ready.

Having discovered this evolving reality of human life, we have attempted to determine whether Rousseau's and Locke's ideas can be tested empirically. Two data sets used for this attempt are the "World Values Survey" by Ronald Inglehart and his associates and the "Multilateral Treaties Survey" by Lien T. Q. Le and Takashi Inoguchi. The former deals with global citizens' values and norms, whereas the latter deals with UN multilateral treaties. Based on the results of a systematic and empirical analysis of these two data sets, we argue that rather than concentrating on power competition and ranking and rather than focusing attention on culture, religion, and race in an adversarial way, the world should spend more thinking about consensus, compassion, and their application in better constructing our increasingly digitally globalized international and transnational politics.

This book consists of three parts: Part I, Global Social Contract; Part II, Global Quasi-legislative Behavior; and Part III, Three Varieties of Global Politics After the Cold War. The first part describes how we became interested in multilateral treaties. Two macro-trends of human history, i.e., the drastic decline of war-related deaths and the dramatic permeation of digitalized globalization, have inspired us (IISS 2015; Inoguchi 2015). First, war-related deaths among soldiers have dropped dramatically from previous periods in the history of the civilized world. Second, digitalized globalization has dramatically changed the human diffusion of ideas and emotions in terms of the instantaneous speed and breadth in which content can reach people across the globe. These two phenomenal changes have grown steadily since the late twentieth century. Cognizance of these two phenomena has led us to think about whether two social contract theories by Rousseau and Locke, propounded in the seventeenth and eighteenth centuries, might be remodeled to encompass the world's human population in its entirety. In other words, it might be feasible to think that Rousseau and Locke *can be writ global.*

In Rousseau's direct democratic idea of social contract, he set a clear civilizational limit not to include Corsica and Poland, while in Locke's representative democratic idea of social contract, he excluded those without status and piety (as these attributes make up the dual sovereignty prerequisites for his social contract idea). In other words, Rousseau's and Locke's ideas of democracy can be writ global given the pervasive and instantaneous conditions of democratic information diffusion. This part examines and empirically tests Rousseau's and Locke's social contract ideas against the late twentieth-century and early twenty-first-century world. It is noted that multilateral treaties rest first on sovereign states' ability to aggregate and reflect citizens' preference in values and norms and to join multilateral treaties that are in sync with their national citizens' preferences as well as with global preferences expressed in these multilateral treaties. In the empirical testing that we conducted, the ability of a state to reflect its citizens' preferences is based on relevant analytical results from Christian Welzel's latest work from the "World Values Survey" (Welzel 2013), whereas the sovereign states' multilateral treaties participation is based on the "Multilateral Treaties Survey" (Le/Mikami/Inoguchi 2014; Inoguchi/Le 2016). More specifically, the multilateral treaty participation of sovereign states is based on relevant analytical results of six instrumental variables associated with the pattern of sovereign states' actions on multilateral treaties participation. Broad convergence between a state's ability to reflect citizen preference and ability to join multilateral treaties in sync with that preference is shown as one strident step forward in empirical analysis.

In Part I, our argument does not go so far as to strictly verify that Rousseau's and Locke's social contract theories statistically. Rousseau's world was limited so much geo-culturally to such a great extent as to exclude Corsica and Poland from his civilized world. Today's world is clearly beyond his notions of geography, culture, and technology. Locke's world was limited by two terms: status and piety (Kato 2018 and Waldron 2002)). Those without status and piety are not targeted by Locke's representative democracy.

In Part II, given that sovereign states' participation in multilateral treaties is closely tied to both citizens' preferences and sovereign states' calculus of national and global interest to be joiners of multilateral treaties, we conceptualize sovereign state actions as *global quasi-legislative behavior*, each national set of which can be called external legislative policy. This part examines how sovereign states act when confronted by the legislative possibility of multilateral treaties and presents how they differ when they join treaties in terms of speed, angle, and strategy—when they sign, when they ratify, when they join in view of participatory trends, and to which policy domain (i.e., labor and health, human rights, communications and commerce, the environment, peace and disarmament, intellectual property) of multilateral treaties they choose to belong. Three dimensions of sovereign states' treaty behavior are then presented with spatial locations of sovereign states and their ten geo-historico-religious groups, first devised by Welzel.

On the basis of the three dimensions of sovereign states' *global quasi-legislative behavior*, statistically derived from their modes of participation in multilateral treaties, we develop an evidenced-based typology. Eight types of *global quasi-legislative behavior*—observed in Brazil, Iran, Sweden, New Zealand, Slovakia, South Korea, Nigeria, and Uzbekistan—are presented, and their characteristics are described. In addition, based on this typology, the *global quasi-legislative behavior* of 27 Asian sovereign states is analyzed. In Part II, we argue that the bundle of six instrumental variables (year of membership, year of deposit, number of current members, treaty participation index, ten modified Welzel's regional groups, and six policy domains) represents key aspects and attributes of the *global quasi-legislative behavior* of the 193 states examined in this book. To theoretically further enhance the concept of *global quasi-legislative behavior*, we use the old-fashioned argument by Georg Simmel that the form of interactions (communication style) is different from the content of interactions (communication message) and that the form of interactions, when assembled and accumulated, creates society. He uses the word *Vergesellschaftung* in German or sociation in English (Simmel 1950). In the context of our research, sovereign states' participation in multilateral treaties can be understood as the forms of interactions via multilateral treaties among sovereign states. Our argument a la Simmel (1950), a sociologist, is that the forms of interactions among sovereign states via participation in multilateral treaties generates society through participation in multilateral treaties in terms of modes and attributes. Our argument a la Hidalgo (2016), a physics-trained complex system analyst, is that "what makes our planet special is not that it is a singularity of matter, or information. Our planet is to inform what a black hole is to matter and what a star is to energy—(T)he mechanisms that help information win small battles, prevailing stoically in our universe's only true war: the war between order and disorder; between entropy and information" (Hidalgo 2016, p.x). One might argue that the correlations among the six quantitative and qualitative variables need to be statistically tested to see their significance, which we will do later in Chap. 5. Our argument is that this book is of the first of its kind and that the initial hunch-cum-hypothesis about global quasi-legislative behavior can be further elaborated in terms of data and methods as well as concepts on the basis of this work.

In Part III (authored solely by Takashi Inoguchi), in order to position this attempt in the broad context of post-Cold War international relations research, we compare and contrast three hypotheses of post-Cold War politics: theory of power transition, theory of civilizational conflict, and theory of global legislative politics. Part III proposes a theory of multilateral agreement in view of the difficulties these dominant theories encounter in explaining some aspects of international relations in a post-Cold War world: the theory of power transition and the theory of civilizational clash. Chapter 10 presents how three broad frameworks were used to assess and understand the post-Cold War world (Inoguchi 1999). Chapters 11 and 12 present the author's take on the theory of power transition and theory of civilizational clash, respectively. Inoguchi's criticism of these two theories is that while the theory of power transition is preoccupied with power ranking, leading powers' contestation, and power alternation, it has difficulty accounting for key phenomena in post-Cold

War politics (Inoguchi 2010) and that while the theory of civilizational conflict is preoccupied with the sharp distinction between "us" and "them" in terms of conventional religious-cum-racial fault lines, it also has difficulty accounting for key phenomena in post-Cold War politics (Collet and Inoguchi 2012). Chapter 13 is a culmination of thought and analysis based on Parts I and II and on the critiquing of the two major streams of thinking that prevailed in the fourth quarter of the last century and the first quarter of this century. In Part III, we argue that the thrust of this book becomes clearer and sharper if we compare and contrast some of those theories highlighted before and after 1989, i.e., the theory of power transition, the theory of civilizational conflict, and the theory of global legislative politics.

With Part I, Part II, and Part III developed step-by-step, we argue that perhaps an orthodox and yet old-fashioned approach to global politics—namely, the Westphalian approach that primarily focuses on might, wealth, and ideology—should be replaced by more polished and elaborate schemes and indicators of sovereign states' external engagements, referred to as participation in multilateral treaties, to deal with global conundrums such as peace and disarmament, human rights, health and labor, intellectual property, the environment, and trade and communications, particularly during the new millennium, when sovereign states struggle and survive in the fast-changing digitalized globalization.

Methodological Note

This note is for those interested in the methodological aspects of this study. Since the book is organized along the concepts used, i.e., *a bundle of global quasi-social contracts* and *global quasi-legislative behavior* (Parts I and II), the methodological steps that were adopted are not necessarily presented in an orderly description in the main text. This note serves this purpose.

(1) The perspective adopted in this study is unconventional in mainstream empirical international relations research (e.g., Thompson 2018). It is unconventional in the sense that multilateral treaties are the key data sources for analysis and argument. War occurrence, alliance formation, and diplomatic negotiation are among the most frequently analyzed subjects, while treaties, agreements, and conventions are often left for consideration by international law specialists, academics, and practitioners, who mostly deal with them on a case-by-case basis.
(2) The data sources of this study cover roughly one extended twentieth century for multilateral treaties and roughly three quarters of a century for cross-national opinion polls. The study covers 193 sovereign states. The global citizens of those countries covered by this study constitute 90% of the world's population (Inglehart 2018, p. xviii).
(3) The initial hunch-cum-hypothesis of this study comes from Jean-Jacques Rousseau and John Locke who left their works written mostly in the seventeenth and eighteenth century in Western Europe. The key argument of this

study is that Rousseauesque and Lockean ideas of democracy can be writ global. The two conditions attached to the hypothesis are as follows:

(a) Those scientific and technological breakthroughs achieved in the last quarter of the last century and the first quarter of this century: digitalized globalization permeates each and every part of the globe, enabling instantaneous and massive communications and transactions.
(b) Geographical, sociological, and religious constraints are significantly moderated by today. Geographically, the Rousseauesque world did not include Corsica and Poland, for instance. Sociologically, the Lockean world did not include those persons who were not regarded as the narrowly defined elites, and religiously, the Lockean world did not include those persons who were not pious as Christians.

(4) Multilateral treaties have become a mainstay of international relations along with war occurrence, alliance formation, and international organization. International relations less often resort to violence and more often resolve to agreement. To resolve conflicts among states, agreement often takes the form of multilateralism rather than bilateralism (Hale, Held and Young 2013; Hale and Held 2017).
(5) For Rousseau's and Locke's original ideas of social contract to be writ global, their ideas need to be metamorphized into *a bundle of global quasi-social contracts* and *global quasi-legislation*.

References

Collet, C., & Inoguchi, T. (2012). Is globalization undermining civilizational identities? A test of Huntington's core state hypothesis among the publics of Greater Asia and the Pacific. *Japanese Journal of Political Science, 13*(4), 553–585.

Fukuyama, F. (1992). *The end of history and the last man*. London: Penguin.

Goldstein, J. S. (2011). *Winning the war on war: The decline of armed conflict worldwide*. New York, NY: Penguin.

Guéhenno, J. M. (1993). *La fin de la democratie*. Paris: Flammarion.

Hale, T., & Held, D. (2017). *Beyond gridlock*. Cambridge: Polity Press.

Hale, T., Held, D., & Young, K. (2013). *Gridlock: Why global cooperation is failing when we need it most*. Cambridge: Polity Press.

Held, D., & Maffettone, P. (Eds.). (2019). *Global political theory*. Cambridge: Polity Press.

Hidalgo, C. (2016). *Why information grows: The evolution of order, from atoms to economies*. New York: Penguin.

Inglehart, R. (2018). *Cultural evolution: People's motivations are changing, and reshaping the world*. Cambridge: Cambridge University Press.

Inoguchi, T. (1999). Peering into the future by looking back: The Westphalian, Philadelphian and Anti-Utopian paradigms. *International Studies Review, 1*(2), 173–191.

Inoguchi, T. (2010). World order debates in the twentieth century: Through the eyes of the two-level game and second image (reversed). *Chinese Journal of International Politics, 3*(2), 155–188.
Inoguchi, T. (2015). War occurrence: Hyper-insecurity and multilateral institutions. *Japanese Journal of Political Science, 16*(3), 388–398.
Inoguchi, T., & Le, L. T. Q. (2016). Toward modelling a global social contract: Jean-Jacques Rousseau and John Locke. *Japanese Journal of Political Science, 17*(3), 489–572.
International Institute for Strategic Studies. (2015). *Strategic survey 2014*. London: IISS.
Kato, T. (2018). *John Locke; Kami to ningen to no aida* [John Locke; between god and humans]. Tokyo: Iwanami shoten
Le, T. Q. L., Mikami, Y. & Inoguchi, T. (2014). Global leadership and international regime: Empirical testing of cooperation without hegemonic paradigm on the basis of 120 multilateral conventions deposited to the United Nations system. *Japanese Journal of Political Science, 15*(4), 523–601.
Levy, J. S., & Thompson, W. (2011). *The arc of war: Origins, escalation and transformation*. Chicago: University of Chicago Press.
Locke, J. (1993). *Two treatises of government*. New York: Everyone Paperback.
Mueller, J. (1989). *Retreat from doomsday: The obsolescence of major war*. New York: Basic Books.
Mueller, J. (2004). *The remnants of war*. Ithaca: Cornell University Press.
Pinker, S. (2011). *The better angels of our nature: Why violence has declined*. New York: Penguin.
Pinker, S. (2018). *Enlightenment now: The case for reason, science, humanism, and progress*. New York: Viking.
Rousseau, J.-J., & Cranston, M. (1968). *The social contract*. London: Penguin classics.
Simmel, G. (1950). *The sociology of Georg Simmel*, compiled and translated by Kurt Wolff, Glencoe. Illinois: Free Press.
Waldron, J. (2002). *God, Locke, and equality: Christian foundations in Locke's political thought*. Cambridge: Cambridge University Press
Welzel, C. (2013). *Freedom rising: Human empowerment and the quest for emancipation*. New York: Cambridge University Press.

Contents

Part I Global Social Contract

List of Figures

List of Tables

Part I
Global Social Contract

Chapter 1
Introduction to Part I

Abstract The key concept utilized in this book to understand the international system is neither hegemony, hierarchy, nuclear bipolarity, nor pecking order; instead it is the global social contract. Lamenting the lack of a global polling study on the basis of global sampling theory and the lack of a global quasi-legislative study covering all the multilateral treaties, we have decided to study the link between the citizens' preferences in values and norms and sovereign states' participation in multilateral treaties systematically and empirically. By providing the empirical evidence that global citizens' preference about values and norms converges approximately with sovereign states' participation in multilateral treaties, it can be concluded that the global social contract could be imagined and minimally envisaged. Part I describes how our initial hunch-cum-hypothesis has developed into the conceptual formulation of the problem: Rousseau and Locke Writ Global. Deploying the World Value Survey (R. Inglehart et al) and the Multilateral Treaties Survey (Lien T.Q. Le and Takashi Inoguchi), we present the degree of association between citizens' preference in value orientation and states' preference in treaty participation and argue that our initial hunch-cum-hypothesis has been approximately validated when we formulate states' participation in multilateral treaties as a bundle of global quasi-legislative contracts.

States engage with one another in an environment known as the international system. In the pursuit of understanding the international system, international relations scholars have tried to define the key concepts that detail the history of the international system. Kenneth Waltz's tripartite approach of the individual, the state, and the international system as related to the causes of war occurrence is a classic approach (1957/2001); he broadly defines the concept of the international system as forces beyond the nation-states. Morton Kaplan's structural scheme examines the possession of nuclear weapons that allow possessors to retaliate against enemies with the most devastating results (Kaplan 1957). In his scheme, nuclear unipolarity can be stable or unstable depending on the desire and design of a unipolar nuclear state. In contrast, nuclear multipolarity can lead to chaos and instability because the nuclear calculus among multipolar powers is difficult to determine. Hence, nuclear

T. Inoguchi, L. T. Q. Le, *The Development of Global Legislative Politics*,
Trust: Interdisciplinary Perspectives 3, https://doi.org/10.1007/978-981-32-9389-2_1

bipolarity can be viewed as the most stable structure because the calculus of both bipolar powers cancels one another out. Thus, the Non-Proliferation of Nuclear Weapons Treaty has placed international constraints on the two nuclear powers, the United States and the Soviet Union, and later on the Russian Federation, to reduce their respective nuclear weapons in a balanced fashion so that any imbalance between the two in terms of nuclear weapons would not trigger actions with devastating consequences. Other states are discouraged from going nuclear as the Treaty is associated with many regulatory clauses. The Treaty also restricts newly nuclear-armed states from enhancing nuclear weapons.

Based on the long stability during the Cold War period, Robert Gilpin (1983) uses the concept of hegemony to explain the dynamics of world politics in terms of hegemony's rise and decline. Hegemony is defined as power that has accumulated through the combined strength of gross domestic product; military arsenal; global infrastructure of communication and transportation with technological superiority; and political, diplomatic, and cultural power to induce other states not to oppose its hegemonic power, i.e., soft power (Nye 2005). A hegemon's rise and decline determine the features of the international system; most importantly the occurrence of war, according to Gilpin. In line with this concept, some related concepts—supporter, challenger, and spoiler—have been invented (Krasner 1983, 2009; Lake 2011). Gilpin's emphasis on war occurrence and the associated creation of a hegemony are important.

Not sufficiently satisfied with the simple explanatory scheme for the international system, David Lake (2011) uses hierarchy to analyze the international system. By hierarchy, he means a country ranking derived according to gross domestic product, military arsenal, and soft power. What is important here is that there are multiple sources of power. The explanatory picture of the international system has become less of a determinant. In other words, the picture has become more complex, yet the core concept has remained the power hierarchy.

More recently, Vincent Pouliot (2016) applies pecking orders as the core explanation for multilateral diplomacy. Using elite survey responses, Pouliot specifies that pecking orders in international organizations or habits illustrate the influence of international organizations, such as NATO and the UN. One can see how international organizations and their staff have come to empower themselves by understanding which states are more powerful than depending on their positioning in the hierarchy within the international organization, such as the inclusion in the UN Security Council as a permanent member. In further exploration of global intergovernmental organizations, Dawisson Belem Lopes (2017) analyzes their steady polyarchization (Dahl 2006). Underlying this shift in analysis is the Weberian interpretation of the modernization of international organizations (Steffek 2017).

From the above cited works, it is clear that at the core of the international system are sovereign states and the status of power as perceived among them. Differing radically from those works, this book is an attempt to describe the structure among sovereign states from an alternative perspective. Accordingly, the key concept utilized in this book to understand the international system is neither hegemony, hierarchy, nuclear bipolarity, nor pecking order; instead, it is the *global social contract*.

Through this concept, this book seeks to examine how sovereign states represent global citizens' voices on such globally impactful subjects as climate change, trans-border pollution, and international terrorism. We prioritize the notion of global citizens instead of their own citizenries, the latter of which imparts the strong color of nationally divided citizenries. Specifically, we consider how global citizens' voices can be aggregated when the world consists of over 7 billion people and a global sampling theory and practice do not exist (Cf. Gilani and Gilani 2013; Gilani 2017). We argue in favor of using the best survey that covers as many as 93 sovereign states with the same questionnaire worldwide (as of 2005-2009), i.e., the World Values Survey (WVS) led by Ronald Inglehart and his associates.

Public opinion polls on worldwide issues are conducted conventionally with national sampling based on the national population and demographics, rather than global sampling based on global population and demographics. It is not an exaggeration to say that contemporary social science theory and method were consolidated predominantly in the United States in the third quarter of the last century (Zunz 1998; Inoguchi 2011, 2015). Public opinion surveys made major methodological advances during this period, and, as such, the academic realms of human behavior research—economics, sociology, and political science—use sovereign state as the natural unit of their respective frameworks.

Similar to the lack of global polling on the basis of global sampling, there is a lack of global legislation on the basis of a global legislature; thus, without a world assembly, we lack a world polity. When global polling is required, organizations such as WIN-Gallup International conduct national surveys and assemble these results. When global legislation is called for, global quasi-legislation is carried out in various forms of multilateral treaties. In other words, initiators, drafters of multilateral treaties, platforms of discussion, rules of finalizing agreements, and advertising megaphones — all of these must exist to attract more people and more states to join multilateral treaties by signing and ratifying. The unit of aggregation of popular preference is primarily the sovereign state. Hence, there is no systematic study of global quasi-legislature.

Lamenting the lack of a global polling study on the basis of global sampling theory and the lack of a global quasi-legislative study covering all the multilateral treaties, we have decided to study the link between citizens' preference on values and norms and sovereign states' participation in multilateral treaties systematically and empirically. Obviously, in shaping multilateral treaties, both global citizens' preference about values and norms and sovereign states' participation (and non-participation) matter. Specifically, when the tides of globalization and digitalization have an overwhelming international public presence, global citizens' attitudes about values and norms and world sovereign states' participation in multilateral treaties must be studied and analyzed head on. By proving that global citizens' preference about values and norms converge approximately with sovereign states' participation in multilateral treaties, it can be concluded that the global social contract could be imagined and minimally envisaged (Inoguchi 2018; Inoguchi and Le 2016; Le et al. 2014). One may as well argue that without covering 193 existing sovereign states the empirical testing of global citizen's preferences pertaining to values and norms in relation to sovereign states' preferences about participation in multilateral treaties cannot be fruitfully attested (Cf. Achen and Bartels 2016). Yet one may as well argue that even if the data availability and precision may be less than satisfactory from the methodologically hard liners, it is our argument that if our analysis brings one to get closer to accuracy, it is worth the effort to go through trials and errors. Pinker (2018, pp. 43–44) argues well: "(R)esistance to the idea of progress runs deeper than statistical fallacies. Of course, any dataset is an imperfect reflection of reality, so it is legitimate to question how accurate and representative the numbers truly are. But the objections revealed not just a skepticism about the data but also an unpreparedness for the possibility that the human condition has improved. Many people lack the conceptual tools to ascertain whether progress has taken place or not; the very idea that things can get better just doesn't compute."

Part I is organized as follows: Part I describes how our initial hunch-cum-hypothesis has developed into the current formulation of the problem: Rousseau and Locke Writ Global. Chapter 2: "Global Social Contract Theory" examines Jean-Jacques Rousseau's *Social Contract* and John Locke's *Two Treatises of Government* to see how these two theories of social contract originated with a view of global politics that is currently unfolding in front of our eyes. Our task is to compare and correlate two things: global citizens' preferences on value orientation in the World Values Survey data and sovereign states' participation modes in multilateral treaties in the Multilateral Treaties Survey data. Chapter 3: "Global Citizens' Preferences in Value Orientation", drawn from Christian Welzel's *Freedom Rising* (2013) summarizes the 10 regional groups' locations on two key dimensions: protective versus emancipative and sacred versus secular, to give readers a glimpse at how people's preference differs by region. The World Values Survey has been reputed as the best survey available on value orientation in terms of the wide coverage (90% of world population) and the methods used with competence. Chapter 4: "Sovereign States' Participation in Multilateral Treaties" presents our formulation of multilateral treaties as global quasi-legislative outcomes with sovereign states as global quasi- legislators. Sovereign states have two eyes looking at domestic preferences within and external preferences without as well as decisional environments. Chapter 4 offers readers a summary description of multilateral treaties by policy domains and the ranking of sovereign states and of 10 regional groups by policy domains in terms of preference or the willingness to participate in multilateral treaties. Chapter 5: "Toward Modelling a Global Quasi-Social Contract" presents the degree of associations between citizens' preference in value orientation and states' preference in treaty participation and argues that our initial hunch-cum-hypothesis has been adequately validated when we formulate states' participation in multilateral treaties as a bundle of global quasi-social contracts.

References

Achen, C., & Bartels, L. (2016). *Democracy for realists: Why elections do not produce responsive government*. Princeton: Princeton University Press.

Belem Lopes, D. (2017). Polyarchies, competitive oligarchies or inclusive hegemonies? A comparison of 23 global intergovernmental organizations based on Robert A. Dahl's political theory. *Cambridge Review of International Affairs, 29*(4), 1233–1258.

Dahl, R. (2006). *A preface to democratic theory*. Chicago: University of Chicago Press.

Gilani, I. (2017). How global are global polls? Proposal for hybrid samples of world populations to blend policy concerns (favoring sample of 100 countries) and theoretical concerns (favoring sample of 100,000 people). In Paper presented at WAPOR annual conference, Lisbon, July 15–17, 2017.

Gilani, I. S. & Gilani, B. (2013). Global and regional polls: A paradigmatic shift in from "state-centric" to "global-centric." In Paper presented at WAPOR annual conference at Boston, May 14–16, 2013.

Gilpin, R. (1983). *War and change in world politics*. Cambridge: Cambridge University Press.

Inoguchi, T. (2011). Political theory. In B. Badie, D. Berk-Schlosser, & L. Morlino (Eds.), *International encyclopedia of political science* (Vol. 6, pp. 2050–2063). London: Sage Publications.

Inoguchi, T. (2015). Social science infrastructure: East Asia and the Pacific (Research and Teaching). In J. D. Wright (Ed.), *International encyclopedia of the social and behavioral science* (Vol. 22, 2nd ed., pp. 631–636). Oxford: Elsevier.

Inoguchi, T. (2018). Theoretical underpinnings of global social contract. In W. Thompson (Ed.), *The encyclopedia of Oxford empirical international relations theory* (Vol. 4, pp. 223–240). Oxford: Oxford University Press.

Inoguchi, T., & Le, L. T. Q. (2016). Toward modelling a global social contract: Jean-Jacques Rousseau and John Locke. *Japanese Journal of Political Science, 17*(3), 489–522.

Kaplan, M. (1957). *System and process in international politics*. New York: Wiley.

Krasner, S. D. (Ed.). (1983). *International regimes*. Ithaca: Cornell University Press.

Krasner, S. D. (2009). *Power, the state and sovereignty: Essays on international relations*. London: Routledge.

Lake, D. A. (2011). *Hierarchy in international relations*. Ithaca: Cornell University Press.

Le, T. Q. L., Mikami, Y., & Inoguchi, T. (2014). Global leadership and international regime: Empirical testing of cooperation without hegemony paradigm on the basis of 120 multilateral conventions data deposited to the United Nations System. *Japanese Journal of Political Science, 15*(4), 523–601.

Nye, J. (2005). *Soft power: The means to success in world politics*. New York: Public Affairs.

Pinker, S. (2018). *Enlightenment now: The case for reason, science, humanism, and progress*. New York: Viking.

Pouliot, V. (2016). *International pecking orders: The politics and practice of multilateral diplomacy*. Cambridge: Cambridge University Press.

Steffek, J. (2017). Max Weber, modernity and the project of international organization. *Cambridge Review of International Affairs, 29*(4), 1502–1519.

Waltz, K. (1957/2001). *Man, the state, and war: A theoretical analysis*. New York: Columbia University Press, Revised edition.

Zunz, O. (1998). *Why the American century?* Chicago: University of Chicago Press.

Chapter 2
Global Social Contract Theory

Abstract This chapter describes the nature and potentials of Rousseau's and Locke's social contract theories to be reformulated as global social contract theory. Despite their limits attributed to the seventeenth and eighteenth century western Europe where they lived their lives like Rousseau's geo-cultural exclusion of Mediterranean and eastern Europe and Locke's socio-religious exclusion of those without status and piety, we summarize those subsequent democratic developments in Rosseauesque direct democracy driven by empathy and compassion and in Lockean representative democracy driven by human reasoning and pragmatism. Citing Immanuel Kant's *Eternal Peace* in comparing the year of 1912 when Norman Angell expressed optimism on the basis of free trade-derived peace and prosperity and the year of 2019 when international organizations, democracy and free trade have reached their peaks and the beginnings of a stall.

Of all the philosophers of modern democracy, Jean-Jacques Rousseau and John Locke are among the most commonly read and thus can be seen as the most influential in the twenty-first century (Rousseau and Cranston 1968; Locke 1993). Judith Shkler (1973) notes that although Rousseau did not invent the concept of the *volonté générale,* it was Rousseau who made it famous. John Dunn (2005) notes that although the concept of representative democracy did not originate from Locke, he is perceived as the philosopher who resuscitated democracy in ancient Greece 2000 years later.

When discussing social contract theory, two great philosophers often come to mind: Jean-Jacques Rousseau and John Locke. Rousseau's *Social Contract* and John Locke's *Two Treaties of Government* are two books penned from quite contrasting angles. It is acknowledged that social contracts are formed between the ruler and the ruled, between the state and its citizens; however, according to the philosophers, the ways in which social contracts are formed differ—Rousseau believes they are formed through the communitarian development process and Locke through the utilitarian development process.

Born in and accustomed to how Geneva, a city with some 20,000–25,000 inhabitants, was run, Rousseau imagined social contracts in a communitarian way. This

T. Inoguchi, L. T. Q. Le, *The Development of Global Legislative Politics*,
Trust: Interdisciplinary Perspectives 3, https://doi.org/10.1007/978-981-32-9389-2_2

essentially meant that people knew one another and consensus was formed in debating issues face-to-face with compassion. In contrast, Locke imagined social contracts in a utilitarian fashion. During Locke's lifetime in England, the country was home to some 5–6 million inhabitants ruled by a king and nobility who possessed disputed authority and power over property, tax, and religion. Then, in 1688, via the Declaration, some compromises of power were made. Following this declaration, mundane utilitarian legislative politics have slowly but steadily evolved in England. Under such circumstances, the utilitarian social contract can be seen as being exemplified in the gains and losses calculated by contesting groups for each legislative idea, and in crafting compromises resolve this.

The aim of this chapter is to extend the scope of the social contract concept from cantonal and national to global and international—meaning examining whether a global social contract is even possible. To date, no world government or world assembly has been established that does not make uneasy or cause dissatisfaction among those who believe in national sovereign states having national executive, legislative and judiciary branches. However, by following and extending the two logics of Rousseau and Locke to the world, the authors attempt to show that imagining a global social contract is possible. Such imagined global social contracts may not necessarily enjoy undisputed authority. What we attempt to do is to show that such global social contracts can be empirically and statistically tested. In Rousseau's words, such a global contract is possible with compassion among global citizens. In Locke's words, such a global contract is possible through reason and pragmatism with sovereign states representing national citizens. Rousseau's idea of a global social contract can be realized via Immanuel Kant's moral imperative, Sigmund Freud's unconsciousness, and more recent neuroscientific findings pointing to the empirical reality of compassion by globally ubiquitous digitalization (Azuma 2014). Two recent examples of close-to-unanimous multilateral treaties include: (1) the Paris accord on climate change in 2015, and (2) treaties banning nuclear weapons in 2017. Locke's idea of a global social contract can be realized via global quasi-legislation such as the United Nations Security Council (five permanent and veto-exercising members and the rest), the Paris accord on climate change, and the Permanent Court for Arbitration on the South China Sea.

In the following subsections, theoretical underpinnings drawn from Rousseau's and Locke's metaphors of democracy are provided. Pointing out the insufficient articulation of these two great philosophers of democracy, which reflected the constraints of living in seventeenth and eighteenth century Geneva and England, it must be noted that the authors justify the adaptation of their ideas to what may be called global democracy in the dawn of the new millennium (Inoguchi and Le 2016). Key drivers of Rousseau's and Locke's concepts of democracy are empathy and compassion, and human reason and pragmatism, respectively. Given the technological, economic, political, social, and cultural environments in the dawn of the new millennium, captured by accelerated globalization and digitalization, transnational direct democratic and transnational representative democratic models of a global social contract are feasible and justified. To illustrate this dramatic change, the authors contrast 2 years: 1912, when Norman Angell (1912) forecasted the advent of peaceful years ahead, and 2019, when this chapter was penned.

2.1 Two Metaphors of Democracy

Direct democracy and representative democracy are two key concepts that pervade the study of democracy. Three threads of democracy study were present in the fourth quarter of the twentieth century and remain so in the first quarter of the twenty-first century. First, political science theories produced—mostly in the third quarter of the last century—a bundle of concepts related to the democracy that was unfolding in the United States and the rest of the world. They include: pluralist democracy, liberal democracy, direct democracy, and communitarian democracy (Dahl 2006; Budge 1996; Barber 2004; Putnam 2000). Second, in the fourth quarter of the last century, self-reflective and critical theories emerged. Many of these lean toward the critical category, but they do not necessarily question the assumption of democracy embedded in a national territorial sovereign state and civil society. Instead, they tend to focus on the enhancement of civil society vis-a-vis the state. Democratic maturity often means the resilience of a civil society (Habermas 1991; Badie 2000). Third, in the first quarter of the twenty-first century, theories have emerged that are influenced by the rise of digital communication on the one hand and the burst of transnational communications, business transactions, social movements, and organizations on the other. The marriage of the second and third threads has sometimes generated theories emphasizing the negation of democracy as understood before the onslaught of digitalism and transnationalism (Keane 2009; Rosanvallon 2008; Mair 2013; Achen and Bartels 2016).

What matters here is the fact that Rousseau's and Locke's philosophical beliefs have survived in large part because of their style of articulation. Their style is immensely affected by the historical and cultural contexts of Switzerland and England in the seventeenth and eighteenth centuries. Switzerland was very peripheral in the sense that it was provincial, parochial, and distant from the Vatican and major powers in Europe. England was very peripheral in a similar sense: provincial, parochial, and distant from the Vatican and major powers including Istanbul. Laurence Whitehead (2002) correctly acknowledges that European democracy emerged out of peripheral societies: Switzerland, England, and Sweden. The less discussed reason is that the influence of the Vatican on these countries was not as strong as it was on France, Spain, and geographical entities in Germany and Italy; thus, it was in England and Switzerland that the balance between the secular and sacred was first achieved. Moreover, though a relatively small city with a population of 20–25,000, Geneva, where Rousseau resided, perceived itself as an important autonomous city; while, in England, a country whose population was 5–6 million, Locke witnessed the decline of the power of the king and a steady increase in the power of the parliament.

Three factors have have led to Rousseau's and Locke's philosophies becoming insufficient in terms of their articulation for the twenty-first century context. First, their philosophies were based on demographically sparse societies. The population in Switzerland in the seventeenth and eighteenth centuries was less than 1 million, and as previously mentioned, 5–6 million in England. Since nation-building efforts were slow-moving during that period, traditional political institutions were thriving. In other words, a gerontocracy comprising traditional social leaders was prevalent in Switzerland and England at the time. Second, the influence of religion was waning as the secularization of life was steadily rising. In medieval Europe, that which was sacred was of primary importance while the secular was often disregarded. With the advent of the Renaissance, however, came the slow erosion of the religious dominance in the domain of science. The debate between realism (traditional theology) and nominalism (spearheaded in England by William of Ockham) in Christian theology slowly gave the latter more weight, thus separating politics from religion (Ockham and Brown 1990). Third, territorial sovereign states were slowly consolidated in various parts of Europe while traditional communities and associated political institutions were kept largely intact. In the pre-Industrial Revolution period, international, transnational, and/or supranational phenomena were not recognized in the minds of most people. After all, the age of nation-states had not yet arrived.

Following this brief discussion of the backgrounds of Rousseau and Locke, their concepts of direct democracy and representative democracy will be presented in the subsequent sections of this chapter.

2.1.1 Direct Democracy by Rousseau

Rousseau's writings contain self-contradictions. On the one hand, he argues for the human yearning of freedom; on the other hand, he argues for the perfect fusion of the individual and the state (Azuma 2014, p. 35). The first proposition is not difficult to swallow; after all, for Rousseau, a student of the Encyclopedist on the eve of the French Revolution, freedom is one of the core values that he adores (Diderot and le Rond d'Alembert 1751–1772). The second proposition is, according to him, resolved by introducing the almighty concept of reason, or Vernunft—Reason replaced God; God was waning. Human reasoning prevailed, so thought, for instance, Robespierre, who carried out a dictatorship in the name of the revolution. Rousseau himself even argued that "when the state decrees death, a citizen should unconditionally obey that imperative". The Kantian moral imperative and Robespierresque revolutionary passion were linked, as Azuma (2014, p. 11) argues well.

Born in Geneva, Switzerland, Rousseau's opinions on direct democracy are expected; there as well as in all the cantons in Switzerland at that time (and, as some including Barber (2004) argue, thereafter as well) direct democracy was practiced. The prerequisites of direct democracy include the following:

(a) A relatively small number of residents in geographically small vicinities;
(b) Relatively dense daily interactions among residents/members of a community; and
(c) The relative isolation of a community from other similar communities and political and religious influences.

These circumstances possibly led Rousseau to ponder democracy daily. Among his vast writings, he discusses Corsica and Poland, but the tone of discussion is different than his discussion of Geneva. He regarded Corsica and Poland as not reaching the heightened level of direct democracy that he believed Geneva had reached. The lack of further articulation in achieving the general will is not without reason. After all, "the will of the state is equivalent to the unified will of citizens, and it is infallible by definition" (Azuma 2014, p. 11).

As mentioned in Azuma (2014), a philosopher and critic, Rousseau's ideology leans more toward animal compassion rather than human reason as a driver of human action. This point distinguishes Rousseau from Encyclopedists and from Locke, to whom reason and human reasoning were key drivers. This distinction is illustrated clearly in many of Rousseau's writings beyond the *Social Contract*, such as *New Eroise, Origins of Human Inequality,* and *Emille* (Farr and Williams 2015).

One question that might be raised here is what happens to the Rousseauesque world when digitalized globalization accelerates. Digitalization can be defined as the introduction of the instantaneous, massive, often customized, and even possibly intractable communication tools and bodies. The Economist magazine notes that the social network has turned itself into "one of the world's most influential technology giants" (The Economist 2016b). This is, as Azuma argues, the Rousseauesque world unfolding itself in front of our eyes! What has led some to think that Rousseau's alleged lack of sufficient articulation of how the general will is formed out of citizens' preferences can be resolved once Rousseau's thoughts about the general will are based far more strongly on the theory of animal compassion as a key driver in human action. Rousseau's concept of compassion differs entirely from the concept of reason and human reasoning; his line of thinking in terms of compassion is linked to Immanuel Kant, when Kant talks about the moral imperative (Kant 2013; Russett and Oneal 2001) and with Sigmund Freud when Freud (2010) talks about unconsciousness as a driver of human action (Azuma 2014, pp. 85–99 for Freud, and pp. 155–163 for Kant).

2.1.2 Representative Democracy by Locke

In contrast to Rousseau's, Locke's line of thinking is based on reason and human reasoning. Human reasoning is defined as the human operation of making sense. Locke lived his life in England during a significant period of transition, and lived in self-imposed exile for a time because his writings put his life in danger. Fortunately, English politics evolved in a way that Locke had envisioned; that is, the king's authority was stabilized and legitimized through the Declaration of 1688, a contract between the king and parliament. The Vatican's authority and influence in England were reduced because of the separation of the Anglican Church from the Vatican.

Thus, the prerequisite of representative democracy in England was made possible for a number of reasons:

(a) The separation of the secular from the sacred in the form of the establishment of the Anglican Church, independent of the Vatican.
(b) The despotic king was tamed through the Declaration of 1688 between the king and parliament. The king as envisioned by Thomas Hobbes (2014) for the initial phase of the formation of a sovereign territorial state had almost disappeared.
(c) The prosaically implemented legislative politics of England that steadily evolved with the parliament were made a focal point; thus, many including John Dunn (2005) called this a model of representative democracy. According to Dunn, following the demise of ancient Greece, the 2000-year democratic void was finally over, as democracy was resuscitated.

Legislative politics *a la* Locke is quintessentially English in the sense that the parliament is the platform of politics where parliamentarians are chosen according to the spirit of selecting leaders, from the so-called gentry to a more inclusive class representation (entrepreneurs and workers) plus peripheral areas of Scotland, Wales, and Northern Ireland through democratic elections. (Cf. Mair 2013; Achen and Bartels 2016 for not so democratic practices.)

Of all the democratic models, representative democracy is the most widely practiced in the twenty-first century. Interestingly, the Google search engine indicates that there have been 1,360,000 registered searches of representative democracy, while there have been 4,400,000 registered searches of direct democracy (accessed April 13, 2016). The far greater number of searches of direct democracy is perhaps due to the latent and manifest dissatisfaction with the current forms of representative democracy. (Cf. Keane 2009; Rosanvallon 2008; Mair 2013; Achen and Bartels 2016).

2.2 Global Quasi-Legislation Without a World Assembly

Legislation at the national level has four aspects: representation, debating, log-rolling, and voting at committee and plenary settings. (Martin et al. 2016; Redman and Newstadt 2001; Fenno 2002) National differences are vast; however, to examine the differences between national and global legislative processes and outcomes, a comparison of these four aspects may suffice. It is important to emphasize that global legislation possesses the same aspects as legislation at the national level, although with many variations.

The global legislative process has many different forms of representation: sovereign state, transnational non-governmental organization, and transnational social movement through opinion polls and social networking instruments. The debate stage occurs in institutionalized and non-institutionalized forms. Thus debating exists within international organizations and also within newspapers, magazines, television, etc. The global legislative process shifts next to log-rolling, which occurs at many levels through formal and informal means such as formal diplomatic compromise and non-compromise, as well as log-rolling in international organizations, etc. In a global setting, voting occurs without a formal institutionalized parliament because no such body exists. Nevertheless, quasi-parliamentary functions are played by various bodies—such as the United Nations Security Council and the International Football Association Executive Committee—and social movements.

Legislative outcomes at the national level occur through the passage of bills into laws through committee and plenary meetings. Laws take the form of rule-making and aspirational calling; the former contains regulative aspects while the latter focuses on normative aspects without either awarding or punishing. Outcomes at the global level occur through multilateral treaties, conventions, declarations, and resolutions. Multilateral treaties and conventions are signed primarily by sovereign states, while declarations and resolutions are issued mostly by the collective wills of participants in various international gatherings.

Legislative effects at the national level tend to be strong and binding depending on the nature of laws. Moreover, these legislative effects tend to vary at the global level, as quasi-legislative outcomes tend to be highly dependent on the legislative environments. Bonding and binding power is variable according to the strength of passion, interest, and power of the participants in quasi-legislative processes.

2.3 Transnational Direct Democracy

Rousseau resorts to empathy and compassion, feelings which are bound to arise when human suffering is witnessed. With the advances in digital communication and artificial intelligence, transnational digital democracy is something one can envisage (Rosanvallon 2008; Kriesi et al. 2013). Transnational domains of direct democracy are categorized as transnational communication, transnational movements, transnational organizations, and transnational transactions.

2.3.1 Transnational Communication

Transnational communication has evolved remarkably through the years. The days when the International Postal Union prevailed in the domain of international communication are gone; now, the internet has taken over with its high speeds and instantaneous results. When physical communication is required over digital, the international logistics company known as DHL has taken over. With seamless networks of delivery for physical objects such as letters and documents and the help of Google Earth, DHL delivers far and wide when the internet is an inappropriate vehicle for communication. Another aspect of transnational communication is the unfortunate occurrence of terrorism. Needless to say, hazards such as terrorist attacks cannot be precluded as a result of the evolution of communication.

The increased speed and density of transnational communication has subsequently increased the degree to which direct democracy is experienced. In order for the majority to perceive transnational direct democracy as a reality, direct participation is key. For this to occur, the establishment of air travel networks with higher flight frequency, lower financial costs, and decreased flight hours will make all the difference. While frequency and cost have seen great improvements over the years, flight hours have not decreased much since technological innovation for jet aircrafts has been stagnant for the last 50 years. However, the introduction of very low priced flights has made air travel more accessible to a wider range of people. Overall, the progress in transnational communication, and especially in participation, has moved transnational direct democracy a step or two forward.

2.3.2 Transnational Social Movements

The latest book by Russell Dalton and Christian Welzel (2015), *The Civic Culture Transformed: From Allegiant to Assertive Citizen*, and Sidney Tarrow's (Tarrow 2011) *Power in Movement: Social Movements and Contentious Politics* have noted the spectacular rise of social movements where people take direct action. The tide of globalization swayed Latin American societies in the new millennium. After the Group of Seven agreed on the Plaza accord in 1985 whereby the currency trade flourished 50–100 times thenceforth in comparison to the trade of goods and services. Latin American social forces were defensive as their economies were on the whole weaker in manufacturing and monetary service sectors. On the one hand they wanted to defend their vested interests by bureaucratic authoritarian protection from external and internal liberalizing forces while on the other hand they wanted to enhance the power of democratizing forces in civil societies. Massive and largely defensive social mobilization took place across Latin American countries. Transnational advocacy networks across Latin American countries played an important creative role of advancing the cause of the poor, women and socially handicapped coping with the sway of globalization (Johnston and Almeida 2006).

2.3.3 Transnational Organizations

Multilateral treaties are one of the key aspects of transnational organizations. Legitimated by multilateral treaties and conventions, some transnational organizations grow as an institutional body while others may not (Tallberg et al. 2013; Abbott et al. 2015, 2016; Abbott and Snidal 1998). The speed with which the number of transnational organizations has grown since 1945 has been phenomenal (Le et al. 2014). Transnational organizations come in two types: aspirational yearning type and rule-making type. The former resolves to achieve a certain set of goals as if they were part of transnational social movements; the United Nations Conference on Trade and Development (UNCTAD) is such an example, as it resolves to address the gaps between the developing South and the industrial North. As time goes by and the per capita income level increases among the developing South, the UNCTAD has reduced its erstwhile fervent political rhetoric. The latter type of transnational organization, that emphasizes strict bindings by clauses with associated rewards and punishments, focuses on rule-making and the regulations among sovereign states normally manned by professional experts specializing in science, technology, medicine, nuclear energy, development, and finance. The International Atomic Energy Agency (IAEA) is an organization of experts in nuclear energy that monitors nuclear energy production. While it helps in nuclear generated energy production and utilization, together with sovereign states' representatives, it also defines rules and regulations whereby the prospect for nuclear weapons non-proliferations would shine. Therein the IAEA constitutes a platform of transnational direct democracy in a very narrowly limited, yet highly specialized, domain.

2.3.4 Transnational Transactions

Business transactions used to comprise simple transactions of goods and services. Until 1985, the external trade of goods and services occupied approximately 90% of total business transactions. With the Plaza Accord by the Group of Seven, currency trade became a mainstream way of doing business externally. Trade and investments have continued as before, but large profits have been made from currency trade by making use of the variable currency exchange rates and losses with sophisticated machines. By deliberately exaggerating or underestimating currency exchange rates, currency trade has come to play a key role in driving the world economy. Some now say that capitalists have ended their useful and progressive role, while investors who manipulate the currencies of the world with a large amount of money in hand reign supreme (Mizuno 2014). Investors of the world are latently united in the sense that they can fathom each other's moves in currency markets as if conducting transnational direct democracy. For instance, Japanese businesses, which acquire enormous benefits from overseas investments in comparison to their benefits from domestic investments, are sensitive to currency markets and exchange rate movements. Domestic production and consumption carry less weightage in their calculus and their relative insensitivity to the governmental call for the increase in domestic consumption and the union's call for wage increase (Jesper 2019).

In sum, the three mechanisms of initiative, referendum, and recall are embedded in direct democracy to allow for the investigation and reassessment of executive incumbents regarding illegal, immoral, or otherwise inappropriate actions. A certain number of signatures are required to start the process, and in transnational settings, a variety of rules apply; one good example of this involves the International Football Association's president. For example, the International Football Association Board unanimously approved video assistant referees (VARs) to help increase integrity and fairness in the game at its 132nd Annual General Meeting taking place at its headquarters in Zurich on March 3, 2018. The President then signed off on the board's approval.

2.4 Transnational Representative Democracy

2.4.1 Subnational Local Election

In envisioning transnational representative democracy, subnational local elections loom increasingly large (Barber 2014). For example, mayoral positions are becoming increasingly important as seen in the prominence of mayoral summits where leaders of key global cities gather to discuss and present resolutions for issues of global importance. Although their agreements and prescriptions do not have any binding power, the fact that the mayors of the world's major cities come together over concern for perceived problems of global importance is constructive; it provides an opportunity for fresh and possibly useful perspectives to be exchanged, as each city is often confronted by similar, and possibly acute, problems. Additionally, mayors of the world's major cities are often leaders with illustrious careers who have exemplary achievements. Thus, in addition to what they say and how they act, how they are elected by citizens from various walks of life should be closely examined (Jain forthcoming). No less important are subnational elections of a local nature. After all, such local characteristics are often more transnationally observed. For example, when a decision was made to divert water supplies from Haryana to New Delhi, the country as a whole as well as outside observers had a stake in the Haryana residents' respective decision to protest; even though the riots—as collective protest—were unrelated to an election, it was clear that the riot participants and representatives exerted enormous influence on the present status and future of New Delhi and India (The Economist 2016a).

2.4.2 National Election

Transnational representative democracy has been mostly envisioned as being constituted by national representatives acting as delegates of sovereign states, making summit meetings of national leaders momentous occasions. Therefore, a national leader's willingness to travel abroad affects how confident the citizens are with his or her ability to lead the country in an age of a fledgling transnational representative democracy. Consider, for example, that Japanese Prime Minister Eisaku Sato (r. 1964–1972) did not travel abroad during the first year of his tenure because he was apprehensive of the possibility of disquieting moves unfolding while abroad. Prime Minister Shinzo Abe (2006–2007 and 2012-today), however, scheduled 74 trips abroad between December 2012 and April 2019. He has been to the capital cities, as well as those cities that accommodate multilateral meetings of various sorts including the UN General Assembly, Asia Pacific Economic Conference, East Asia Summit, and ASEAN Plus Three (Japan, China, and South Korea). Prime Minister Abe's extensive participation in transnational representative democracy and the citizen's selection of the Liberal Democratic Party in the 2012, 2014 and 2017 general elections, indirectly led to Abe's position as Prime Minister.

2.4.3 Regional and International Platforms

Transnational representative democracy also functions when those democracies perform within a variety of platforms, such as regional, international, and Asian platforms. Such platforms often begin modestly as entities or groups that grow over time into institutions and organizations. In other words, with the increase in participants and the consolidation of rules and practices, such platforms can become regional and international organizations offering resources, staff legitimacy, and power. The Shanghai Cooperation Organization is such an example for which China has been a prime driver; the East Asia Summit, encompassing the ASEAN plus three (China, Japan, and South Korea) and two (Australia and India), is another example for which Japan has been a prime driver. Initiating a platform and then institutionalizing it means that those initiators are members in good standing. In transnational representative democracy, being a member in good standing is very important; when several such platforms arise, having characteristics that potential users would like to see is important. This lesson can be seen in the downfall of Yahoo following the introduction of Google as an internet search engine—potential users liked Google as a platform better than Yahoo.

2.4.4 Non-governmental Organizations

In transnational representative democracy, non-governmental organizations are relevant. The UN began as an organization comprised of a small number of sovereign states in 1945. When the UN building was designed and constructed along the Hudson River, architects imagined that the number of members would reach 50 by the end of the 1950s and into the hundreds by the end of the 1960s. Neither of these estimates proved correct; membership rolls exceeded these estimates by leaps and bounds. In the 1940s and 1950s, Asia and Latin America were key member contributors and, in the 1960s, Africa and the Middle East played a similar role. In the 1970s and beyond, non-governmental organizations have maintained an important role in the United Nations. The growth of United Nations member states eventually stalled (with 193 sovereign states); however, non-governmental organizations have attained their high status by bringing in fresh and novel perspectives and pushing new energy and power outside of the United Nations' organizations (Grigorescu and Baser 2019). Symbolic of the growing legitimacy and power of the NGO is its ability to spearhead social movements. For example, the movement to ban landmines was headed by Jody Williams, who was awarded a Nobel Peace Prize in 1997.

Both legislators and executives possess the ability to refresh their goals and objectives. Legislators can force the executives led by the prime minister to resign if they are able to mobilize majority votes; additionally, executives can call for a general election whereby all legislators face an election or re-election. In transnational settings, however, this has never occurred. WIN-Gallup International (World-Independent-Network-Gallup International), which polls people worldwide, annually surveys respondents from approximately 50 countries. In 2012, the question asked was: "When the United States exerts influence on matters of global importance, some people are thinking that not only American citizens but also citizens of other countries should have voting rights on US presidential election. Do you agree or disagree? Choose one: agree very much; agree; neither agree nor disagree; disagree; disagree very much." Although such voting rights would never be implemented, in this artificial setting, Kenya, Afghanistan, and China were the top three countries where far more than the majority of respondents chose "agree very much" or "agree." WIN-Gallup International conducted a similar global poll in 2016 (WIN-Gallup International 2016). The rankings of the countries based on the difference of the percentage of respondents choosing Trump versus Clinton was Russia (23%), China (−9%), the US (−7%), and India (−22%) (Inoguchi 2017). The point here is that non-governmental organizations sometimes conduct what may be called artificial elections under the umbrella of transnational representative democracy.

2.5 Comparison of Global Politics Between 1912 and 2019

If this book had been penned one century ago, say in 1912 when Norman Angell (1912) published a book entitled *The Great Illusion: A Study of the Relation of Military Power to National Advantage*, would readers have been receptive to our ideas? Initially, Norman Angell's book was applauded by many readers, but, in tandem with the outset of war in 1914, eventually came to be seen as a great disappointment. Angell envisaged that the slow, steady development of economic transactions across nations would prevail in the world, resulting in the idealized liberal peace that Immanuel Kant had depicted one century before in his *Eternal Peace*. Ironically, it turned out to be a great illusion; at the height of the growing economic interdependence, a great war erupted in 1914. Furthermore, economic interdependence did not advance between the First World War and the Second World War, which ravaged the entire world, resulting in the deaths of 60 million people between 1938 and 1945.

In 2018, a century later, as this book is being written, economic interdependence in terms of the transactions of goods and service trade have stalled. In fact, such transactions have stagnated since 2008, when the Lehman Brothers-originating recession occurred. In contrast, currency trade has increased substantially since 1986. When comparing 2018 to 1912, the level of economic interdependence in terms of free trade has increased astronomically. This is due, in part, to the expectation that in currency trade, as distinguished from goods and service trade, a most noteworthy difference is present: the massive amount of transactions and their instantaneous speed. Furthermore, the level of interdependence has proliferated from more narrowly confined economic interdependence to a wide range of human activities.

If one focuses on Western Europe, one of the core geographical areas of world prosperity in the twentieth century, the development of interdependence from mostly goods and service trade across borders to many other areas is most pronounced. First, an energy community was constructed to share the meager energy resources. Second, free trade among selected countries was implemented. Third, free movement of people was implemented across borders among selected countries, which were called the Schengen Five: France, Germany, Belgium, the Netherlands, and Luxemburg. Fourth, free transactions with foreign currencies was implemented in 2000 via the Maastricht Treaty among select countries who joined the Maastricht Treaty and adopted the euro as their national and international currency. Globally, free movement of men and women across borders has increased substantially—due in part because the European Union, especially Germany, and selective northwestern European countries have been "progressive" in accommodating refugees and immigrants. Needless to say, other countries have been moving in the same direction, but the speed and range of their progress is incomparable to that of the European Union.

What can be said about global legislation? Immanuel Kant said that signing and ratifying agreements and treaties among similar-minded nations would contribute to peace, free trade, and democracy. This has been the initial hunch of the authors of this book. Through the concept of global legislation, the authors tried to express the mechanism through which global citizens' preferences are transformed into global legislative products called multilateral treaties. Since global legislative processes and outcomes are qualitatively different from national legislative processes and outcomes, the term "quasi-legislative processes and outcomes" is adopted.

There are two theoretical agendas pertaining to global quasi-legislative processes and outcomes. First, it is absolutely necessary to provide evidence systematically and scientifically on the basis of extant empirical data to illustrate that the global citizens' preferences and global quasi-legislative outcomes more or less match. Second, it is absolutely necessary to show that multilateral treaties are shaped by sovereign state actors whose political regime characteristics influence legislative outcomes.

These two tasks are what this book aims to undertake. For the first task, to empirically examine the possibility of a social contract within a global setting, two sets of data are used: one is global citizens' preferences about values and norms as gauged by the World Values Survey, while the other is sovereign states' participation in 120 multilateral treaties deposited to the UN. The details of these two set of data will be presented in Chaps. 3 and 4, respectively.

References

Abbott, K., & Snidal, D. (1998). Why states act through formal international organizations. *Journal of Conflict Resolution, 42*(1), 3–32.

Abbott, K., Genschel, P., Snidal, D., & Zangl, B. (Eds.). (2015). *International organizations as orchestrators*. Cambridge: Cambridge University Press.

Abbott, K., Green, J., & Keohane, R. (2016). Organizational ecology and institutional change in global governance. *International Organization, 70*(2), 247–277.

Achen, C., & Bartels, L. (2016). *Democracy for realists: Why elections do not produce responsible government*. Princeton: Princeton University Press.

Angell, N. (1912). *The great illusion: A study of the relation of military power to national advantage, paperback edition*. New York: Bottom of the Hill Publishing.

Azuma, H. (2014). *General Will 2.0: Rousseau, Freud, Google*, New York: Vertical.

Badie, B. (2000). *The imported state: The westernization of the political order*. Stanford: Stanford University Press.

Barber, B. (2004). *The death of communal liberty: A history of freedom in a Swiss Mountain Canton*. Princeton: Princeton University Press.

Barber, B. (2014). *If mayors ruled the world: dysfunctional nations, rising cities*. New Haven: Yale University Press.

Budge, I. (1996). *The new challenge of direct democracy*. Cambridge: Polity.

Dahl, R. (2006). *A preface to democratic theory, expanded edition*. New Haven: Yale University Press.

Dalton, R., & Welzel, C. eds. (2015). *The civic culture transformed: From allegiance to assertive citizens*. New York: Cambridge University Press.

Diderot, D., & le Rond d'Alembert, J. (1751–1772). *Encyclopédie ou Dictionnaire Raisonné des Sciences, des Arts et des Métiers* (Vol. 28). Sydney: Wentworth Press.

Dunn, J. (2005). *Setting the people free: The story of democracy*. London: Atlantic Books.

Farr, J., & Williams, D. L. (Eds.). (2015). *The general will: The evolution of a concept*. New York: Cambridge University Press.

Fenno, R. (2002). *Home style: House members in their districts*. New York: Pearson; Longman Classics edition.

Freud, S. (2010). *The interpretation of dreams: The complete and definitive text*. New York: Basic Books.

Grigorescu, A., & Baser, C. (2019). The choice between intergovernmentalism and nongovernmentalism: Projecting domestic preferences to global governance. *World Politics, 71*(1), 88–125.

Habermas, J. (1991). *The structural transformation of the public sphere: An inquiry into category of bourgeois society*. Cambridge, MA: MIT Press.

Hobbes, T. (2014). *Thomas Hobbes: Leviathan*. Oxford: Oxford University Press, 1st edition of Clarendon Edition of the Works of Thomas Hobbes.

Inoguchi, T. (2017, January 27). Non-US and US citizens' polling in US presidential election 2016: A hierarchical Bayesian model. In *Paper prepared for the conference organized by Asian journal of comparative politics (SAGE publications)*. Tokyo: International House of Japan.

Inoguchi, T., & Le, L. T. Q. (2016). Toward modelling a global social contract: Jean-Jacques Rousseau and John Locke. *Japanese Journal of Political Science, 17*(03), 489–522. https://doi.org/10.1017/S1468109916000207.

Jain, P. (forthcoming). Asian subnational governance in foreign affairs. In T. Inoguchi (Ed.), *The Sage handbook of Asian foreign policy, Vol. 1, Chapter 16*. London: Sage Publications.

Jesper, K. (2019). "Japan is back as a top global contender." *The Japan Times*, Feb. 3.

Johnston, H., & Almeida, P. (Eds.). (2006). *Latin American social movements: Globalization, democratization, and transnational networks*. New York: Rowman & Littlefield Publishers.

Kant, I. (2013). *Eternal peace and other internal essays*. New York: The Classicus.us.

Keane, J. (2009). *The life and death of democracy*. London: Simon and Schuster.

Kriesi, H., Lavenex, S., Esser, F., Matthes, J., Bühlmann, M., & Bochsler, D. (2013). *Democracy in the age of globalization and mediatization*. Basingstoke, Hampshire: Palgrave Macmillan.
Le, T. Q. L., Mikami, Y., & Inoguchi, T. (2014). Global leadership and international regime: Empirical testing of cooperation without hegemonic paradigm on the basis of 120 multilateral conventions deposited to the United Nations System. *Japanese Journal of Political Science, 15*(4), 523–601.
Locke, J. (1993). *Two treaties of government*. New York: Everyman Paperback.
Mair, P. (2013). *Ruling the void: The hollowing of Western democracy*. London: Verso.
Martin, S., Saafeld, T., & Strøm, K. (2016). *The Oxford handbook of legislative studies*. Oxford: Oxford University Press.
Mizuno, K. (2014). *Shihonshugi no Shuen to Rekishino Kiki (The end of capitalism and the crisis of history)*. Tokyo: PHP Institute.
Ockham, W., & Brown, S. (1990). *Ockham-philosophical writings: A solution*. New York: Hackett Publishing Company.
Putnam, R. (2000). *Making democracy work: Civic traditions in modern Italy*. Princeton: Princeton University Press.
Redman, E., & Newstadt, R. (2001). *The dance of legislation: An insider's account of the workings of the United States Senate*. Seattle: University of Washington Press.
Rosanvallon, P. (2008). *Counter-democracy: Politics in an age of distrust*. Cambridge, MA: Cambridge University Press.
Rousseau, J.-J., & Cranston, M. (1968). *The social contract*. London: Penguin Classics.
Russett, B. M., & Oneal, J. (2001). *Triangulating peace: Democracy, interdependence, and international organizations*. New York: Norton.
Shkler, J. (1973). General will. In P. Wiener (Ed.), *Dictionary of the history of ideas* (p. 275). New York: Charles Scribner's Sons.
Tallberg, J., Sommerer, T., Squatrito, T., & Jonsson, C. (2013). *The opening up of international organizations: Transnational access in global governance*. Cambridge: Cambridge University Press.
Tarrow, S. (2011). *Power in movement: Social movements and contentious politics*. Cambridge, MA: Cambridge University Press.
The Economist. (2016a). "*Caste in India: Backward ho!*" February 27–March 4, pp. 21–22.
The Economist. (2016b). "*How to win friends and influence people*" April 9–15, p. 18.
Whitehead, L. (2002). *Democratization: Theory and practice*. Oxford: Oxford University Press.
WIN-Gallup International. (2016). *Global poll on the American election: Region-wise results, demographics-wise results and U.S. results*, Vienna: WIN-Gallup International.

Chapter 3
Global Citizens' Preferences for Value Orientation

Abstract For our data on global citizens' preferences for value orientation, we use the World Value Survey. Before we link, in Chap. 5, between global citizens' preferences for value orientation on the one hand and sovereign states' preferences for participation in multilateral treaties on the other hand, Chap. 3 describes the nature and merits of the data used for global citizens' preferences. Along the key two dimensions, protective vs emancipative and secular vs sacred, yielded by factor analysis of the World Value Survey data, ten geo-historico-cultural groups are plotted on graphs: Sub-Saharan Africa, Sinic East, Returned West, Reformed West, Orthodox East, Old West, New West, Latin America, Islamic East, Indic East. Branco Milanovic's (Shadows and lights of globalization. Globalinequality Blog. http://glineq.blogspot.com/. Accessed 25 Apr 2019, 2019) rebalancing between the West and the Rest gives a fresh insight into ten geo-historico-cultural graphs.

How are World Values Surveys conducted in close to 100 countries (whose population covers 90% of the world population, Inglehart 2018, p. i)? First, the WVS (www.worldvaluessurvey.org) is a global network of social scientists studying changing values and their impact on social and political life, led by an international team of scholars, with the WVS association and secretariat headquartered in Stockholm, Sweden. Second, methodologically, three criteria are mandatory: (1) WVS are required to cover all residents in a country in the age of 18 years older and older; (2) Principal Investigators in each country can lower the minimum age limit as long as the minimum required sample size for the 18+ population is achieved; (3) Obtained sample should be representative, i.e., should reflect the main distribution observed in the country population (gender, age groups, urban/rural population etc. Thus, a full probability sample of the population aged 18 years and older, allowing a national representative random sample based on multi-stage territorial stratified selection. Third, interviewing respondents and registering data are required to be as follows. The main method of data collection in the WVS survey is face-to-face interview at respondent's home/place of residence. Respondent's answers could be recorded in a paper questionnaire (PAPI) or via CAPI (Computer Assisted Personal Interview). The latest (WVS-7) questionnaire comprises 14 thematic subsections:

T. Inoguchi, L. T. Q. Le, *The Development of Global Legislative Politics*,
Trust: Interdisciplinary Perspectives 3, https://doi.org/10.1007/978-981-32-9389-2_3

(1) social values, attitudes and stereotypes (45 items); (2) societal well-being (11 items); (3) social capital, trust and organizational membership 849 items); (4) economic values (6 items); (5) corruption (9 items); (6) migration (10 items); (7) post-materialist index (6 items); (8) science & technology (6 items); (9) religious values (12 items); (10) security (21 items); (11) ethical values & norms (23 items); (12) political interest and political participation (36 items); (13) political culture and political regime (25 items); (14) demography (31 items), thus amounting to 290 questions in WVS-7. The number of questions in WVS-6, which we have used for our analysis, is slightly smaller than 290.

The World Values Survey (WVS) has been determining how global citizens express their preferences for value orientation on a very large scale. Since the early 1980s, it has conducted global surveys six times: 1981–1984, 1990–1994, 1995–1998, 1999–2004, 2005–2009, and 2010–2014. Ronald Inglehart has led the WVS since the 1970s (Inglehart 1976, 1997, 2018), while more recently Pippa Norris, Christian Welzel, Miguel Basanez, and many others have enriched their products in various ways.

We have used the latest analysis results by Welzel (2013) in this research. Our aim is to determine the link between global citizens' preferences for value orientation and sovereign states' participation in multilateral conventions. When factor-analyzing the data of the WVS, Welzel (2013) has labeled the first and second dimensions as *protective versus emancipative* and *sacred versus secular*. In Ronald Inglehart's original version, the labels were *materialist versus post-materialist* and *sacred versus secular* (Inglehart 1997) and *modernist versus post-modernist* and *sacred and secular* (Inglehart 2018).

The first dimension *protective versus emancipative* captures the closed, protectionist, and defensive orientation versus the open, liberal, and cooperative orientation. In the original version, the *materialist versus post-materialist* orientation captured the survival versus leisure orientation. In the 1990s version, the *modernist versus post-modernist* orientation captured the impulse to modernize life versus the composure after modern economic growth. The current version focuses specifically on those oriented toward a borderless, globalized, and digitalized world. Thus, the topics of enterprise, trade, migration, climate change, navigation, freedom of speech and assembly, gender equality, and human rights have come to the forefront in the WVS questionnaire as well.

The second dimension is the *sacred versus secular* orientation. The secular orientation of human kind, at least in the West, had increased by the third quarter of the twentieth century. In the last quarter of the last century, however, the weight of religion and religiosity in human life has steadily increased. This direction has been masterly analyzed by Norris and Inglehart (2004). In addition, Putnam and Campbell (2012) comprehensively traced the broad trends of American religion and religiosity and their cultural and sociological impacts. The dimension labels change over time as citizens' preferences for values and norms change, yet some span half a century.

Moreover, the number of societies that the WVS covers has notably increased extensively, contributing to the change in labels. When the WVS began in cooperation with the European Value Systems Study group, only seven countries (the United States, Argentine, Australia, Japan, South Korea, and South Africa)—aside from European countries—participated. By 2019, the WVS covered close to 100 countries whose combined population amounts to about 90% of the world population. (Inglehart 2018, p. xvii)

Based on the results of his research, Welzel has placed countries into ten geo-historico-cultural groups as presented in the following sections.

3.1 Sub-Saharan Africa

Sub-Saharan Africa refers to the following countries: Nigeria, Mali, Burkina Fasso, Rwanda, Uganda, Ghana, Zambia, Zimbabwe, Tanzania, South Africa, and Ethiopia. Ethiopia, South Africa, Tanzania, Zimbabwe, and Zambia, located in Southern and Eastern Africa, were found to be the most emancipative Africa. Nigeria, Mali, and Burkina Fasso, located in Western Africa, and Rwanda and Uganda, located near Lake Victoria were found to be the most protective. In terms of the sacred versus secular dimension, Ghana, Zimbabwe, and Tanzania are stronger in their secular orientation, while the sacred orientation is stronger in the rest; for instance, Christians and Muslims compete in Nigeria.

3.2 Sinic East

Sinic East includes the countries of China, Vietnam, Japan, and South Korea. The most emancipative of these are South Korea and Japan, and the most protective are China and Vietnam. It must be noted that Vietnam is more emancipative in part because the southern parts are governed more in harmony with the market economic system. Additionally, South Korea has been more in harmony with the market economic system particularly since the Asian Financial Crisis of 1997–1998. In terms of the sacred versus secular dimension, it is noteworthy that Japan and China are very secular; furthermore, these two countries contribute to the fact that Sinic East is overall very secular. Sinic East competes with the Reformed West, especially Scandinavia, in this respect, and is so distant from the United States. The United States has a relatively high score in the sacred direction on the sacred versus secular dimension, and is closer to Indic East, Latin America, and Sub-Sahara Africa. Vietnam and South Korea have strong Christian and Buddhist communities.

3.3 Returned West

Returned West refers to those countries that switched from the East to the West in 1989. They include Poland, Slovenia, Estonia, Croatia, Hungary, Slovakia, Latvia, and Lithuania. In terms of the protective versus emancipative dimension, Slovenia is the most emancipative. The most protective are Lithuania, Latvia, and Slovakia, as they are smaller and act with strong neighbors. In terms of the sacred versus secular orientation, the most secular countries are Latvia and Lithuania, whereas the sacred orientation is strong in Poland and Slovenia.

3.4 Reformed West

Reformed West refers to the West European countries shaped after the Reformation, including Germany, the Netherlands, the United Kingdom, Switzerland, Finland, Sweden, and Norway. The most emancipative are Sweden, Norway, and the Netherlands, whereas the most protective are the United Kingdom, Germany, Switzerland, and Finland. In terms of the sacred versus secular dimension, the most secular are Norway, Finland, Switzerland, and Sweden where the Reformation led by Luther, Calvin, and many others was solidly carried out. The Netherlands, the United Kingdom, and Germany are less secular.

3.5 Orthodox East

Orthodox East covers both the former Soviet Union members and bloc members, or the Orthodox Christian countries. They include Russia, Ukraine, Belarus, Armenia, Georgia, Azerbaijan, Uzbekistan, Kyrgyzstan, Kazakhstan, Moldova, Montenegro, Albania, Bosnia, Bulgaria, Serbia, and Romania. The most emancipative of the Orthodox East are Serbia and Bulgaria, while the most protective are the trans-Caucasian (Armenia, Georgia, Azerbaijan) and Central Asian states (Kyrgyzstan, Uzbekistan). In terms of the sacred versus secular orientation, the most secular are Moldova, Montenegro, and Bulgaria, while the most sacred orientation is manifested in Armenia (Armenian Christian), Romania (Catholic), Kyrgyzstan (Islam), and Uzbekistan (Islam).

3.6 Old West

Old West refers to those countries that were shaped after the fall of the Roman Empire. They include Italy, France, Spain, Andora, and Cyprus. The most emancipative are Andora, Spain, and France, while the most protective are Italy and Cyprus.

In terms of the sacred versus secular dimension, the most secular is Andora whereas the most sacred are Cyprus and Spain. France is worthy of a special note as France is proud of abiding by *laïcité* (secular in public places), and thus is located between secular and sacred.

3.7 New West

New West refers to the countries with new settlers such as the United States, Canada, New Zealand, and Australia. Being new settlement societies, they are all emancipative in principle. Ranked from the highest to the lowest in terms of emancipation, among them, however are Australia, New Zealand, the United States, and Canada, in this order. In terms of sacred versus secular dimension, their difference is noteworthy. The United States is the most extreme in its sacred orientation (Putnam and Campbell 2012), and New Zealand is the most secular of the four.

3.8 Latin America

Latin America refers to those countries in the Americas except for the United States and Canada. The most emancipative is Uruguay, making it an ideal location for the Uruguay free trade negotiation round two. Argentina and Chile are next, and both of these used to thrive on agricultural and mining products exported to Europe and North America in the century between the American Civil War and the Second World War. Brazil and Mexico, both large countries, are in between emancipative and protective. In terms of the sacred versus secular dimension, the most secular are Uruguay, Argentina, and Chile while Guatemala, Trinidad-Tobago, Ecuador, and Venezuela are strongly religious.

3.9 Islamic East

Islamic East includes those in the Middle East and North Africa whose dominant religion is Islam. They are Iran, Saudi Arabia, Bahrain, Lebanon, Albania, Turkey, Iraq, Tunisia, Egypt, Yemen, Jordan, Libya, Algeria, Iraq, Tunisia, Kuwait, Qatar, Kuwait, Morocco, Syria, and Afghanistan. The most emancipative of the Islamic East countries are Iran, Saudi Arabia, Bahrain, and Lebanon. The most protective of the Islamic East are Qatar and Morocco. The most secular are Lebanon, Morocco, Turkey, and Kuwait while religiosity is strong in Iran, Saudi Arabia, Egypt, Yemen, and Jordan.

3.10 Indic East

Indic East refers to those countries in South Asia and Southeast Asia that were impacted by the ancient Indian civilization (especially religion and language). They are Bangladesh, Pakistan, Indonesia, Malaysia, India, Thailand, the Philippines, and Singapore. The most emancipative are Singapore, Thailand, and the Philippines. The most protective are Bangladesh, Pakistan, Indonesia, and Malaysia. In terms of the sacred versus secular dimension, the most secular are Indonesia, India, Singapore, and Thailand, whereas the most religious are the Philippines, Bangladesh, Malaysia, and Pakistan.

3.11 Rebalancing: Ten Geo-Historico-Cultural Groups

The two key dimensions of the World Values Survey as presented in Welzel (2013) is one of the most interesting findings and gives deep insights into the evolution of human culture (Inglehart 2018). We have followed the Welzel grouping scheme when we examine the list of 120 multilateral treaties and the list of 193 sovereign states. Most striking is the pronounced weight of the broader West in the multilateral treaties cosmos. The Welzel ten group scheme has four Wests and four Easts plus Sub-saharan Africa and Latin America. Orthodox East is a complex creature of Russian Orthodox combined with the East Roman Empire and the Soviet Empire. No less striking, though, is the slow and steady increase of the rest, or the non-West (Rachman 2017). The number of sovereign states in the rest or the non-West has grown very steadily since 1945. According to B. Milanovic's (2019) recalculation of the Maddison Project (2018), it is not confined to the great reversal of the number of countries but also no less great rebalancing of the size of per capita gross national product is taking place. Whereas the ratio of Britain and China in early nineteenth century and early twentieth century in terms of per capita gross national product is three versus one and eight versus one respectively, into the late twentieth century onward the ratio has been dramatically rebalancing itself. In the 1980s, the per capita gross national product the ratio between Britain and China, between Indonesia and the Netherlands, and between Britain and India has been changing favorably to former colonial countries. Milanovic (2019) attributes this reversal to globalization. The first globalization between early nineteenth century and early twentieth century ended in imperialism and World War I. The second globalization between the fourth quarter of the twentieth century and the first quarter of the twenty-first century has been materializing the great rebalancing. Though the process of rebalancing has been still in the midway, one keeps this in mind when they examine the locations of 193 sovereign states in global citizens' value orientation (and their treaty orientation).

References

Inglehart, R. (1976). *The silent revolution: Changing values and political styles among western publics*. Princeton: Princeton University Press.

Inglehart, R. (1997). *Modernization and postmodernization: Cultural, economic, and political change in 43 societies*. Princeton: Princeton University Press.

Inglehart, R. (2018). *Cultural evolution: People's motivations are changing, and reshaping the world*. Princeton: Princeton University Press.

Maddison Project Database. (2018). https://www.rug.nl/ggdc/historicaldevelopment/maddison/releases/maddison-project-database-2018. Accessed 25 Apr 2019.

Milanovic, B. (2019). Shadows and lights of globalization. *Globalinequality Blog*. http://glineq.blogspot.com/. Accessed 25 Apr 2019.

Norris, P., & Inglehart, R. (2004). *Sacred and secular: Religion and politics worldwide*. Cambridge, MA: Cambridge University Press.

Putnam, R. D., & Campbell, D. E. (2012). *American grace: How religion divides and unites us*. New York: Simon & Schuster.

Rachman, G. (2017). *Easternization: Asia's rise and America's decline from Obama to Trump and beyond*. New York: Other Press.

Welzel, C. (2013). *Freedom rising: Human empowerment and the quest for emancipation*. New York: Cambridge University Press.

Chapter 4
Sovereign States' Participation in Multilateral Treaties

Abstract In this chapter we use the Multilateral Treaties Survey data. Each treaty is described using six attributes: policy domains, year of deposit, year of membership, regional group, number of current members, treaty participation Index. The core of the Treaty Participation Index, is constituted by the number of years lapsed between sovereign states' signing and ratifying multilateral treaties. The Treaties Participation Index is shown for 193 sovereign states as well as for ten geo-historico-cultural groups (Sub-Saharan Africa, Sinic East, Returned West, Reformed West, Orthodox East, Old West, New West, Latin America, Islamic East, and Indic East) and for six policy domains (human rights, peace and disarmaments, trade, commerce and communications, the environment, intellectual property, labor).

4.1 Multilateral Treaties as a Source of Global Quasi-Legislative Outcomes

There is no institutionalized government for the whole world; nevertheless, our increasingly interdependent world is constantly facing a daunting array of threats that transcend national boundaries, such as climate change and environmental degradation, nuclear proliferation, and terrorism. Most countries have acknowledged that national governments alone cannot ensure adequate and effective solutions to face what former UN Secretary-General Kofi Annan called "problems without passports" (Annan 2009). How is the world governed without a world assembly?

In a national parliamentary democratic setting, the legislative branch takes care of legislation while the executive branch takes care of policy implementation. The members of the legislative branch are elected by citizens or electors. Electors' preferences are reflected and materialized in legislated bills. Therefore, outcomes in a national setting take the form of legislation of bills to laws through committee and plenary meetings. This is an ideal than a reality. Otto Bismarck once remarked that if you like laws and sausage, you should never watch either one being made.

In the real world, a formal institutionalized parliamentary body does not exist. Therefore, there is no global legislative mechanism with legislative and executive

T. Inoguchi, L. T. Q. Le, *The Development of Global Legislative Politics*,
Trust: Interdisciplinary Perspectives 3, https://doi.org/10.1007/978-981-32-9389-2_4

branches. There is no legal mechanism whereby global citizens' preferences are fed into laws, which in turn function as a set of global public policies. Yet if one envisages that those public opinions expressed and those multilateral treaties and conventions signed, ratified, and further implemented are equivalent to nationally surveyed citizens' preferences and nationally legislated bills respectively, there emerges global quasi-legislative politics. Therefore, it can be seen that the most concrete instances of global quasi-legislative outcomes are multilateral treaties.

A multilateral treaty is a written instrument entered into by sovereign states through a legislative process of negotiation, signing, and ratification, by which states establish rights and obligations among themselves. A government that has ratified the treaty is expected to apply its provisions through legislation or other appropriate means, as indicated in the text of the treaty (Alli 2008). Through these, states work together to establish common standards of behaviors in spheres such as trade and security, embedding norms and rules in international institutions charged with providing global goods and mitigating global ills (Patrick 2014). These regulatory regimes have helped facilitate international cooperation among states to address various aspects of the problems associated with global governance. In addition to their initial goals of protecting human rights, safeguarding peace, establishing a framework for international trade, and promoting economic and social progress, multilateral treaties are now being formulated to tackle the new generation of global matters, from intellectual property protection and labor laws to issues associated with peaceful uses of nuclear energy, armaments and proliferation, combat against terrorism, and cybercrime. More than 500 multilateral treaties are deposited with the Secretary-General Office of the UN that cover a broad range of subject matters such as human rights, disarmament, and protection of the environment (United Nations n.d.-a; -b). The speed with which the number of treaties has grown since 1945 has been phenomenal (Hale and Held 2017; Le et al. 2014). From the middle of the twentieth century, an expansion of formal global government has taken place. In the twenty-first century, the number of international organizations and their offshoots has only increased from 7000 to 8000 (Hale and Held 2017, p. 4).

Despite the ever increasing variety of multilateral agreements, conventions, and treaties, a comprehensive picture has not been provided in any systematic and statistical format (Kajima Institute of Peace 2015; Iriye 2004; Rosenberg 2012; Shaw 2017). Important observations include the works by Hale et al. (2013) and Hale and Held (2017). These ambitious studies attempt to answer the following question: In the twenty-first century, when global cooperation is most earnestly needed, why has multilateralism been failing? Hale et al. (2013) analyze the causes of failure, while Hale and Held (2017) present seven pathways through and beyond gridlock across areas of world politics examined in eleven policy areas: finance, monetary policy, trade, investment, energy, humanitarianism, human rights, health climate, cyber security, and weapons of mass destruction. This study is an attempt to construct an analytical framework for a more comprehensive and systematic examination of the attitudes and behaviors of sovereign states who have participated in these multilateral treaties; thus, 120 multilateral agreements deposited in the UN, which is the only truly universal and inclusive multilateral institution, were chosen for this study. In what follows, a survey of these 120 UN multilateral treaties will be described in detail.

4.2 Multilateral Treaties Survey

With the intent of producing a holistic database rather than a narrow view in any specific regime, this collection extends its coverage to a range of issues in today's world, including: human rights, peace and disarmament; trade, commerce, and communication; environment; intellectual property; and labor health and safety. These six categories of policy domains of multilateral treaties have been set by the UN and each of the 120 multilateral treaties to our analysis has been categorized by the UN. Each area includes different but related issues; for instance, arms control and disarmament, non-nuclear zones, non-nuclear proliferation, and prevention of cybercrime and terrorism all fall under the peace and disarmament category. Most of the treaties are registered in the UN, while some are also registered in the League of Nations (1918–38), and a few are from before 1918. The global legislative outputs of more than 560 are based on its entirety, except for those that do not fit the major multilateral treaty definition. For our analysis, we have chosen 120 multilateral treaties out of the UN-deposited 560 multilateral treaties. The difference between them is because in our analysis those multilateral treaties that are more regional and less global in geographical coverage, more procedural and less substantive in content, and more universal and less particularistic in orientation, are not included. Each treaty is described using six attributes as follows:

- *Policy Domain:* Treaties are categorized into six areas: human rights (H); peace and disarmament (P); environment (E); intellectual property rights (I); trade, commerce, and communication (C); and labor, health and safety (L).
- *Year of Deposit:* The year that a treaty was registered with the relevant international body.
- *Year of Membership:* Information on the ratification year of each sovereign state on a given treaty is recorded.
- *Regional Group:* The name of the ten geo-historico-cultural groups by Christian Welzel (2013) in a modified and extended form: (1) Indic East, (2) Islamic East, (3) Latin America, (4) New West, (5) Old West, (6) Orthodox East, (7) Reformed West, (8) Sinic East, (9) Sub-Saharan Africa, and (10) Returned West (see Appendix 1 for the Welzel list and the extended list or so-called Le/Inoguchi list).
- *Number of Current Members*: The number of current member countries of a treaty as of 2014.
- *Treaty Participation Index*: A quantitative index to measure the willingness of a state participating in a treaty and is calculated based on the number of elapsed years between the promulgation of a treaty and a state's ratification act (see Sect. 4.5.1).

Table 4.1 reveals all the multilateral treaties covered in our survey, listed in their abbreviated forms. A brief profile of each is listed in Appendix 2.

Table 4.1 List of multilateral treaties covered by the survey

Domain	Sub-Category	Treaties in acronyms or shortened names
Human Rights (H)	Human Rights	Slavery, Genocide, ICERD, ICESCR, ICCPR, ICCPR Protocol 1, War Crimes, ICSPCA, CEDAW, CAT, Apartheid in Sports, CRC, ICCPR Protocol 2, MWC, CRPD, Disappearance
Peace and Disarmament (P)	Arms Control and Disarmament	Hague 1899, Hague 1907, Geneva, PTBT, BWC, CCW, CWC, CTBT, APM, NPT, IAEA
	Non-Nuclear Zones	Tlatelolco, Rarotonga, Bangkok, Pelindaba, CANWFZ
	Prevention of Cybercrime and Terrorism	Aircraft, Unlawful Seizure, Civil Aviation, Diplomatic Agents, Hostages, Airport Protocol, Maritime, Fixed Platform, Plastic Explosives, Terrorist Bombings, Terrorist Financing, Nuclear Terrorism, Nuclear Materials, Cybercrime
Trade, Commerce, & Communication (C)	Trade and Commerce	IMF, WB, GATT, WTO
	Transportation and Communication	ITU, UPU, IMO, ICAO
	Measurement and Technical Standards	Metre, ISO, IEC, TBT
Environment (E)	Environment	FAO, ICRW, WH, CITES, LC72, Ramsar, Air Pollution, LOS, CMS, Vienna, Montreal, Basel, CBD, FCCC, Kyoto, PIC, POPs
	Nuclear Safety	CEENA, CACNARE, CNS, JCS
Intellectual Property (I)	Intellectual Property	Paris, Berne, Madrid, Hague, UCC, Rome, UPOV, WIPO, Phonograms, PCT, TRIPS, TLT, WPPT, WCT
Labor (L)	Basic Labor Rights	C29, C87, C98, C100, C105, C111, C138, C182
	Occupational Health and Safety	C13, C45, C62, C115, C119, C120, C127, C136, C139, C148, C155, C161, C162, C167, C170, C174, C176, C184, C187

4.3 Description of Multilateral Treaties by Policy Domain

4.3.1 Human Rights

The concept of human rights has a rich history, beginning with early discussions in the seventeenth century (Sweet 2005). However, it was not until the twentieth century that human rights became a central issue at the global discussion table (Sikkink 2017; Borgwardt 2005; Donnelly 1989, and Risse 1999). The issue of suppressing slavery and the slave trade first received international attention at the 1926 Slavery Convention (Slavery), created under the auspices of the League of Nations. It was then followed by a series of conventions that formed the global human right regimes. Undoubtedly, one of the great achievements of that century was making human rights and fundamental freedoms a domain of law that has radically transformed the thinking of humankind. Such an achievement could not have materialized without human rights conventions proclaiming rights and freedoms for all (Smis 2004).

With the purpose "to achieve international co-operation in solving international problems of an economic, social, cultural, or humanitarian character, and in promoting and encouraging respect for human rights and for fundamental freedoms for all without distinction as to race, sex, language or religion" (United Nations Charter, United Nations 2014), the UN is the main international organ by which the international standards of human rights have been established. Additionally, this organization helps to supervise the implementation of these rights. Since the adoption of the Universal Declaration of Human Rights in 1948, an extensive set of declarations and conventions containing detailed standards on human rights have come into being at both the global and regional level.

The most comprehensive development of the Universal Declaration of Human Rights can be found in the two international covenants and in their optional protocols adopted by the General Assembly in 1966: the International Covenant on Economic, Social, and Cultural Rights (ICESCR) and the International Covenant on Civil and Political Rights (ICCPR). The first optional protocol of ICCPR (ICCPR Protocol 1) was adopted in 1966 and implemented in 1976, and the second optional protocol (ICCPR Protocol 2) against the death penalty was adopted by the General Assembly in 1989 and implemented in 1991.

In addition to the Universal Declaration and the two covenants, which cover human rights in general, the General Assembly has, over the years, adopted a large number of declarations and conventions with regard to specific subjects. One of the first was the prohibition of crimes against humanity that is clarified in the Convention on the Prevention and Punishment of the Crime of Genocide in 1948 (Genocide), the International Convention on the Elimination of All Forms of Radical Discrimination in 1966 (ICERD), the Convention on the Non-Applicability of Statutory Limitations to War Crimes and Crimes Against Humanity in 1968 (War Crimes), the International Convention on the Suppression and Punishment of the Crime of Apartheid in 1973 (ICSPCA), and the International Convention against Apartheid in Sports in 1985 (Apartheid in Sports).

Furthermore, human rights associated with individual groups have received significant attention. Discrimination on the basis of gender was addressed in 1979, when the General Assembly adopted the Convention on the Elimination of All Forms of Discrimination against Women (CEDAW). Additionally, in 1959, the General Assembly adopted a declaration on the rights of the child, and more than 30 years later (in 1990), a binding convention on that subject was realized in the Convention on the Rights of the Child (CRC). Another topic in which the General Assembly has been active is the protection of rights of individual persons who are subject to arrest or detention and of all migrant workers. The Declaration against Torture or Cruel, Inhuman or Degrading Treatment or Punishment, adopted in 1975, was followed by a binding Convention against Torture (CAT) in 1984. The International Convention on the Protection of the Rights of All Migrant Workers and Members of Their Families (MWC) was adopted in 1990 and implemented in 2003. In addition, other major human rights treaties have been recently drafted under the auspices of the UN, such as the Convention on the Rights of Persons with Disabilities in 2006 (CRPD) and the International Convention for the Protection of All Persons from Enforced Disappearance in 2006 (Disappearance).

4.3.2 Environment

4.3.2.1 Environmental Movements

Recently, global environmental issues have become a top concern for world leaders. The post-World War II era has witnessed a steady increase in environmental awareness, along with an increase in the severity and incidence of environmental problems (Schwabach 2004). These issues, including ozone depletion, climate change, and loss of biodiversity across borders, endanger the global population and also pose a long-term obstacle for all of humanity.

The mid-twentieth century, which ushered in the era of globalization, experienced a serious degradation of the global environment, and the world recognized the importance of working together to solve this transboundary issue. This is strongly illustrated through the historical conference in Stockholm in 1972 that attracted representatives from 114 countries. The Stockholm Conference transformed micro- and macro-perceptions of environmental issues, firmly placed it on the international political agenda, and raised it in prominence, emphasizing the environment as a universal concern. The conference was the catalyst that continues to shape the international convention related to environmental protection today (Varfis and Wilson 2004).

The second major milestone in international action on environmental issues was achieved in June 1992. More than a hundred heads of states gathered in Rio de Janeiro for the UN Conference on Environment and Development (UNCED), popularly known as the "Earth Summit" where the "Agenda 21" action plan was proposed (French 2004). Governments, international organizations, and non-governmental organizations (NGOs) again met to find a common response to transboundary environmental issues, such as climate change and loss of biodiversity.

The "Agenda 21" action prioritized the conservation and management of resources for development, which includes different issue-areas such as: (1) protection of the atmosphere; (2) nature conservation and protection of terrestrial resources and all kinds of seas; (3) conservation of biological diversity and environmentally sound management of biotechnology; (4) promotion of the safe management of toxic wastes to prevent air and water pollution. These environmental movements provided the catalyst that shape and strengthen the system of collective international environmental agreements (IEAs) today. Additionally, the action taken to protect the atmosphere represents one of the most important groups of multilateral conventions, and includes the 1985 Vienna Convention for the Protection of the Ozone Layer (Vienna), the 1987 Montreal Protocol on Substances that Deplete the Ozone

Layer (Montreal), the 1992 Framework Convention on Climate Change (FCCC), and the 1997 Kyoto Protocol (Kyoto).

To deal with nature conservation and protection of terrestrial resources and all kinds of seas, a list of IEAs have been adopted to form another important regulatory framework for environmental protection. Among them, the International Convention for the Regulation of Whaling (ICRW) has the longest history; it was signed in 1946 and enforced two years later. From being an international convention with a small number of members, it has now expanded with the participation of 86 nations to regulate commercial whaling and conservation of the remaining whale populations. Other IEAs, including the 1971 Ramsar Convention on the Conservation of Wetlands (Ramsar), the 1972 World Heritage Convention concerning the Protection of the World Cultural and Natural Heritage (WH), the 1973 Convention on International Trade in Endangered Species of Wild Flora and Fauna (CITES), the 1979 Convention on the Conservation of Migratory Species of Wild Animals (CMS) are all linked to the regulatory area of nature conservation.

Another group of IEAs focuses on environmentally sound management of toxic wastes in order to prevent air and water pollution. They include the 1972 Convention on the Prevention of Marine Pollution by Dumping of Wastes and Other Matter (LC72), the 1979 Convention on Long-range Transboundary Air Pollution (LTAP), the 1989 Basel Convention on the Control of Transboundary Movements of Hazardous Wastes and Their Disposal (Basel), the 1998 Rotterdam Convention on the Prior Informed Consent Procedure for Certain Hazardous Chemicals and Pesticides in International Trade (PIC), and the 2001 Stockholm Convention on Persistent Organic Pollutants (POPs).

Another critical issue, despite mounting efforts over the past 20 years, is the loss of the world's biological diversity, which is the result of habitat destruction, over-harvesting, pollution, and the inappropriate introduction of foreign plants and animals (UNCED). To address this issue, the 1992 Convention on Biological Diversity (CBD) was finalized and adopted in Montreal in 2000. It provides a comprehensive and holistic approach to the conservation of biological diversity, the sustainable use of natural resources, and the fair and equitable sharing of benefits deriving from the use of genetic resources (Zedan 2005). Biosafety is one of the main topics addressed by this convention. As one of the twin aspects of biotechnology, aside from providing great potential for food, agriculture, and health care, this modern technology can also pose a potential threat to human health and the environment. In looking toward sustainable management and use of biological resources, the Cartagena Protocol on Biosafety to the Convention on Biological Diversity adopted in 2000 seeks to protect biological diversity from the potential risks posed by genetically modified organisms resulting from modern biotechnology (Secretariat of CBD 2000).

4.3.2.2 Nuclear Safety

In acknowledgment of the environmental impact of nuclear energy after the Ukrainian nuclear power plant accident of Chernobyl in the former USSR in April 1986, an international legal framework for nuclear energy safety was developed.

The promotion of nuclear safety is achieved mainly through the adoption of legally binding agreements focusing on two basic aspects of nuclear energy: (1) prevention of accidents, and (2) communication and management of their effects. Currently, there are five key international conventions regulating these aspects, and the IAEA is the depositary of these legal agreements. Adopted in 1986, the Conventions on the Early Notification of Nuclear Accident (CEENA) and the Convention on Cooperation and Assistance in Cases of Radiological Emergencies (CACNARE) deal with responses to communication and management of nuclear accidents or radiological emergencies. Later, other critical conventions were issued to cover matters related to accident prevention. The Convention on Nuclear Safety (CNS), which was adopted in 1994, is an incentive-based instrument that requires the states operating nuclear power plants to establish and maintain a regulatory framework to govern the safety of nuclear installations. Enforced in 2001, the Joint Convention on the Safety of Spent Fuel Management and on the Safety of Radioactive Waste Management (JCS) was the first international instrument to focus on minimizing the effects of hazardous radioactive waste materials and developing the best practices to promote an effective nuclear safety culture.

4.3.3 Intellectual Property Protection

In the late twentieth century, economists and critical theorists recognized that in many developed countries, long-dominant industrial economies based on the manufacturing, distribution, and consumption of tangible goods were being eclipsed in size and social impact by an emerging economic system based on the creation, commodification, exploitation, and control of intangible (or information-based) goods (Coombe and Turcotte 2012). This shift elevated the importance of intellectual property (IP) in an increasingly globalized information economy. When valuable technology is transferred through trade, it is likely to be copied or imitated; therefore, intellectual property rights that regulate legal protection for investors from outside use or implementation without consent have increasingly become an important issue in multilateral trade negotiations. They provide encouragement for the development of subsequent innovations by granting successful inventors a temporary monopoly over their innovations. Through this mechanism, intellectual property rights can foster creativity in advanced technology. Accordingly, strengthening IP protections has been a priority for many nations and has increasingly been the focus of attention for policymakers (Bird and Jain 2008).

An extensive international system has been established for defining, protecting, and enforcing intellectual property rights, comprising of both multilateral treaty schemes and international organizations (Marsh 2014). Intellectual property treaties regulate the protection and management of copyright, trademark, patent rights, and related areas such as trade secrets, geographical indications, and rights of publicity. They also conserve the originality of industrial designs, plant varieties, databases, and integrated circuit topography. In mainstream policy discourses, IP policy is advanced as a means to provide incentives for creativity and innovation, and to secure economic rewards for investment in research and development while providing a socially optimal level of creative and technological goods (Coombe and Turcotte 2012). This explains why the last two decades have attracted heightened attention and concern toward the IP community.

The most important international governmental organization that promotes the protection of intellectual property is the World Intellectual Property Organization (WIPO)—a specialized UN agency established in 1967 in Geneva, Switzerland under the constituent instrument called the WIPO Convention. The WIPO currently manages 26 international treaties; however, the origins of the WIPO can be traced back to one of the first intellectual property treaties: the 1883 Paris Convention for the Protection of Industrial Property (Paris), which established the Union for the Protection of Industrial Property, or the so-called Paris Union. Other key conventions in this arena include the 1886 Berne Convention for the Protection of Literary and Artistic Works (Berne), the 1891 Madrid Agreement Concerning the International Registration of Marks (Madrid), the 1925 Hague Agreement Concerning the International Deposit of Industrial Designs (Hague), and the Universal Copyright Convention (UCC). The UCC, adopted in 1952 and enforced in 1955, introduced the idea that culture (literary, scientific, and artistic works) embodies universal values that require uniform protection, and accordingly, is a shared responsibility to be assumed by the international community. The UCC is an alternative for those countries that disagreed with aspects of the Berne Convention, but still wished to participate in some form of multilateral copyright protection. Extending the regulations for the protection of industrial property in the Paris Convention, the Patent Cooperation Treaty (PCT) came into effect in 1978 and facilitated patent protection for the same invention in member countries through centralized filing and standardized application procedures (Moschini 2004).

Whereas previous copyright law had been written to regulate the circulation of printed materials, there was no equivalent protection for sound recordings. In the 1930s, the use of magnetic tape for recording made the reproduction of sounds and images easier and cheaper than ever before. In response to these new technologies, the Rome Convention for the Protection of Performers, Producers of Phonograms, and Broadcasting Organizations (Rome) was accepted in 1961. The convention expands the coverage of copyright protection from the author of a work to the creators and owners of specific physical instances of intellectual property, such as audiocassettes or DVDs. Later, in 1971, the Convention for the Protection of Producers of Phonograms against Unauthorized Duplication of Their Phonograms (Phonograms) was created as a new international treaty that was designed to give music producers, separate from composers and performers, additional powers to combat copyright infringement. This gave them standing to prosecute makers of unauthorized copies of their tapes or records in other countries (Baskerville 2006). The 1994 Agreement on Trade Related Intellectual Property Issues (TRIPS) administered by the WTO achieved further progress in this field by creating a framework of uniform standards for the protection of a wide range of intellectual property on a near-universal basis. The agreement covers seven areas of intellectual property, including (1) copyright and related rights (rights of performers, producers of sound recordings, and broadcasting organizations), (2) trademarks, (3) geographical indications including appellations of origin, (4) industrial designs, (5) patents, including the protection of new varieties of plants, (6) layout-designs of integrated circuits, and (7) undisclosed information including trade secrets. In each of these areas, the agreement establishes minimum standards of protection, provisions relating to the domestic enforcement of IP rights, and provisions concerning international dispute settlement (Safadi 2004). Other instruments in the field of copyright protection include the well-known International Convention for the Protection of New Varieties of Plants (UPOV), WIPO Performances and Phonograms Treaty 1996 (WPPT), and WIPO Copyright Treaty 1996 (WCT).

4.3.4 Peace and Disarmament

4.3.4.1 Arms Control and Disarmament

The first international negotiations concerning disarmament can be traced back to a series of treaties and declarations negotiated at two international peace conferences that were held at The Hague in the Netherlands. The first and second Hague Conferences were held in 1899 and 1907, respectively. As a result, the Hague Convention on the Laws and Customs of War on Land in 1899 (Hague 1899) and the Hague Convention on War on Land in 1907 (Hague 1907) were among the first formal statements of the laws of war and war crimes in the body of secular international law.

The twentieth century was the most disastrous era in the history of humankind due to World Wars I and II. Toward the end of the twentieth century, approximately 90% of casualties from war were civilians, as opposed to just 10% at the beginning (Fast 2004). Technological development has led to nuclear, biological, and chemical weapons, which have potentially devastating effects as they have the capacity to kill an unbelievable number of people and destroy the natural environment. The alarm has been sounded across the entire globe regarding the need for a framework to safeguard and protect civilian lives in times of war. Assigned as the organization that aims to promote peace, stability, and well-being, the UN has responded to these challenges by strengthening the arms control and disarmament regimes. Multilateral arms control and disarmament agreements are typically exercised through restrictions and/or reductions on the development, production, stockpiling, proliferation, and usage of weapons, especially weapons of mass destruction (Kolodkin 2012).

The Protocol for the Prohibition of the Use in War of Asphyxiating, Poisonous or Other Gases, and of Bacteriological Methods of Warfare signed in Geneva on June 17, 1925, usually referred to as the Geneva Protocol, is a treaty prohibiting the use of chemical and biological weapons. It strictly regulates the use of chemical and biological weapons but does not mention anything about their production, storage, or transfer. Subsequently, two conventions, namely, the 1972 Convention on the

Prohibition of the Development, Production, and Stockpiling of Bacteriological (Biological) and on Toxin Weapons and their Destruction (BWC) and the 1993 Convention on the Prohibition of the Development, Production, Stockpiling, and Use of Chemical Weapons and on their Destruction (CWC) were created to cover the previously overlooked concerns.

Since nuclear weapons entered the realm of world politics during World War II, issues relating to the control of nuclear materials, technology, and knowledge have formed one of the most important dimensions of international security. After the atomic bombing of Hiroshima revealed the existence of nuclear weapons to the general public, a mass non-violent protest forced the creation of the first nuclear arms control agreement—the 1963 Partial Test-Ban Treaty (PTBT). The PTBT banned nuclear tests in the atmosphere, outer space, and under water but not underground. A major step toward this goal came with the signing of a key agreement: the Non-Proliferation Treaty in 1968 (NPT). A total of over 190 parties have joined the treaty, with five states being recognized as nuclear weapons states: the United States, Russia, the United Kingdom, France, and China. Under the regulation of NPT, non-nuclear weapon states were prohibited from possessing, manufacturing, or acquiring nuclear weapons or other nuclear explosive devices. The subsequent decades witnessed little progress in nuclear disarmament legislation. It was not until the end of the Cold War in 1991 that intensive efforts were made to adopt the 1996 Comprehensive Test-Ban Treaty (CTBT) by which states agree to ban all nuclear explosions in all environments, for military or civilian purposes.

The global Nuclear Non-Proliferation Treaty and other treaties against the spread of nuclear weapons are the responsibility of the International Atomic Energy Agency (IAEA) as the nuclear inspectorate regulated under the Safeguard Agreement. Under this agreement, IAEA can verify that a state is meeting its international commitments to not use nuclear programs for nuclear weapons purposes. Within the world's nuclear non-proliferation regime, the IAEA's safeguards system functions as a confidence building measure, an early warning mechanism, and a trigger that sets in motion other responses by the international community if and when the need arises (IAEA n.d.).

4.3.4.2 Non-nuclear Zones

In Article VII of the NPT, the following is stated: "nothing in this Treaty affects the right of any group of States to conclude regional treaties in order to assure the total absence of nuclear weapons in their respective territories" (IAEA 1970: 4). Based on that, the establishment of Nuclear Weapons-Free Zones (NWFZ) was a regional approach to strengthen global nuclear non-proliferation and disarmament norms, and to consolidate international efforts toward peace and security (Gillis 2009). An NWFZ is a specified region in which countries commit themselves not to manufacture, acquire, test, or possess nuclear weapons (Gillis 2009). Five such zones exist today, with four of them spanning the entire Southern Hemisphere. The regions currently covered under NWFZ agreements include Latin America (1967 Treaty of

Tlatelolco), the South Pacific (1985 Treaty of Rarotonga), Southeast Asia (1995 Treaty of Bangkok), Africa (1996 Treaty of Pelindaba), and Central Asia (2006 Treaty on CANWFZ). It is said that these five land zones cover 84 million square kilometers, representing more than one-half of the earth's surface.

4.3.4.3 Prevention of Cybercrime and Terrorism

The concept of "international security" is no longer confined to traditional issues of war and peace, but additionally covers topics such as terrorism and criminal law. Terrorism has been on the international agenda since 1934, when the League of Nations took the first major step toward outlawing the scourge by discussing a draft convention for the prevention and punishment of terrorism. Although the Convention was eventually adopted in 1937 under the League of Nations, it was not enforced until the establishment of the UN (United Nations 2014). During the second half of the twentieth century, many countries in Europe, Latin America, Africa, and Asia confronted a diversity of movements that were using violence against innocent civilians to obtain their goals (O'Donnell 2006). In response, the establishment of effective international regimes to combat criminal terrorism and cyber penetration has taken on a new urgency. Currently there are thirteen international treaties against terrorism, and one treaty has been adopted for cybercrime prevention.

The Convention on Offences and Certain Other Acts Committed on Board Aircraft (Aircraft), adopted in Tokyo in 1963, is considered to be the first international treaty against terrorism (O'Donnell 2006). Five more were adopted during the 1970s: the 1970 Convention for the Suppression of Unlawful Seizure of Aircraft (Unlawful Seizure); the 1971 Convention for the Suppression of Unlawful Acts against the Safety of Civil Aviation (Civil Aviation); the 1973 Convention on the Prevention and Punishment of Crimes against Internationally Protected Persons, including Diplomatic Agents (Diplomatic Agents); the 1979 International Convention against the Taking of Hostages (Hostages); and the 1979 Convention on the Physical Protection of Nuclear Material (CPPNM). Three treaties were adopted in 1988: the Convention for the Suppression of Unlawful Acts against the Safety of Maritime Navigation (Maritime), the 1988 Protocol for the Suppression of Unlawful Acts against the Safety of Fixed Platforms Located on the Continental Shelf (Fixed Platforms), and the Protocol for the Suppression of Unlawful Acts of Violence at Airports Serving International Civil Aviation (Airport Protocol). The 1990s saw the adoption of the 1991 Convention on the Marking of Plastic Explosives for the Purpose of Detection (Plastic Explosives), the 1997 International Convention for the Suppression of Terrorist Bombings (Terrorist Bombings), and the 1999 International Convention for the Suppression of Financing of Terrorism (Terrorism Financing). On April 13, 2005, the UN General Assembly adopted the International Convention for the Suppression of Acts of Nuclear Terrorism (Nuclear Terrorism). These treaties define crimes against civil aviation, shipping, or continental platforms, crimes involving the use, possession, or threatened use of "bombs" or nuclear materials, and crimes concerning the financing of terrorism.

Over the past decade, cybercrime, one of the fastest growing areas of crime, has also posed a serious threat to national and international security (Interpol n.d.). The widespread use of the Internet has enabled criminals to carry out illegal activity throughout the world via cyberspace. Vulnerabilities include not only information systems and the computer systems of government and major companies but also critical national infrastructures such as power plants or electrical grids. The Convention on Cybercrime (Cybercrime) in 2014 is the only binding international instrument on this issue in existence; it serves as a guideline for any country developing comprehensive national legislation against cybercrime and as a framework for international cooperation between state parties with regard to this treaty (Council of Europe n.d.).

4.3.5 Labor, Health and Safety

4.3.5.1 Basic Labor Rights

Although the concept of protecting workers from the perils of labor environments dates all the way back to fourteenth-century Europe, the first example of the modern labor rights movement came in response to the brutal working conditions accompanying the onset of the Industrial Revolution in the eighteenth and nineteenth centuries (Brown 2001). In 1802, the UK Parliament passed the English Factory Act that restricted working hours to 12 hours per day (Brown 2001). However, it was evident that the support for the rights of workers in these early days was inconsistent across international boundaries. It was not until the end of World War I that the International Labor Organization (ILO) was established (in 1919) to implement uniform standards on an international scale. Leaders of the world met at Versailles and agreed to set up this completely new type of international organization, represented not only by governments but also by representatives from businesses and by workers. One of the main functions of the ILO is to develop international labor conventions that cover labor matters, such as the protection of basic worker rights, job security enhancement, and workplace democracy and empowerment, as well as social matters such as child labor, bullying, discrimination, and gender inequality.

One of the most important parts of the ILO Convention is the Governing Body, which identified eight conventions as fundamental to the rights of human beings at work. These rights are a precondition for all others in that they provide the necessary framework from which to strive freely for the improvement of individual and collective work conditions (International Labor Office 2002). These rights cover four main areas: (1) freedom of association and collective bargaining regulated in the 1948 Freedom of Association and Protection of the Right to Organize a Convention (C87) and the 1949 Right to Organize a Collective Bargaining Convention (C98); (2) abolition of forced labor governed in the 1930 Forced Labor Convention (C29) and the 1957 Abolition of Forced Labor Convention (C105); (3) abolition of child labor determined in the 1973 Minimum Age

Convention (C138) and the 1999 Worst Forms of Child Labor Convention (C182); and (4) elimination of discrimination at work handled by the 1951 Equal Remuneration Convention (C100) and the 1958 Discrimination (Employment and Occupation) Convention (C111).

4.3.5.2 Occupational Health and Safety

Increased productivity and social wealth worldwide in recent decades are largely the result of advances in technology. However, in addition to bringing great benefits to mankind, technological advances are frequently accompanied by undesirable social consequences such as health or safety hazards. A recent trend has emerged in which the magnitude of the consequence of each individual incident, whether it involve an air, train, or shipping disaster, or a chemical or nuclear plant, is growing considerably (IAEA Bulletin 1987). As overseers and protectors of the public interest, governments must play a direct role in preventing such tragic accidents through effective planning, controls, and regulations. The last decades of the twentieth century have seen multinational cooperation in establishing a regulatory framework in the form of international treaties to tackle universal safety issues.

Over the years, occupational health and safety (OHS) has received increased attention from the international community. OHS encompasses the social, mental, and physical well-being of workers in the workplace environment (ILO n.d.). Yet, most countries and industries still scarcely recognize occupational health and safety practices as a crucial determinant of national development. Some of the main tasks assigned to the International Labor Organization (ILO) through its set of international OSH conventions are to enhance the protection of the worker against sickness, disease, and injury arising from employment, and to achieve strong preventive safety cultures. The conventions embody principles that define the rights of workers in the field, as well as allocate duties and responsibilities to competent authorities, employers, and workers (Alli 2008). Based on scope or purpose, the OSH conventions can be categorized into the following groups.

The first group consists of fundamental principles to guide policies for OSH promotion, action, and management as presented in three international labor conventions (Occupational Health Services Convention in 1985 [C161], Promotional Framework for Occupational Safety and Health Convention in 2006 [C187], Occupational Safety and Health Convention in 1981 [C155]). These provide the groundwork for the adoption of a national occupational safety and health policy, and describe the actions to be taken by governments and within enterprises to promote occupational safety and health and improve the working environment (Alli 2008). The second OSH convention group comprises a set of general protection measures; for example, actions such as the guarding of machinery (Guarding of Machinery Convention in 1963 [C119]) or limiting the weight of loads to be transported by a single worker are included (Maximum Weight Convention in 1967 [C127]). The third group regulates the protection of workers in specific branches of economic activity such as the building industry (Safety Provisions Building Convention in

1937 [C62], Safety and Health in Construction Convention in 1988 [C167]), commerce and dock work (Hygiene [Commerce and Offices] Convention in 1964 [C120]), mining (Safety and Health in Mines Convention in 1995 [C176]), or agriculture (Safety and Health in Agriculture Convention in 2001 [C184]). The protection of specific types of workers who have specific occupational health needs, such as women (Underground Work [Women] Convention in 1935 [C45]), is another aspect of OSH conventions.

A final aspect of OSH is the protection of workers against specific risks and substances in the workplace, including ionizing radiation, benzene, and asbestos (White Lead [Painting] Convention in 1921 [C13], Radiation Protection Convention in 1960 [C115], Benzene Convention in 1971 [C136], Asbestos Convention in 1986 [C162]). This aspect also addresses the prevention of occupational cancer (Occupational Cancer Convention in 1974 [C139]); the control of air pollution, noise, and vibration in the working environment (Working Environment [Air Pollution, Noise and Vibration] Convention in 1977 [C148]); measures to ensure safe chemical use (Chemicals Convention in 1990 [C170]); and major industrial accidents (Prevention of Major Industrial Accidents Convention in 1988 [C174]).

4.3.6 Trade, Commerce and Communication

4.3.6.1 Trade and Commerce

The growth of cross-border trade of products and services is a driving force behind the creation of a global system of tariffs and technical standards. Tariffs, as well as technical and safety standards, have become one of the main areas for coordination among those countries in dispute on tariffs services. Tariffs have been the central and uppermost concern for all members. Countless tariff unions and agreements have been formulated throughout history and can be traced over centuries. However, before the twentieth century, these agreements had been regional in terms of geographical scope; it was not until World War II ended that a truly global tariff emerged—the General Agreement on Tariffs and Trade (GATT). A global coordination mechanism seems to have appeared in other aspects of international trade, such as measurement standards and quarantine procedures.

Standards facilitate international trade by ensuring the compatibility and inoperability in different markets. Standards also have an important role to play in supporting the competitiveness of each country in the global market by helping to improve the products and services. They help to harmonize the technical specifications of products and services, making the industry more efficient and breaking down barriers to international trade (ISO n.d.). Many existing global standards are developed and regularly revised to ensure that they remain fit for their purpose as new materials, technologies, and processes become available (European Commission n.d.). The first ever globally uniform measurement convention was established in 1875 based on the Metric System. As a central organ vital to the implementation of the Convention, the

International Bureau of Weights and Measures (French acronym BIPM is commonly used) was established in Paris at the same time to ensure world-wide uniformity of measurements and their traceability to the International System of Units (SI).

Other well-known organizations, such as the International Telecommunications Union (ITU), the International Electrotechnical Commission (IEC), and the International Organization for Standardization (ISO), are involved in the development and adoption of international standards. Being one of the oldest international organizations, ITU is a specialized agency of the United Nations that is specifically responsible for coordinating standards for shared global use of the telecommunication infrastructure and for assisting in the development and coordination of worldwide technical standards. IEC is a non-governmental organization that acts as the principal body coordinating the development and promulgation of international standards for electrical, electronic, and related technologies. It publishes 300 to 500 international standards each year, covering a wide range of technologies from power generation, transmission, and distribution to home appliances and office equipment (European Commission n.d.). ISO is the principal body coordinating the development and promulgation of formal international standards. ISO standards are developed in almost all industry sectors, with the exception of electrotechnical and telecommunications standards (developed by IEC and ITU, respectively) (European Commission n.d.).

For the commercial aspects of international development, numerous international organizations involved in the regulation of international trade have been developed. The Bretton Woods Conference in 1944 is recorded as an important milestone due to the creation of the International Bank for Reconstruction and Development (IBRD), which is part of today's World Bank (WB) and International Monetary Fund (IMF). GATT came next, and was signed at an international conference in Geneva in October 1947. GATT's aim was to expand international trade and raise world welfare by promoting non-discrimination among member nations and by adhering to a policy of national treatment (Tiefenbrun 2004). It provided a regulatory framework for world trade (Tiefenbrun 2004); however, GATT was not followed consistently by each of its member nations until the WTO was formed in 1995 (Tiefenbrun 2004).

The World Trade Organization (WTO), GATT's successor body, serves to exemplify the methods and practical measures adopted by an organized global trading system to regulate international trade in support of national aspirations for international development (Sucharitkul 2004). The WTO currently has more than 130 members, accounting for over 90% of world trade. The WTO represents a legal framework for the organization of international trade, consisting of a binding set of technical regulations and product standards governing the Agreement on Technical Barriers to Trade (TBT). In recognition that differing regulations and standards among countries make trade difficult for producers and exporters, the TBT exists to promote the development of regulations, standards, testing, and certification procedures that countries use to regulate markets, while also providing members with the right to protect their consumers, preserve their natural resources, and protect domestic industries.

4.3.6.2 Communication

A connected world requires continued coordination efforts to establish and maintain connectivity. This is true for all stages of communication, from postal mail to the Internet, and for all venues of transportation including ships, railways, and airlines. In the area of postal communication, experts organized an international congress in Berne, Switzerland in 1874 to discuss how to facilitate a global postal system by regarding the whole world as a single postal territory. This meeting marked the birth of another international organization, the Universal Postal Union (UPU) in 1874. Through the UPU, postal authorities agree on the rules for what and how items should be mailed, and they compensate each other for handling each other's mail (Alleyne 2004).

In other areas of global communication, the International Maritime Organization (IMO) and the International Civil Aviation Organization (ICAO) constitute the current participants in the law-making process for international transport by air, sea, and other international waterways (Alleyne 2004). In response to the need for international standards to regulate shipping that can be adopted and accepted by all countries, the IMO was formally created in 1948. Meanwhile, the ICAO was established in 1944 to promote a safe and orderly development of international civil aviation throughout the world. It currently serves as a forum for cooperation among its 190 member states, and creates standards and regulations necessary for aviation safety, security, efficiency, and regularity, as well as for aviation environmental protection.

4.4 Steady Increase of Global Quasi-Legislative System

When there is no formally instituted global polity, multilateral treaties are produced to manage quasi-legislative works of transnational nature. The question that arises is how we can trace and observe the steady increase in these legislative endeavors changing over time and in different policy domains, and in particular, the attitudes and behavior of a particular sovereign state toward these multilateral agreements? A comprehensive view of the current global quasi-legislative system should be particularly interesting to scholars, yet this is still not provided in any systematic and statistical format. However, as a single exception, an analysis of the nuclear non-proliferation regime (Brenner 1981/2009) has been undertaken to shed new light on quasi-legislative processes of impulses, interactions, and impacts in statistical terms. One of the most important findings is the positive correlation between the assistance provided by technologically advanced countries to less technologically advanced countries in the area of nuclear power generations for peaceful purposes and nuclear proliferation. This is one strong step forward in making regime analysis more holistic. More recently, some noteworthy, innovative, and important works on multilateral treaties have been published, although the scope of time and domain is not very comprehensive (Milewicz and Snidal 2016; Denemark and Hoffmann 2008; Glas et al. 2018; van der Wusten et al. 2011; Keene 2012).

For the purpose of providing a comprehensive view of how the sovereign states in the world have supported different multilateral agreements according to different policy domains setting the global legislative system, we have analyzed the increase in membership of the multilateral treaties over time. By analyzing the data on the treaty ratification year, we found that some treaties, after their declaration, appear to attract more attention particularly from the international community than others and then quickly reach a global consensus and commitment by the majority of states. Therefore, these treaties achieve their peak membership numbers in just a couple of years, whereas others grow gradually. The global effort required for a given transnational issue to reach a multilateral consensus from a large number of sovereign states strongly depends on the quickness or reluctance of national policy in response to a global calling for cooperation.

In other words, the speed with which high international consensus is achieved for a multilateral treaty can be used to reflect the steady increase in legislative endeavors of transnational nature. This can be used to answer the following question: how long does it take for a given topic of global governance to be expanded and consolidated among the international community? To answer this question, data has been analyzed to determine how many years it takes for a treaty to receive ratification from 50% of its current members. This way, the length of time it takes to implement legislative endeavors related to shared global matters can be measured and compared among various global issue-areas.

The following series of figures (Figs. 4.1, 4.2, 4.3, 4.4, 4.5, and 4.6) show the duration it took for the multilateral treaties in different domains of the global quasi-legislative system to achieve ratification from 50% of its current members.

It is clear that there is a significant difference in the duration required for various key domains of global governance to be expanded and gain the multilateral consensus from 50% of member parties. The analysis reveals that the environmental movements embedded in the form of multilateral treaties have received the speediest boost of support from the international community. The biological diversity issue materialized in the Convention for Bio-Diversity, in addition to the atmospheric protection issue regulated in a set of UN Framework Convention on Climate Change, Vienna, Montreal, and Kyoto Protocol, are among the top global issues that have drawn the attention of more than 100 member states in the first four years after promulgation. In fact, issues such as climate change, global warming, ozone layer depletion, and biodiversity loss are among the most serious dangers that threaten human beings worldwide. There is an urgent need for a prompt and effective international law that regulates global action to mitigate these threats. This is highly recognized by the majority of nations worldwide and explains why a significant number of sovereign states have taken initiatives by committing themselves to those agreements in a short period of time. The same fact can also be observed with respect to the issue of pollution control (embedded in the convention of LC72, LTAP, Basel, PIC, and POPs). Nearly 70 states, which account for 50% of current

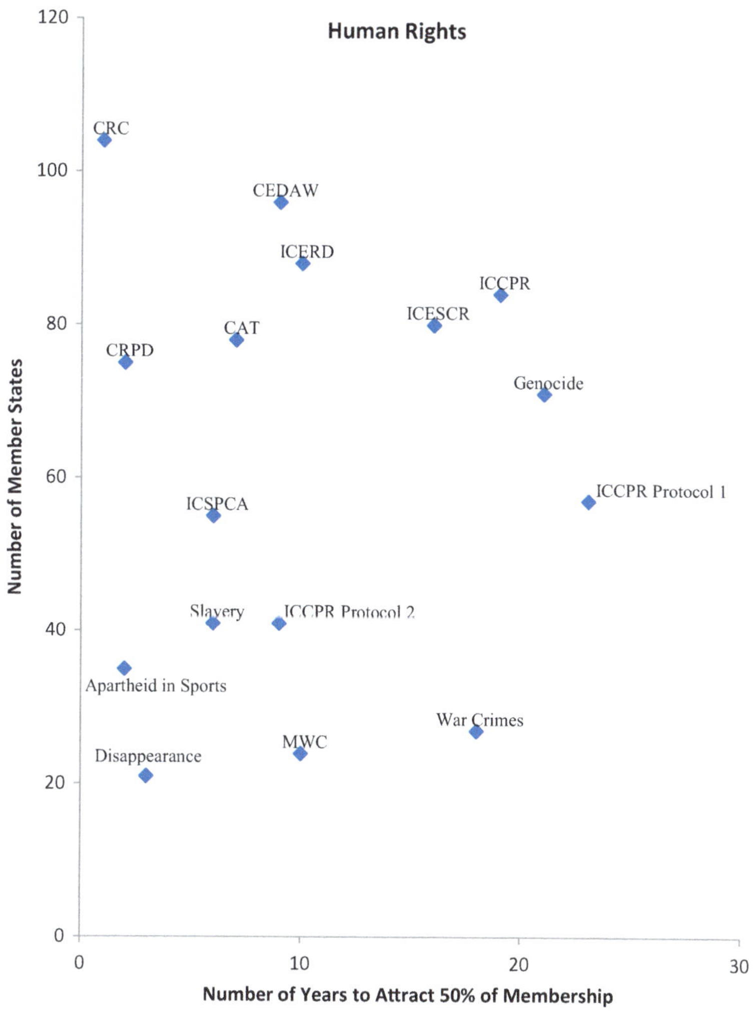

Fig. 4.1 Duration for expanding cooperation to 50% of membership (Human Rights Domain)

membership, made their decision to adopt the regulation of treaties on pollution control during the first four years.

Outside of the environmental domain, topics related to nuclear technology, including nuclear technology control and nuclear safety management, are also highly ranked topics in world affairs. While 50% of members committed to nuclear weapons-related regulations in the first nine-year period, it took only eight years to reach this number for the nuclear safety issue. Interestingly, the other safety issue, occupational health and safety, received the international consensus of 50% of members around 10–15 years after their adoption. For another key topic, the control of chemical and biological weapons, it took 18 years for nearly 90 member coun-

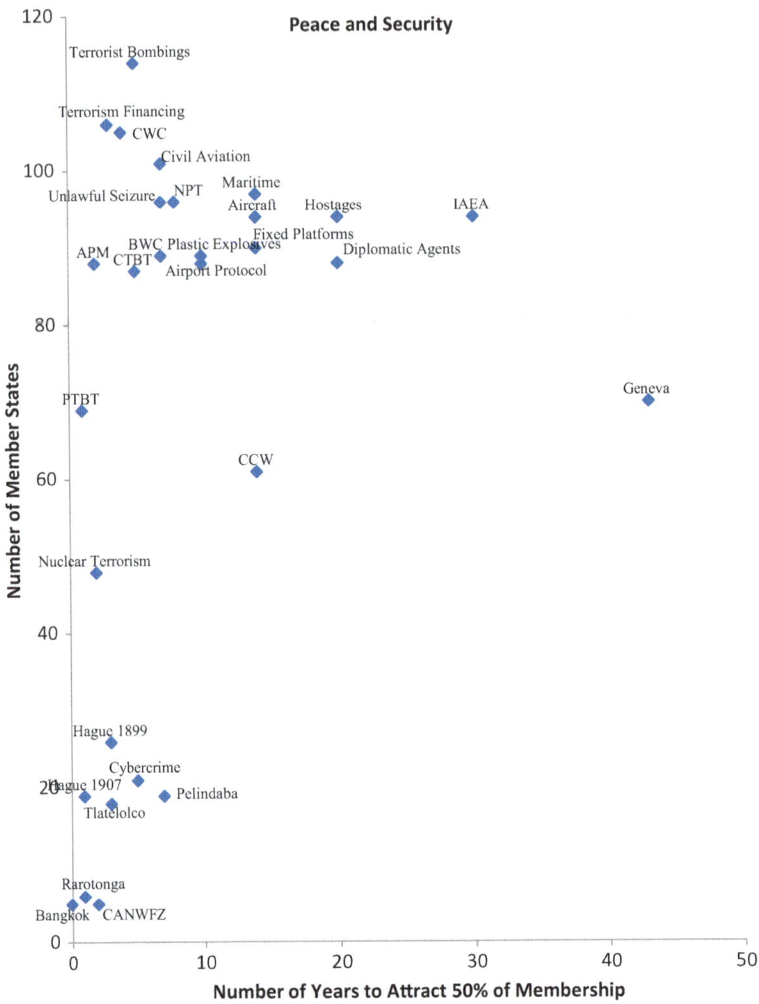

Fig. 4.2 Duration for expanding cooperation to 50% of membership (Peace and Security Domain)

tries to commit to the relevant regulatory regime. Nature conservation took longer, approximately 23 years, to gain agreement from nearly 80 states.

It is most surprising to find that regulations related to the issue of technological standards and intellectual property of the global trade system took the most time (from 35 to 39 years) to extend the consensus to 50% of their membership. This indicates that it is more difficult to obtain unified agreements on regulations for the topics of standards and intellectual property than others due to the nature of global trade competitiveness among states.

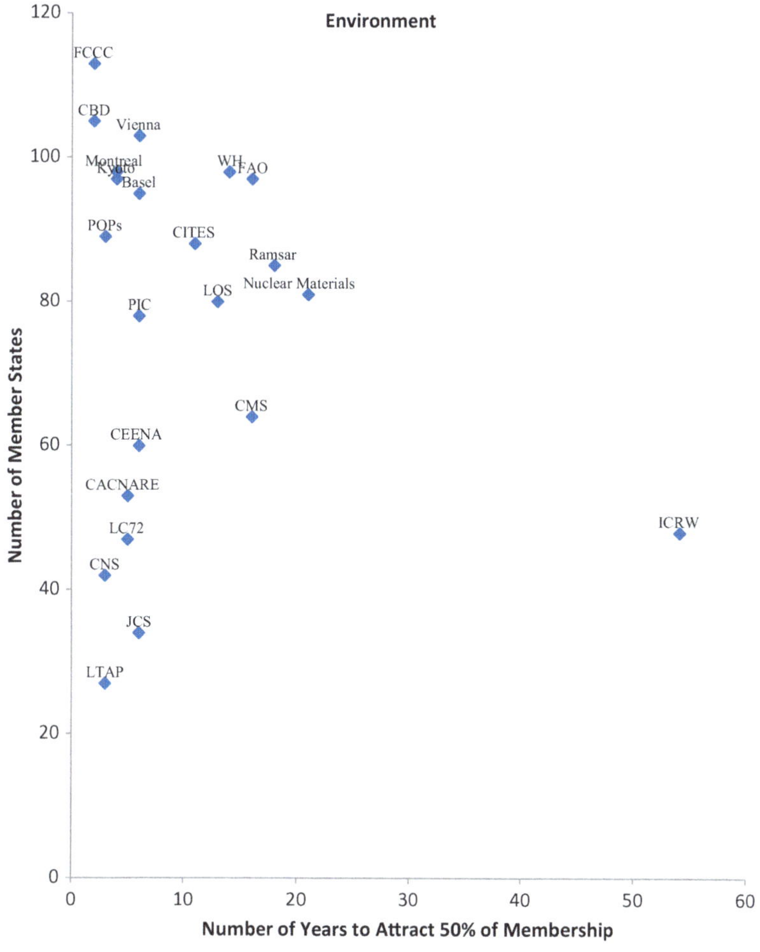

Fig. 4.3 Duration for expanding cooperation to 50% of membership (Environment Domain)

Overall, the duration for a group of multilateral treaties to be expanded globally correlates with the difficulty in achieving multilateral consensus for a given issue-area of global governance. While environmental protection actions receive significant attention from the majority of the international community, other critical issues such as occupational health and safety or intellectual property protection still face some constraints in the manner in which countries cooperate universally. This is reflected both through limited membership and their reluctance to take action.

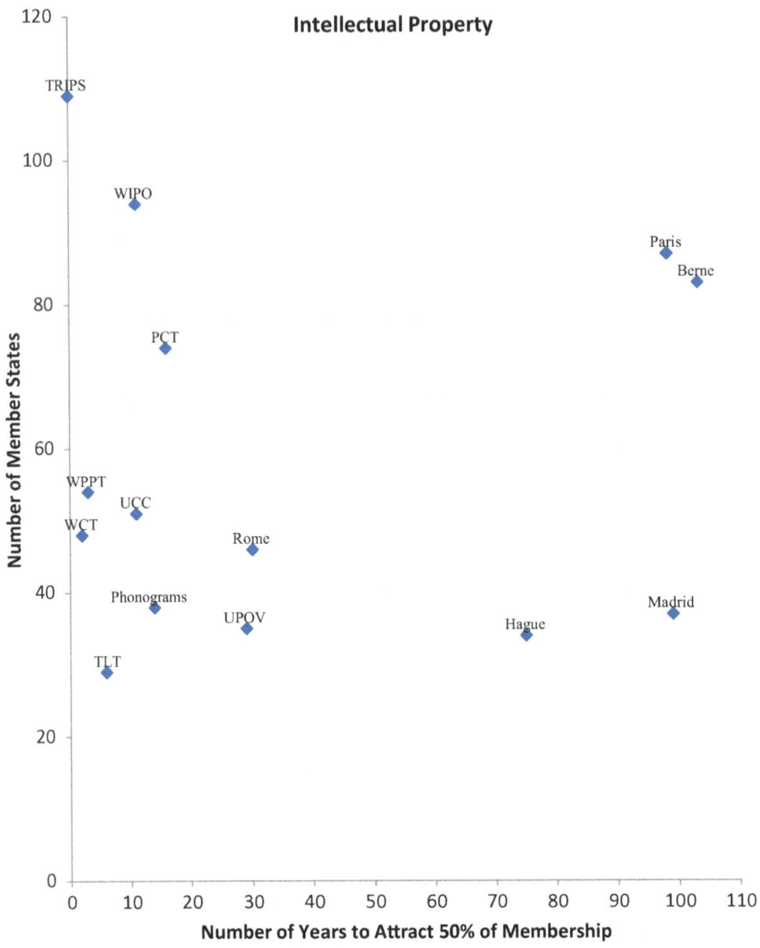

Fig. 4.4 Duration for expanding cooperation to 50% of membership (Intellectual Property Domain)

4.5 Sovereign States' Participation in Multilateral Treaties

4.5.1 How to Measure the Willingness of a State to Participate in Multilateral Treaties

As previously mentioned, global politics has quasi-legislative mechanisms whereby citizens' preferences are selectively chosen to generate multilateral treaties in which sovereign states either join or do not join. In other words, for the state, the decision to ratify a treaty represents the citizens' preferences in a certain policy area, and then reflects the willingness on the part of the ratifying country to comply with

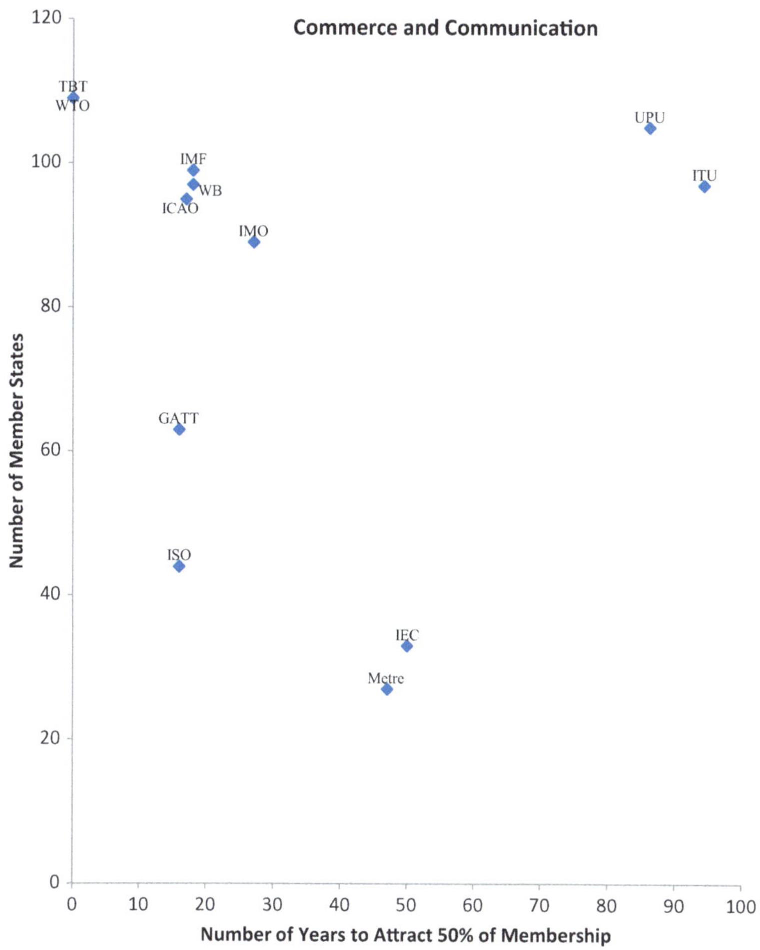

Fig. 4.5 Duration for expanding cooperation to 50% of membership (Trade, Commerce, and Communication Domain)

global legislation and thus to cooperate with other partners in governing the given transnational and global activity. Needless to say, this is often an ideal than a reality. Take the US' exit from the Paris climate change accord announced by President Donald Trump in 2017 as an example. Those who favored US participation in the US are greater in number than those who did not favor participation. However, the sovereign state's action was to withdraw. Thus it was not in harmony with the majority of US citizenry. Yet one has to consider the influence from within and without simultaneously when considering sovereign states' decision regarding joining multilateral treaties. What we call global social contract is an initial hunch-cum-hypothesis. According to our formulation preference in value orientation from within and preferences in treaty participation from without as seen from sovereign

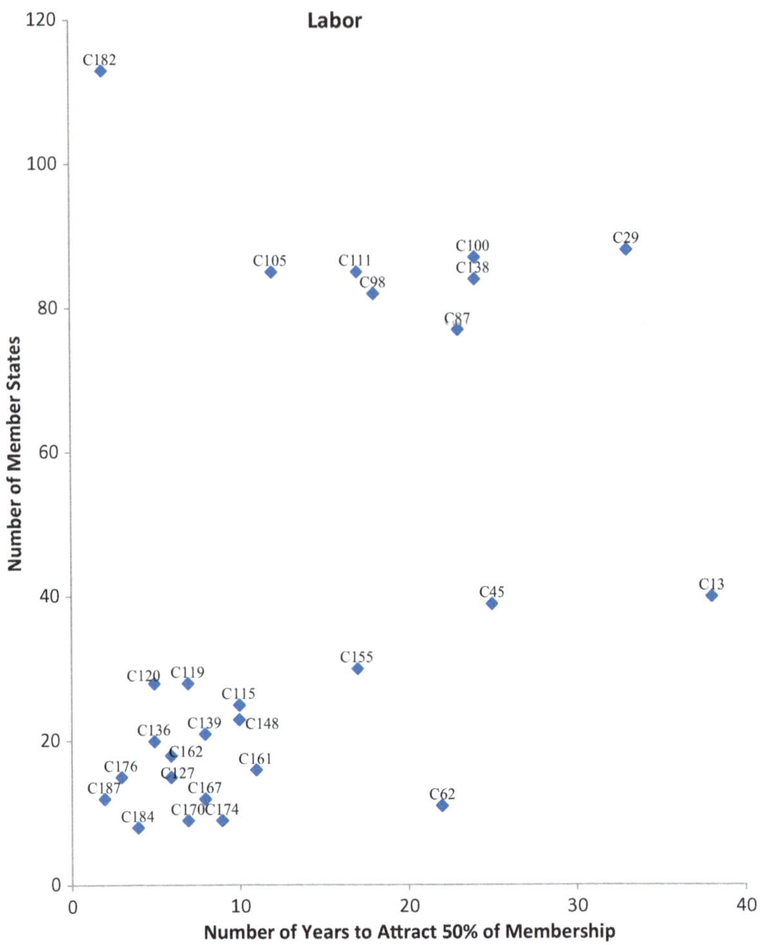

Fig. 4.6 Duration for expanding cooperation to 50% of membership (Labor Domain)

states and as decided upon by sovereign states have been observed to be correlated. This is what we call *a bundle of global quasi-legislative social contracts* with sovereign states placed between citizens' preference in value orientation and sovereign states' preference in treaty participation. Contract does not require causality. Correlation is required to identify whether both global citizens and sovereign states have decided to join or not join a treaty. This is the best we can do with the relevant data being not easily available over time. In *terra incognita*, which is the subject of *global quasi-legislative behavior*, one cannot be overambitious about entering into the problem of causality.

In fact, multilateral treaties have no binding legal power unless and until states decide to join them through ratification action. Hence, understanding why some states ratify an agreement immediately after it opens for signature, whereas others wait for years to approve it is important to understand the willingness of states to cooperate with other partners in governing the transnational processes. The swifter the ratification act, the stronger the country's willingness for cooperation to behave in actor-negotiated international regimes. In other words, the ratification timing itself has meaning as it reflects the intense desire and eagerness or reluctance of a sovereign state to *de novo* legislate or revise domestic laws to comply with international law. Therefore, the following analysis has focused on the treaty ratification years by states to produce a quantitative measurement of states' participation in different issue-areas of global governance. Moreover, we go much deeper to analyze each of the state-actor's behavior to measure their willingness or reluctance in participating in the global legislation system.

For each country, rather than considering only its ratification for a certain treaty, this study presents an empirical analysis focusing on the time patterns of its ratification action to identify the first movers, and thus, leaders in a given global quasi-legislative process. To measure how fast a national policy responds to a typical multilateral treaty, we counted the delayed years between the promulgation of a treaty and its ratification. For a typical treaty, let $\boldsymbol{D_i}$ denote gap in years between promulgation of a treaty and its ratification by country *i*. If $\boldsymbol{Y_P}$ is the year of treaty's promulgation, and $\boldsymbol{Y_i}$ the year of ratification by country *i*, then $\boldsymbol{D_i} = \boldsymbol{Y_i} - \boldsymbol{Y_P}$ takes account of delayed policy making decisions of a state towards a treaty. It is clear that the ratification pattern differs extensively among treaties. Some treaties quickly reached their peak member number in the first ten years, whereas others were gradually changing, especially in some cases where countries were still pursuing ratification more than three decades after a treaty was promulgated.

Policy making, such as the decision to ratify a multilateral treaty, is a type of decision that takes place over several years and is considered intertemporal decision making. Intertemporal decision making over time is a type of future-oriented decision making that has been extensively investigated in the field of neuroeconomics (Cajueiro 2006; Takahashi 2009). In order to capture the essential features of this type of decision over time, the following q-exponential temporal discounting model from neuroeconomics has been adopted (Cajueiro 2006; Takahashi 2009):

$$V(D) = \frac{V(0)}{\left(1 + k_q(1-q)D\right)^{\frac{1}{1-q}}} \tag{4.1}$$

where *V(D)* is the subjective value of a reward that the subject received with delay *D*, and *V(0)* is the subjective value of a reward that the subject received with delay D = 0. k_q and q are free parameters indicating impulsivity impatience at $t = 0$ (t is a delay until the receipt of the delayed reward) and deviation from neoclassical rationality in intertemporal choice, respectively. Larger k_q values represent greater temporal discounting (impulsivity) at $t=0$. If $q = 1$, Eq. (4.1) corresponds to the exponential discount function originally proposed in neoclassical economics (Samuelson 1937):

$$V(D) = V(0)\exp(-k_e D) \tag{4.2}$$

If $q = 0$, the time discount function is the following (simple) hyperbolic function (Mazur 1987):

$$V(D) = \frac{V(0)}{1 + k_h D} \tag{4.3}$$

We have adopted Eq. (4.1) for modeling the state's participation in a multilateral treaty through its ratification act. What is important to consider when applying this model is how to give an appropriate weight (i.e., the value for q in the intertemporal choice model) to capture the time of delay in the ratification decision of a state. We have examined three cases of q, including: $q = 1$, $q = 0$ and $q = -1$, for our dataset and found that multilateral treaties attract 50% of their memberships in an average of 20 years. The rational for adopting this model of q-exponential, (q = 1) is the best fit with the threshold of on average 20 years for treaties to attract 50% of members. Therefore, a duration of 20 years of delay can be used as the threshold to differentiate between the initiative ratifiers and non-initiative members. As Fig. 4.7 illustrates, the hyperbolic model with $q = 0$ is the best fit model for our dataset to express the distinctive behavior between a state that ratified an agreement promptly and the others that ratified it with more than 20 years of delay. Then, in order to model the state's ratification decision, the hyperbolic model with $q = 0$ was chosen to capture the essential feature of the state's ratification decision over time.

A quantitative indicator, namely, the Treaty Participation Index (***TPI***), is constructed based on the hyperbolic model of the intertemporal choice (Fig. 4.8). A state that ratified a given treaty immediately without any delay was rewarded the highest value of score of 1 (i.e., $V(0) = 1$). The metric of willingness of a given

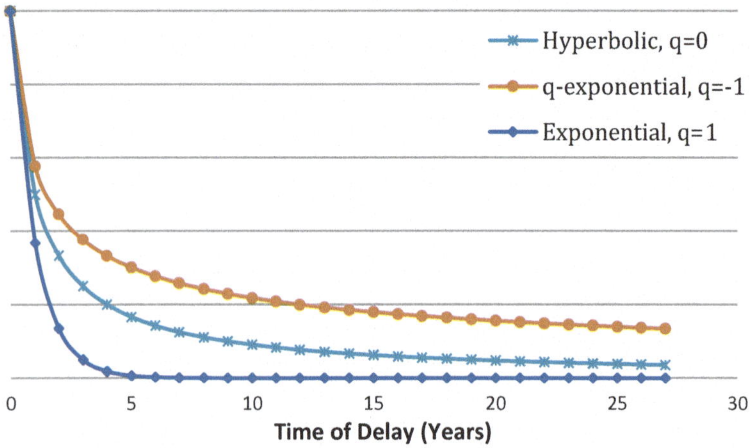

Fig. 4.7 The q-exponential Temporal Discounting Model

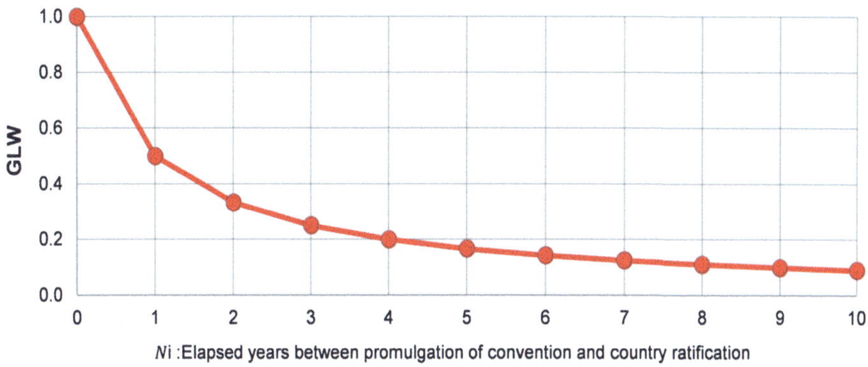

Fig. 4.8 Treaty Participation Index

country *i* will take account of the delayed time of the state *i*'s ratification decision by the inverse in the number of delayed years D_i, and is expressed as follows:

$$TPI = \frac{1}{1 + D_i}$$

This indicator was then applied to our collective data of 120 multilateral treaties that have regulated the quasi-legislative works of a transnational nature since the late nineteenth century, from peace and disarmament, environment, trade, communication, transportation, and intellectual property protection to human rights and labor rights. The goal is to systematically and comprehensively trace and compare the sovereign state's willingness to join the multilateral treaties and how the willingness is changing over domains and over regional groups. By comparing the metric results of TPI for the top ten initiative actors in different policy domains, we can identify the divergence in powers that are bound to shape the twenty-first century global politics.

The following sections detail, changes in the sovereign states' willingness to join multilateral treaties for different regimes. For each category of treaties, the top 10 countries that performed outstandingly well are listed along with their achieved TPI score.

4.5.2 *Peace and Disarmament*

Rank	Country	TPI
1	Hungary	0.49
2	Mexico	0.38
3	Austria	0.38

Rank	Country	TPI
4	Sweden	0.36
5	UK	0.35
6	Denmark	0.35
7	Norway	0.35
8	Bulgaria	0.34
9	Spain	0.32
10	Russia	0.32

Rank	Region	TPI
1	Reformed West	0.28
2	Old West	0.18
3	Returned West	0.17
4	Sinic East	0.15
5	Latin America	0.13
6	Orthodox East	0.13
7	New West	0.12
8	Islamic East	0.11
9	Indic East	0.10
10	Sub-Saharan Africa	0.10

For the multilateral treaties within the peace and disarmament domain, the most active performances were from Hungary and Mexico. European states such as Austria, Sweden, the United Kingdom, Denmark, Norway, Bulgaria, Spain, and Russia also had high achievements in this domain. The fact that the initiative positions belong to an array of Western countries, especially the Reformed West countries, explains why these regions hold the highest ranks that indicatethe strongest willingness to join the multilateral treaties in the field of global peace and security protection. Reformed West ranked first, followed by Old West and Returned West. On the contrary, Islamic East, Indic East, and Sub-Saharan Africa scored lowest among the 10 regions.

4.5.3 Environment

Rank	Country	TPI
1	Norway	0.56
2	Canada	0.47
3	Sweden	0.46

Rank	Country	TPI
4	USA	0.46
5	Denmark	0.40
6	Australia	0.39
7	Mexico	0.38
8	UK	0.38
9	Russia	0.37
10	Finland	0.36

Rank	Region	TPI
1	Reformed West	0.39
2	Old West	0.21
3	New West	0.19
4	Sinic East	0.19
5	Returned West	0.18
6	Latin America	0.16
7	Islamic East	0.15
8	Indic East	0.13
9	Orthodox East	0.13
10	Sub-Saharan Africa	0.11

Among the top 10 countries to take a leading position in the environmental domain, five are representatives of the Reformed West region: Norway, Sweden, Denmark, the UK, and Finland. This explains why the Reformed West is holding the initiative position in managing quasi-legislative works of global environmental protection. Other countries from the G8 group, such as Canada, the USA, the UK, and Russia also scored high. Mexico also shows remarkable achievement in this global regime category.

Throughout our analysis of multilateral treaty data, it was apparent that Western societies, including the Reformed West, Old West, New West, and Returned West, are the most active participants in promoting the environmental protection regime. It is commonly known that multilateral environmental agreements adopted in the period after 1945 targeted efforts to build coherence among countries as the first step in strengthening environmental management in diverse areas, including freshwater and land resource management, the conservation and sustainable use of biodiversity, and marine and coastal ecosystem management (UNEP 1999). These conventions were concerned with the nature component of the environment, and therefore, have widespread support and receive a quick response from the international community, especially the Western societies. CITES, the Montreal Protocol, and the Basel Convention, among others, all have 170 or more parties.

4.5.4 Trade, Commerce and Communication

Rank	Country	TPI
1	Belgium	0.82
2	Norway	0.80
3	France	0.79
4	USA	0.78
5	UK	0.76
6	Netherlands	0.75
7	Canada	0.68
8	Denmark	0.67
9	Italy	0.66
10	Sweden	0.64

Rank	Region	TPI
1	Reformed West	0.57
2	Old West	0.40
3	Latin America	0.26
4	Indic East	0.21
5	New West	0.18
6	Returned West	0.17
7	Sub-Saharan Africa	0.15
8	Islamic East	0.15
9	Sinic East	0.14
10	Orthodox East	0.11

International trade in the years after 1945 entered an unprecedented rapid pace. Commercial policy and technological factors help explain the causes behind this enormously rapid growth. However, it is largely recognized that the Bretton Woods international monetary system played an important role in providing a stable environment for trade to flourish. The Bretton Woods Accord, along with the IMF and World Bank over other parts of the world trading system (ICAO, IMO, and ISO), were institutions that were formed under the critical role played by the G7 group; among them, some are the New West countries, such as the USA and Canada, as well as some from the Old West region, including France and Italy, and others from the Reformed West, such as the UK. Outside of the G7, the active players were from Europe and included Belgium, Norway, the Netherlands, Denmark, and Sweden.

Therefore, our analytical results reveal the dominance of Reformed and Old West regions in initiating and promoting the growth of the world trade system. The Latin America and Indic East countries also have important roles in supporting and maintaining these world trade organizations.

4.5.5 Intellectual Property Protection

Rank	Country	TPI
1	UK	0.68
2	Switzerland	0.60
3	Germany	0.59
4	Spain	0.58
5	France	0.55
6	USA	0.50
7	Sweden	0.44
8	Mexico	0.40
9	Japan	0.40
10	Denmark	0.40

Rank	Region	TPI
1	Reformed West	0.38
2	Old West	0.25
3	Returned West	0.22
4	Latin America	0.17
5	Sinic East	0.14
6	Orthodox East	0.13
7	Sub-Saharan Africa	0.11
8	Indic East	0.10
9	New West	0.08
10	Islamic East	0.07

A similar scenario to that experienced with environmental issues has unfolded in the domain of intellectual property. Several European leaders bore the leadership mantle for the establishment of basic protection mechanisms of intellectual works, including the UK, Switzerland, Germany, Spain, France, Sweden, and Denmark. Therefore, Western societies, including Reformed West, Old West, and Returned West, once again hold the top three critical roles in promoting the intellectual property rights protection regime. In particular, several trends in global international property regulation that emerged in the 1970s and accelerated in the early 1980s began to weigh heavily on US policy-makers' minds. TRIPS is the most typical example of a norm that has become an integral part of the identity of the United States in the global political economy. It is indicated in our analysis by the high score for the US in this domain. The period after 1989 marks the outstanding willingness to support intellectual property treaties from Japan who is one of the Sinic East region representatives.

4.5.6 Human Rights

Rank	Country	TPI
1	Bulgaria	0.49
2	Ecuador	0.48
3	Sweden	0.42
4	Hungary	0.40
5	Costa Rica	0.38
6	Egypt	0.36
7	Philippines	0.35
8	Mexico	0.34
9	Australia	0.33
10	Norway	0.33

Rank	Region	TPI
1	Reformed West	0.21
2	Latin America	0.19
3	Returned West	0.16
4	Old West	0.15
5	Sinic East	0.13
6	Orthodox East	0.13
7	Islamic East	0.13
8	Sub-Saharan Africa	0.13
9	Indic East	0.11
10	New West	0.07

One may be puzzled to see states such as Hungary and Bulgaria scoring well on the rank order of participation in human rights. Three reasons are noted. First, the human rights-related multilateral treaties and conventions tend to be tied to the strategy of aspirational bonding rather than mutual binding. In other words, the preamble and clauses of such treaty or convention do not contain the elements of punishment in case of violation. Second, the definition of human rights sometimes differs across countories. Some focus on freedom for an individual citizen. Others emphasize freedom from poverty in a collectivist society. Third, those states that are active in such organizations as the United Nations Educational, Scientific and Cultural Organization (UNESCO) participate in human rights domains. Bulgaria produced one of the recent Director-Generals of the UNESCO, Irina Bokova, whereas Hungary ranks 4th in all-time medal count at the International Mathematical Olympiad with a total of 336 medals, dating back to 1959. The domain of human rights has witnessed active participants from Latin America, especially Ecuador and Costa Rica. This explains Latin America's rise to the second position among the ten regions in the human rights regime. The highest position still belongs to the

Reformed West region, and surprisingly, the New West holds the lowest rank. As a member of the New West region, the United States resists international rights cooperation out of concern that it might harm business, infringe on autonomy, or limit freedom of speech (Council on Foreign Relations 2013). These concerns are reflected in the US's attitude and willingness to commit to human rights conventions in the years from 1945 to 1989. Therefore, a very modest score representing a low willingness to join the human rights agreements is assignes to the US.

4.5.7 Labor, Health and Safety

Rank	Country	TPI
1	Sweden	0.63
2	Norway	0.33
3	Finland	0.28
4	Cuba	0.25
5	UK	0.24
6	Spain	0.24
7	Mexico	0.22
8	Ecuador	0.20
9	Hungary	0.19
10	Switzerland	0.17

Rank	Region	TPI
1	Reformed West	0.23
2	Old West	0.09
3	Returned West	0.08
4	Latin America	0.07
5	Islamic East	0.07
6	Orthodox East	0.05
7	Sub-Saharan Africa	0.05
8	Sinic East	0.04
9	Indic East	0.03
10	New West	0.02

In contrast to the relatively high score in the level of willingness that the international community showed in other domains, the labor regime appears to receive insufficient attention from states. A very moderate value of the TPI (lower than 0.1, i.e., countries ratified more than 10 years after the treaty's promulgation) for all regions, except for the Reformed West countries, can be observed throughout the history of international labor treaties. Sweden in comparison has an incredibly active attitude with a TPI score of 0.63, which is much higher than that of the world average of 0.06. Sweden is followed by other Reformed West members—Norway, Finland, and the UK. Other active levels of commitment on labor rights come from Latin America, including Cuba, Mexico, and Ecuador.

4.5.8 Overall Assessment

Rank	Country	TPI
1	Sweden	0.49
2	Norway	0.41
3	UK	0.39
4	Hungary	0.38
5	Mexico	0.35
6	Spain	0.35
7	Denmark	0.34
8	France	0.34
9	Germany	0.32
10	Switzerland	0.30

Rank	Region	TPI
1	Reformed West	0.32
2	Old West	0.19
3	Returned West	0.15
4	Latin America	0.15
5	Sinic East	0.13
6	Islamic East	0.11
7	Orthodox East	0.11
8	New West	0.10
9	Indic East	0.10
10	Sub-Saharan Africa	0.10

Throughout the history of the formation and development of the UN multilateral treaty system, the overall picture is that the Western societies, including the Reformed West, Old West, and Returned West, are among the top three active regions who take initiative in managing and promoting the quasi-legislative works of transnational and global governance. Sweden, Norway, and the UK hold a top leading position in almost every domain of regimes. Latin American is ranked fourth, followed by the Eastern societies, including Sinic East, Islamic East, and Orthodox East, respectively. The New West, Indic East, and Sub-Saharan Africa hold the lowest ranks among the 10 regions with a 0.1 TPI score.

4.5.9 *Sovereign State Profile towards Multilateral Treaties*

We have characterized a sovereign state's political attitude towards the UN multilateral treaties using a hexagonal graph that plots six measurements of its willingness to participate in the multilateral treaties in six regime domains. The plotting point in each angle of the hexagonal graph reflects how many standard deviations above or below the world mean a state exercised, which is called the z-score. Thus, a positive score represents a country that has a TPI value above the world mean, whereas a negative score represents a country that has a TPI value below the world mean. This kind of score is called standardized or normalized and is used to capture the comparative evaluation among countries. As our set of data is under normal distribution, if we have the world mean μ ("mu") and standard deviation σ ("sigma") of all country scores, we can standardize each TPI value, by converting it into a z-score using the following formula:

$$\mathbf{z} = \frac{TPI - \mu}{\sigma}$$

Thus, a z-score represents a state's comparative position to the world's mean; thus, it can illustrate whether a state is leading the world or not on a given global issue. For instance, if a state A has a z-score of 1.0 (A is noted as A (1.0) with the z-score in parentheses), in the normal distribution, we can infer that A achieved better than 68% of countries in the world and ranked roughly among the top 60 countries (32% × 200). Similarly, B (2.0) means that Country B achieved better than 95% of the countries in the world and is among the top 10 countries of the world. Using the same type of interpretation, when C achieved better than 99.7%, C will be written as (3.0), and presented as the best global performer. With that scale of measurement, it can be interpreted that a state having a z-score in a given regime domain of 2.0 or higher has outstanding initiative in the global legislative process. The full list of 193 countries' z-scores on six domains of treaties is presented in Appendix 6.

Figure 4.9 is one example of a generated hexagonal graph. The solid line represents the z-score values achieved by a given state and the dotted line shows the world's average. They highlight the comparable evaluation of the state's policy attitude, categorized by six global subject matters of Peace and Security (P); Human Rights (H); Environment (E); Intellectual Property (I); Labor, Health and Safety (L); and Trade, Commerce, and Communication (C),

Next, the number of regime categories in which countries had achieved a z-score of more than 2 (e.g., they are the initiative states in multilateral treaties) was calculated. The results show that in total, 15 states were found to be leaders in the global quasi-legislative process of at least two categories of international regimes. Among them, the most active state is from a Reformed West region: Sweden, who has achieved superlatively in all six global arenas (the z-scores in all six categories is more than 2). Other Reformed West members included the United Kingdom who has also been leading the world in five different regime categories, Norway (four

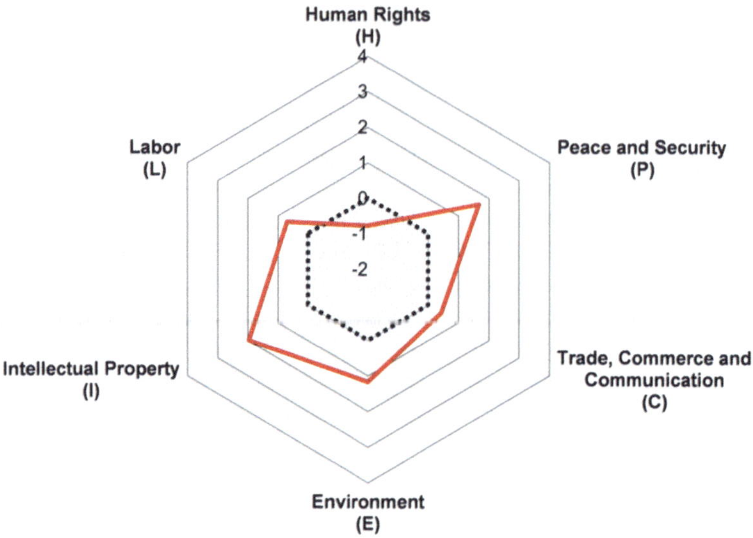

Fig. 4.9 Example of hexagonal profile of a country

domains), Denmark (three domains), and Finland (two domains). From the New West group, the initiative positions belong to the United States (three domains), Australia (two domains), and Canada (two domains). France and Spain of the Old West have taken leadership in three domains, while Austria has leadership in two domains. Outside of the Western societies, the active representatives are from Latin America and include Mexico, who has shown outstanding leadership in five domains. The two Orthodox East members, Russia and Bulgaria, both achieved two domains; from the Returned West group, Hungary has taken leadership initiative in two domains. Additionally, 12 other states have taken a leading position in one regime domain, and include Belgium, Costa Rica, Cuba, Egypt, Germany, India, Italy, Luxembourg, Mongolia, the Netherlands, the Philippines, and Switzerland. The full listing of hexagonal graphs from the 193 member states of the UN can be found in Appendix 3. Chapter 8 takes up the eight ideal-types states that represent each of the eight types. Chapter 13: The Theory of Global Legislative Politics takes into the summary, description and explanation of what has been examined at theoretical and empirical level.

References

Alleyne, M. D. (2004). International communication and world affairs. In R. Luthra (Ed.), *Journalism and mass communication* (Encyclopedia of Life Support Systems (EOLSS), Developed under the Auspices of the UNESCO). Oxford: EOLSS Publishers.

Alli, B. O. (2008). *Fundamental principles of occupational health and safety* (2nd ed.). Geneva: International Labour Office.
Annan, K. A. (2009). "Problems without passports," *Foreign Policy*, November 9. http://foreign-policy.com/2009/11/09/problems-without-passports/. Accessed 18 August 2016.
Baskerville, D. (2006). *Music business handbook and career guide* (pp. 542–546). Thousand Oaks: Sage.
Bird, R. C., & Jain, S. C. (2008). *The global challenge of intellectual property rights*. Cheltenham/Northampton: Edward Elgar Publishing.
Borgwardt, E. (2005). *A new deal for the world: America's vision for human rights*. Cambridge, MA: Belknap Press of Harvard University Press.
Brenner, M. (1981/2009). *Nuclear power and non-proliferation: The remaking of US policy*. Cambridge, MA: Cambridge University Press.
Brown, D. K. (2001). Labor standards: Where do they belong on the international trade agenda? *The Journal of Economic Perspectives, 15*(3), 89–112.
Cajueiro, D. O. (2006). A note on the relevance of the q-exponential function in the context of intertemporal choices. *Physica A: Statistical Mechanics and its Applications, 364*, 385–388.
Coombe, R. J., & Turcotte, J. F. (2012). Cultural, political, and social implications of intellectual property laws in an informational economy. In UNESCO-EOLSS Joint Committee (Ed.), *Culture, civilization and human society* (Encyclopedia of Life Support Systems (EOLSS), Developed under the Auspices of the UNESCO). Oxford: EOLSS Publishers.
Council of Europe. (n.d.). "*Council of Europe action against economic crime*." https://www.coe.int/t/dg1/legalcooperation/economiccrime/Default_en.asp. Accessed October 2018.
Council on Foreign Relations. (2013). *The global human rights regime*. http://www.cfr.org/humanrights/global-human-rights-regime/p27450
Denemark, R. A., & Hoffmann, M. J. (2008). Not just scraps of paper: The dynamics of multilateral treaty-making. *Cooperation and Conflict, 43*(2), 185–219.
Donnelly, J. (1989). *Universal human rights in theory and practice*. Ithaca: Cornell University Press.
European Commission. (n.d.). *Using standards to support growth, competitiveness and innovation*. http://ec.europa.eu/enterprise/policies/sme/regional-sme-policies/documents/no.2_sme_standards_en.pdf
Fast, L. A. (2004). Peace and security. In M. J. Marquardt (Ed.), *Human resource management* (Encyclopedia of Life Support Systems (EOLSS), Developed under the Auspices of the UNESCO). Oxford: EOLSS Publishers.
French, H. (2004). The role of The United Nations in environmental protection and sustainable development. In I. L. Murphy (Ed.), *Democratic global governance* (Encyclopedia of Life Support Systems (EOLSS), Developed under the Auspices of the UNESCO). Oxford: EOLSS Publishers.
Gillis, M. (2009). *Disarmament – A basic guide*. New York: United Nations.
Glas, A., van der Linden, C., Hoffmann, M. J., & Denemark, R. A. (2018). Understanding multilateral treaty-making as constitutive practice. *Journal of Global Security Studies, 3*(3), 339–357.
Hale, T., & Held, D. (2017). *Beyond gridlock*. Cambridge: Polity Press.
Hale, T., Held, D., & Young, K. (2013). *Gridlock: Why global cooperation is falling when we need it most*. Cambridge: Polity Press.
IAEA. (1970). *Full text of treaty on the non-proliferation of nuclear weapons*. International Atomic Energy Agency Publications. http://www.iaea.org/Publications/Documents/Infcircs/Others/infcirc140.pdf
IAEA. (n.d.). *IAEA safeguards overview: Comprehensive safeguards agreements and additional protocols*. International Atomic Energy Agency Publications. http://www.iaea.org/Publications/Factsheets/English/sg_overview.html
International Atomic Energy Agency (IAEA) Bulletin. (1987). *Nuclear power and safety*. http://www.iaea.org/Publications/Magazines/Bulletin/Bull294/29402092526.pdf

International Labour Office. (2002). *The international labour organization's fundamental conventions*. http://www.ilo.org/wcmsp5/groups/public/—ed_norm/—declaration/documents/publication/wcms_095895.pdf

International Standard Organization. (n.d.). *Benefits of international standards*. http://www.iso.org/iso/home/standards/benefitsofstandards.htm

Interpol. (n.d.). *Cybercrime*. http://www.interpol.int/Crime-areas/Cybercrime/Cybercrime

Iriye, A. (2004). *Global community: The role of international organizations in the making of the contemporary world*. Oakland: University of California Press.

Kajima Institute of Peace. (2015). *Gendai kokusai kankei no kihon monjo (Basic documents of contemporary international relations)*. Tokyo: Nihon hyoronsha.

Keene, E. (2012). The treaty-making revolution of the nineteenth century. *The International History Review, 34*(3), 475–500.

Kolodkin, B. (2012). "What is arms control?" *US Foreign Policy*, The New York Times Company.

Le, T. Q. L., Mikami, Y., & Inoguchi, T. (2014). Global leadership and international regime: Empirical testing of cooperation without hegemony paradigm on the basis of 120 multilateral conventions data deposited to the United Nations System. *Japanese Journal of Political Science, 15*(4), 523–601.

Marsh, U. S. A. (2014). *The importance of intellectual property valuation and protection*. http://usa.marsh.com/NewsInsights/ThoughtLeadership/Articles/ID/5228/The-Importance-of-Intellectual-Property-Valuation-and-Protection.aspx#

Mazur, J. E. (1987). An adjusting procedure for studying delayed reinforcement. In *Quantitative analysis of behavior: Effects of delay and of intervening events on reinforcement value* (Vol. 5, pp. 55–73). Hillsdale: Erlbaum.

Milewicz, K., & Snidal, D. (2016). Cooperation by treaty: The role of multilateral powers. *International Organization, 70*(4), 823–844.

Moschini, G. C. (2004). Patents and other intellectual property rights. In M. A. Azzeddine (Ed.), *Public policy in food and agriculture* (Encyclopedia of Life Support Systems (EOLSS), Developed under the Auspices of the UNESCO). Oxford: EOLSS Publishers.

O'Donnell, D. (2006). International Treaties against Terrorism and the Use of Terrorism during Armed Conflict and by Armed Forces. *International Review of the Red Cross, 88*, 864.

Patrick, S. (2014). The unruled world: The case for good enough global governance. *Foreign Affairs, Jan/Feb*, 58–73.

Risse, T. (1999). *The power of human rights: International norms and domestic change*. New York: Cambridge University Press.

Rosenberg, E. (Ed.). (2012). *A world connecting: 1870–1945*. Cambridge, MA: Harvard University Press.

Safadi, R. (2004). Policy-making in a globalising world economy. In I. Sirageldin (Ed.), *Sustainable human development* (Encyclopedia of Life Support Systems (EOLSS), Developed under the Auspices of the UNESCO). Oxford: EOLSS Publishers.

Samuelson, P. A. (1937). A note on measurement of utility. *The Review of Economic Studies, 4*(2), 155–161.

Schwabach, A. (2004/Rev.2006). International environmental law. In Aaron S. & Cockfield A. J. (Eds.), *International law and institutions* (Encyclopedia of Life Support Systems (EOLSS), Developed under the Auspices of the UNESCO). Oxford: EOLSS Publishers.

Secretariat of the Convention on Biological Diversity. (2000). *Cartagena protocol on biosafety to the convention on biological diversity: Text and annexes*. Montreal. https://www.cbd.int/doc/legal/cartagena-protocol-en.pdf

Shaw, M. N. (2017). *International law*. Cambridge: Cambridge University Press.

Sikkink, K. (2017). *Evidence for hope: Making human rights work in the 21st century*. Princeton: Princeton University Press.

Smis, S. (2004). Human rights treaties and agreements. In A. Schwabach & A. J. Cockfield (Eds.), *The role of international law and institutions* (Encyclopedia of Life Support Systems (EOLSS), Developed under the Auspices of the UNESCO). Oxford: EOLSS Publishers.

Sucharitkul, S. (2004). The nature and sources of international development law. In A. F. Munir Maniruzzaman (Ed.), *Some aspects of international development law* (Encyclopedia of Life Support Systems (EOLSS), Developed under the Auspices of the UNESCO). Oxford: EOLSS Publishers.

Sweet, W. (2005). Human Rights. In M. Sekiguchi (Ed.), *Government and politics* (Encyclopedia of Life Support Systems (EOLSS), Developed under the Auspices of the UNESCO). Oxford: EOLSS Publishers.

Takahashi, T. (2009). Theoretical frameworks for neuroeconomics of intertemporal choice. *Journal of Neuroscience, Psychology, and Economics, 2*(2), 75–90.

Tiefenbrun, S. (2004). Business and trade law. In A. Schwabach & A. J. Cockfield (Eds.), *Law* (Encyclopedia of Life Support Systems (EOLSS), Developed under the Auspices of the UNESCO). Oxford: EOLSS Publishers.

United Nations. (2014). *United Nation action to counter terrorisms*. http://www.un.org/en/terrorism/instruments.shtml

United Nations. (n.d.-a). *Treaties deposited in the United Nations*. https://treaties.un.org/. Access in February 2017.

United Nations. (n.d.-b). *United Nations charter*. https://www.un.org/en/documents/charter/

United Nations Conference on Environment & Development., Rio de Janerio, Brazil, 3 to 14 June 1992, AGENDA 21, http://sustainabledevelopment.un.org/content/documents/Agenda21.pdf

United Nations Environment Programme (UNEP). (1999). *Economic instruments for the sustainable management of natural resources*. New York and Geneva: United Nations.

van der Wusten, H., Denemark, R. A., Hoffmann, M., & Yonten, H. (2011). The map of multilateral treaty-making 1600–2000: A contribution to the historical geography of diplomacy. *Tijdschrift voor economische en sociale geografie, 102*(5), 499–514.

Varfis, C.-Z., & Wilson, L. M. (2004). International agreements. In G. M. Kutting (Ed.), *Conventions, treaties and other responses to global issues* (Encyclopedia of Life Support Systems (EOLSS), Developed under the Auspices of the UNESCO). Oxford: EOLSS Publishers.

Welzel, C. (2013). *Freedom rising: Human empowerment and the quest for emancipation*. New York: Cambridge University Press.

Zedan, H. (2005). *Convention on biological diversity, the WIPO seminar on intellectual property and development*, Geneva, Switzerland. http://www.wipo.int/edocs/mdocs/mdocs/en/isipd_05/isipd_05_www_103974.pdf

Chapter 5
Toward Modeling a Global Social Contract

Abstract The task of linking global citizens' preferences in value orientation and sovereign states' preferences in treaty orientation is carried out in this chapter. The key two dimensions (protective vs emancipative and secular vs sacred) of the World Value Survey data and the key three dimensions (agile vs cautious, global commons vs individual citizens' interests, and aspirational bonding vs mutual binding) of the Multilateral Treaties Survey data are correlated to show that their links are fairly robust, indicating that our initial hunch-cum-hypothesis is basically correct.

Political science often holds itself out as queen of social sciences so long as economics is king. However, political philosophers and political scientists from their respective schools have historically not been in agreement; the former concentrates on what ought to be, whereas the latter focuses on what is. In other words, the normatively oriented political philosophers and empirically oriented political scientists do not have a history of conversing extensively. Even if they did talk to one another, the fusion of normative political philosophy and empirical political science has occurred only within the last quarter of the last century and the first quarter of this century (Inoguchi 2008). As a matter of fact, both Jean-Jacques Rousseau and John Locke have never been systematically and scientifically modeled prior to this work (Le et al. 2014; Inoguchi and Le 2016; Inoguchi 2018).

The theoretical underpinnings of the global social contract drawing from the two great philosophers, Jean-Jacques Rousseau and John Locke, have been provided in Chap. 2. Both Rousseau and Locke formulated their versions of social contract theories in the national context of seventeenth and eighteenth-century Europe. This chapter attempts to extend their theories from cantonal and national to the global context. In other words, this chapter sets out to answer the question: Is a global social contract possible? In what follows, an attempt is made to construct a global model of social contract extended from the two metaphors of Rousseau and Locke by using two sets of data: the global citizens' preferences about values and norms as gauged by the results of the World Values Survey (WVS), which are presented in Chap. 3, and sovereign states' participation in 120 multilateral treaties deposited to the United Nations, which have been presented in Chap. 4. By establishing the relationship between these two datasets, this chapter theoretically reveals that imagin-

T. Inoguchi, L. T. Q. Le, *The Development of Global Legislative Politics*,
Trust: Interdisciplinary Perspectives 3, https://doi.org/10.1007/978-981-32-9389-2_5

ing a global social contract is possible and that empirically validating such ideas is feasible. Moreover, to clarify the correlation between citizens and treaties (quasi-legislative outcomes, in a sense), dimensional similarities between the cosmos of citizens' preference and the cosmos of sovereign states' willingness to join multilateral treaties are examined. Once done, the sovereign states are located in one of the two cosmoses, citizens' or states', and the correlation coefficients between them are measured. On the basis of these empirical results, the nature of the global quasi-legislative process is clarified; additionally, conclusions and implications are drawn.

5.1 Introduction

Global politics employs quasi-legislative processes similar to national legislative processes (Volgy 1973; Popovski and Fraser 2014) with the following differences: (1) there is no institutionalized world government; hence, none claims sovereign power in global politics; and (2) there is no formal institutional legislative body unlike a national parliament that aggregates citizens' preferences into government policy. However, there are mechanisms whereby citizens' preferences are selectively chosen to generate multilateral treaties in which sovereign states either join or not join.

It is widely accepted that signing and ratifying agreements and treaties among similar-minded nations helps facilitate cooperation among states for solving global issues, i.e., increasing free trade and democracy. In forming a global legislation system, global citizens' preferences are expressed and transformed into global legislative products called multilateral treaties. Notably, the term "quasi-legislative processes and outcomes" has been adopted since global legislative processes and outcomes are qualitatively very different from national legislative processes and outcomes.

On what we refer to as the global quasi-legislative process and outcome, there have been an abundance of studies: examining how global climate policy initiatives have been attempted in Tokyo, Copenhagen, and Paris (Kutney 2013; Sovacool and Dworkin 2014); analyzing how the global trade liberalization scheme has been agreed upon only with a less than global and comprehensive scope, i.e., bilateral, regional, and partial (Jones 2015); examining how the nuclear non-proliferation treaty has experienced the diffusion of new nuclear powers (Joyner 2013; Solingen 2013); and tracing how a multilateral agreement on fire-control radar was crafted during the meeting of navies of some 22 countries assembled in Shandong, China amidst the Japanese-Chinese disputes in the East China Sea in 2013 (Inoguchi 2015). When the quasi-legislation process and outcome is focused on one policy area, this genre of academic research is often called regime theory (Krasner 1983; Yamamoto 2008). There are many regimes, including the nuclear non-proliferation regime, climate change regime, free trade regime, intellectual property regime, public health regime, and human rights regime. Regime research provides a view of global quasi-legislative processes when they are digested as a whole in terms of quasi-legislative impulses, interactions, and impacts. Yet so far, no research has been conducted in this genre to see how these three key knots in the global quasi-legislative processes are related in numerical terms. One exception to this, however, is nuclear non-proliferation regime analysis (Brenner 1981/2009), which has been conducted to shed new light on quasi-legislative processes in terms of impulses, interactions, and impacts in statistical terms. Among the most important findings is the positive correlation between technologically advanced countries' assistance to less technologically advanced countries in the area of nuclear power generation for peaceful purposes and nuclear proliferation. This is one strong step forward in making regime analysis more holistic.

The framework proposed here aims to clarify the nature of global quasi-legislative processes in a vast array of regime domains of global politics today, from not only the human rights; peace and disarmament; and trade, commerce, and communication regimes but also the environment, intellectual property, and labor health and safety regimes. The main task is empirically and statistically analyzing the links between citizens' preferences and states' joining in multilateral treaties to posit a model of global social contract using the metaphors of Rousseau and Locke.

The Rousseauesque metaphor focuses on citizens' preferences and sovereign states' participation in multilateral treaties, setting aside intermediaries of quasi-legislative bodies. Regarded as a direct democracy, Rousseau's Social Contract does not envisage any legislative bodies even in the national setting. The Locke metaphor, however, focuses on the gradual expansion of parliamentary power and the politics therein, i.e., the growth of a representative democracy. The Lockean metaphor of representative democracy in global social contract consists of three knots: (1) citizens' preferences, (2) quasi-legislative bodies, and (3) states' participation in multilateral treaties. A new element is the quasi-legislative bodies. How should we define this? As regime research has amply shown, a bundle of intermediaries exist in the global quasi-legislative processes: some 200 sovereign states and members of the United Nations, tens of thousands of non-governmental organizations, UN specialized institutions, non-UN affiliated international and transnational organizations, etc. Thus, an important question to be answered is the following: How should we generate numerical indicators for quasi-legislative bodies?

We must recall that Rousseau and Locke are used as metaphors. They were immensely constrained by the historical background of seventeenth and eighteenth century Europe; therefore, there are some conceptual difficulties when attempting to introduce their models writ large on a global scale. Our proposed model, which is inspired by their philosophical thrusts, is not necessarily strict in distinguishing Rousseau and Locke for two reasons: first, because they did not imagine the world of globalization and digitalization; second, because neither of them articulated or specified how their models of direct or representative democracy would possibly function in a steadily globalizing world.

In this book, citizens' preferences are linked with states' participation in multilateral treaties. Performing a factor analysis of the two separately enables us to see whether their dimensionalities are more or less the same. To carry out this analysis, the correlation coefficients between the factor scores of citizens' preferences and the factor scores of states' participation in multilateral treaties are useful to see the similarity of dimensionalities. Additionally, the states' locations on those dimensions derived from two factor analyses will be used to understand with two dimensional locations of states that citizens' preferences and states' participation in multilateral treaties function on similar dimensionalities. If these operations are carried out successfully, then the idea of a global social contract extended from Rousseauesque and Lockean metaphors will be roughly useful.

5.2 Gauging Links Between Citizens' Preferences and States' Treaty Participation

The focus so far has been on describing the procedure of linking global citizens' preferences and states' participation in multilateral treaties. The question that should be tackled before gauging such links is as follows: Should one assume the scheme of a global quasi-legislative process in a global political system, where there are no sovereign institutions, with democratically elected representatives and professionally chosen bureaucrats who together construct agreements and execute laws facing seven billion citizens without borders? The answer is no. The first task—the most important task—is to describe citizens' preferences in terms of collectively unconscious desires and passions. Since the WVS continues to inquire about values and norms, or in other words, about what citizens aspire to and want to materialize, the fairly strong collective desires are highlighted via statistical methods. Secondly, since the Multilateral Treaties Survey continues to register the common ground between states in treaties and conventions, the fact that fairly strong collective passions are part of such multilateral treaties and conventions is highlighted via statistical methods. After these two tasks are carried out, the next task is to assess their connection methodically.

The kind of statistical procedure that best fit these tasks was factor analysis via varimax rotation. By carrying out this analysis, the correlation coefficients between the factor scores of citizens' preferences and the scores of states' participation in multilateral treaties will allow us to know whether their dimensionalities are more or less of the same kinds. Citizens' preferences have been most intensively studied by the WVS team (Inglehart and Welzel 2005; Welzel 2013; Basanez 2015); states' participation in multilateral treaties has been studied by the Multilateral Treaties project team (Le et al. 2014). The former task has been carried out by Welzel (2013); his results are summarized only to the extent to which they are pertinent to the present task.

Welzel utilizes the data of World Values Survey executed in 2005–2009 that cover 95 societies (including Hong Kong and Taiwan) spreading all around the globe, and including the largest populations and biggest economies from each world region. Thus the data represents almost 90% percent of the world's population. Welzel places the previously mentioned ten geo-historico-cultural country groups into these two dimensions. The first dimension is *Emancipative versus Protective* and the second dimension is *Secular versus Sacred*. Welzel's grouping focuses on the West, and therefore, the differences among the West are sharply delineated, whereas the non-West is less so. Nevertheless, the most striking is the predominance of the West. The rough order of high scores in the *Emancipative versus Protective* dimension is as follows: Reformed West → Old West → New West → Latin America → Returned West → Sub-Saharan Africa → Orthodox East → Sinic East → Indic East → Islamic East. Similarly, in the *Secular versus Sacred* dimension, the rough order is as fol-

Table 5.1 Six variables of the factor analysis on multilateral treaties data

Variable	Description
Year of membership [YrMember]	The year when a state ratified a treaty is identified
Year of deposit [YrDeposit]	The year when a treaty is deposited to the relevant international body
Number of current members [CurrentMember]	The number of current member countries of a treaty as of 2014
Treaty participation index [TPI]	A quantitative index to measure how quickly a state participates in a treaty and is calculated based on the number of elapsed years between the promulgation of a treaty and a state's ratification act
Modified Welzel regional group [Region]	A country is classified in one of the ten geo-historico-cultural groups by Christian Welzel (2013) in its modified form by the Le/Inoguchi scheme (see Appendix 1)
Policy domain [Domain]	The six policy domain categorizations based on the main purpose of a treaty

lows: Sinic East → Reformed West → Returned West → Orthodox East → Old West → New West → Indic West → Islamic West → Latin America → Sub-Saharan Africa.

Notably, the most secular position is occupied by the Sinic East. It is not widely known as the origin of meritocracy (Young 2011). Contrary to what is widely believed in the West meritocracy, i.e., merit-based bureaucracy, was practiced in the Sinic East, centuries before civil service examination emerged in the West (Woodside 2006). Next in line for secular is the Reformed West (those countries established after the Reformation). Non-Catholic populations in the Reformed West are placed at this level of secularity. In terms of secularity, the Returned West (post-Cold War Central and Eastern Europe) comes in third. The Orthodox East comes next. Seven decades of communist rule resulted in very secularized societies. Yet, the post-communist societies have revived non-secularity significantly. Following the Orthodox East is the Old West (those countries established after the Roman Empire). The Republic of France's culture for *laïcité* leads it to endeavor for secularity in schools and other institutions. The Old West, with new settler societies, is the most religious of the West; in particular, the United States of America is known for high religiosity. Next comes a whole range of non-Western countries, albeit not including the Sinic East. Religiosity was higher in the order of the Indic East, Islamic East, Latin America, and Sub-Saharan Africa. The Indic East is the most religious in Asia, but outside of Asia it is the least religious.

Next, the data pertaining to the Multilateral Treaties Survey about states' participation in multilateral treaties was factor-analyzed. For that purpose, the principal component analysis with varimax rotation, and Kaiser normalization based on six variables that represent six attributes of multilateral treaties was implemented (Table 5.1).

Table 5.2 lists the three most important dimensions that emerged from the factor analysis of the multilateral treaties data. These dimensions explain nearly 70% of cumulative variance. The two items *Year of Membership* and *Year of Deposit* tap the first component that is named *Agile versus Cautious*. The second dimension, the

Table 5.2 Factor analysis of six instrumental variables with varimax rotation and Kaiser normalization: Sovereign States' participation in multilateral treaties

	Component		
	1	2	3
YrMember	.899		
YrDeposit	.919		
CurrentMember		.746	
TPI			−.836
Domain		−.797	
Region			.587

so-called *Global Commons versus Individual Citizens' Interests,* is based on the two items *Policy Domain* and *Number of Current Members.* Thirdly, the two items *Treaty Participation Index* and *Modified Welzel Regional Group* form the third dimension that is labeled as *Aspirational Bonding versus Mutual Binding.*

The first dimension *Agile versus Cautious* has to do with how nimble or prudent the country is regarding joining multilateral treaties. Naturally those countries that became independent immediately after the Second World War and those countries that became independent in the fourth quarter of the last century are cautious—always apprehensive of the possibility of being constrained by such treaties when their precious national independence has only been recently obtained. The accumulation of skills of professional expertise and organizational leadership by Western countries has made a huge difference in joining multilateral treaties. The rough order of high scores on the first dimension is as follows: Reformed West → Old West → Sinic East → Latin America → Islamic East → Indic East → New West → Sub-Saharan Africa → Returned West → Orthodox East.

The second dimension that is labeled as *Global Commons versus Individual Citizens' Interests* is concerned with whether primary concerns are the environment, peace and disarmament, and intellectual property rights on the one hand, or labor health and safety and human rights on the other. The rough order of those country groups is as follows: Returned West → Reformed West → Orthodox East → Old West → Latin America → Islamic East → Sinic East → Sub-Saharan Africa → Indic East → New West.

Most striking are the most global positions held by the Returned West and the Reformed West. Their concern about global commons is reflected in the generation of highly skilled professionals manning UN and other special international organizations and transnational social movements. The Nobel peace prize, Copenhagen initiative in environmentalism, and yearning for Ikea-style innovation and invention are some of the features of the Reformed West. Then follow the Orthodox East, Old West, and Latin America; these areas balance the global commons with the individual citizen's interests. Not surprisingly the New West (including the United States) leans toward individual citizen's interests. The Islamic East, the Sinic East, the Indic East, and Sub-Saharan Africa reveal their yearning for independence and state sovereignty.

The third dimension is called *Aspirational Bonding versus Mutual Binding*. Multilateral treaties are often qualitatively different from national laws in terms of the degree of binding. They often contain those appealing to aspirational bonding. They try to appeal their common desires and dreams and to achieve them together. High on Aspirational Bonding are Sub-Saharan Africa, Latin America, the Sinic East, the Islamic East, the Indic East, and the Orthodox East; all of these regions represent the Global South's collective voice, registering their yearning rather than being mutually bound. In contrast, the Returned West, the Old West, the New West, and the Reformed West quietly generate rules that bind the rest as much as possible. The rough order from high to low on the third dimension is as follows: Sub-Saharan Africa → Latin America → Sinic East → Islamic East → Indic East → Orthodox East → Returned West → New West → Old West → Reformed West (Table 5.3).

To gauge the link between the *Two-Dimensional Cultural Map of the World (CMW)* produced from Welzel's World Values Survey data and the *Three-Dimensional Legislative Map of the World (LMW)* obtained from factor-analyzed of Multilateral Treaties Survey, the relationships between citizens' preferences and sovereign states' multilateral treaties participation are examined. Data are available for 93 countries in the Welzel dataset (after excluding Hong Kong and Taiwan), while data of states' participation in multilateral treaties are available for 193 countries. To match these two sets of data, we extracted the data of sovereign states' multilateral treaties participation for 93 states (from the original dataset of 193 states of the Multilateral Treaties Survey) that are correspondent with Welzel' s data of World Values Survey. Next, the correlation coefficients between the two major dimensions of CMW and the three major dimensions LMW are calculated and presented in Table 5.4.

Table 5.3 The major dimensions that emerged from the CMW factor-analyzed data (Welzel 2013) and LMW factor-analyzed data, listed along with their abbreviated forms

The CMW factor-analyzed with varimax rotation yields two major dimensions	(1) Protective versus Emancipative (Pr-Em)
	(2) Sacred versus Secular (Sa-Se)
The LMW factor analyzed with varimax rotation yields three major dimensions	(1) Agile versus Cautious (Ag-Ca)
	(2) Global Commons versus Individual Citizens' Interests (Gc-Ic)
	(3) Aspirational Bonding versus Mutual Binding (Ab-Mb)

Table 5.4 Correlation coefficients among the CMW and the LMW

	Pr-Em	Sa-Se	Ag-Ca	Gc-Ic	Ab-Mb
Pr-Em	1.000				
Sa-Se	0.129	1.000			
Ag-Ca	−0.443	0.059	1.000		
Gc-Ic	−0.438	−0.287	0.183	1.000	
Ab-Mb	0.559	0.452	−0.558	−0.340	1.000

In order to see the relationship between the CMW and the LMW in our sample data of 93 countries is strong enough to represent the relationship in the whole population, the significance of each correlation coefficient is examined and displayed in Table 5.5. The significance level (or *p-value*) is the probability of obtaining results as extreme as the one observed. The results show that the significance level for the correlation coefficient between Pr-Em and Ag-Ca, Pr-Em and Gc-Ic, Pr-Em and Ab-Mb, Sa-Se and Gc-Ic, Sa-Se and Ab-Mb are very small (less than 0.01), then the correlations are significant. It is important to note that the significance level for the correlation coefficient between Sa-Se and Ag-Ca is relatively large (0.579), then the correlation is not significant and the two variables are not linearly related. In general, this test statistically reveals that imagining a global social contract is possible and that empirically validating such ideas is feasible.

Next, we have mapped the ten modified Welzel groups' locations on the CMW and the LMW as follows (Figs. 5.1, 5.2, 5.3, 5.4, 5.5, and 5.6).

Table 5.5 The significance of the correlation coefficient among the CMW and the LMW

	Pr-Em	Sa-Se
Ag-Ca	0.000	0.579
Gc-Ic	0.000	0.006
Ab-Mb	0.000	0.000

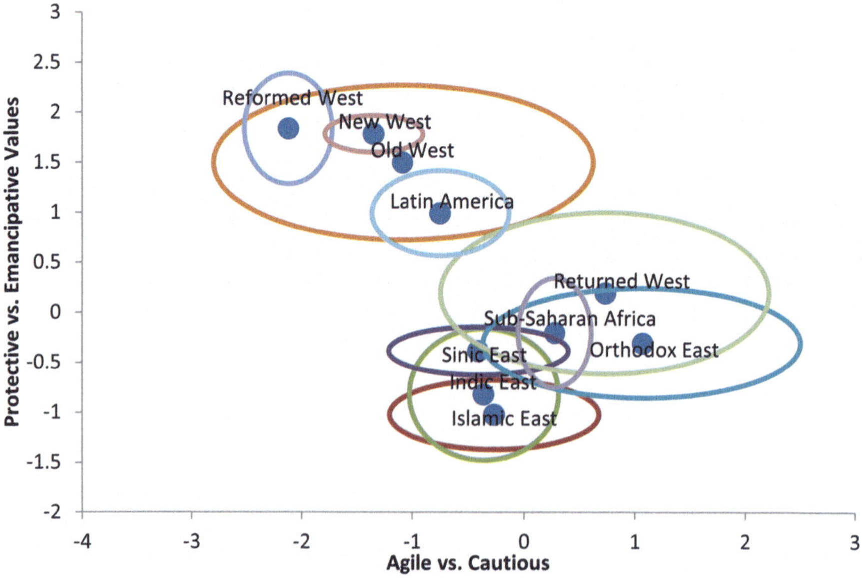

Fig. 5.1 Ten groups of countries located onto dimensions (Ag-Ca x Pr-Em)

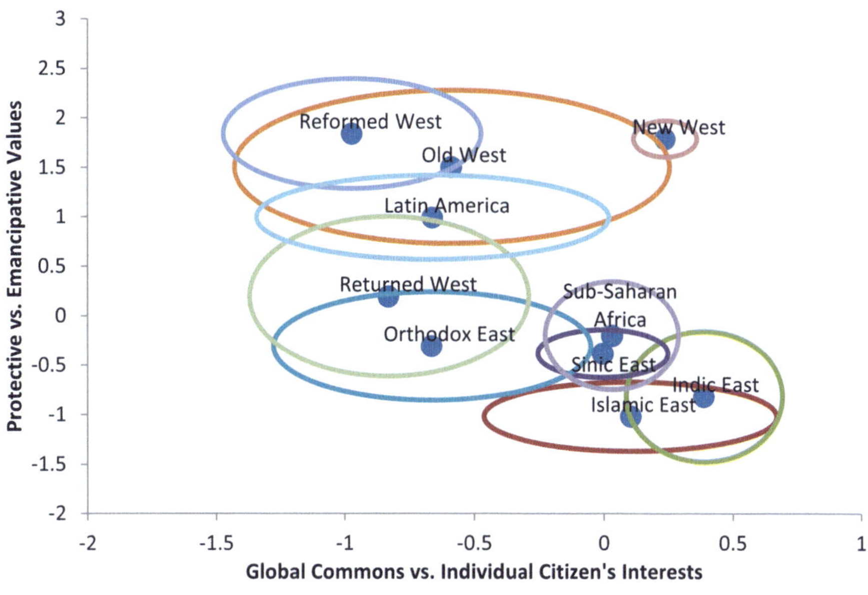

Fig. 5.2 Ten groups of countries located onto dimensions (Gc-Ic x Pr-Em)

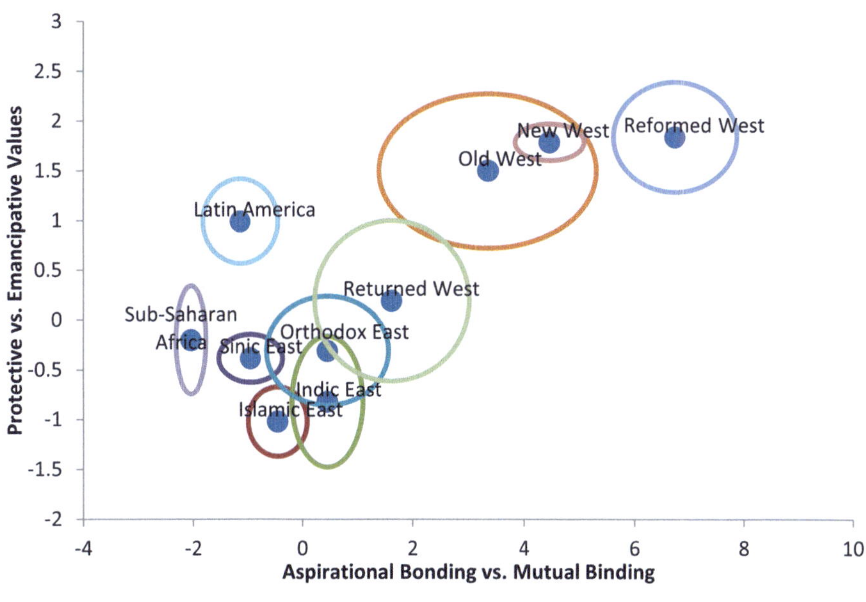

Fig. 5.3 Ten groups of countries located onto dimensions (Ag-Mb x Pr-Em)

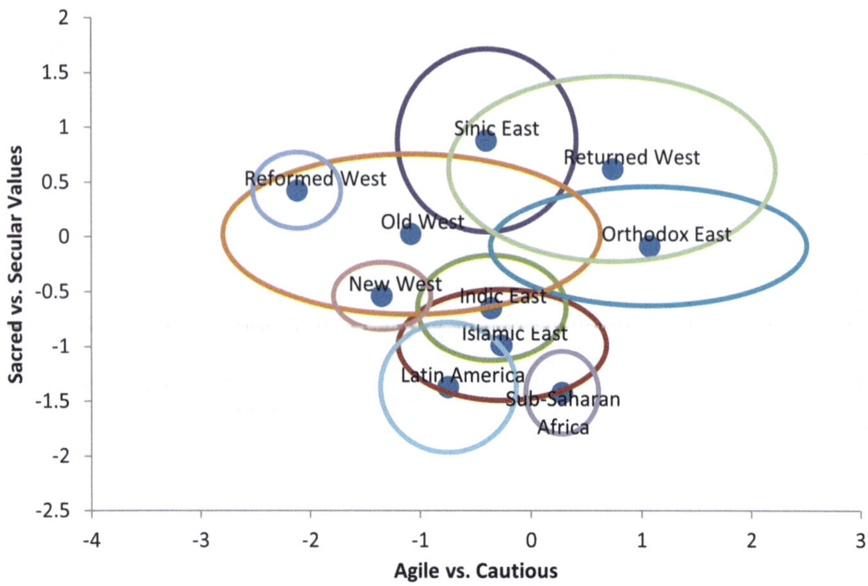

Fig. 5.4 Ten groups of countries located onto dimensions (Ag-Ca x Sa-Se)

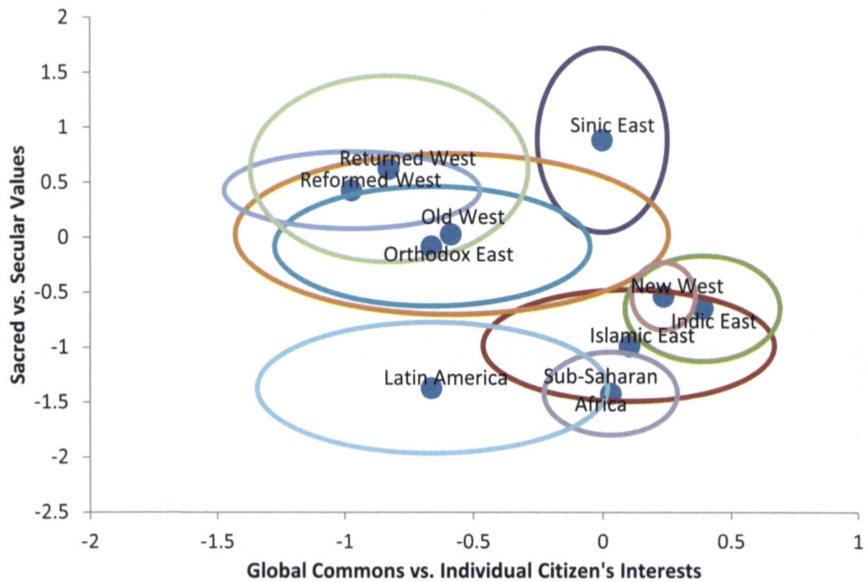

Fig. 5.5 Ten groups of countries located onto dimensions (Gc-Ic x Sa-Se)

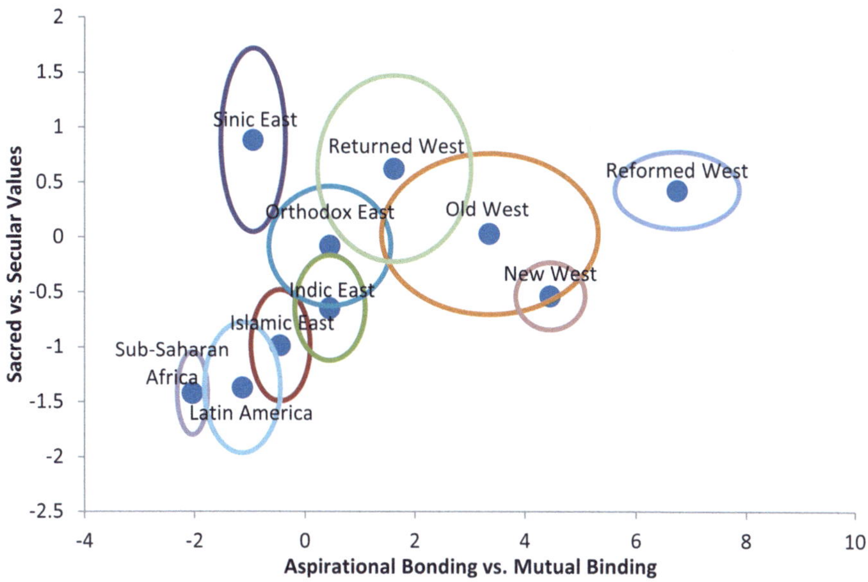

Fig. 5.6 Ten groups of countries located onto dimensions (Ab-Mb x Sa-Sc)

5.3 Conclusion

We have proposed a model of global social contract derived from Rousseau's and Locke's metaphors by linking global citizens' preference and states' participation in multilateral treaties. The results show that global citizens' preferences on norms and values as represented by the WVS (Welzel 2013) and sovereign states' participation in multilateral treaties as represented by the Multilateral Treaties Survey (Le et al. 2014) work in tandem. In other words, the key dimensions of each of the citizen's data and the states' data are more or less parallel. More specifically, the emancipative versus protective dimension is reasonably correlated with the agile versus cautious participation; the sacred versus secular orientation and the global commons versus individual citizens' interests orientation run more or less parallel. The correlation coefficients between the citizens' preference scores and the states' participation scores are reasonably high. Simultaneously, we have found that Rousseau's and Locke's ideas of direct democracy and representative democracy are not easily amenable to operationalization. Rather, Rousseau's and Locke's metaphors will continue to help us envisage a more sophisticated model of global quasi-legislative processes and outcomes. This is simply the first result in our search for global quasi-legislative politics.

The next task is to see what national regime type and national characteristics will make a difference. It is absolutely necessary and important to show that multilateral treaties are shaped by sovereign state actors whose political regime characteristics influence legislative outcomes. In Chap. 7, some positive empirical evidence will be presented to show that the states' locations on these key dimensions provide quite succinct and excellent snapshot-like profiles. For example, Sinic East as a whole is cautiously agile and well mixed between global commons orientation and the national interest orientation. The United States, one of the New West countries, manifests a good mix of emancipative and protective orientation as well as the significantly religious and secular orientation. Sovereign states' participation requires a deeper analysis of what might be called the states' treaty behavior. Each of the 193 sovereign states and each of the 10 geo-culturally similar groups needs to be researched further to gain a deeper understanding of treaty behavior.

References

Basanez, M. (2015). *A world of three cultures: How values impact development*. Oxford: Oxford University Press.

Brenner, M. (1981/2009). *Nuclear power and non-proliferation: The remaking of US policy*. Cambridge, MA: Cambridge University Press.

Inglehart, R., & Welzel, C. (2005). *Modernization, cultural change, and democracy: The human development sequence*. Cambridge, MA: Cambridge University Press.

Inoguchi, T. (2008). Political theory. In B. Badie, D. Berg-Schlosser, & L. Morlino (Eds.), *International encyclopedia of political science* (Vol. 6, pp. 2050–2063). Thousand Oaks: SAGE.

Inoguchi, T. (2015). War occurrence: Hyper-insecurity and multilateral institutions. *Japanese Journal of Political Science, 16*(3), 388–398.

Inoguchi, T. (2018). Theoretical underpinnings of global social contract. In W. Thompson (Ed.), *The Oxford encyclopedia of empirical international relations theory* (Vol. 4, pp. 209–220). Oxford: Oxford University Press.

Inoguchi, T., & Le, L. T. Q. (2016). Toward modelling a global social contract: Jean-Jacques Rousseau and John Locke. *Japanese Journal of Political Science, 17*(3), 489–522.

Jones, K. (2015). *Reconstructing the World Trade Organization for the 21st century: An institutional approach*. Oxford: Oxford University Press.

Joyner, D. H. (2013). *Interpreting the nuclear non-proliferation treaty*. Oxford: Oxford University Press.

Krasner, S. (Ed.). (1983). *International regimes*. Ithaca: Cornell University Press.

Kutney, G. (2013). *Carbon politics and the failure of the Kyoto protocol*. London: Routledge.

Le, T. Q. L., Mikami, Y., & Inoguchi, T. (2014). Global leadership and international regime: Empirical testing of cooperation without hegemony paradigm on the basis of 120 multilateral conventions data deposited to the United Nations system. *Japanese Journal of Political Science, 15*(4), 523–601.

Popovski, V., & Fraser, T. (2014). *The security council as global legislator (global institutions)*. London: Routledge.

Solingen, E. (2013). *Regional orders at century's dawn*. Princeton: Princeton University Press.

Sovacool, B. K., & Dworkin, M. H. (2014). *Global energy justice: Problems, principles, and practices*. Cambridge, MA: Cambridge University Press.

Volgy, T. (1973). The role of the 'outsider' in quasi-legislative systems: The potential utility of a legislative model. *International Organization, 27*(1), 85–98.

Welzel, C. (2013). *Freedom rising: Human empowerment and the quest for emancipation*. New York: Cambridge University Press.

Woodside, A. (2006). *Lost modernities: China, Vietnam, Korea and the hazards of world history*. Cambridge: Harvard University Press.

Yamamoto, Y. (2008). *Kokusai regime to governance* (International regimes and governance). Tokyo: Yuhikaku.

Young, M. (2011). *The rise of the meritocracy*. New York: Transaction Publishers.

Part II
Global Quasi-legislative Behavior

Chapter 6
Introduction to Part II

Abstract Part I conceptualizes Rousseau's and Locke's ideas of social contract to be writ global and formulated as a bundle of global quasi-social contracts. Part II formulates sovereign states' participation in multilateral treaties as global quasi-legislative behavior. Factor-analyzing six instrumental variables of sovereign states' participation in multilateral treaties yields three dimensions of speed, angle and strategy whereupon the typology of global quasi-legislative behavior by sovereign states is constructed. Chapter 7 presents the rankings of 193 sovereign states and ten geo-historico-cultural groups on three dimensions, i.e., speed, angle, and strategy when sovereign states join or opt not to join multilateral treaties. Chapter 8 presents the hexagonal profiles of sovereign states, first globally, then regionally focusing on Asia. Hexagonal profiles are constructed to show the distance from world mean by six policy domains.

In Part I, we argued that a state's decision to join or not join multilateral treaties can be conceptualized as a social contract, as envisaged by Rousseau and Locke writ global on the basis of convergence between the global citizens' preference for value orientation, on the one hand, and sovereign states' participation in multilateral treaties, on the other. In Part II, we examine how each of the 193 states manifests *global quasi-legislative behavior* by factor-analyzing six instrumental variables: (1) year of membership, (2) year of deposit, (3) number of current members, (4) treaty participation index (In our calculation based on the number of elapsed years between promulgation and ratification of a treaty), (5) modified Welzel regional group, (6) six policy domains of multilateral treaties, namely, peace, communications and commerce, human rights, intellectual property, environment, and health. The yielded dimensions of behavior are related to sovereign states' speed, angle, and strategy. In other words, they pertain to the following: (1) agile vs cautious, (2) global common good vs individual interests, and (3) aspirational bonding vs mutual binding. *Global quasi-legislative behavior* differs from country to country. While Chap. 5 focuses on the products, i.e., multilateral treaties, Chap. 7 focuses on the agents of multilateral treaties, i.e., sovereign states. Patterns of sovereign states' participation in multilateral treaties are analyzed, producing the so-called states' *global quasi-legislative behavior*. If Chap. 5 adopts a system perspective, Chap. 7 (and Chap. 8) adopts each country's national perspective. Chapter

T. Inoguchi, L. T. Q. Le, *The Development of Global Legislative Politics*,
Trust: Interdisciplinary Perspectives 3, https://doi.org/10.1007/978-981-32-9389-2_6

7 describes different patterns of states' *global quasi-legislative behavior*, and Chap. 8 outlines eight states representing eight types of *global quasi-legislative behavior*, i.e., Brazil, Sweden, New Zealand, Slovakia, South Korea, Nigeria, and Uzbekistan. It can be compared to a kind of foreign policy. The key word is agreement. Agreement here refers to whether sovereign states concur or not with the spirit, clauses, and consequent benefits and regulations, which multilateral treaties apply to signatory sovereign states. Considering that international politics was regarded as consisting of might, wealth, and ideology until the late twentieth century, it provides a fresh perspective to look at and examine global politics. Instead of being always preoccupied with conflict and competition, animosity and antagonism, hierarchy and dominance, this perspective allows one to view sovereign states' participation in multilateral treaties as their foreign policy on the basis of agreement. In an age of digitalization and globalization, in which speed, uncertainty, and complexity relentlessly plague or occasionally please global citizens and sovereign states, multilateral treaties are one of the forms through which the spirit of international collaboration and rules are as open and inclusive as possible. A review of recent studies of multilateral treaties allows one to see how lawyers and academics strive to identify solutions for gridlock faced by these treaties against the speed, uncertainty, complexity, and associated risks that plague the international system (Hale et al. 2013; Hale and Held 2017; Katzenstein and Seybert 2018). Setting aside the salience of the problem-solving approach of recent studies, this book proposes and presents a study of multilateral treaties as the subject of joiners' foreign policy and transnational policy combined. In other words, Part II presents 193 sovereign states' foreign policy and transnational policy with their consequential implications for the future of global politics.

Chapter 5's factor-analysis yielded three dimensions, namely, speed, angle, and strategy of the global quasi-legislative behavior of 193 states, which we typologized into eight types by the combination of speed (agile vs cautious), angle (global commons vs individual citizens' interests), and strategy (aspirational bonding vs mutual binding) using binary coding. In each of the three dimensions. The higher-scoring top 20 out of 193 states were ranked to identify the states that are well performing. Similarly, all the ten regions were ranked on each of the three dimensions. "Chapter 8: Eight Types of *Global Quasi-legislative Behavior*" features of eight states (Brazil, Iran, Sweden, New Zealand, Slovakia, South Korea, Nigeria and Uzbekistan), representing each of the eight types as an ideal type. The beauty of these eight types is to enable readers to be cognizant of the many styles of engagement with the world when we register multilateral treaties participation as if they were outcomes of *a bundle of global quasi-social contracts*.

References

Hale, T., & Held, D. (2017). *Beyond gridlock*. Cambridge: Polity Press.

Hale, T., Held, D., & Young, K. (2013). *Gridlock: Why global cooperation is failing when we need it most*. Cambridge: Polity Press.

Katzenstein, P. J., & Seybert, L. (Eds.). (2018). *Protean power: Exploring the uncertain and unexpected in world politics*. Cambridge: Cambridge University Press.

Chapter 7
Patterns of States' Global Quasi-Legislative Behavior

Abstract This chapter shows the rankings of global quasi-legislation behavior of 193 sovereign states and ten geo-historico-cultural groups (Sub-Saharan Africa, Sinic East, Returned West, Reformed West, Orthodox East, New West, Latin America, Islamic East, Indic East) on three dimensions, i.e., agile vs cautious (speed), global commons vs individual citizens' interests (angle), aspirational bonding vs mutual binding (strategy).

In contemporary global politics, sovereign states are in a sense legislators in a non-existent world assembly—they have the option to join or not join multilateral treaties. Before legislative bills or multilateral treaty drafts are discussed and negotiated, states shape and share the products of legislation.

7.1 Introduction

When deciding to join or not join multilateral treaties, what considerations and calculations must states make? Based on our factor analysis of the data from the Multilateral Treaties Survey about states' participation in multilateral treaties, the following are the three most important dimensions:

Dimension 1: Agile versus Cautious behavior
Dimension 2: Global commons versus Individual citizens' interests
Dimension 3: Aspirational bonding versus Mutual binding

The first dimension encapsulates speed, preparedness, and progressiveness. Speed is defined as being prompt in examining treaty drafts and acting fast in signing and ratifying. When documents are examined by nations, such proficiency is sometimes lacking. Since English has been a *lingua franca*, societies weak in English proficiency are bound to be slow. Even if bureaucratic examinations proceed steadily, political actions can be slow. The Paris Climate Change agreement was shaped decisively by the bilateral talk between the US and China. Having not been well-informed

T. Inoguchi, L. T. Q. Le, *The Development of Global Legislative Politics*,
Trust: Interdisciplinary Perspectives 3, https://doi.org/10.1007/978-981-32-9389-2_7

about this move in advance, Japan has failed to ratify the agreement in time to be qualified as a founding member. Being well-prepared thus translates into speed; being non-progressive about multilateral treaties tends to lead to hesitation and reluctance.

The second dimension is global commons versus individual citizens' interests. In our data from the Multilateral Treaties Survey, the six domains of multilateral treaties, i.e., human rights (H), peace and disarmament (P), trade, commerce, and communication (C), environment (E), intellectual property (I), and labor, health and safety (L), possess varying weights in terms of dealing with global commons and individual citizens' interests. This dimension reflects the sovereign states' angle from which multilateral conventions' legislative focus is examined: global commons versus individual citizens' interests. In other words, it answers the question of whether the state is interested in the global angle or the angle of national interest. For instance, the Climate Change agreement leans toward global commons, whereas the Trans-Pacific Partnership agreement concerns the sectors that are highly impacted, e.g., rice and beef.

The third dimension is aspirational bonding versus mutual binding. Multilateral treaties are burdened by an inherent dilemma; since membership is voluntary, treaty drafters think about the content from two perspectives—on one hand, they want to create numerous strict rules and regulations to establish and enforce solid global governance, while, on the other hand, they want to create generous, flexible rules and regulations that will persuade the most number of members to join multilateral treaties. Essentially, the two schools of thought involve those states that wave their burning passions and bonding spirits and those states that strictly feel obliged to observe duties and responsibilities. For example, the non-proliferation of nuclear weapons has been in force for many years. Compromise was struck between nuclear weapons states and non-nuclear weapons states; the former wanted to constrain and restrict non-nuclear weapons states such that nuclear weapons development could proceed only under specific rules and regulations, whereas the latter wanted to require nuclear weapons states to steadily disarm themselves of nuclear weapons. The spirit of the treaty is that of aspirational bonding for disarmament by nuclear weapons states, juxtaposed by that of mutual binding for the non-diffusion of nuclear weapons to non-nuclear weapons states. The reality is that disarmament discussions among nuclear weapons states, such as the US and Russia, do not progress far, whereas the non-proliferation rules are tightly governed when it comes to non-nuclear weapons states: such regulations disregard the desire of some non-nuclear weapons states to go nuclear for peaceful and non-peaceful purposes. Because of this asymmetrical pattern of compromise, the number of nuclear weapons states has been slowly rising.

Based on our factor analysis results on these above three dimensions, this chapter will answer the question: Which states have high or low scores within the key dimensions? Specifically, for each dimension, we list the top twenty states with the highest score and provide a ranking of ten regional groups of states. Moreover, we measure the distance among these ten groups on these key dimensions to provide a comparative and insightful glimpse of the states' global quasi-legislative behavior.

7.2 Ranking States on the Key Dimensions of Global Quasi-Legislative Behavior

7.2.1 Agile Versus Cautious Dimension

The top ten states for agile behavior are all European, and many of them are familiar with the theory and practice of international law. This is because they are accustomed to the management of international organizations where specialized personnel with language expertise, often from Europe, are dominant. The top ten, listed top-down, are Norway, France, Italy, Sweden, Switzerland, the Netherlands, Spain, the United Kingdom, Denmark, and Germany. The next ten (i.e., 11–20) are also dominated by European countries, most of which are in the eastern part of the continent, with only two being outside of Europe. Listed top-down, the positions from 11 to 20 are the United States, Mexico, Austria, Egypt, Belgium, Hungary, Romania, Bulgaria, Greece, and Portugal.

On the other side, the top twenty states on cautious behavior tend to be small and peripherally located in and near Europe. Listed top-down are Montenegro, Bosnia and Herzegovina, Moldova, Kazakhstan, Armenia, Serbia, Macedonia, Georgia, Kyrgyzstan, Slovenia, Lithuania, Slovakia, Tajikistan, Albania, Estonia, Croatia, Czech Republic, Bahrain, Azerbaijan, and Palau.

Evident from these lists is the fact that diplomacy, international law, international organizations, and international commerce have been most densely developed in modern Europe; its strength via accumulation cannot be denied. It is a vindication of European strength apart from its military might, which may have been substantial or hegemonic in the era of Westphalia (Table 7.1).

7.2.2 Global Commons Versus Individual Citizens' Interests Dimension

The top ten countries listed top-down on global commons (1–10) are Bosnia and Herzegovina, Uruguay, Luxemburg, Brazil, Sweden, Serbia, Spain, Finland, Belgium, and Germany. Further listed are Slovakia, Czech Republic, Poland, Montenegro, Hungary, Ukraine, Croatia, Mexico, Russia, and Macedonia. Those states with high scores on global commons are predominantly European or European-originated.

Listed top-down on individual citizens' interests are Palau, Bhutan, Marshall Islands, Tonga, Brunei, Myanmar, Qatar, Oman, Guinea-Bissau, Saint Lucia, Grenada, the Maldives, Saint Kitts Nevis, United Arab Emirates, Nauru, Comoros, Botswana, Democratic People's Republic of Korea, Bahrain, and Samoa. Those states with high scores on individual citizens' interests are either predominantly small maritime island states in the Pacific Ocean, the Caribbean, the Indian Ocean, or the Persian Gulf (Table 7.2).

Table 7.1 Top twenty states on *agile vs. cautious* dimension

Top 20	Agile	Cautious
1	Norway	Montenegro
2	France	Bosnia & Herzegovina
3	Italy	R.Moldova
4	Sweden	Kazakhstan
5	Switzerland	Armenia
6	Netherlands	Serbia
7	Spain	Macedonia
8	UK	Georgia
9	Denmark	Kyrgyzstan
10	Germany	Slovenia
11	USA	Lithuania
12	Mexico	Slovakia
13	Austria	Tajikistan
14	Egypt	Albania
15	Belgium	Estonia
16	Hungary	Croatia
17	Romania	Czech Republic
18	Bulgaria	Bahrain
19	Greece	Azerbaijan
20	Portugal	Palau

7.2.3 Aspirational Bonding Versus Mutual Binding Dimension

Multilateral treaties are often called multilateral conventions. Conventions often contain those articles that wave the flag of aspiration for equality of race and religion or of income—appealing to those who aspire and those who suffer before their dreams are realized. Accordingly, these conventions often bond together all those who suffer. This is called aspirational bonding. In contrast, multilateral treaties often aim at binding joiners with the same rules and regulations. This is called mutual binding.

The top ten states listed top-down on aspirational bonding are Cape Verde, Mauritania, Mozambique, Benin, Lesotho, Tanzania, Djibouti, Rwanda, Core D'Ivoire, Togo, Guinea-Bissau, Burkina Faso, Comoros, Saint Vincent Grenadines, Swaziland, Sao Tome Principe, Guinea, Ghana, Nigeria, and the Democratic Republic of Congo. Small and large states in Western Africa and the Caribbean tend to dominate the top 20.

Listed top-down on mutual binding are Sweden, Norway, the United Kingdom, Denmark, Germany, Switzerland, Finland, the Netherlands, Spain, the United States, France, Canada, Hungary, Australia, Ireland, Austria, Iceland, Belgium, Portugal, and Italy. Predominant are Europeans once more, sticking to the principle of universal and reciprocal binding (Table 7.3).

Table 7.2 Top twenty states on *global commons vs. individual citizen's interests* dimension

Top 20	Global commons	Individual citizen's interests
1	Bosnia & Herzegovina	Palau
2	Uruguay	Bhutan
3	Luxembourg	Marshall Islands
4	Brazil	Tonga
5	Sweden	Brunei
6	Serbia	Myanmar
7	Spain	Qatar
8	Finland	Oman
9	Belgium	Guinea-Bissau
10	Germany	Saint Lucia
11	Slovakia	Grenada
12	Czech Republic	Maldives
13	Poland	St. Kitts &Nevis
14	Montenegro	UAE
15	Hungary	Nauru
16	Ukraine	Comoros
17	Croatia	Botswana
18	Mexico	D. P. R. Korea
19	Russia	Bahrain
20	Macedonia	Samoa

7.3 Ranking Ten Groups on the Key Dimensions of Global Quasi-Legislative Behavior

Ranking 193 states on the key dimensions gives clear and precise locations on key dimensions. Yet one might as well see big picture pertaining to these countries' with similar culture, geography, and history. Ranking the 10 groups of states categorized by Christian Welzel (2013) and revised by Lien Le and Takashi Inoguchi meets this purpose.

7.3.1 Ranking Ten Groups on the Agile Versus Cautious Dimension

The following represents the top ten groups listed from cautious to agile: Orthodox East, Returned West, Sub-Saharan Africa, New West, Indic East, Islamic East, Latin America, Sinic East, Old West, and Reformed West. The most cautious are the Orthodox East and Returned West, i.e., Central and Eastern Europe, which changed from communism to capitalism in the last quarter of the last century. Then come the broad areas of Asia, Africa, and Latin America. One of the most striking results is the location of the New West, i.e., Canada, Australia, New Zealand, and most

Table 7.3 Top twenty states on *aspirational bonding vs. mutual binding* dimension

Top 20	Aspirational bonding	Mutual binding
1	Cape Verde	Sweden
2	Mauritania	Norway
3	Mozambique	UK
4	Benin	Denmark
5	Lesotho	Germany
6	Tanzania	Switzerland
7	Djibouti	Finland
8	Rwanda	Netherlands
9	Cote d'Ivoire	Spain
10	Togo	USA
11	Guinea-Bissau	France
12	Burkina Faso	Canada
13	Comoros	Hungary
14	St. Vincent & the Grenadines	Australia
15	Swaziland	Ireland
16	São Tomé and Príncipe	Austria
17	Guinea	Iceland
18	Ghana	Belgium
19	Nigeria	Portugal
20	D.R.Congo	Italy

importantly the United States. After all, in George Washington's words, disentanglement from extended alliance and affairs is a key to the United States. The US comes next to sub-Saharan Africa in terms of cautiousness in joining multilateral treaties. Following the New West come the Indic East, the Islamic East, and Latin America. Next come the Sinic East, the Old West, and the Reformed West. The latter two are founders of multilateral treaties in a sense; therefore it is not surprising to find them being the most agile. The Sinic East is quite a surprise, with its busy trade and economic vigor with China, Japan, South Korea, Singapore, Hong Kong, and Taiwan included, which bodes well for Asia's future (Rachman 2017) (Table 7.4).

7.3.2 Ranking Ten Groups on Global Commons Versus Individual Citizens' Interests Dimension

Listed top-down on the individual citizens' interests to global commons are the New West, the Indic East, Sub-Saharan Africa, the Sinic East, the Islamic East, Latin America, the Old West, the Orthodox East, the Reformed West, and the Returned West. Most striking is the top spot of the New West, especially the United States, with emphasis on individual citizens' interests as contrasted to global commons. In addition, it is striking that the Returned West is ranked as having the

Table 7.4 Ranking ten groups on *agile vs. cautious* dimension (From *cautious* to *agile*)

Rank	Group	Score
1	Orthodox East	0.98
2	Returned West	0.81
3	Sub-Saharan Africa	0.27
4	New West	0.17
5	Indic East	0.02
6	Islamic East	−0.15
7	Latin America	−0.22
8	Sinic East	−0.23
9	Old West	−0.86
10	Reformed West	−1.82

Table 7.5 Ranking ten groups on *global commons vs. individual citizen's interests* dimension (From *individual citizen's interests* to *global commons*)

Rank	Group	Score
1	New West	0.65
2	Indic East	0.54
3	Sub-Saharan Africa	0.30
4	Sinic East	0.16
5	Islamic East	0.14
6	Latin America	−0.13
7	Old West	−0.41
8	Orthodox East	−0.54
9	Reformed West	−0.75
10	Returned West	−0.89

highest emphasis on global commons. Adjacent to the Reformed West, the core of Western Europe, the Returned West naturally takes positions closest to the Reformed West (Table 7.5).

7.3.3 *Ranking Ten Groups on Aspirational Bonding Versus Mutual Binding Dimension*

Listed top-down on Mutual binding are the Reformed West, the Old West, New West, the Returned West, the Orthodox East, the Indic East, the Islamic East, the Sinic East, Latin America, and Sub-Saharan Africa. Within this dimension, all the Wests, i.e., the Reformed West, the Old West, the New West, and the Returned West, are ranked very similarly. The

Table 7.6 Ranking ten groups on *aspirational bonding vs. mutual binding* dimension (From *mutual binding* to *aspirational bonding*)

Rank	Group	Score
1	Reformed West	6.19
2	Old West	2.84
3	New West	1.99
4	Returned West	1.61
5	Orthodox East	0.38
6	Indic East	0.16
7	Islamic East	−0.49
8	Sinic East	−0.85
9	Latin America	−1.38
10	Sub-Saharan Africa	−2.04

remaining six groups take the positions of aspirational bonding rather than mutual binding. The West likes to bind the rest whereas the rest want to enhance solidarity without being bound by rules of the game initiated and consolidated by the West (Table 7.6).

7.4 Measuring Distance Among Ten Groups in the Key Dimensions

7.4.1 Measuring Distance Among Ten Groups in the First and Second Dimensions

It is important to consider the distance on key dimensions in order to gauge the propensity to join or not join multilateral treaties, as groups are defined as similar entities in terms of geographic, historical, cultural, political, and economic elements.

The first dimension is *Agile versus Cautious*, while the second dimension is *Global Commons versus Individual Citizens' Interests*. These angles are the two most important angles, as the distance between them significantly impacts sovereign states' global quasi-legislative behavior. Groups whose distance on these two dimensions are close behave similarly in their legislative space. From these combined angles, Islamic East is closest to Sinic Asia in terms of distance. Similarly, the Indic East is the closest to New West in terms of distance. Orthodox East is the closest to the Returned West in terms of distance. It is natural to see this, after all, because they used to adopt communist regimes. The Old West is closest to Latin America in terms of distance; it is natural to see the close distance between the Old West and Latin America due to the strong influence of France and other southern Europe countries on Latin America. In particular, many Latin American countries achieved independence after the French Revolution and the Napoleonic War. The Reformed West is closest to the Old West in terms of distance, and the New West is closest to Indic West in terms of distance. This is explained by the common thread of disentanglement (the US) and non-entanglement (Indic). The Returned West is closest to Orthodox East in terms of distance, and Sub-Saharan Africa is closest to Indic East in terms of distance. It may be explained, though only in part, by the relationship between British colonialism and its legacy in Sub-Saharan Africa and India's tendency to call eastern and southern Africa as "near abroad" with two million Indians living in Africa. Latin America is closest to Islamic East in terms of distance (Table 7.7).

7.4.2 Measuring Distance Among Ten Groups in the First and Third Dimensions

The first dimension is *Agile versus Cautious*, while the third dimension is *Aspirational Bonding versus Mutual Binding*. The third dimension enables multilateral treaties to have an extremely important future. Underlying the third dimension is the key difference in the orientations: the developing South tries to bond amongst themselves while trying to evade the North's binding of the South through rules. In other words, the developed North tries to bind the South while the North tries to evade joining the South's dreams. From these combined angles, the Islamic East is closest to the Sinic East in terms of distance. The Indic East is closest to the Islamic East in terms of distance, and the Sinic East is closest to Latin America. The Orthodox East is closest to the Returned West in terms of distance, and the Old West is closest to the New West. The Reformed West is closest to the Orthodox East in terms of distance, and the New West is closest to the Returned West. The Returned West is closest to Orthodox East in terms of distance, and Sub-Saharan Africa is closest to Latin America in terms of distance (Table 7.8).

7.4.3 Measuring Distance Among Ten Groups in the Second and Third Dimensions

The second dimension is *Global Commons versus Individual Citizens' Interests*, whereas the third dimension is *Aspirational Bonding versus Mutual Binding*. From these combined angles, the Islamic East is closest to the Sinic East in terms of distance, and the Indic East is closest to the Islamic East. Sinic East is closest to the Islamic East in terms of distance, and the Orthodox East is closest to the Returned West. The Old West is closest to the Returned West in terms of distance, while the Reformed West is closest to the Old West in terms of distance. The New West is closest to the Indic West in terms of distance, and the Returned West is closest to the Orthodox East in terms of distance. Sub-Saharan Africa is closest to the Sinic East in terms of distance, while Latin America is closest to the Sinic East (Table 7.9).

Table 7.7 Measuring distance of ten groups on *agile vs. cautious* and *global commons vs. individual citizen's interests* dimensions

Region	Islamic East	Indic East	Sinic East	Orthodox East	Old West	Reformed West	New West	Returned West	Sub-Saharan Africa	Latin America
Islamic East	**0.00**	0.60	0.08	1.42	1.02	1.99	0.78	1.71	0.44	0.40
Indic East	0.60	**0.00**	0.59	1.78	1.58	2.50	0.20	2.17	0.42	0.99
Sinic East	0.08	0.59	**0.00**	1.49	1.00	1.95	0.79	1.77	0.50	0.42
Orthodox East	1.42	1.78	1.49	**0.00**	1.69	2.58	1.85	0.52	1.36	1.24
Old West	1.02	1.58	1.00	1.69	**0.00**	1.00	1.78	1.68	1.45	0.71
Reformed West	1.99	2.50	1.95	2.58	1.00	**0.00**	2.70	2.42	2.43	1.71
New West	0.78	0.20	0.79	1.85	1.78	2.70	**0.00**	2.27	0.50	1.17
Returned West	1.71	2.17	1.77	0.52	1.68	2.42	2.27	**0.00**	1.77	1.43
Sub-Saharan Africa	0.44	0.42	0.50	1.36	1.45	2.43	0.50	1.77	**0.00**	0.76
Latin America	0.40	0.99	0.42	1.24	0.71	1.71	1.17	1.43	0.76	**0.00**

Table 7.8 Measuring distance of ten groups on *agile vs. cautious* and *aspirational bonding vs. mutual binding* dimensions

Region	Islamic East	Indic East	Sinic East	Orthodox East	Old West	Reformed West	New West	Returned West	Sub-Saharan Africa	Latin America
Islamic East	**0.00**	0.32	0.17	1.10	1.59	3.29	1.12	1.27	0.77	0.39
Indic East	0.32	**0.00**	0.49	0.88	1.42	3.12	0.81	0.96	0.98	0.71
Sinic East	0.17	0.49	**0.00**	1.23	1.71	3.40	1.29	1.43	0.69	0.23
Orthodox East	1.10	0.88	1.23	**0.00**	2.00	3.60	1.02	0.56	1.24	1.34
Old West	1.59	1.42	1.71	2.00	**0.00**	1.70	1.02	1.62	2.36	1.93
Reformed West	3.29	3.12	3.40	3.60	1.70	**0.00**	2.58	3.13	4.07	3.61
New West	1.12	0.81	1.29	1.02	1.02	2.58	**0.00**	0.61	1.76	1.51
Returned West	1.27	0.96	1.43	0.56	1.62	3.13	0.61	**0.00**	1.67	1.61
Sub-Saharan Africa	0.77	0.98	0.69	1.24	2.36	4.07	1.76	1.67	**0.00**	0.53
Latin America	0.39	0.71	0.23	1.34	1.93	3.61	1.51	1.61	0.53	**0.00**

Table 7.9 Measuring distance of ten groups on *global commons vs. individual citizen's interests* and aspirational bonding vs. mutual binding dimensions

Region	Islamic East	Indic East	Sinic East	Orthodox East	Old West	Reformed West	New West	Returned West	Sub-Saharan Africa	Latin America
Islamic East	**0.00**	0.64	0.16	1.04	1.65	3.18	1.30	1.73	0.71	0.55
Indic East	0.64	**0.00**	0.70	1.55	1.79	3.21	0.81	2.14	1.02	1.18
Sinic East	0.16	0.70	**0.00**	1.13	1.80	3.33	1.42	1.84	0.56	0.48
Orthodox East	1.04	1.55	1.13	**0.00**	1.09	2.55	1.83	0.73	1.60	0.96
Old West	1.65	1.79	1.80	1.09	**0.00**	1.54	1.55	0.87	2.36	1.88
Reformed West	3.18	3.21	3.33	2.55	1.54	**0.00**	2.71	2.01	3.89	3.42
New West	1.30	0.81	1.42	1.83	1.55	2.71	**0.00**	2.20	1.83	1.84
Returned West	1.73	2.14	1.84	0.73	0.87	2.01	2.20	**0.00**	2.33	1.69
Sub-Saharan Africa	0.71	1.02	0.56	1.60	2.36	3.89	1.83	2.33	**0.00**	0.68
Latin America	0.55	1.18	0.48	0.96	1.88	3.42	1.84	1.69	0.68	**0.00**

References

Rachman, G. (2017). *Easternization: Asia's rise and America's decline from Obama to Trump and Beyond*. New York: Other Press.

Welzel, C. (2013). *Freedom rising: Human empowerment and the quest for emancipation*. New York: Cambridge University Press.

Chapter 8
Eight Types of Global Quasi-Legislative Behavior

Abstract This chapter shows the hexagonal profiles of sovereign states' legislative behavior, first globally (Brazil, Sweden, Iran, New Zealand, Slovakia, South Korea, Nigeria, Uzbekistan), then regionally on Asia (Japan, China, North Korea, Indonesia, Bangladesh, South Korea and Uzbekistan). Hexagonal profiles are constructed to show the distance from world mean by six policy domains, i.e., human rights, peace and security, trade, commerce and communication, environment, intellectual property, labor, health).

8.1 Eight Types of Global Quasi-Legislative Behavior

In this chapter, attention shifts from *a bundle of global quasi-social contracts* to *global quasi-legislative behavior*. In other words, after theoretically and empirically justifying the concept of *a bundle of global quasi-social contracts* from a systemic perspective, we shift our focus to *global quasi-legislative behavior* for each of the participants in multilateral treaties. Eight types of *global quasi-legislative behavior* are first categorized on the basis of deviations from the world mean (See Appendix 5: Global Quasi-Legislative Behavior and All the Participating Countries Categorized into Eight Types). Eight states are selected to illustrate their perspective on *global quasi-legislative behavior* in terms of speed, angle, and strategy. Those eight countries are Brazil, Iran, Sweden, New Zealand, Slovakia, South Korea, Nigeria, and Uzbekistan.

The empirical results of the previous chapters show that the three dimensions identified by the factor analysis of 120 multilateral treaties in terms of legislative data are: (1) agile versus cautious; (2) global common good versus individual citizens' interests; and (3) aspirational bonding versus mutual binding. Each of these dimensions is concerned with the three perspectives of sovereign states' global quasi-legislative behavior, including: (1) *speed,* (2) *angle*, and (3) *strategy*. It can be clearly seen that the first dimension is concerned with the speed of sovereign states' behavior. Here, *speed* is referred to as the willingness of the state to participate in multilateral treaties. Next, the second dimension focuses on the primary angle of the

T. Inoguchi, L. T. Q. Le, *The Development of Global Legislative Politics*,
Trust: Interdisciplinary Perspectives 3, https://doi.org/10.1007/978-981-32-9389-2_8

sovereign states. The term *angle* is intended to mean the direction of the state's looking glass—specifically, whether that direction leans toward global common good versus individual citizens' interests. Finally, the third dimension deals with the primary strategy of sovereign states in multilateral treaties. *Strategy* is the method used for appealing to and attracting members for the cause of multilateral treaties; such strategies can be: (3a) a passionate call for solidarity whereby the prospect for the long-term construction of norms and rules in future multilateral treaties can be enhanced; or (3b) a pragmatic and somber calculus of participation whereby merits and demerits of commitments to rules and norms, that is, constraints imposed by treaties, are gauged for the short and long term. In deciding whether to join multilateral treaties, all three are indispensable. In tackling foreign policy behavior, substance and the adversary/partner in bilateral relations tend to be the focus. For example, substance is divided into two categories: high politics and low politics, or security and commerce. Adversary/partner is categorized as a friendly ally versus unfriendly foe or good versus evil. These varied and intertwined dimensions are what make the study of foreign policy behavior about multilateral treaties, in contrast to the study of foreign policy behavior about bilateral treaties, so complex. Fortunately, speed, angle, and strategy can be examined closely when discussing external policy behavior in relation to multilateral treaties.

Speed Speed is relevant. Diplomats present at the Palace of Versailles with European aristocrats and politicians discussing post-Napoleonic war settlements signed after an endlessly prolonged conference, noted that the "conference's dance" was almost indefinite. Trade liberalization talks under the World Trade Organization have failed to bring about any liberalizing and globalizing action despite its long rounds of negotiation. For over a decade, climate change talks appear to be on a similar trajectory. Similar to the United States-China sudden rapprochement amid the Vietnam War, the multilateral agreement was prompted by the same bilateral decisions to join the Paris Agreement, whereby the Paris Agreement became effective with the addition of some other joiners. Then, in 2017, President Donald Trump expressed his disdain of the Paris Accord from which the United States eventually withdrew. In the Balkan peace negotiations, the United States' chief negotiator withheld airline tickets until the negotiation was agreed upon. In the Iran-US-EU nuclear negotiation, very long negotiations were necessary. A positive aspect of that three-way negotiation was that there were similar nuclear scientists on both sides, similar in the sense that they were US-trained. Many Iranian negotiators were US-trained while many of the US negotiators were Iranian-American scientists.

Angle Multilateral treaties address all kinds of human activities. Yet, the angle adopted by sovereign states in tackling such issues makes an enormous difference. The most salient is a global common good versus individual citizens' interests. This is not to say that big powers adopt the global angle, whereas small powers adopt the angle focused on narrow national interests. An often cited example is the United States who frequently acts to dodge and disentangle itself from multilateral treaties. The 2016 US presidential election campaign highlighted this propensity within US foreign policy;

the two major candidates, Hillary Clinton and Donald Trump, argued that once elected they would oppose the multilateral free trade agreement called the Trans-Pacific Partnership Agreement. In contrast, one of the smallest countries, the Maldives, argues very ardently in support of the Paris Climate Change Agreement and has adopted the clear and forceful position of establishing a global common good. Yet another example gives a completely different impression of big powers: both the United States and China bilaterally forged and signed an agreement on non-carbon emission and proceeded to participate in the Paris Climate Change Agreement to demonstrate that they are great powers who have realized that the time to act decisively has arrived. The proposition is that the higher the stakes placed on free trade, the more liberal international order is adopted. Thus the hegemon, the supporter, the free rider, and the challenger exist almost in proportion to the size of their stake in free trade. Since the liberal international order has appeared only recently, empirical validation is pending.

Strategy Aspirational bonding versus mutual binding is most often seen as a strategic difference in multilateral treaties. Participating in multilateral treaties can be compared to a strategy of forging interpersonal trust. Robert Putnam contrasts American-Japanese strategic encounters as follows: in the prisoner's dilemma game in which players are left incommunicado, how the first move of cooperation is responded to by the adversary is the most important (Inoguchi 2000, pp. 383–384). The observed tendency of reciprocating with cooperation among Americans and Japanese is striking: while Americans tend to reciprocate with a cooperative move, the Japanese tend to ignore the sign of cooperation at least at first. Joining multilateral treaties is like joining a game in which norms and rules are shaped and shared by those who have joined. Joiners may be one of two kinds: (1) those who join anticipating that all norms and rules are to be practiced universally and that they should be strictly binding; and (2) those who join anticipating that articles are more or less of a longer term nature—that there are goals to be materialized in a nebulous future and that in the short term it is of utmost importance to be bonding with others with similar aspirations. High-income countries tend to prefer the former strategy, whereas low-income countries tend to prefer the latter. The Paris Climate Change Agreement used to include two kinds of countries: those whose carbon emission target is specified and those whose carbon emission target is not specified. In the latest version, the carbon emission target has become a solid obligation, although the developing countries' increase in carbon emission during the early phase of economic modernization is accommodated. Thus the West tends to broadly adopt a mutually binding strategy, whereas the rest of the world tends to adopt an aspirational bonding strategy. Among the West, the divergence between the developing West and the developed West has led to a cleavage amongst the European Union with regard to one common unified currency. Among the rest, the divergence has become extremely large: even among Southeast Asia, the divergence between Brunei and Singapore, on the one hand, and Laos and Myanmar, on the other, is a three or four digit difference in terms of per capita income in US dollars. In proportion to per capita income level, the multilateral treaties strategy differs.

Table 8.1 Types of global quasi-legislative behavior

	Type of global quasi-legislative behavior	Code
1	Agile behavior Global common good Aspirational bonding	abc
2	Agile behavior Individual citizens' interests Aspirational bonding	aBc
3	Agile behavior Global common good Mutual binding	abC
4	Agile behavior Individual citizens' interests Mutual binding	aBC
5	Cautious behavior Global common good Mutual binding	AbC
6	Cautious behavior Global common good Aspirational bonding	Abc
7	Cautious behavior Individual citizens' interests Aspirational bonding	ABc
8	Cautious behavior Individual citizens' interests Mutual binding	ABC

To categorize the countries based on their global quasi-legislative behavior, this analysis has recorded three dimensions with the following letters:

1. **a** for agile versus **A** for cautious (or **a** versus **A** in short): the higher the accumulation of multilateral treaties, the more agile a state is. The lower the accumulation of multilateral treaties, the more cautious a state is.
2. **b** for global common good versus **B** for individual citizens' interests (or **b** versus **B**): the more globally spread out the state's interests are, the more global of an angle is present. The less globally spread out the state's interests are, the more focus on individual citizens' interests.
3. **c** for aspirational bonding versus **C** for mutual binding (or **c** versus **C**): the more conscious the state is of being peripheralized, the more protective the state is in terms of being constrained by multilateral treaties. The more conscious the state is of being a global stakeholder, the more vocal the state is about effective rules and regulations of multilateral treaties.

With the binary distinction of each dimension, eight different combined patterns have emerged: abc, aBc, abC, aBC, AbC, Abc, ABc, and ABC. These patterns represent eight types of global quasi-legislative behavior exhibited by states. The description for each type of behavior is found in Table 8.1.

Table 8.2 Illustration of eight types of global quasi-legislative behavior (world) with deviations from world mean in each of the six policy domains

Type	Country	Human rights	Peace and security	Trade, commerce and communication	Environment	Intellectual property	Labor
abc	Brazil	.485	.799	1.532	.658	1.232	1.232
aBc	Iran	–.326	.248	.220	.071	–1.032	–.415
abC	Sweden	2.850	3.130	2.253	3.183	2.288	8.243
aBC	New Zealand	.886	.945	.953	1.611	–.193	–.414
AbC	Slovakia	–.696	.095	–.106	.304	.989	1.063
Abc	South Korea	–.190	.055	.059	–.047	.021	–.254
ABc	Nigeria	.661	.183	–.016	1.158	–.380	–.366
ABC	Uzbekistan	–1.013	.296	–.991	–.630	–.792	–.732

8.2 Illustrations of the Eight Types

For each state, we have measured its willingness to participate in the multilateral treaties in six regime domains by proposing the Treaty Participation Index. To reflect how many standard deviations above or below the world mean a state exercised its participation, we have also proposed the z-score that is the standardized or normalized measurement of the Treaty Participation Index to capture the comparative evaluation among countries (See Sect. 4.5.9 of Chap. 4). Appendix 6 provides the full listing of 193 states' z-scores indicating positive or negative deviations from the world mean for six policy domains.

By combining the type of global quasi-legislative behavior and the z-score, we have chosen eight states to illustrate their respective global quasi-legislative behavior in terms of speed, angle, and identity. The eight states are Brazil, Iran, Sweden, New Zealand, Slovakia, South Korea, Nigeria, and Uzbekistan (Table 8.2 and Fig. 8.1).

abc

Brazil As a member of BRICS, the acronym for the combined emerging economies of Brazil, Russia, India, China, and South Africa, Brazil is confident of its economic potential. This multi-cultural country has abundant water, forest, and mineral resources, significant space, a large population, an advanced science and technology industry (manufacturing and well selling small-scale business flight airplane). Moreover, it is one of the leaders of the regional economic group, Mercosur. Self-confidence encourages agility in perception and action with a self-claimed leader of the Post-Western World (Stuenkel 2016). Its angle is that of the developing South and developed South combined. Its strategy is that of a leader of the developing South, thus emphasizing the strategy of aspirational solidarity in treaty behavior. Therefore, those policy domains of trade, intellectual property, and labor are three of its national interest-focused domains, whereas human rights and the environment are perceived very important but are not regarded as its banner-waving domains.

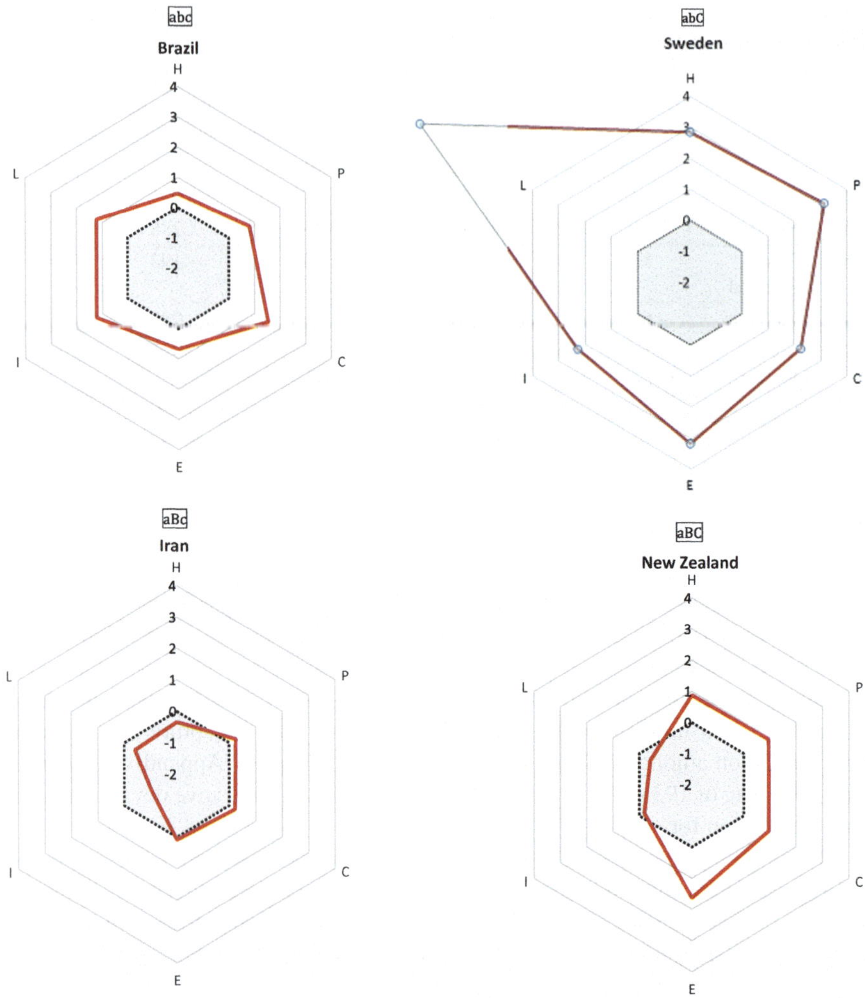

Fig. 8.1 Hexagonal profiles of eight type of Sovereign states' global quasi-legislative behavior The solid line representing the actual values achieved by a given state and the dotted line representing the world's average in each of six policy domains: Human rights (H), Peace and Security (P), Trade, Commerce and Communication (C), Intellectual Property (I) and Labor and Health (L)

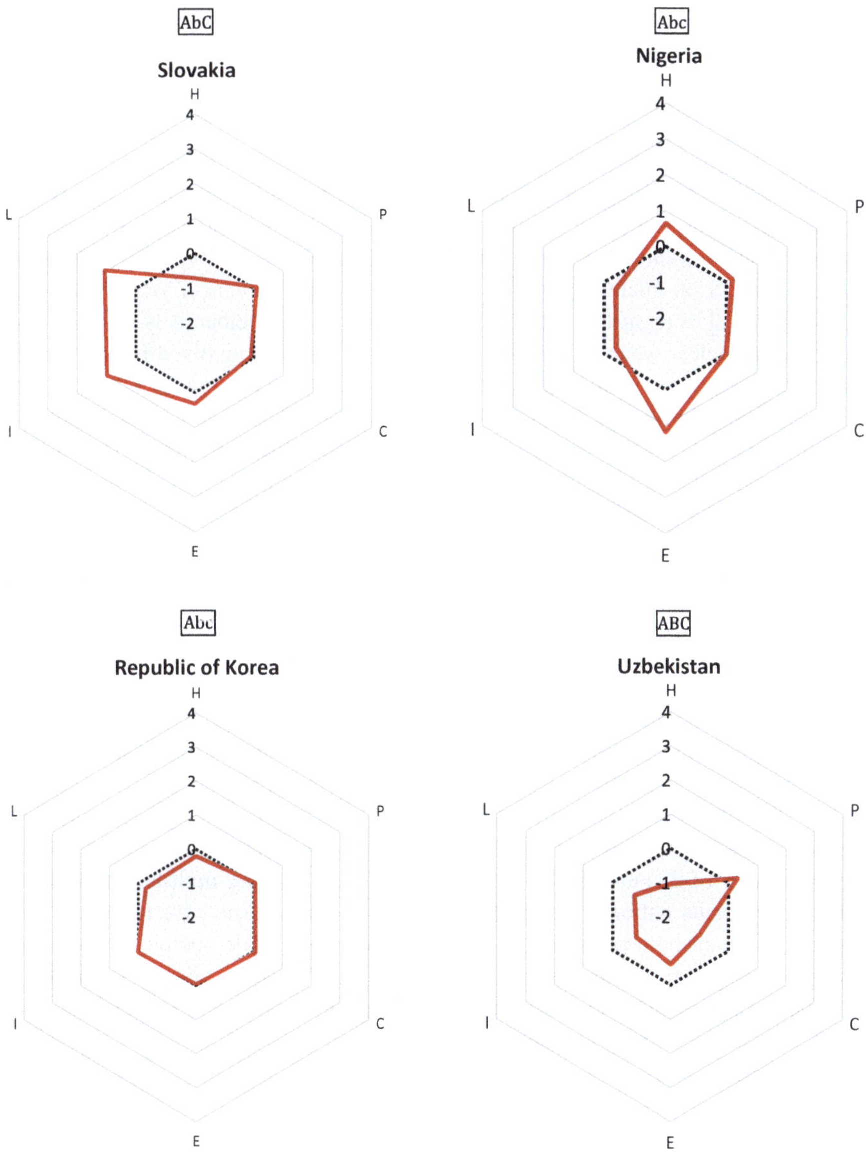

Fig. 8.1 (continued)

This is especially true, given that the West, the Reformed West, and the Old West are the self-proclaimed leaders of human rights and the environment, and often criticize the developing South's poor efforts in these two domains.

aBc

Iran As an oil producing country with a historic and proud civilization, Iran is full of distinctive treaty behavior. Its action is agile with its negotiation style of vigorous argumentation and shrewd give-and-take calculation. The Iranian agreement with the EU and the US on nuclear power generation shows its influence. When Iran held talks with the US regarding nuclear power generation, whether it is for peaceful purposes or nuclear weapons production, the circumstances involved Iranian scientists and Iranian American scientists talking to each other. Its strategy is global oriented, befitting the legacy of an ancient civilizational holder and most recently a quasi-hegemonic regional leader of the Middle East. When the Soviet Union collapsed in 1989–1991, Iranian religious leader, Khomeini, said that it was because Khomeini persuaded both the American and Soviet leaders that the West and the East should not confront each other. Being vehemently anti-Western, human rights and intellectual property policy domains register negative deviations from the world mean. Peace and trade are two domains whereas Iran is agile and globally strategic.

abC

Sweden Sweden registers agile in action with a global minded angle and universal contractualism. It is one of the champions of multilateral treaties in the core of the Reformed West. Having been defeated in the Northern War against Russia, resulting in the loss of continental territories, Sweden maintains a policy of neutrality. Because neutrality has been observed for so long, Sweden has a reputation of being a good arbiter of disputes and a good contributor in drafting multilateral treaties. While keeping its national niche of design and manufacturing, for items such as engines and household furniture, Sweden has built its social democracy on the basis of high taxes, high welfare, and high participation. Thus, Sweden registers high positive deviations in all six domains of peace, trade, intellectual property, human rights, the environment, and labor.

aBC

New Zealand If the United States is known as a free trade champion, then New Zealand is known for freedom and fairness. When migrants from England settled in new societies, those choosing North America were distinctively those who had been religiously persecuted in England and other places in the seventeenth century, whereas those settling in New Zealand in the nineteenth century were distinctively those who had experienced the rise of the working class in England (Fisher 2011). Thus, similar to how early American settlers emphasized freedom, New Zealand's new settlers emphasized freedom and fairness. Gentle to the original inhabitants, Maoris, New Zealanders are practitioners of multi-culturalism. New Zealand spearheaded the non-nuclear principle nationally, regionally, and globally. New Zealand is agile in treaty behavior while its angle is national interest-minded. Both features are reflective of its size and location—a small country on the big Pacific Ocean. Its strategy is that of a universal contractualist. When the regional free trade multilateral agreement in the Pacific was about to reach an overall consensus, it was New Zealand and Canada that introduced the notion to consider whether or not room for compromise existed for domestic political reasons.

AbC

Slovakia Slovakia's treaty behavior is cautious. As a small, landlocked, former communist and former Nazi-allied country, that was formerly half of Czechoslovakia and is now more recently the Slovak Republic and a member of the European Union and of the Schengen, Slovakia is naturally cautious, always going along with its bigger neighbors. With a high per capita income level, it registers 40th in the world. It accommodates many automobile manufacturing factories including Volkswagen, Porsche, Audi, Citoroen, and Kia Motors. Slovakia's angle is global minded. With this environmental setup, Slovakia broadly views world market trends. Its strategy is naturally universal contractualism.

Abc

South Korea South Korea's treaty behavior is cautious. President Lee Myung-bak proudly noted that although South Korea's land space is limited, the space in which South Korea conducts free trade via bilateral and multilateral free trade agreements is No. 1 in the world. This naturally leads South Korea to develop a global mindset in treaty behavior. South Korean businesses travel to even the smallest markets after learning the languages of somewhat esoteric and small countries with tiny populations. In fact, to support these innovative efforts, the Korean University of Foreign Languages employs native-speaking professors for 76 languages, whereas in contrast Japan's Tokyo University of Foreign Languages and International Studies offers courses on only 27 foreign languages. With North Korea sitting heavily armed just north of the Armistice Line, South Korea is no less heavily armed, however, its focus on peace is superior. Being ranked the fourteenth largest economy in the world, South Korea pays a lot of attention not only to trade but also human rights and the environment. Its action, however, tends to be cautious. Its strategy is that of aspirational solidarism. As a member of the G20, South Korea adopts the strategy of aligning itself with the developing South even though its economic and industrial power is way above that of the average member of emerging economies.

ABc

Nigeria As the demographically largest country in Africa, producing mineral resources, agricultural products, and some industrial products like automobiles, Nigeria is fairly busy with multilateral legislative activities. Basically cautious (speed), national interest-focused (angle), and a solid contractualist (strategy), Nigeria's deviations from world mean in each of the six policy domains show: (1) that they are positive in human rights and environment, indicating Nigeria is a generally responsible stakeholder: (2) that trade, intellectual property, and labor are weakly negative; and (3) that Nigeria's deviation from world mean on peace policy domain is slightly positive, indicating that Nigeria requires peace at home and with its neighbors in order to prioritize economic and social development. Overall figures show that Nigeria is a large emerging power, acting as a stakeholder not only regionally but also globally. Nigeria's caution was visible in the recent (March 2018) African Union negotiation that involved 55 members negotiating an ambitious free trade agreement. While 44 states signed, 11 states, including Nigeria, did not (*The Economist* 2018, March 24–30, p. 7).

ABC

Uzbekistan A doubly landlocked country (i.e., surrounded by other landlocked countries), Uzbekistan is a cotton-focused agricultural country that also relies economically on mineral resource excavation—gold and natural gas, in particular. Its treaty behavior is characterized by caution (speed), national interest focus (angle), and aspirational solidarity (strategy). Except for the peace policy domain, Uzbekistan deviates negatively from the world standards. Human rights and the environment are two of the policy domains where Uzbekistan's deviations from the world standard are significant. Though not as significant, it also deviates from the world standard in the market economy-focused domains of trade, intellectual property, and labor. Under Islam Karimov, Uzbekistan's first president, the country was hostile to industrial entrepreneurship because it was not easy to control from above. Under the current president, Shaykat Mirziyoyev, market economic policies have gradually been studied and practiced.

8.3 Twenty-Seven Asian States and Eight Types of Global Quasi-Legislative Behavior

In this section, *the global quasi-legislative behavior* as the combination of the three perspectives in terms of *speed*, *angle*, and *strategy* of 27 typical Asian states is described in detail. As explained in this chapter, the eight types of global legislative behavior of a given state are noted as follows:

abc: agile, global, and aspirational
abC: agile, global, and contractual
aBC: agile, individual, and contractual
aBc: agile, individual, and aspirational
AbC: cautious, global, and contractual
Abc: cautious, global, and aspirational
ABc: cautious, individual, and aspirational
ABC: cautious, individual, and contractual

Table 8.3 Types of global quasi-legislative behavior of twenty-seven Asian states

Type	Country
abc	Japan, China
aBc	Democratic People's Republic of Korea
abC	India
aBC	Indonesia, Pakistan, the Philippines, Sri Lanka, Thailand
AbC	Not found in any of the 27 Asian states
Abc	Republic of Korea, Kazakhstan, Kyrgyzstan, Tajikistan
ABc	Bangladesh, Bhutan, Brunei, Cambodia, Laos, Singapore, Timor-Leste, Turkmenistan, Mongolia, Vietnam
ABC	Uzbekistan, Malaysia, the Maldives, Myanmar

Table 8.4 Illustration of eight types of global quasi-legislative behavior with deviations from world mean in each of the six policy domains

Type	Country	Human rights	Peace and security	Trade, commerce and communication	Environment	Intellectual property	Labor
abc	Japan	−0.762	1.680	0.434	1.149	1.966	0.691
	China	0.194	−0.095	0.160	0.830	−0.726	0.049
aBc	DPR Korea	−0.569	−1.201	−0.976	−0.707	−0.747	−0.865
abC	India	1.018	0.504	2.047	0.897	−0.068	−0.193
aBC	Indonesia	−0.279	−0.551	0.315	−0.344	0.526	−0.223
AbC	Not found in any of 27 Asian States						
Abc	R. Korea	−0.190	0.055	0.059	−0.047	0.021	−0.254
ABc	Bangladesh	0.261	−0.518	−0.079	−0.017	−0.448	−0.528
ABC	Uzbekistan	−1.013	0.296	−0.991	−0.630	−0.792	−0.732

Based on our analytical results, we can categorize the Asian states based on their types of *global legislative behavior* as follows (Tables 8.3, 8.4 and Fig. 8.2).

When examining the global quasi-legislative behavior of 27 Asian states, one has to keep in mind the length of their existence as a sovereign state as recognized by membership in the UN. A significant number of Asian states obtained national independence after World War II, especially in the 1950s and 1960s. Other regions outside of the West gained independence on the following timelines. Many Latin American states gained independence after the Napoleonic War in the early nineteenth century. Most Eastern and Central European states gained independence after World War I. A large portion of Middle Eastern and North African states gained independence in the 1960s and 1970s. Sub-Saharan African states gained independence in the 1960s and 1970s. Many Southern Pacific states gained their independence in the 1970s and 1980s. In other words, a large majority of Asian states became independent relatively early when compared to other non-Western states, with the exception of Latin American states. The history of multilateral treaties was based on the West, in the broad sense of the word. Therefore, those Western states have long been accustomed to participating in them.

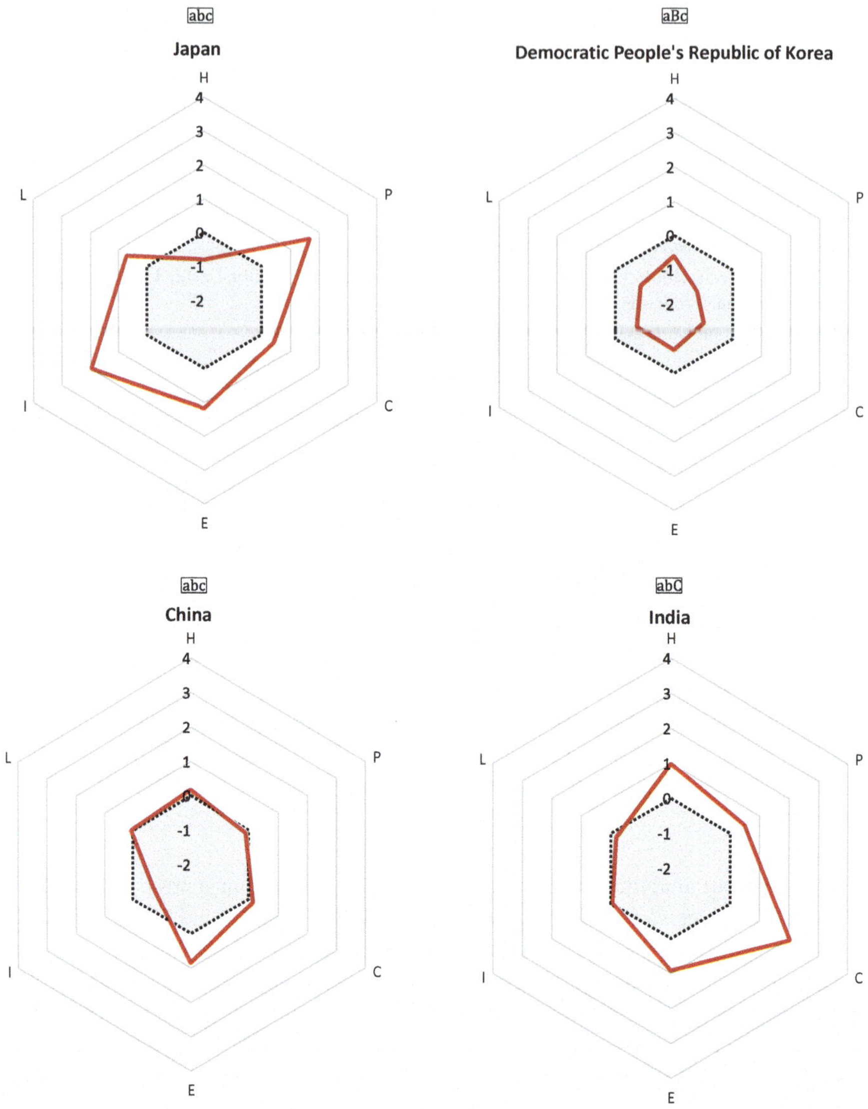

Fig. 8.2 Hexagonal profiles of eight type of Asian Sovereign states' global quasi-legislative behavior
The solid line representing the actual values achieved by a given state and the dotted line representing the world's average in each of six policy domains: Human rights (H), Peace and Security (P), Trade, Commerce and Communication (C), Intellectual Property (I) and Labor and Health (L)

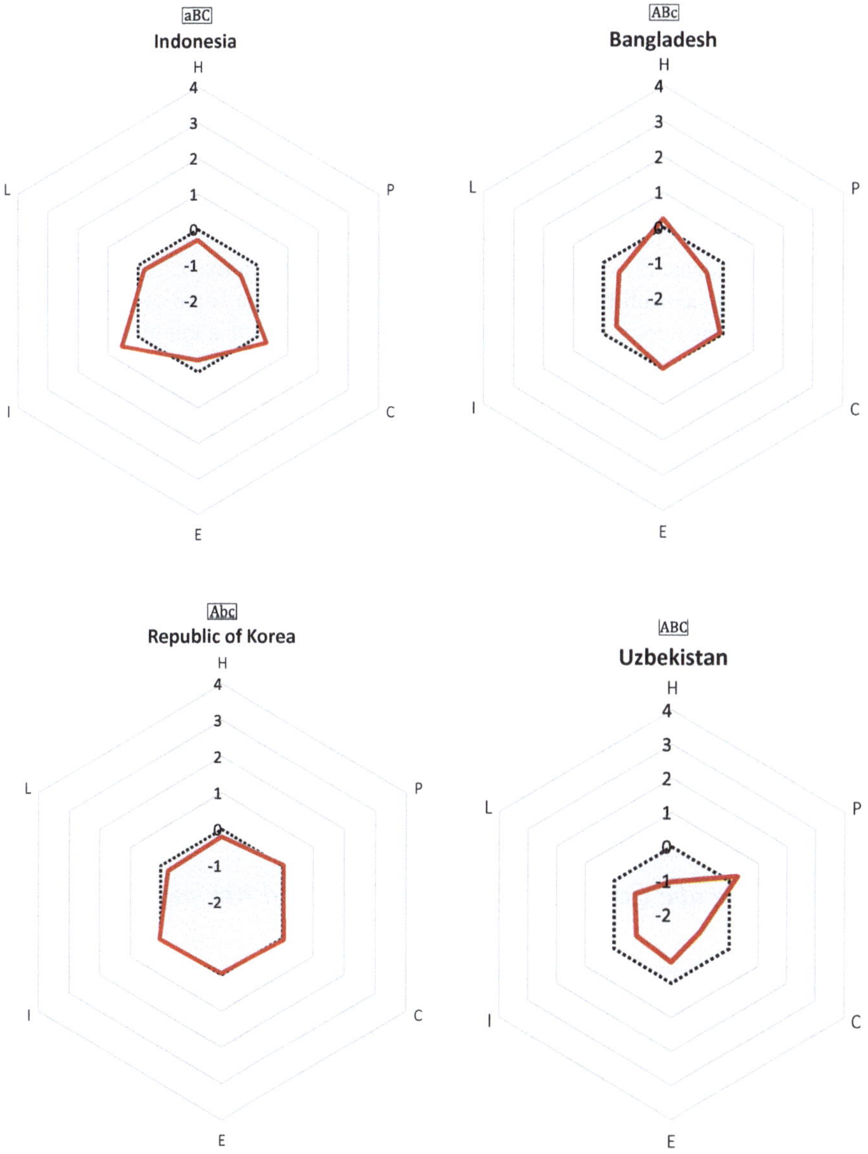

Fig. 8.2 (continued)

Why do we take up the eight types of Asian states in addition to the eight types of the world? Three reasons are given here. First, because we like to avoid giving the impression that the cosmos of multilateral treaties is that of the West versus the Rest, given the historical prevalence of the West: the West predominant and the Rest feeble. It is of utmost importance to recall that the history of multilateral treaties is a brief one: starting from the late nineteenth century through the advent of World War II. It was the story of the preponderance of the West virtually without the Rest. Thus, its preponderance was ironically a feeble one. Only after World War II has the cosmos of multilateral treaties become a massive force in global politics. It may as well be argued that it may grow into the force of self-sustainability and robust connectivity in another three quarters of a century, given the strident economic growth of the Rest including Asia and the steady improvement of quality of life of the Rest including Asia in the last quarter of a century (UN 2018; Pinker 2018; Estes and Sirgy 2017; Michalos 2013; Kamau et al. 2019).

Second, we like to avoid giving the impression that the Rest is economically stagnant poverty-stricken and politically dictatorial, a strong image tenaciously held since the times of G. Hegel and K. Marx. In the Thirty Years' crisis after the Cold War, it has becoming a little clearer that the Rest including Asia has been remarkably improving many of thirty seven sustainable development goals of the United Nations.

Third, focusing on Asia, the kind of diversification in terms of global quasi-legislative behavior is of most welcoming sort, given that most Asian states got a national sovereignty recently, mostly around half a century ago on average.

Let us examine selective Asian states that fit within each of the eight types of global quasi-legislative behavior.

8.3.1 Type abc Called "Ambitious Global and Regional Power"

Japan and China are of type abc, meaning they possess the combination of agility in speed, global in angle, and aspirational in strategy. Japan and China are "intimate rivals" (Smith 2016), meaning that they are large powers in the same region, but they are also similar in their orientation. They are swift in judgment and action, and their angle is wide rather than narrowly focused on national benefits. Their strategy is not just contractual, meaning being interested in norms and rules stipulated in multilateral treaties, instead they are also interested in enhancing solidarity among like-minded states in order to promote the cause stipulated in the concerned multilateral treaty. In this sense they are called "ambitious global and regional powers." Japan and China are relatively new members of multilateral treaties. Japan, punished for its defeat in World War II, was not permitted to enter the UN until 1956. China remained outside of the UN until the United States shifted its support for representation from Taiwan to mainland China in 1972.

When considering type abc, it is not surprising to see Brazil belonging to this type. Brazil is number one among emerging economies and is one of the leaders of the G20. Both Japan and China aspire to become a global power like Brazil. Although China caught up to Japan's GNP in the 2010s, Japan's global quasi-legislative behavior is to seek friends and markets from near and far. Japan has been cautious in reforming domestic laws in policy domains such as human rights and labor. Japan's lower score in human rights may be a small surprise to some readers. It is in part because of the solid opposition in Japan to revise the Civil Law, originally legislated in the late nineteenth century when parental authority was very widely exerted in Civil and Family laws. Similarly, China has been cautious in reforming its own domestic laws in policy domains such as intellectual property, human rights, and labor. In the context of Intellectual property rights, China has been resisting hard against the US and often G7 countries. China's business firms are dominated by state-owned firms. In accommodating foreign capital in Chinese business firms, they often or sometimes make it obligatory to transfer highly valued technologies to them without much respect to intellectual property rights of original inventors and innovators of highly valued technologies. China has been aggressively seeking "great power status" in word and action, whereas Japan has been cautious in becoming more autonomous from the United States in security tasks. While China has been building its armed forces by leaps and bounds with the slogan of no more humiliation since mid-nineteenth century onward by the West and Japan, Japan has been building self-defense forces closely tied to the US armed forces for over 70 years with the slogan of keeping peace with the alliance with the US and the friendship and cooperation with neighbors.

8.3.2 Type abC Called "Multilateral Non-alignment Power"

India is type abC, meaning agile in action, global in angle, and contractual in strategy. It is not surprising to see that Sweden represents this type of global quasi-legislative behavior; although Sweden represents one of the more active multi-lateralists, in contrast to India who is far less active in initiating and implementing multilateral treaties. More generally, those Northwestern European states, called the Reformed West belong to this type. Sweden has been pursuing the principle of neutrality since Russia dealt Sweden a heavy blow in the Northern War, depriving Sweden of its continental territories. India, having pursued a non-alignment policy during the Cold War period and beyond, has been steadly transforming its policy from non-alignment to multilateral non-alignment of late.

India is more cautious in such policy domains as labor and intellectual property. This approach is a partial reflection of the slow process of domestic reforms from state dominance to market force as well as the small size of its professional corps of diplomats and foreign affairs bureaucrats per its slogan of multilateral non-alignment.

8.3.3 Type aBC Called "Defensive Self-Assertive Power"

Indonesia is type aBC, meaning agile in action, individual interests in angle, and contractual in strategy. Fellow Asian states of this same type are Pakistan, the Philippines, Sri Lanka, and Thailand. Type aBC is called "defensive self-assertion." Indonesia has long been defensive since Sukarno fell in the mid-1960s. A dominant member of ASEAN (established in 1968), accounting for more than one-half of the ASEAN population, Indonesia had been far less vocal in expressing its preference in the organization's public forum before Suharto fell in 1998. This may have to do with the decentralized nature of Indonesian society. Fellow Asian states belonging to type aBC have been plagued by a centrifugal nature of sorts, such as Pakistan ("strong society" by Anatol Lieven), the Philippines ("big family-dominance"), and Thailand ("Bangkok dominance of monarchy, the military, bureaucrats, big business, and Buddhism"). Outside of Asia, those states belonging to the type aBC are New Zealand, Australia, Canada, and the United States—all part of the New West, meaning they are new settler states.

Based on the types of society in Asia, these states belong to societal types where the centrifugal constellation of society pushes states to an extreme monopolization of power or to the incessant striving of, and collusion among, societal sectors.

8.3.4 Type aBc Called "Agile Defensive-Aggressive Power"

The Democratic People's Republic of Korea is agile in speed, extremely self-centered in angle, and aspirational in strategy. Behavioral agility is combined with defensive-cum-aggressive postures. Sandwiched by China and the United States, North Korea finds only meager space within which to maneuver and manipulate. Coping with extreme difficulties to create resources for survival and to use ways and means to influence foreign states, North Korea changes its position so frequently that it often becomes confusing to foreign states. Its participation in multilateral treaties has not been very active. It has focused on trade and communications, especially since the 1970s. After the Sino-Soviet conflict erupted in the 1960s, North Korea's survival depended on its trade and communications with the Third World from the 1970s onward. Getting agricultural and manufactured products through foreign trade with developing states has been critical for its survival. North Korea has also been active in multilateral treaties in the policy domain of human rights since the1950s. A bulk of multilateral treaties in human rights possess an aspirational spirit without any strict obligatory clauses. Human rights NGOs have been gaining access and increasing their involvement in UN organizations, including the UN General Assembly and the Human Rights Council. Many Third World states that are not necessarily proud of their suppression of human rights have tended to invest time and energy in this policy domain in battling human rights NGOs in the UN and transnational fora. Multilateral treaties in the policy domain in peace and disarmament are not regarded by North Korea as reliable. As in the case of the Nuclear Non-Proliferation Treaty and the six party talks of nuclear power plants, states seem to provisionally agree, discover the aspects of the treaty that may inconvenience their states, and then suddenly exit the negotiations. Although we have not included Iran in our definition of Asia, the Islamic Republic of Iran is also of this legislative type.

8.3.5 Type Abc Called "Cautious Supportive Stakeholder"

The Republic of Korea belongs to type Abc, meaning cautious in speed, global in angle, and aspirational in strategy. Fellow states of type Abc are Kazakhstan, Kyrgyzstan, and Tajikistan. Common to these four states are an extraordinary dependence on, and vulnerability to, overseas markets and external forces for their survival. Caution is always important; global sensitivity is a must. The strategy must be to minimize the commitment of being further constrained; hence, instead of scrupulously complying with stipulated norms and rules of multilateral treaties, it is more appealing to enhance solidarity among those like-situated and like-minded states. Type Abc states are called "cautious supporters." The Republic of Korea ranks number 7 in the world in terms of GDP, with the largest bilateral free trade agreement implemented with those countries occupying the world largest space under bilateral free trade. Kazakhstan is full of mineral resources with gigantic neighbors sandwiching it. Kyrgyzstan's airport has been changing its host-cum-user from the Soviet Union/Russian Federation to the United States, and most recently China. Tajikistan is poverty-stricken and mountainous, surrounded on all sides by strong neighbors.

8.3.6 Type AbC Called "Small, Cautious, and Contractual Power"

This type cannot be found in the 27 states in our definition of Asia. Instead, this type is found mostly in small European states such as Cyprus, Malta, Albania, Moldova, Croatia, Czech Republic, Estonia, Latvia, Slovakia, and Slovenia. Surrounded and influenced by big European powers, these states manifest their legislative behavior pattern focusing on treaties with mutually obligatory contractual clauses. After all, strategy C is predominantly Northwest European.

8.3.7 Type ABc Called "Cautious Defensive Aspirant Power"

Bangladesh belongs to type ABc, meaning cautious in speed, individual in angle, and aspirational in strategy. Fellow states of type ABc are Bhutan, Brunei, Cambodia, Laos, Singapore, Timor-Leste, Turkmenistan, Mongolia, and Vietnam. Common to the type ABc is that the hexagonal profiles are small and close to the world mean in six policy domains. Type ABc states can be called states of "cautious defensive aspiration." It may come as a surprise to find such states as Bangladesh, Singapore, and Vietnam, known for being economically vigorous of late, do not manifest the hexagonal profile much larger than the world mean in six policy domains. One of the key reasons is that they are very new states, having just recently gained independence: Bangladesh seceded from Pakistan in 1971; Singapore seceded from the Malaysian Federation in 1965; and Vietnam reunified South and North Vietnam in 1976. Another of the key reasons is that unlike Africa, Latin America, or Western Europe, Asia does not have a strong regional drive for integration. ASEAN was established in 1968, but it has been loath to interfere in the internal affairs of its members. It declared the formation of an economic community building in commemoration of its 50th anniversary in 2018. Western Europe has been the strongest in terms of regional integration: free trade, free movement of people, common currency, and above all, a very gigantic technocratic bureaucracy called the European Union. Latin America is full of regional multilateral treaties in terms of free trade, common opinion polls, and regional sports events. Latin America has a long history of independence and a common and semi-common language of Spanish and Portuguese. Africa is full of regional multilateral treaties, led by the African Union established in 2002, by reforming the Organization of African Unity, established in 1963. It has regional armed forces to carry out regional peacekeeping operations.

8.3.8 Type ABC Called "Cautious Defensive Stakeholder"

Uzbekistan belongs to type ABC, meaning cautious in speed, individual in angle, and contractual in strategy. Fellow states are Malaysia, the Maldives, and Myanmar. Type ABC states can be called states of "cautious defensive self-constraints." They are handicapped by geographical conditions. For example, Uzbekistan is doubly land-locked. Malaysia is ethnically divided. The Maldives are a group of small islands in the Indian Ocean. Myanmar is a vast space with persistent ethnic strife between Yangon and ethnic tribes. Common to them is the energy and attention devoted to domestic problems, especially internal strife. To mitigate internal strife, dictatorships have tended to be the response in these countries.

8.4 Conclusion

Illustrations of global quasi-legislative behavior have shown that this type of behavior can be categorized into eight types based on the available combinations of *speed*, *angle*, and *strategy*. They have also shown that in an era of globalization and digitalization, studying global quasi-legislative behavior is enormously useful for understanding a country's foreign policy behavior because global quasi-legislative behavior is built on a country's accumulated legislative records. In other words, what may well be called global quasi-legislative culture of countries and groups of countries can be used productively to explain and predict global quasi-legislative behavior of those countries who face the choice of joining or not joining, for example, the Paris climate change accord, the treaty prohibiting the use of nuclear weapons, or the Trans-Pacific Partnership agreement.

Turning back to the three Waltzian causes of war and peace (Waltz 1959) and the three Singeresque levels of analysis (Singer 1961), we argue that those causes of the mixed domestic-transnational and those levels of the mixed domestic-transnational should be utilized for understanding foreign policy direction and behavior. In an era of globalization and digitalization that lacks a single global legislative body, the systematic and empirical study of global quasi-legislative behavior of countries and groups of countries cannot be over-exaggerated for its increasing significance in better understanding global politics.

References

Estes, R. J., & Joseph Sirgy, M. (Eds.). (2017). *The pursuit of human well-being: The untold global history*. New York: Springer.

Fisher, D. H. (2011). *Fairness and freedom: A history of two open societies, New Zealand and the United States*. Oxford: Oxford University Press.

Inoguchi, T. (2000). Broadening the basis of social capital in Japan. In R. D. Putnam (Ed.), *Democracies in flux: The evolution of social capital in contemporary society* (pp. 383–384). New York: Oxford University Press.

Kamau, M., et al. (2019). *Transforming multilateral diplomacy: The inside story of the sustainable development goals*. London: Routledge.

Michalos, A. (2013). *Encyclopedia of quality of life and well-being* (12 volumes). Dordrecht: Springer.

Pinker, S. (2018). *Enlightenment now: The case for reason, science, humanism, and progress*. New York: Viking.

Singer, J. D. (1961). The level-of-analysis problem in international relations. *World Politics, 14*(1), 77–92.

Smith, S. (2016). *Intimate rivals: Japanese domestic politics and a rising China*. New York: Columbia University Press, Reprint edition.

Stuenkel, O. (2016). *Post-western world: How emerging powers are remaking global order*. Cambridge: Polity.

The Economist. (2018, March 24–30). *The world this week: Politics* (p. 7).

United Nations. (2018). *The sustainable development goals*. New York: UN publications.

Waltz, K. (1959). *Man, the state and war*. New York: Columbia University Press.

Part III
Three Varieties of Global Politics After the Cold War

Chapter 9
Introduction to Part III

Abstract In this Part III, we attempt to locate the previous two Parts, i.e., Part I: Global Social Contract and Part II: Global Quasi-Legislative Behavior, in the broader context of global politics, focusing on the post-Cold period of Thirty Years Crisis (1989–2019). Chapter 10 presents three paradigms of post-Westphalian politics, Westphalian, Philadelphian and Anti-Utopian, whose core concept is sovereignty, whether it is state sovereignty, popular sovereignty or the loss of sovereignty. This chapter gives the basis for our comparison of three post-Cold War global politics in Chap. 11 (Theory of Power Transition), Chap. 12 (Theory of Civilizational Clash), and Chap. 13 (Theory of Global Legislative Politics). Contrasting the three theories shows that whereas the theory of power transition underestimates vulnerability when hegemons' mishaps and mistakes of exercising power over those oppressed and marginalized by merely increasing the potentials of imploding and exploding (McNeill and Carrol) and whereas the theory of civilizational clash underestimates the subtlety and complexity of culture which needs apt taxonomical minds (Foucault) and subtle and even cynical handling (Bagehot), the theory of global legislative politics presents the theory that astutely captures the essentials of the ongoing global politics by conceptualizing it as a bundle of global quasi-social contracts under digitalized globalization.

In this Part, we attempt to locate the previous two Parts, i.e., Part I: *Global Social Contract* and Part II: *Global Quasi-legislative Behavior*, in the broader context of global politics, especially focusing on the post-Cold War period since 1989. "Chapter 10: Three Frameworks of Global Politics" sets the scope of this Part in terms of the tri-paralleled frameworks of global politics: The Westphalian, the Philadelphian, and anti-Utopian frameworks. In the Westphalian framework, state sovereignty is pivotal; in the Philadelphian framework, popular sovereignty is central; in the anti-Utopian framework, the loss of sovereignty is primordial. In the following Chaps 11, 12 and 13, we identify three theories: the theory of power transition, the theory of civilizational conflict and the theory of global legislative politics. The task of these three chapters is to compare and contrast their thrusts and to argue that the theory of global legislative politics has the distinctive feature of

T. Inoguchi, L. T. Q. Le, *The Development of Global Legislative Politics*,
Trust: Interdisciplinary Perspectives 3, https://doi.org/10.1007/978-981-32-9389-2_9

"perspective revolution"(Zakaria 1997, cited in Funabashi 2019, p. 227). Why the perspective revolution of the theory of global legislative politics in post-Cold War global politics is distinctive is explained here.

In the conventional Westphalian framework, two elements of global politics are distinguished: might and wealth. Otto Bismark, a statesman who first ruled Prussia and then Germany in the late nineteenth century, used "iron and bread", meaning that unified Germany was able to produce weapons and to feed populace. These two elements were considered to be primordial in global politics. Those states abundant with such resources were regarded as a strong power. In the conventional Cold War framework, one more element stole into this equation of global politics. That is ideology: meaning capitalist democracy vs communist dictatorship. With the infusion of ideology into global politics equation, the confrontation between each camp of the West and the East intensified. In the whirlwinds of the post-Cold War world, the ideological battles took place as to who would carry the *zeitgeist*, the ideology of the era. Francis Fukuyama (1992) took a lead proclaiming that liberal democracy would be the only game in town, whose song would be chanted in the whole world. Rushing into this battle of shaping *zeitgeist* of post-Cold War politics was Samuel Huntington. As if recalling the *zeitgeist* of the post-Vienna conference after the Napoleonic War, which Henry Kissinger (1985) portrayed as the suppression of one power dominance, revolutionary fervor and religious resurrection, Samuel Huntington (1997) discovered that the coming *zeitgeist* would be the clash of civilizations with a religious flavoring. He must have felt convinced that the time had come for religion to go in the opposite direction predicted by Max Weber in the early twentieth century: less secular and more gods in each of his eight civilizations. What is common with Fukuyama and Huntington is that both regarded that the ideological element of the Cold War politics would be replaced by something which can be conceptualized in an universalistic concept, i.e., democracy and civilization. During the post-Cold War's 30 years crisis while this ideological battle was waged, all the three key elements of the Westphalian framework underwent dramatic metamorphosis. Scientific revolutions and technological innovations have been swaying the world with early runners and late comers changing their respective members with alarmingly diversified configurational maps under the galloping tides of digitalized globalization. The world has become enormously complex, uncertain and unpredictable. To better fathom this complex, uncertain and unpredictable world and furthermore to better equip with observers and analysts of the complex world full of unknown knowns or unknowns, the theory of global legislative politics has been presented in this book. Instead of analyzing might, wealth, and ideology, we propose to look into a bundle of global quasi-legislation in the form of multilateral treaties and conventions. As long as Rousseauesque and Lockean social contracts can be imagined as a bundle global quasi-social contracts on the basis of digitalized globalization and transnational social movements, we can undertake a systematic recording, analysis, and synthesizing of a bundle of multilateral treaties and conventions each of which constitutes global quasi-legislative actions with sovereign states wagering the calculus of joining or not joining multilateral treaties and conventions by gauging preferences within (society of a sovereign state) and preferences without (other sovereign states and transnational entities). Here, how difference and diversity are gauged is of utmost importance.

When works such as *Every Nation for Itself* (Bremmer 2013), *No One's World* (Kupchan 2013), and *Pax Technica* (Howard 2015) portray the world as uncertain, complex, and changing relentlessly fast, the responding query is why bother with multilateral treaties that are legal agreements signed and ratified by sovereign states about peace, trade, intellectual property, human rights, health, and environment? To answer the question, we must start with the characterizations of global change during the 30 years' crisis of 1989–2019. Once the East-West confrontation ceased between 1989 and 1991, the United States became confused about which direction the world was heading. Amidst the whirlwind of the Soviet deployment of Intermediate Range Nuclear Missiles targeted at Western Europe but not at the United States, Henry Kissinger said in a speech in Brussels on January 13, 1984: "The Soviet Union must decide whether it is a country or a cause." (Kissinger 1985, cited by Roberts 2010, p. 534). Given this ultimatum, Gorbachev chose to be a country. The irony is that "[w]hen the USSR ceased to be a cause, it rapidly ceased to be a country" (Roberts 2010, p. 534). The fall of the Berlin Wall was followed by the subsequent Soviet implosion. Poignantly, another prediction that would impact the US was made, this time by Georgi Arbatov on December 8, 1987. Arbatov, from the Soviet Academy of Sciences, registered his thoughts about the United States in a *New York Times* piece: "the Kremlin was going to deprive America of The Enemy" (cited in Fettweis 2018, p. 1). This meant that without the Enemy, the United States would face unforeseen problems.

All the rumors about the imminent American decline preoccupied commentators, consultants, pundits, and prophets long before 1989. Some found consolation in the history of the Roman Empire, which lasted 200 years after its imminent decline was widely forecasted (Nye 1990). Nevertheless, a pressing question arose: Who would replace the United States as the hegemonic leader?

Once communism was declared dead by Mikhail Gorbachev, the triumph of democracy was announced (Fukuyama 1992), "democracy is the only game in town." The number of UN member states reached 193 by the end of the twentieth century, and among those states, 120 were characterized as democracies. It seemed that after America's long-time enemy, communism, had been essentially eradicated, the question became: which enemy replaces communism in the eyes of the Americans?

The first question is about power transition; the latter is about value transition. The most noteworthy quality of the literature dominated by Americans is its preoccupation with power ranking. As the end of the Cold War brought about the advent of unipolarity, the concern revolved around how long unipolarity could be sustained. Practically speaking, the question was how fast is China ascending to replace the United States? However, no less pervasive than power is the nature of values entertained by new leaders. Whether the next leader is China, Russia, or some other nation, the American preoccupation with a possible change in value would permeate what they regard as the liberal world order, composed of such key words as rule of law, democracy, free market, and human rights.

Of the hundreds of schools of thought that pondered possible post-Cold War scenarios along the above-mentioned lines, we focus our energies on two specific schools: the opinions generated by Robert Gilpin (1983) and Samuel Huntington (1997). On the basis of our previous publications on power transition (Inoguchi 2010) and value changes (Collet and Inoguchi 2010), we argue that much of American thinking about post-Cold War politics lacks a sober recognition of power and its nature. Power entails vulnerability (McNeill and Kindleberger 1989); if one pushes hard with power, those oppressed and marginalized by over-exercised power tend to express themselves when the mishaps and mistakes of the powerful are inadvertently laid bare.

In the same vein, we argue that culture or a set of values is a complex organic whole, inherently difficult to deal with when attempting to examine the subject of culture in a Cartesian manner of logic and causality. Geography, history, and context are all deeply embedded within culture, making it difficult to argue for the "us-vs-them" dichotomy in terms of civilizational conflict. We argue that much of American thinking after the post-Cold War politics lacks a deep understanding of culture and its nature. Culture is so intricately embedded with geography, history, and context that without a good understanding of culture and an apt taxonomical mind (Foucault 1994), culturally affected phenomena would become beyond one's reach.

In what follows, as we explore quasi-legislation of multilateral treaties, we illuminate qualities of post-Cold War global politics. Accordingly, we present the following three phenomena as key indicators of post-Cold War politics:

1. Three key events, namely, the signing of the 1985 Plaza Accord, the 1991 invention of the World Wide Web, and the 2008 economic recession, significantly impacted the speed, rate, and range of digitalization and globalization such that the entire globe has become a fairly integrated whole. When Jean-Jacques Rousseau envisioned *The Social Contract*, he argued that the force of compassion would immediately enable the formation of *le volonté générale*. Due to global integration of certain systems, the conditions in the twenty-first century, compared to those in the seventeenth and eighteenth centuries when Rousseau was alive, are ripe for the formation of *le volonté générale* (The Economist Corporate Network Asia 2018; Goldsmith and Posner 2007)
2. Use of violence has decreased in frequency and volume. When one compares the number of annual war-related deaths of soldiers (intentionally excluding civilian deaths), using the International Institute of Security Studies (London) for the following three periods, 1938–1945, 1945–1989, and 1989–2014, i.e., the great war period, the Cold War period, and the post-Cold War period, there is a striking decrease in the number of deaths of military personnel from five million per annum for the great war period, to 100,000 per annum for the Cold War period, and to 10,000 per annum for the post-Cold War period (Inoguchi 2010; Pinker 2012).

3. Legislation has become an indispensable tool on the global stage for dispute avoidance and settlement. There is no world polity, no world parliament. Yet there are more than 8000 international organizations and their off-shoots as of 2014 (Hale and Held 2017), 120 consolidated multilateral treaties (based on our strict definition; see Appendix 2), 193 UN member states, and 73 states that accept the obligatory jurisdiction of the International Court of Justice (2018). Less than 10 years after John Locke envisioned *Two Treaties of Government* (circa 1680), arguing for representative democracy by curtailing the power of the monarchy and reducing the authority of church in politics, conventional legislative politics surrounding parliament in England were provisionally established. Now in the new millennium, (quasi-) legislative politics evolve on multiple levels, such as subnational, national, regional, international, transnational, and multiple domains such as peace, communications and commerce, human rights, intellectual property, the environment, and health.

"Chapter 10: Three Frameworks of Global Politics" presents the three types of post-Cold War politics: the Westphalian, the Philadelphian and the anti-Utopian whose core concept is sovereignty, whether it is state sovereignty, popular sovereignty or the loss of sovereignty. In post-Cold War politics the weight and variety of sovereignty presents different theories. Chapter 11 examines the theory of power transition criticized from the viewpoint of McNeill's vulnerability of power, whereas Chap. 12 examines theory of civilizational conflict criticized from the viewpoint of the excessive emphasis on the "us against them" in adversarial terms. When the succeeding three chapters on theories of power transition, of civilizational conflict, and of global legislative politics are compared and contrasted in terms of key concepts, i.e., vulnerability, religion, and agreement respectively, the degree of power-associated adversarial weight is stronger in the former two theories whereas the last one carries less weight. "Chapter 13: Theory of Global Legislative Politics" presents its findings with illustrations of 27 Asian states fitted in with eight types of global quasi-legislative behavior. The strength of the last theory of global legislative politics is: (1) less adversarial and less power-associated competitiveness are embedded; (2) more sophisticated varieties of sovereign states' engagement in global quasi-legislative behavior are presented to help better fathom the nature of global politics.

The succeeding Chapters stand to rethink the theory of power transitions (Chap. 11), rethink the theory of civilizational conflict (Chap. 12), and propose the theory of global legislative politics (Chap. 13). Table 10.3 summarizes the structure of these subsequent Chapters. The idea of using the "pathways" concept is taken from Hale and Held's (2017) *Beyond Gridlock* (Table 9.1).

Table 9.1 Structure of the subsequent Chaps. 11, 12, and 13

		Power transition	Civilizational clash	Global quasi-legislation
Name	Key concepts	Power and vulnerability	Religion and incompatibility	Agreement and sharing/ shaping
	Driving forces	Apprehension about decline	Us-and-them adversary	Ubiquitous gridlock
	Solution	Security cooperation	Multiple modernity	Minimizing agreement target and criterion
	Pathways	Share of some hegemonic responsibility	Exposure to daily life of other religions	Shifts in major powers' core interests
		Skirt some of hegemonic responsibility	Stay/study in foreign cultures	Autonomous and adaptive institutions
		Stick to stakeholders' privilege	Working with colleagues of diverse cultures	Technical groups with effective and legitimate processes
		Divert replaceable functions to allies and friends	Set up forum for civilizational dialogue	Multiple, diverse organizations and institutions around common goals/norms
		Shifts of global constituencies	Curb civilizational hatred	Mobilization of domestic constituencies
		Civil society coalitions	Global opinion polls carried out	Civil society coalitions
		Innovative leadership for provision to alternative to decline	Innovative leadership of multiple modernities	Innovative leadership as a reaction to gridlock

References

Bremmer, I. (2013). *Every nation for itself: Winners and losers in a G-zero world.* New York: Portfolio.

Collet, C., & Inoguchi, T. (2010). Is globalization undermining civilizational identities? A test of Huntington's core state hypothesis among the public of greater Asian and Pacific. *Japanese Journal of Political Science, 13*(4), 553–585.

Fettweis, C. (2018). *Psychology of a superpower: Security and dominance in U.S. foreign policy.* New York: Columbia University Press.

Foucault, M. (1994). *The order of things: An archaeology of human sciences.* New York: Vintage Books.

Fukuyama, F. (1992). *The end of history and the last man.* London: Penguin.

Funabashi, Y. (2019). *Think Tank towa nanika-Seisakukigyouryoku no jidai* [what is think tank – The era of policy entrepreneurship]. Tokyo: Chuokoronshinsha.

Gilpin, R. (1983). *War and change in world politics.* Princeton: Princeton University Press.

Goldsmith, J., & Posner, E. (2007). *The limits of international law.* Oxford: Oxford University Press.

Hale, T., & Held, D. (2017). *Beyond gridlock.* Cambridge: Polity Press.

Howard, P. (2015). *Pax Technica: How the internet of things may set US free or lock us up*. New Haven: Yale University Press.
Huntington, S. (1997). *The clash of civilizations and the remaking of world order*. New York: Simon and Schuster.
Inoguchi, T. (2010). World order debates in the twentieth century: Through the eyes of the two-level game and second image (reversed). *Chinese Journal of International Politics, 3*(2), 155–188.
International Court of Justice. (2018). *Declarations recognizing the jurisdiction of the Court as compulsory*. Available from https://www.icj-cij.org/en/declarations. Accessed 1 June 2018.
Kissinger, H. (1985). *Observations: Selected speeches and essays, 1982–1984*. London: Michael Joseph and Weidenfeld & Nicolson.
Kupchan, C. (2013). *No one's world: The west, the rising rest, and the coming global turn*. Oxford: Oxford University Press.
McNeill, W., & Kindleberger, C. (1989). Control and catastrophe in human affairs. *Daedalus, 118*(1), 1–15.
Nye, J. S. (1990). *Bound to lead: The changing nature of American power*. New York: Basic Books.
Pinker, S. (2012). *The better angles of our nature: Why violence has declined* (reprinted ed.). New York: Penguin Books.
Roberts, A. (2010). An 'incredibly swift transition': Reflections on the end of the cold war. In M. P. Leffler & O. A. Westad (Eds.), *The Cambridge history of the cold war* (Vol. III, pp. 513–534). Cambridge: Cambridge University Press.
The Economist Corporate Network Asia. (2018). *Digital Asia: Asia's digitally transforming economies*. London: The Economist.
Zakaria, F. (1997). The rise of illiberal democracy. *Foreign Affairs, 76*(6), 22–47.

Chapter 10
Three Frameworks of Global Politics

Abstract This chapter examines three types of those paradigms of global politics, Westphalian (state-centric), Philadellphian (global republican) and Anti-Utopian (post postcolonialist and multicultural). In each of the three paradigms, geo-political framework, geo-economic foundations and geo-cultural networks are laid out with key concepts, principal authors, institutional unit, behavior principle, driving force, critical variable, key purpose and key effect being characterized. Principal authors are Henry Kissinger, Alexander Gerschenkron, and Benedict Anderson in the Westphalian paradigm, Francis Fukuyama, Robert Reich, and Benjamin Barber in the Philadelphia paradigm and Samuel Huntington, David Landes, and Robert Kaplan in the Anti-Utopian paradigm.

In the preceding Chapters of Parts I and II, we have found that the two social contract theories laid out by Jean-Jacques Rousseau and John Locke are writ global in the galloping tide of digitalization and globalization and that sovereign states' participation in multilateral treaties are conceptualized as *global quasi-legislative behavior*, on the basis of two surveys, the *World Values Survey* and the *Multilateral Treaties Survey* against the background of having neither a world polity nor world assembly. On the basis of the three frameworks of global politics (Inoguchi 1999), the following three theories, i.e., theory of power transition (Chap. 11), theory of civilizational clash (Chap. 12), and theory of global legislative politics (Chap. 13) which were embraced in the last quarter of the last century and the first quarter of this century, are compared and contrasted in this Chapter (Chap. 10). One of the most cited theories of power transition was authored by Gilpin (1983). One of the most dramatically received theories of civilizational conflict and cooperation was authored by Huntington (1997). This Chapter prepares readers to place the three Chapters within the three broader frameworks of global politics.

We compare and contrast the three theories, i.e., the power transition theory as set forth in Inoguchi (2010), written with an attention to Gilpin's work (1983), Huntington's civilizational clash theory (1997) as empirically tested in Collet and Inoguchi (2010), and the legislative politics theory (Inoguchi and Le this volume). Common to all three is that their births were triggered by multi-layered, multi-level

T. Inoguchi, L. T. Q. Le, *The Development of Global Legislative Politics*,
Trust: Interdisciplinary Perspectives 3, https://doi.org/10.1007/978-981-32-9389-2_10

transformations in the 70-odd years of US-led liberal international order since 1945, and in particular since 1989. The long anticipated decline of the US-led liberal international order is the short answer to the question of their births. More specifically, the power transition theory is an effort to slow down or prevent the decline of US world leadership through military supremacy and the soft power of institutional design and policy planning; the civilizational clash theory is a response to the increasingly menacing forces of non-Western civilizations or non-Anglo-American civilization; and the legislative theory is the response to the alarmingly steady trends of digitalization and globalization, on the one hand, and interdependence and vulnerability, on the other, which are unfolding globally.

The three theories of global politics have sprung up from the broader frameworks of global politics established at the end of the last century (Inoguchi 1999): the Westphalian, Philadelphian, and Anti-Utopian frameworks. To show how these theories originated from these preceding frameworks and how the theories have adapted at the dawn of this century, the gist of the frameworks is summarized below.

The key concept upholding the Westphalian framework is state sovereignty; for the Philadelphian framework, it is popular sovereignty; and for the Anti-Utopian, it is the loss of sovereignty. The leading works of Henry Kissinger (1994), Francis Fukuyama (1992), and Samuel Huntington (1997) frame these three paradigms. In harmony with the three geopolitical frameworks, we articulate the geo-economic frameworks backed by three leading economists, Alexander Gerschenkron (1965), Robert Reich (1991), and David Landes (1998), as well as the geo-cultural frameworks backed by three leading experts, Benedict Anderson (1991), Benjamin Barber (1993), and Robert Kaplan (1998).

As is clear from the above, the three paradigms evolve around state sovereignty. As Krasner (1983) astutely argues and Spruyt (1993) amply demonstrates, the picture of global politics did not change dramatically over the last two centuries. Only in the mid-nineteenth century did sovereign states come to occupy a central place in global politics, with territorial states born one after another within Europe (Germany and Italy) as well as in its peripheries (the United States and Japan). Furthermore, the European sovereign state overflowed to colonialist empires worldwide during the nineteenth and twentieth centuries as well as during the sixteenth and seventeenth centuries. Only during World War II and thereafter did colonialism begin to relinquish its grip, unleashing a proliferation of newly sovereign states, which was unprecedented in human history. At the end of World War II, there were 51 sovereign states; these were mostly European states and white-settled former colonies. Although the architect of the United Nations building envisaged it accommodating a maximum of 100 countries, his prediction fell dramatically short. By the dawn of the new millennium, states numbered close to 200. Given this dramatic increase and the conventional views of international law, it was still not unnatural to think that global politics was essentially "inter-national" politics, i.e., politics among nations (Morgenthau 1959). This is what makes up the Westphalian framework.

In the dusk of the twentieth century, at least two other frameworks, which were not centered on the sovereign state, began to develop inconspicuously: the Philadelphian and the Anti-Utopian. The Philadelphian framework is the framework that governed the United States from its independence until its Civil War in the mid-nineteenth century and has been in a process of revival on a global scale beyond the end of the twentieth century. Its manifestation can be seen in the dramatic increase in the number of liberal democracies that subscribe to the norms and rules of the free-market economy and democratic politics. One of the principles leading to this increase is that democracies rarely war with each other (Doyle 1986, 1997; Russett 1994; Keane 1998; Cox et al. 2000; Russett and Oneal 2011). By Anti-Utopian, we refer to the framework that governs the failed and failing states and that has been structurally veiled by other frameworks. The term, Anti-Utopian, derives from the colonialist legacy. During the twentieth century, the universalist forces that sought to "civilize" the world through territorial expansion in the colonial age shifted to international efforts aimed at global governance, human security, and humanitarian assistance. However noble these utopian objectives, the outcomes of their implementation have included prolonged strife, exploitative regimes shored up by international aid, and failed states.

The growing Philadelphian influence is evidenced by the number of sovereign states that adopt in their constitutions adherence to the conventions and declarations on freedom, democracy, equality, equity, and human rights of 1776 (the United States), 1789 (France), and Japan (1946). The Philadelphian influence now extends to some 150 states (those UN member states minus those states far less committed) with multilateral treaties and declarations on key principles of freedom, democracy, equality, and human rights. The growing influence of the Anti-Utopian framework is evidenced by the number of humanitarian assistance and peacekeeping or peace-enforcing operations that are occasioned by large scale famine and intermittent civil strife. In 2017, the UN peacekeeping operations budget amounted to $658 million (in US dollars), 10% of the annual UN budget. Additionally, in 2017, the UN recruited 100,000 peacekeepers from 125 states. The UN deployed more than one million peacekeepers for more than 70 peacekeeping operations from 1948 to 2017 (United Nations 2018; Yomiuri Shimbun 2018). Thus, while state sovereignty has become the zeitgeist of the twentieth century and beyond, it has also been accompanied by the steady erosion of state sovereignty in the growing tide of globalization and digitalization as well as the steady growth of civil society (Biersteker and Weber 1996). In short, these three frameworks have been growing in tandem (Inoguchi 2002).

These frameworks consist of three domains—political, economic, and cultural. An outline of the three frameworks with respect to the three domains are summarized in Table 10.1.

We will now articulate the elements attributed to the three frameworks of global politics, the Westphalian, Philadelphian, and Anti-Utopian. As seen in Table 10.1, geo-political frameworks can be measured using six yardsticks: principal author, key concept, institutional unit, behavioral principle, peace, democracy; the geo-economic foundations can be measured using four yardsticks: principal author, key concept, driving force, critical variable; and the geo-cultural networks can be measured by four yardsticks: principal author, key media, key purpose and key effect.

In the Westphalian framework, the actors are "normal states" and the basic premise is state sovereignty. In the Philadelphian framework, the actors are liberal democracies as politico-economic systems, and the basic premise is the ideology of liberal democracy. In the Anti-Utopian framework, the actors are failed and failing

Table 10.1 Outline of Westphalian, Philadelphian, and Anti-Utopian Legacies

Geo-political framework	Westphalian (state-centric)	Philadelphian (global republican)	Anti-Utopian (post postcolonial multicultural)
Principal author Key concept	Kissinger State sovereignty	Fukuyama Popular sovereignty	Huntington Post-sovereignty loss of sovereignty
Institutional unit	Nation-state	Liberal democracy	Civilizational superstate & failed/failing state
Behavioral principle	Balancing/ bandwagoning	Building/hiding	Fortifying, hollowing out/ collapsing
Peace	Peace by War	Liberal democratic peace	Neither war nor peace
Democracy	Indifference	Aggressive export or opportunistic silence	Military intervention or cynical neglect
Geo-economic foundations			
Principal author Key concept	Gerschenkron National economy	Reich Global market	Landes Economic development
Driving force	State-led industrialization	Market-driven megacomposition	World cultures that guide the inner values and attitudes of a population
Critical variable	Large input of capital and labor	Critical input of technology	Invention and know-how
Geo-cultural networks			
Principal author Key media	Anderson State-run radio/TV	Barber Cable TV network	Kaplan Underground network
Key purpose	Nation building	Global penetration	Anti-state reaction & dissident communication, reconstituting order in cultural sphere
Key effect	Video legitimization	Video globalization Homogenization	Subversive operations Legitimization of civilizational superstates

states, and the basic premise is loss of sovereignty. Normal states are characterized by a clear distinction of "order within" versus "anarchy without." They are especially sensitive to infringements on sovereignty and territory. They abhor interference in internal affairs (Biersteker and Weber 1996). Liberal democracies are characterized by firmly entrenched popular sovereignty and broad acceptance of universal norms and values, such as the free market and democratic politics—however incompatible such norms may be at times. They seek to downplay emphasis on protectionism, state sovereignty, and the potentially volatile politics of marginalized segments of the globe. Failed and failing states are those that have suffered from "hollowing out" in terms of sovereignty and have become economically marginalized. They are very vulnerable in the face of global economic changes and security instability and are prone to suffer from internal disorder and civil strife. They tend to be ripe for outside intervention, whether it comes in the form of colonialism, humanitarian relief, armed aggression, or economic penetration and exploitation.

The behavior modalities of normal states are balancing and bandwagoning (Walt 1987; Schweller 1997). The aim of balancing is to contain the potentially explosive assertiveness of other normal states. The capability to engage in war must nevertheless be maintained in case it is necessary. In the case of an overwhelmingly powerful normal state (or coalition thereof), a state may resort to bandwagoning: if you cannot beat them, join them. The behavior modalities of liberal democracies are binding and hiding (Deudney 1996; Onuf 1998; Keane 1998). Like-minded actors band together in order to achieve a larger and stronger union. However, when faced with forces that might jeopardize the foundation of liberal democratic norms, concealment may be expedient. The behavioral modalities of failed and failing states are hollowing out and collapsing. These actors no longer function autonomously; they are associated with anarchy within and intervention from without, yet they are so amorphous that their strength is not significantly affected by such outside intervention (IFRCRCS 1998; UNHCR).

The four yardsticks of the geo-economic bases are principal author, key concept, driving force, and critical variable. Principal authors for the geo-economic bases of the Westphalian, the Philadelphian, and the Anti-Utopian frameworks are Alexander Gershenkron, Robert Reich, and David Landes, respectively. Gershenkron's key concept is the national economy supported by the sovereign state as key actor driven by its own late-comer's status and economic backwardness. His protagonists are Russia and Germany. Reich's key concept is the global market supported by an anonymous and amorphous set of all the speculators in the world as the key actors, whose watchful eyes are on the lookout for opportunities that can be exploited. Reich's future is to be sustained by the fortunate few who can adapt to, and excel in, global megacompetition. His premise is that further liberalization will lead to globally higher incomes and more general happiness. Regarding the majority, who see a *de facto* decline in their income, he argues that it can be rescued through massive training schemes financed by the privileged minority. Government intervention, especially if it takes the form of protectionism, will necessarily reduce the general standard of living. The Reich world is the modernization theory writ large with the United States as the model for liberalization and globalization. Landes's key concept is economic development supported by groups of entrepreneurs with the propensity to make the best use of technological breakthrough as the key actors. The driving force are the supportive attitudes and norms of such entrepreneurs regarding innovation and enterprise in the cultural environment. Therefore, the critical variable is the cultural predisposition to advance invention and know-how in the context of economic development.

Gershenkron's transformative mechanism is a large input of capital and labor, which entails a system of stockholding to collect capital, state-led industrialization to guide entrepreneurs, and long working hours in exchange for permanent employment status or high wages. The transformative mechanism of the Reich world is the straightforward input of technological innovation. As Paul Romer (1990) cogently argues, technology itself is endogenized in the market here, in contrast to that of Gershenkron's view, where technology tends to be treated as exogenous.

The global market began to flourish after telecommunications devices became available to all speculators and after opportunities for currency trading were dramatically amplified by the Plaza Accord of 1985. It will further flourish at some future time when telemanufacturing and teledistribution devices are invented and utilized globally. Landes's transformative mechanism is Weberian. The inner values and attitudes that guide a population are depicted as fundamental to preparing, advancing, and sustaining economic development. Certain kinds of values and attitudes cherished by a population are more conducive to invention and innovation and to enterprise and development.

Four yardsticks of the geo-cultural networks are as follows: principal author, key media, key purpose, and key effect. Principal authors on geo-cultural networks are Benedict Anderson, Benjamin Barber, and Robert Kaplan. Anderson describes how the state radio network of Indonesia serves a primary role in the country's nation building efforts. Barber describes the starkly different networking technologies and strategies of the Philadelphian and Anti-Utopian worlds—which he denotes are symbolized by McWorld and Jihad, respectively. CNN and Samizdat (samoizdatel'stvo or self-publication) symbolize another aspect of the opposing elements of these two different networks. Kaplan focuses on networking techniques and the strategy of the Anti-Utopian worlds.

Networks are important for nurturing, cementing, sharing, and creating solidarity; therefore, they are self-strengthening. The rise or decline of the three frameworks depends in part on how they flourish, compete, or degenerate. In the Anderson network, the state-owned radio and television play key networking roles in Indonesia. Indonesia comprises over 17,000 islands where almost countless native languages are spoken and where the newly independent nation's standard tongue, Bahasa Indonesia, was created on the basis of a somewhat artificial and very local language spoken mostly in Malay Peninsula coastal areas and their vicinities for commercial purposes. It is a sort of Malayo-Polynesian Esperanto. The leaders of the independence deliberately chose this language instead of Javanese, the predominant language on the island of Java where most of the Indonesian founding fathers originated. For the sake of unity and solidarity of the Republic of Indonesia, it was decided that the dominant language of the dominant population should not be imposed on the rest of the population. Efforts are made to disseminate the national language on all possible occasions through the public radio, Radio Indonesia. Thus, for instance, children born in Eastern and Central Java islands, where their native language is Javanese, study Bahasa Indonesian in primary school, English in high school, and another foreign language in college.

Networks in the region are also very important to Indonesia. A telling event was President Suharto's visit to Tokyo in 1993 during the Group of Seven (G-7) summit. During the visit, Suharto asked to join the G-7, giving the impression that the country was interested in attaining the heightened status and prestige afforded to G-7 members. At that time, *Televisi Indonesia*, knowing that one of the co-authors, Takashi Inoguchi, had lectured on Japanese politics at the University of Gadjah Mada in Jogjakarta, approached Inoguchi for an interview. Given Inoguchi's background and experience in Indonesia, which presumably entailed a certain level of understanding of Indonesia's nation-building efforts, the interview was in essence an invitation to "video legitimize" their cause, as they hoped to depict a more positive view thereof.

If McWorld is the symbol of global penetration, then CNN is its television networking counterpart. CNN is characterized by prompt, live, global reporting with dramatic, well-calculated visual effects. Drawing from a co-author's experience, when Inoguchi appeared on CNN with Diet member Wakako Hironaka during the June 1993 Japanese general elections in which the Liberal Democratic Party was trounced, everything was live—there was no script, no rehearsal. CNN TOKYO's Eileen O'Conner simply appeared shortly before broadcasting and said that she would ask certain questions. The setting was also deliberately selected; the backdrop of the interview was a vote-monitoring room located in the building that houses Japanese television stations and CNN Tokyo. Against the background noise of the busy vote-monitoring room, we sat and discussed the general election and its impact on Japanese politics; this environment was calculated to give the strong visual impression that Japan was experiencing a dramatic change and that TV viewers were witnessing history. This is perhaps what the US government wanted to see in the context of the ongoing trade negotiations and in light of Japan's limited participation in the Gulf War of 1991.

Samizdat is the symbol of dissident communication from the old days of the Soviet regime. Today, fax and predominantly e-mail are the latest devices for dissident communication. These modes of communication are used for underground or subversive operations or for clandestine intelligence activities. Back in 1989, one of the co-authors, Inoguchi received a fax some weeks after the June 4 Tiananmen Square massacre when anti-Chinese government demonstration and meetings were taking place in Tokyo. The message was a call for solidarity from Chinese students at the University of Tokyo. Inoguchi recognized one of the names, as this student had come to him a couple of years earlier with a letter of recommendation from Yan Jiaji, the then director of the Institute of Political Science at the Chinese Academy of Social Sciences. Inoguchi had known Yan Jiaji through correspondence related to the publication of a political science book series in Chinese published by the University of Tokyo Press, of which Inoguchi was editor (Inoguchi 1989–92). In his Introduction to the Chinese edition, he acknowledged the efforts of a number of colleagues including Yan Jiaji. The massacre took place before the Chinese translation was released, and when it appeared, in late 1990, my reference to Yan Jiaji had been deleted.

10.1 Future Directions

Geo-economically, it is not entirely clear that globalization at its extreme will bring peace and prosperity. If everything is subject to market forces, then two obstacles may emerge. First, instability may emerge from market turbulence as globalization could create conditions in which market forces may not function well. Second, due to the growing disparities that result from globalization and marginalization, the pursuit of market efficiency would further accelerate the marginalization of non-competitive segments. Therefore, globalization and integration are not likely to enforce the Philadelphian trend in a unilateral direction; instead, there is likely to be movement in both directions, forward and backward. Atrophy of the Philadelphian framework may take place if the geo-economic foundations are not assured at an optimal level. Once globalization and liberalization reach the extreme, internal dis-

Table 10.2 Directions of change in terms of three key variables

1. Key technological innovations Philadelphian direction	Information technologies steadily combined with manufacturing technologies, creating the conditions in which the law of increase of marginal profits would apply.
2. Demographic-environmental deterioration Anti-Utopian direction	Short-term deterioration and long-term stagnation without vigorous, concerted efforts to stem the tide, creating the conditions in which a self-contained North stagnates and an exploding and imploding South rocks the so-called Spaceship Earth.
3. Resilience of nation-states Westphalian direction	The state as the provider of identity, stability, and fulfilment, more symbolically and culturally than the more conventional Westphalian conception allows.

parities may develop into something that cannot be easily contained. They could well precipitate internal strife and even chaos. The Anti-Utopian framework flourishes in such environs. Similarly, globalization and integration taken to the extreme may bring about a revival of state sovereignty with vehement nationalist assertiveness because the state is counted on as the last defense against the relentless tide of market forces. State sovereignty under such circumstances could easily stress the symbolic and cultural aspects rather than the more conventional Westphalian conception of territorial integrity, military might, and economic wealth.

In light of the potential for negative consequences arising from globalization, the question becomes: How pervasive will globalization be in the next quarter century or so? To get a clearer view of this situation, it is necessary to identify—at least—the following three variables, which are likely to play major roles in determining the vicissitude of the three geopolitical frameworks. They are:

1. key technological innovations
2. deterioration of demographic-environmental conditions
3. resilience of nation-states (Table 10.2)

1. Nikolai Kondratieff, Joseph Schumpeter, and other business-cycle economists (Goldstein 1988; Saito 1998) enumerate the key technological innovations that bring about total factor productivity. Starting at the beginning of the nineteenth century, these innovations include canals (such as the Suez and Panama), railroads, electric power, automobiles, and information technologies. Respectively, each was the driving force in business prosperity for the following (roughly estimated) periods: 1800–1848, 1848–1895, 1885–1941, 1941–1989, 1990-today. What we observe now is the explosion of technological innovation in the information technologies. Starting with telecommunications, computers, and financial services, innovation in these areas has steadily begun to penetrate the operations of the manufacturing and marketing sectors to bring about new revolutions in business. It is not entirely clear whether these innovations will sustain the law of increase of marginal profit (Arthur 1994), in contrast to the law of

decline of marginal profit, which is said to have been the case in the past with respect to the effects of new technologies. If that is the case, the arguments in support of the advent of a new economy without the cycles of business depressions might be credible (Weber 1997). If these things evolve sufficiently well, it may be possible to sustain the geo-economic foundations of the Philadelphian framework reasonably well. Similarly, the geo-cultural networks sustaining the Philadelphian framework will develop further.

2. The deterioration of demographic-environmental conditions is the old Malthusian problem. Technological optimists argue that biochemical and biomedical technologies will make breakthroughs to cope with the expected scenario. Environmental pessimists argue that, in view of the prospect of further population expansion and deterioration of the environment, the basis of food production as well as the fundamental conditions for clean air and water will be undermined, putting human life in jeopardy. Demographically, the proportion of the aged in the world is becoming alarmingly large in comparison to the productive population in the advanced democracies. No less seriously, those developing countries whose demographies are alarmingly skewed to the young are prone to resorting to internal strife and external war (Brooks et al. 2019).
3. The resilience of nation-states will be sustained for the next half century. A whole world awash in the tide of globalization and driven everywhere by market forces is unlikely to take permanent root as that would ultimately mean the obliteration of most organized units other than markets, and this is highly unlikely. The more plausible future is that the more globalized and the more market-force-driven, the more likely that developmental forces will compel us to restore stability and security, and the more reliance there will be with regard to national identity and solidarity as sources of meaning and fulfillment. Yet the traditional prerogatives of sovereign states (i.e., the ability to raise tax revenues and to conscript soldiers) are becoming more difficult; as market liberalization and globalization further expand, globally competitive firms rely less and less on the state. They find ways to pay relatively less tax by expanding offshore accounts and securing tax havens. Conscription is increasingly out of favor, and military reserves are now made up of volunteers. Internationally, mobilizing soldiers for peacekeeping and disaster relief operations will tend to be based on standby agreements.

From what we have argued so far, our best educated speculation is as follows:

Global market forces will make definite advances because of their Prometheus unbound (technology) the opposite to Prometheus bound as the historian David Landes describes how human beings were given fire from Prometheus who stole it from the Heaven and punished, and bounded to rocks of a mountain, whose liver was eaten by eagles, but their durable permeation will not be ensured because when globalization swings to the extreme, counterbalancing forces may offset the Philadelphian direction. Yet, in an enlarged North with its higher income, the Philadelphian framework will prevail more or less. In an exploding and imploding South, the Anti-Utopian direction will include a greater emphasis on global governance that is more likely to work as a mixture of idealistic individual-centered humanism, the vigorous pursuit of global market integrity and consolidation by those globalists, and those cynical "civilizationists" who extend assistance to fend off the negative contamination of alien "civilizations." The Westphalian direction will focus more on the symbolic and cultural aspects of state sovereignty than the conventional Westphalian conception allows, thus, rewarding conditions in which states will be more like "imagined communities," not in stages of nation building, but in stages of nation fragmentation or weakening under the growing forces of global markets and the threat of demographic and environmental deterioration.

If the above speculations make the future seem very near, it is important to remind ourselves that half a century is not so far away. The most important message from the above exercise is that looking back helps us peer into the future, perhaps more clearly, because we can trace the tenuous yet critical threads all the way back. Therefore, we can better understand the path that has been trod for much longer periods of time than conventional wisdom allows.

References

Anderson, B. (1991). *Imagined communities: Reflections on the origin and spread of nationalism* (2nd ed.). London: Verso.

Arthur, B. (1994). *Increasing returns and path dependence in the economy*. Ann Arbor: University of Michigan Press.

Barber, B. (1993). *Jihad vs. McWorld*. New York: Times Books.

Biersteker, T., & Weber, C. (Eds.). (1996). *State sovereignties as social contract*. Cambridge: Cambridge University Press.

Brooks, D. J., Brooks, S. G., Greenhill, B. D., & Haas, M. L. (2019). Demographic transition theory of war: Why young societies are conflict prone and old societies are the most peaceful. *International Security, 43*(3), 53–95.

Collet, C., & Inoguchi, T. (2010). Is globalization undermining civilizational identities? A test of Huntington's core state assumptions among the publics of greater Asia and the Pacific. *Japanese Journal of Political Science, 13*(4), 553–585.

Cox, M., John Ikenberry, G., & Inoguchi, T. (Eds.). (2000). *American democracy promotion: Impulses, strategies and impacts*. Oxford: Oxford University Press.

Deudeney, D. (1996). Binding sovereigns: Authorities, structures, and geopolitics in Philadelphian systems. In Biersteker & Weber (Eds.), *State sovereignty as social construct* (pp. 190–239). Cambridge: Cambridge University Press.

Doyle, M. (1986). Liberalism and world politics. *The American Political Science Review, 80*, 1151–1169.

Doyle, M. (1997). *Ways of war and peace: Realism, liberalism and socialism*. New York: Norton.

Fukuyama, F. (1992). *The end of history and the last man*. London: Penguin.

Gershenkron, A. (1965). *Economic backwardness in historical perspective*. Cambridge, MA: Harvard University Press.

Gilpin, R. (1983). *War and world politics*. Princeton: Princeton University Press.

Goldstein, J. (1988). *Long cycles: Prosperity and war in the modern age*. New Haven: Yale University Press.

Huntington, S. (1997). *The clash of civilizations and the remaking of world order*. New York: Simon and Schuster.

IFRCRCS (International Federation of Red Cross and Red Cross Societies). (1998). *World disasters report 1997*. Oxford: Oxford University Press.

Inoguchi. T. (1989–1992). *Book series: contemporary political science* (in Japanese, Gendai seijigaku sosho, 20 vols. by Tokyo daigaku shuppankai (University of Tokyo Press); in Chinese Xiantai zhengzhixue conshu, 19 vols. by Zhongguo jingji ribao chubanshe (Chinese Economic Journal Press).

Inoguchi, T. (1999). Peering into the future by looking back: The Westphalian, Philadelphian and Anti-Utopian paradigms. *International Studies Review, 1*(2, Summer), 173–191.

Inoguchi, T. (2002). Three Japanese scenarios for the third millennium. In I. Wallerstein & A. Clesse (Eds.), *The world we are entering, 2000–2050* (pp. 189–2002). Amsterdam: Dutch University Press.

Inoguchi, T. (2010). World order debates in the twentieth century: Through the eyes of the two-level game and second image (reversed). *Chinese Journal of International Politics, 3*(2, Summer), 155–188.

Inoguchi, T., & Le, L. T. Q. (this volume). *The development of global legislative politics: Rousseau and Locke writ global.* Singapore: Springer Nature Singapore.

Kaplan, R. (1998). *The end of the earth.* New York: Random House.

Keane, J. (1998). The Philadelphian model. In T. Inoguchi, E. Newman, & J. Keane (Eds.), *The changing nature of democracy* (pp. 231–243). Tokyo: United Nations University.

Kissinger, H. (1994). *Diplomacy.* New York: Simon and Schuster.

Krasner, S. D. (Ed.). (1983). *International regimes.* Ithaca: Cornell University Press.

Landes, D. (1998). *The wealth and poverty of nations.* New York: Norton.

Morgenthau, H. (1959). *Politics among nations* (2nd enlarged ed.). New York: Knopf.

Onuf, N. (1998). The new culture of security studies. *Mershon International Studies Review, 42*(1), 132–134.

Reich, R. (1991). *The work of nations.* New York: Knopf.

Romer, P. (1990). Endogenous technical change. *Journal of Political Economy, 102*, 71–102.

Russett, B. (1994). *Grasping the democratic peace: Principles for a post-cold war world.* Princeton: Princeton University Press.

Russett, B. M., & Oneal, J. (2011). *Triangulating peace: Democracy, interdependence, and international organizations.* New York: W. W. Norton.

Saito, S. (1998). *Junen defure (a decade of deflation).* Tokyo: Nihon Keizai Shimbun.

Schweller, R. (1997). New realist research on alliances: Refining, not refuting, Waltz's balancing proposition. *The American Political Science Review, 91*, 927–935.

Spruyt, H. (1993). *The sovereign state and its competitors: An analysis of systems change.* Princeton: Princeton University Press.

UNHCR (United Nations High Commissioner for Refugees). http://www.unhcr.org/.

United Nations. (2018). *United Nations peace keeping operations.* Available from: https://www.unmissions.org/. Accessed 8 June 2018.

Walt, S. (1987). *The origins of alliances.* Ithaca: Cornell University Press.

Weber, S. (1997). The end of the business cycle? *Foreign Affairs, 76*(July/August), 65–82.

Yomiuri Shimbun. (2018, May 31) *PKO nanajunen masu kikendo* (*70 years of UN peace keeping operations: Risks on the rise*) (p. 6).

Chapter 11
Theory of Power Transition

Abstract The theory of power transition focusing on Robert Gilpin (War and change in world politics. Princeton University Press, Princeton, 1981) It has been paid special attention after the Cold War because the question of who will be a next hegemon dominates global politics as the United States manifests the symptoms of confusion and decline. Instead of highlighting top leaders, this chapter presents the dialectical power transition whereby hegemonic decline due to their mishaps and mistakes leads their vulnerability inadvertently laid bare. Conceptually, the dialectical power transition makes use of the two-level game (Putnam) and the second image reversed (Gourevitch).

11.1 A Literature Review of Power Transition Theory

The theory of power transition focuses on the leading powers in the international system and the struggle from which the next hegemon will emerge. The marginalized have-nots do not play an explicit role in this transition. In his writings on power transition theory, Inoguchi (2010) distinguishes between the dominant leading powers and those on the periphery, the marginalized have-nots. In Gilpin's (1981) writings, he develops a theory of hegemonic leadership being determined through military conflict from which the leader emerges from a limited group of contenders. Lake (1983) theorizes on the preparatory stages of becoming a hegemonic leader and examines US economic foreign policy, beginning in the late-nineteenth century through 1933. In this examination, Lake explores relative scale (GNP) and relative productivity (labor productivity), arguing that these elements are the two key indicators that reveal whether the nation states are (based on his labels) "do nothings" (free riders, spoilers, and supporters) or "leaders" (hegemons).

There are two major weaknesses of the current power transition theory. First, many academics, including Gilpin and Lake, concentrate on the leading powers, excluding the marginalized have-nots from the explanatory scheme. This is not right, as these leading states were often, at one time, some of the marginalized have-nots. Hegemonic transition proceeds well when domestic consolidation is articulated positively in external action. Conversely, hegemonic transition unfolds

T. Inoguchi, L. T. Q. Le, *The Development of Global Legislative Politics*,
Trust: Interdisciplinary Perspectives 3, https://doi.org/10.1007/978-981-32-9389-2_11

negatively toward decline when domestic stagnation and confusion are articulated negatively in external action. The other major weakness of transition power theory is that domestic politics and economics are underestimated or are treated as a black box. In other words, they are not regarded as something that does not need serious explanation. The impact of small and at times marginalized states should be considered in the explanatory scheme. For instance, the start of a hegemon's decline can begin with a miscalculation or misstep by a leading power, when, for example, interacting with small, marginalized states.

11.2 The Dialectics of Power Transition Theory

Aware of the existing weaknesses in power transition theory, Inoguchi (2010) seeks to address the current deficit by engaging two concepts: the two-level game (Putnam 1988) and the second image reversed (Gourevitch 1978). The two-level game refers to the strategy of state leaders to engage simultaneously at the domestic and international levels. The second image reversed concept refers to reversing Waltz's (1959) second image and thereby analyzing how international politics affect domestic structure. Waltz employed three levels of analysis or images to explain the occurrence of war: the first image focuses on human nature as a cause of international aggression (UNESCO Charter 1955); the second image views domestic politics as the impetus behind states going to war (Moore 1964); and the third image posits that war breaks out because of international rivalry among states (Kissinger 2000).

The extended twentieth century (1890–2025) has been an exceptional period in power transition. The world population has grown exponentially from 1.6 billion in 1900 to 6 billion in 2000 to nearly 7.5 billion in 2018. Also staggering in growth is military technological advancement: from Kalashnikovs to military tanks to stealth bomber aircrafts to aircraft carriers to underwater-launched long-range nuclear missiles to unmanned stealth fighter aircrafts or the *army of none* (Scharre 2018). The rapid development and sophistication of how war is waged has reached a point that unmanned war machines designed by artificial intelligence are becoming feasible. As the efficacy of war machines has continued to grow, the number of soldier war deaths (excluding civilian deaths) has dramatically decreased from 5 million per year (1938–1945) to 100,000 per year (1945–1989) to 10,000 per year (1989–2018) as noted by the International Institute of Strategic Studies. In this sense, the twentieth century witnessed a remarkable period in power transition.

Dialectics are part of the power transition theory scheme. While Gilpin's scheme of power transition theory places its thrust on the birth, development and decline of a hegemon with the rest of a hegemonic system left to the black box of might and wealth as a consequence of big war occurrence, Inoguchi (2010) highlights the anger and anguish of the peripheries directed at the hegemon whenever the hegemon commits mishaps and mistakes, and lays bare its vulnerability to the peripheries. Leading states interact with the marginalized have-nots that engage in grassroots-level activities, and in doing so they influence each other. The end result

Table 11.1 The Scheme of Power Transition in Dialectics

The state strategies of leading power states posed by haves	Grassroots-level game (antithesis posed by have-nots)	Images reversed (synthesis posed by haves to "accommodate" have-nots)
Balance of power	People's war	Colonial indifference
Collective security	People power	Humanitarian assistance
Primacy	Global terrorism	Humanitarian intervention plus nuclear disarmament
Global governance	Mirrored global terrorism	Mirrored humanitarian intervention plus nuclear primacy

is that leading states change state policies because of this engagement. To understand the dialectic, it is helpful to examine the concept of conservation of catastrophe (McNeill and Kindleberger 1989). Power is vulnerable but seeks to hide its vulnerability, thereby containing and prolonging the eventuality of a potential catastrophe (McNeill and Kindleberger 1989; McNeill 2001; Tenner 2004). The Red Queen in *Alice's Adventures in Wonderland* articulates this exact notion of the conservation of catastrophe principle when she observes: "It takes all the running you can do, to keep in the same place" (Carroll 2016). For leading state actors, this means that to "keep running," they must maintain and support policy directions and commitments, regardless of costs, until there is a transition, violent or non-violent, to a new institutionalized security regime. Examples in the twentieth century are as follows: World War I marked the violent transition from balance of power to collective security; World War II marked another violent transition from one type of collective security to another; and the end of the Cold War marked a non-violent transition from post-World War II collective security to primacy (Table 11.1).

11.3 Balance of Power

Balance of power has some basic qualities. A somewhat limited number of states (five to six) with similar levels of demographics, industrialization, and military strength participate in this international security regime. (It must be noted that Kissinger (2000) and Kaplan (1957) take into account a somewhat limited number of five to six states in their respective writings of balance of power. However, some other theorists of balance of power place no importance on numerical figures about participants. Instead, power configuration and distribution in the balance of power system are paid more attention.) The rationale is that there is no one state strong enough to dominate others. Once there is the likelihood of the emergence of one or two instances of disrupting power, the dynamics of balance of power work to prevent the disruption from occurring. Through this game, international order and peace are maintained. In the decades preceding World War I, England, France, Prussia, Russia, and Turkey formed a balance of power. Russia and Turkey were demographically stronger than the other states, but their distance from the center of Western Europe counterbalanced this strength. Industrially strong England had its continental ambition curbed by the nineteenth-century Crimean War, and its maritime hegemony was satisfied with its off-shore balancing role in Europe.

A balance of power works best among a limited number of states. The period from the Congress of Vienna to the ascendance of Wilhelm II of Germany is viewed as exemplifying a classical balance of power. In this period, the involved conservative state actors pursued the following three accords: (1) to restore and maintain a balance of power *ante bellum*, in order to block one or more states from growing too strong; (2) to halt the spread of French revolutionary ideas and institutions into the rest of Europe; and (3) to avert a repeat occurrence of overly religious conflation as quietly advocated by Alexander II of Romanov Russia. The rationale behind the third accord was that the non-ideological flexibility and maneuverability of the balance of power needed to be maintained.

11.3.1 Basic Structural Conditions of Balance of Power in Transition

Marginalized space, also referred to as a colony or sphere of influence, is associated with leading powers involved in a balance of power. Therefore, the leading states are colonial powers. The colonies give the major powers room to shift within the balance of power when that room is not available on home territory. The marginalized space allows the leading powers to be more at ease as it gives them a space that is beyond the reach of the normative, prevailing concerns of their governments. A clear division exists to this day between the colonialist thinking of sovereign states in the West and colonies in the non-West. Robert Cooper (2004) captures some of these geo-temporal civilizational distinctions and the associated behavior patterns among post-modern, modern, and pre-modern zones.

The decision of the German monarch, Wilhelm II, to initiate a naval arms race with Britain was the beginning of the end for this balance of power. As leading powers rushed to adjust and consolidate their power through the colonization of Africa, the balance of power lost it foundational grip. By 1906, territorial expansion had run out of land in Africa, Polynesia, and Asia, and in doing so the state actors in the balance of power lost the space and system they needed to achieve their goals.

11.3.2 Collective Security

Collective security is another strategy employed by states to achieve international order and peace. Collective security entails a group arrangement for dealing with a threatening actor. Actors join together to protect the status quo, and as a group they are willing to collectively defend, deter, and dissuade those willing to threaten or challenge the accepted international system. This system is based on the belief that collective action for normative and operational situations is the best means to respond and cope with perceived threats. Normative values that change with the times legitimize the rallying together of leading powers against an identified threat to the established international order. Shared normative beliefs at the time of the Vienna Congress include support for the old ruling families of Europe, opposition to revolutionary movements, and opposition to nationalist forces. Normative values shifted; at the time of the Treaty of Versailles, they included freedom, democracy, national self-determination, and non-aggression. Twenty-five years later at the Yalta Conference, international normative values had shifted again; this time they included freedom, democracy, anti-fascism, anti-colonialism, and human rights. On the 60th anniversary of the Allied victory, US President George W. Bush, in Riga, Latvia, noted that once again normative values had shifted over time to the point that it was now democracy battling against tyranny in all its forms.

Collective security through the establishment of institutions legitimizes joint operational schemes. At the Vienna Congress, monarchs employed classical diplomacy and relied on their representatives to persuade and influence others through eloquent oratory skills and keen social and character judgment. The view of nineteenth-century Europe was that the pen was mightier than the sword, and hence, diplomacy was institutionalized. Mercenaries of the pen, such as scholar and diplomat Friedrich von Grenz, were deployed to tip or restore the desired balance through his contacts with kings, princes, and politicians. At the Treaty of Versailles, the League of Nations became the *du jour* choice of institutionalization. The League's role was: to identify threats; to assess, advise, and offer resolution to threats; and conduct counter-threat operations. The League and its embodied values failed to curtail those states that did not adhere to the same norms and values despite all the commitment with the Kelogg-Brian disarmament treaty that outlawed war in 1928 (Hathaway and Shapiro 2016; Mimaki 2016). The 1928 treaty did not carry "teeth" anywhere in the treaty, which could have been used to compel would-be-violators to repent or to resort to war. Once the US Federal Government was taken by the Democratic Party in 1930s replacing the Republican Party dominant in the 1920s after the great depression, "teeth" were added to the idea of outlawing war, meaning concerted economic sanctions to deter violators from resorting to war. James Hornbeck, in charge of the Far East in the US State Department, uttered a cry upon hearing about the Japanese Pearl Harbor attack that no country resorted to war with no prospect of winning it. At the Yalta Conference, collective security was institutionalized through the formation of the United Nations. The UN General Assembly, the general body with world membership, is responsible for passing resolutions on non-conforming and threatening state actors. The UN Security Council (SC), composed of five permanent members with veto power and ten non-permanent members elected for two-year periods, decides on the action required to respond to rogue actors and unacceptable situations. Due to the veto power of the five permanent member states, the UN has only mobilized it forces once in its history. The Soviet Union boycotted the UN and an SC meeting, and in doing so allowed the other permanent members to pass a resolution that North Korea had broken world peace and needed to be stopped. The Korean War (1950–1953) is the only time UN forces have engaged in launching a military assault in response to a threat posed by a state actor.

11.3.3 Collective Security in Political Transition

Collective Security is operationalized when the major powers feel that certain actors—by not supporting the normative values and collective spirit embodied in the international system—threaten it. Collective security devices, including ideological warfare, target the so-called bad guys of international politics. Historical examples are the French Revolution, the German Imperial Reich, and the Axis Alliance. For collective security to be successful, military strength must be such that potential and real enemies of the system are dissuaded and deterred from acting out and that those in danger are defended. Another consideration in collective security involves its structural components, i.e., the mobilization and deployment of military power, the institutional devices used, and the number of troops committed. After Japan's 1941 attack on Pearl Harbor, Winston Churchill response was "[w]e have won the war." Churchill realized that US participation was a critical link in the European and Asia-Pacific theaters of war. Another important and difficult operational consideration for collective security is "who commands the joint forces?" With the North Atlantic Treaty Organization (NATO), France objected to the United States commanding NATO forces. NATO intervention in Kosovo also raised the contentious issue of who commands the troops. In the case of the United States, even with its military predominance in weaponry and troop training, the general consensus and practice is that the armed forces of other countries are not brought under US military command.

11.4 Primacy

11.4.1 Basic Features of Primacy

Announcements and compliance are qualities associated with primacy. According to the Director-General of the World Trade Organization (WTO), Pascal Lamy (2005), the metaphorical equivalent of state communication style at international gatherings is the United States making announcements by megaphone, and in comparison, Western European states employing telephonic negotiations. In the case of Japan, the preferred method is *tête-à-tête* discussions with bureaucratic representatives representing domestic interests. This style of communication results in a strong unilateral United States, a skillful multilateral Europe, and a sometimes "nullilateral" (i.e., no vector) Japan.

Primacy is characterized by strong convictions, grounded in an unwavering belief system, which causes the actor to be blind to the cost of realizing its goals or implementing its policies. The United States is known for its zest to act regardless of cost. Much of this behavior comes from the US position as sole superpower and its determination to maintain this status. The insistence of the United States to wage war against global terrorism at any cost is similar to Winston Churchill's tenacious words to achieve "victory at any cost" in World War II. Primacy is confident of its own invincibility and, therefore, acts to block any possible or premature decline in its international position of dominance. To again draw parallels to the British experience, just as the Boer War waged by Britain, regardless of cost, is thought to have hastened the British decline, the US wars in Iraq and Afghanistan are thought to be playing a similar role in hastening US decline. State actors in the position of primacy act based on national interests—a strategy that involves purely national interest calculus and largely excludes multilateral diplomacy unless advancing or coinciding with national policy objectives. John Bolton, the US ambassador to the UN, in 2005–2006, was explicit in his message that the UN was viewed by the United States as no more than a diplomatic tool to be called on when needed. The US inclination towards multilateral institutions is characterized as negative when these institutions are seen as constraints on its actions, and positive when seen as instruments that enable the United States to act with global influence. Yet this mindset does not preclude the United States from being one of the most multilaterally equipped countries, ranking alongside the Netherlands, Scandinavian countries, Iran, Mexico, and Hungary—countries that place their brightest and best in the diplomatic corps, leading them to the forefront of multilateral diplomacy.

11.4.2 Basic Structural Conditions in Political Transition

The military supremacy of the United States is irrefutable. The United States has the largest air force in the world. Though this is common knowledge, what is not as widely known is that the second largest air force belongs to the US navy, not Russia, China, France, Britain, or Japan. The US military strength is vigorously reinforced by US expenditure on research and development (R&D) of weapons. In fact, the US accounts for 85% of the total world expenditure on military R&D, including weaponry and supporting systems. The sheer size of this expenditure guarantees US military dominance and primacy for the next 15–25 years, regardless of US missteps or mistakes that it makes in the interim.

The pursuit of primacy and unilateralism sets the United States apart. According to American exceptionalism, the United States is different from other states because it does not suffer from old ideas of discrimination and exploitation related to race, class, wealth, and religion. The United States tends to view itself as a unique source of ideas and while this anti-historical, missionary idealism/realism is not a unanimous view, the United States, through policies like the Patriot Act, seems willing to sacrifice US "rights" in its war on terrorism. As part of the American exceptionalism psyche, the United States offers other countries the opportunity to import (and reap the benefits from) its ideas on capitalism, democracy, freedom, and human rights. The US export of democracy to the rest of the world is grounded in this belief system. The US psyche is fixated on primacy, and the United States is convinced that—before it experiences decline—its mission is to introduce this US belief system into other states and institutional cultures. The slow US decline is evidenced by three symbolic indicators: (1) the cancellation of the international convertibility of the US dollar to gold; the practice since 1985 of large amounts of US dollars being held by major foreign states, such as Britain, Germany, Japan, and China, meaning its balance is supported by foreign governments; the introduction of the Euro in 2001 and its use in many large international trade transactions; (2) the continuous scientific advancement of major countries as supported in journal publications, like *Chemical Abstracts*; and (3) the insistence on unilateralism as well as on enormous expenditures and reckless actions in its war on terrorism.

11.5 Three Popular Strategies Often Developed by Marginalized Have-Nots

Marginalized states attempt to make themselves heard on the international stage with antithetical strategies, such as people's war, people power, and global terrorism. Marginalized have-not states and their ideas on international relations have failed to be satisfactorily expressed in international relations theory.

11.5.1 People's War

11.5.1.1 Basic Features of People's War

States that are invaded, occupied, and colonized are humiliated and marginalized in the process. As a result, some states respond by engaging in a people's war, sometimes called guerrilla warfare. Spain's response, supported by Continental powers, to Napoleon's invading army, was a people's war to thwart Napoleon's conquest. Depicted as Napoleon's "bleeding ulcer," the guerrilla war resulted in the deaths of 300,000 French soldiers. Before the term was coined, American Indians employed guerrilla warfare tactics in the First Nations War in North America, both pre- and post-independence. Marginalized people's wars occur on the peripheries and major powers' wars occur in the core. For instance, the Boer War (1899–1902) was a people's war, and was sparked when the colonizing country, Britain, tried to end Boer opposition to land confiscation. The Boers countered British military action with resolve and persistence. In modern history, the two best-known instances of guerrilla warfare took place against the 2 million strong occupying Japanese army in China and against the French and Americans who tried to stymie Vietnamese independence. Violence is a central feature of a people's war. Mao Zedong understood this well when he said, "Political power grows out of the barrel of a gun." People's wars also require physical space, and their efficacy usually parallels the difficultly of the terrain on which they take place—meaning that guerrilla warfare is often more effective in mountains, deserts, and jungles and urban ghettoes. These potentially treacherous physical spaces provide a refuge for guerrilla strategists to retreat and recuperate.

11.5.1.2 Basic Structural Conditions and Political Transition

Difficult terrain is an asset in people's wars as mountains, deserts, jungles and urban ghettoes slow foreign armies while providing sanctuary for the defending people. Support from the common people is an important asset of those waging a people's war. Mao Zedong noted, "The guerrilla must swim in the people as the fish swims in the sea." Popular support is nurtured through exemplary attitudes and policies, i.e., being respectful and courteous toward people and distributing food to those who need it the most. Creating this image and reputation, at home and abroad, was probably best achieved by the Chinese communists at Yan'an and other sanctuaries. Agnes Smedley, a Western sympathizer and journalist, depicted the Chinese communists as morally minded reformers. If the rebels are fighting their own government, then they need a weak and corrupt government to be the "bad guys." Rebels and revolutionaries secure new recruits and sympathizers by giving the impression that their friends are rich and powerful. These qualities mixed with a bit of luck create a formidable opposition to leading powers, which may in turn trigger a political transition.

11.5.2 People Power

11.5.2.1 Basic Features of People Power

The mantra of people power is non-violent action, even when confronted and provoked by opponents with overwhelming military strength. The rationale behind people power is that violence usual prompts governments to initiate strong suppressive measures against the public. Mahatma Gandhi was successful in securing Indian independence from British rule, in part because he adhered to the principle of passive resistance.

Competent leaders are needed for people power to succeed. Competent leaders must possess the following traits to attract and maintain supporters: charisma, passion, ability to clearly articulate their positions, skill in transforming words into action and results, composure in the face of adversity, and magnanimity with respect to the failings of others in the group. A good example of such a leader is Corazon Aquino, who was instrumental in the people power movement of the Philippines to oust Ferdinand Marcos from power. These movements also require international environments that are receptive to justice being done. Those in the people power movement should bring any barbaric or violent acts committed by those in power (be it governments, occupiers, or invaders) to the attention of the world. In South Korea, two US soldiers, who were driving an armored vehicle, hit and killed two Korean high school girls. The Korean public demonstrated in the streets when the military court found them not guilty. In the next national election, Roh Moo-Hyun, a presidential candidate, campaigned using the residual anti-American sentiment to win the election, albeit with only a 2% majority.

11.5.2.2 Basic Structural Conditions and Political Transition

Non-violent protests can only occur if the public and the government exercise self-restraint and agree to the merits of non-violence. Such a situation existed in 1930–1931, when Mahatma Gandhi organized and led a non-violent protest in the form of satyagraha (power of truth) against the British salt tax. In the 1940s, the Indian National Congress led non-violent action while supporting Britain in the war against Japan. In World War II, Indian communists supported the Soviet Union. Subhas Chandra Bose led the Indian National Army in a protest in the main square of Singapore, British Malaya, which was then invaded and occupied by the Japanese Imperial Army. The slogan chanted during the protest was "on to Delhi." The National Indian Army and the Japanese Imperial Army fought their way through Burma, a part of British India, where they engaged in hostilities with the British Indian Army.

Civil society is often associated with non-violent action at the societal level when the rule of law is fairly well established. Even under a colonial government, civil society can survive if indigenous colonial elites belong to it. Even in situations where the colonial government practices discriminatory policies, the seeds of civil society can be planted and nourished to emerge. In his book, *History of India* (Mill 2007), James Stuart Mill argues that the determined efforts of the colonial government to civilize British India prompted the development of a fledgling civil society.

11.5.3 Global Terrorism

11.5.3.1 Basic Features of Global Terrorism

Violence is the hallmark of global terrorism. Transnational, non-governmental terrorist groups instigate this violence. Well-behaved citizens can be transformed into terrorists capable of extreme acts when called on to fulfill their mission's goals. Global terrorism is based on transnational networks of groups who share convictions and are willing to plot and execute terrorist acts. Built globally but implemented locally, transnational networks are key to global terrorism. As in the case of Afghanistan, groups from these transnational networks can take over and control an entire state apparatus. Another example is the Hezbollah organization in Lebanon, which provides social services and has its own political party with representatives in the national parliament. Deeply embedded in southern Lebanese society, the Hezbollah is strong militarily with its own long-range missiles, supplied by Iran.

Global terrorism preys on human misery and injustice. Terrorists aim to kill and harm civilians, undermining the population's belief in the government's ability to protect its citizens. Terrorists do not seek to engage national armies but instead play on the power disparity between those governing and the governed. Thus, one objective of terrorist activities is to embarrass. To reach the "infidels" in power, terrorists attempt to harm the general populations that are so closely and structurally embedded in global politics and economics. To reach these targets, terrorist attacks must be well designed, comprehensively thought out, and fearlessly carried out.

11.5.3.2 Basic Structural Conditions of Global Terrorism and Political Transitions

A sense of oppressive suffocation from the global structure of human interactions is at the root of global terrorism. The utter saturation and overwhelming domination of political, economic, cultural, and military spheres extinguishes the ability to offer a counter balance of any sort. Marginalized have-nots are unable to separate themselves from the regimes that make up the world economy. The embedded rules and practices, shaped and shared by select citizens of the hegemony, are oppressive and suffocating to those on the outside, the have-nots. Based on a subjective perception of reality, those involved in global terrorism seek to lift the veil of oppressive suffocation, which exists in developed countries as well as developing countries as demonstrated by the fact that just as many terrorists emerge from advanced industrialized states as developing states under repressive regimes.

Solid communication networks play a critical role in how global terrorism reaches its targets, trains its adherents, and executes its plans. High tech and high mortality weapons also are necessary for global terrorists to overcome and compensate for their lack of regular or guerilla troops. A third important factor involved in global terrorists reaching their targets is a set of comprehensive theoretical/theological principles that the group wishes to disseminate as their efforts intend not only to embarrass, disrupt, and undermine governing elites but also to serve as a recruitment tool. To achieve their objectives with maximum effect, terrorists must meticulously study and assess global politics and economics to ensure that the target is well selected and the plan well executed. When these three conditions are met and sustained, the impact of these attacks can cause the governing elites to falter, sometimes leading to a political transition within the leading powers.

11.6 Three Modified Strategies of Leading Powers Often Taking Place as a Synthesis

Over the extended twentieth century, the strategy of major powers and that of marginalized have-nots have unfolded in broad parallel strokes. As the strategy of the major powers transitioned from balance of power (1890–1918) to collective security I (1918–1945) to collective security II (1945–1989) to primacy (1989–2016), the strategy of the marginalized have-nots transitioned from people's war to people power to global terrorism. If the strategy of major powers can be termed a synthesis and the strategy of marginalized have-nots can be termed an antithesis, then the modified strategies of major powers can be examined as a synthesis that occurs in the tension between theses and antitheses. These modified strategies can be labeled: colonial indifference, humanitarian assistance, and humanitarian intervention. All three denote a response by major powers to those who are destitute, living a life of misery, or are victims of disasters. Colonial indifference is the cold-hearted colonialist orientation to those at the nadir of society. Humanitarian assistance applies to the urgent aid sent to those in need, without political strings attached. Humanitarian intervention is the active response of military power to those places experiencing human disasters. These three modified policies or strategies are a synthesis to the have-not challenges to the political security framework. The have nation-states have primarily imposed these responses in a concerted effort to accommodate, appease, placate, and suppress challenges from the marginalized.

11.6.1 Colonial Indifference

11.6.1.1 Basic Features of Colonial Indifference

Colonial indifference denotes a non-caring attitude by the governing structure toward the colonized people. The colonialist state does not view the colonized as equal, and therefore, does not consider the people's needs, wishes, or life conditions. Conflict and disaster among the colonized population does not prompt the colonialist state to act responsibly in securing the population's well-being. Colonialism has been characterized and justified as a civilizing force. It is the mission of advanced people to carry out this task. In his book *History of India*, James Stuart Mill depicts a progression of India toward a more civilized state as it moves from the Hindu period to the Muslim period (ruled by the Mughal empire) to the British Raj period (ruled by the British empire). Colonized people are not in control of their own well-being. As observed by Amartya Sen (Sen 1981), colonial India suffered from famines, but since independence, India has not had one. As an independent state, India tracks local situations and makes informed decisions depending on crop conditions and food production. The success of the Indian government in protecting its people from famine reveals the care the national government takes in estimating the required levels of food production. This was all the more evident in the initial years after independence.

Similarly, colonialist states do not generally intervene in civil strife, unless stakes are high. A prime example is the Persian experience in the early twentieth century. Civil strife raged, and yet the colonialist government responded with indifference. In the words of one British officer, "let them stew in their own juices" (Axelrod 1976). Other examples include, the killing fields of Cambodia in the 1980s and the Rwandan genocide of the mid-1990s—the major powers were largely disinterested and unwilling to get involved. In contrast, when ethnic cleansing occurred in Kosovo, the major powers were robust in their efforts to intervene. However, colonialists were quick to respond when the foundations of their rule were threatened or were being undermined through famine, civil strife, demonstrations, or labor strikes. Good examples of this behavior include the colonists' responses to the Sepoy Mutiny in 1857–1858 and to the Algerian Revolution in 1954–1962. The Sepoy Mutiny was a revolt against the British East India Company by its own sepoys who were dissatisfied with British rule. After more than 1 year, the munity was suppressed and the Company was abolished, imposing the direct rule of the British Crown. The Algerians revolted against French colonial rule in 1954 with a 9 year-long guerrilla war by the Algerian National Liberation Front, finally taking power and achieving independence in 1962.

11.6.2 Humanitarian Assistance

11.6.2.1 Basic Features of Humanitarian Assistance

Compassion is at the center of humanitarian assistance. Above politics, humanitarian assistance appeals to the commonality of people even when political divisions might otherwise prevent such undertakings. Humanitarian assistance is offered to all governments, regardless of how oppressive a regime it may be, if the people are suffering from famine or natural disasters, like an earthquake or tsunami. Humanitarian assistance strives to be non-political, non-intrusive, and effective in the aid it delivers to the vulnerable. Its mission is one of compassion. Yet some governments, such as North Korea, are so sensitive to the donors' delivery method, which generally involves the donor being directly involved in the distribution of medicine and food aid to the people most in need, that the regime rejects assistance. In fact, in 2005, North Korea refused assistance from the World Food Program to alleviate the country's famine because of these concerns.

11.6.2.2 Basic Structural Conditions of Humanitarian Assistance and Political Transitions

To deliver materials and services to those in need, humanitarian assistance typically requires the cooperation of a central government in the affected region to assist in the disbursement of goods, regardless of how incompetent, oppressive, or arbitrary the regime may be. When no such government exists, nongovernmental and international organizations are forced to fill the void, as was the case in Somalia in 2006.

Human compassion motivates humanitarian assistance, but if that assistance prolongs a repressive regime's survival and benefits the ruling elite instead of reducing the suffering of destitute people, then the entire undertaking is undermined. The understanding is that regimes, irrespective of their brutality and disregard for their own people, cannot be ignored. Positive engagement in the form of humanitarian assistance enables outside actors to monitor the situation from within the state. It was this fear that caused North Korea to suspend food assistance from the World

Food Program in 2005. In this way, humanitarian assistance steps into the domain of political and business intelligence.

11.6.3 Humanitarian Intervention

11.6.3.1 Basic Features of Humanitarian Intervention

Humanitarian intervention is based on the concept of forcibly deploying international troops to troubled areas and confronting aggressive actors who contravene international law. It is military intervention limited to surgical operations. The North Atlantic Treaty Organization (NATO) performed such an intervention in Kosovo. The US and UK leadership of NATO-led troops in this operation favored different strategies of intervention: the US advocated for the use of land troops, whereas the UK-led Europeans argued for airstrikes. In this situation, NATO was tasked with halting Serbian Kosovar troops, sent by Belgrade, to persecute Albanian Kosovars.

In cases of humanitarian intervention, the focus of operations is grounded in the notion of universal human rights. Priority is given to the protection of human rights over state rights and popular sovereignty trumps state sovereignty. For example, the impetus of the Afghan war was the overwhelming desire of Western states to extinguish global terrorism, which threatened the lives of civilians potentially everywhere.

On September 11, 2001, terrorists attacked the United States. This targeting of symbolic US buildings that killed thousands, led the United States to retaliate militarily with its own attacks on Kabul and other military/terrorists bases that had served as the power base for global terrorists. Legitimization for such a military operation came from the belief that because global terrorists violate human rights and security, they had to be destroyed. Humanitarian intervention, in the short term, is often an ad hoc coalition of states willing to take collective military action. At times, international resolutions bolster the legitimacy of such initiatives, but often these actions are dependent on the political will and military dominance of the lead state. In general, humanitarian intervention is not well institutionalized on the international political stage.

11.6.3.2 Basic Structural Conditions of Humanitarian Intervention and Political Transitions

The need for humanitarian intervention arises from the global structure and the unremitting market forces that cause some states in the peripheries to fail. This in turn creates a destabilizing and disruptive effect. Fragile states coupled with fragile economies are not able to withstand the tide of globalization, leading to a spiral of decline and failure. The end of the Cold War marked a shift in how the United States prioritized its support of client states and their survival. The end of the East-West confrontation meant that the survival of many client states was jeopardized with the withdrawal of US support. In the early twenty-first century, between 30 and 50 states are either failing or have failed.

In the last quarter of the twentieth century, the pendulum in international relations swung in favor of popular sovereignty, individual freedom, and human rights, and by doing so tilted away from always prioritizing state sovereignty and from the doctrine of non-interference in other states' domestic affairs. Humanitarian intervention is the manifestation of this international swing. This shift is also reflected in the academic research and writings of international relations experts. Approximately 30% of topics covered in international politics textbooks are devoted to human rights, democracy, inequality, gender, global energy, and the environment.

Humanitarian intervention is only possible because the West, with its dominant military force and strong belief in freedom and democracy, support such policies of intervention. The unipolarity of the United States and its conviction to promote and support freedom, human rights, democracy, and equality create a world structure that enables humanitarian interventions.

11.7 Dialectic Moments of the Extended Twentieth Century

A review of the extended twentieth century showcases on a global scale the dialectic moments when the regimes, structures, and mindsets of international political security metamorphosed. It is important to distinguish between the synthesis that emerges from the haves' accommodation, appeasement, placation, or suppression of the have-nots' challenges and the systemic transformations produced by the clashing of thesis and antithesis. A dialectic moment happens when the power resources of the haves is drained by its response to a challenge from the have-nots. If modernity is power and vulnerability, as William McNeill argues, then power saturates the principle of undiminished "conservation of catastrophe." Imperial powers' indifference to colonial people's war created the conditions for imperial decline by allowing the contradictions of colonialism to ferment. At the same time, humanitarian assistance through its support allowed the targeted groups to organize themselves and grow with self-confidence, thereby setting the stage for national liberation and independence. Imperial decline emerges with the simultaneous taxing of imperial resources and humanitarian intervention efforts. How the state power responds to the challenges from the have-nots at home and abroad and how the routinization of its response either weakens or supports the state's systematic functioning are decisive moments for the dominant state.

Three significant dialectic moments characterize the global politics of the extended twentieth century (1890–2025). For much of the nineteenth century, balance of power dominated the international system. The equilibrium of power shifted during the rule of German Kaiser Wilhelm II. Germany was able to link iron and bread; in other words, Germany afforded to achieve the two requirements of expanding military ammunitions and satisfying people's stomachs, and therefore, pose an antithesis to the international system. As a newly unified Germany challenged British naval supremacy, the status quo among major powers also faced the mighty forces of industrialization, nationalism, and rising colonialism as they swept across Europe. The transformation at the level of major states from balance of power to collective security was also marked at the grassroots level among the marginalized and exploited. For the have-nots, the metamorphosis came in the form of a people's war, a generally desperate attempt to resist domination by hegemons both at the local and international level—the antithesis to the balance of power. Among the efforts to resist foreign domination, only three uprisings really gained momentum to seriously challenge the invading or ruling hegemons: the Sepoy Mutiny of India, the Boxer Rebellion of China, and the Boer War of South Africa. Success for the people's war occurred when the armed resistance pushed the major powers to their limit to mobilize their own people as resources. Four empires crumbled in the early twentieth century when faced with such resistance—those belonged to Russia, Germany, Austro-Hungary, and Turkey. The failure of the four empires stemmed from their inattention to their own people at the grassroots level and their failure to mobilize these citizens. This shortcoming represented a critical deterioration of the balance of power system.

For the world at large and Europeans in particular, the unprecedented brutality of World War I triggered the genesis of collective security. Referred to as the war to end all wars, the major signatory powers of the Versailles Treaty in 1919 sought to deter, dissuade, and defeat through legal and institutional means any actor who attempted to violate international norms and values. From the suffering of the Great War, a collective security system arose, known as Wilsonian internationalism and institutionalized as the League of Nations. Remembering George Washington's call for disentanglement after the 1796 defeat of Great Britain, Wilsonian America ironically refused to participate in the newly created institution. The newly formed Soviet Union also refused to participate. This first attempt at a new international system is labeled collective security I, as opposed to the post-1945 system, known as collective security II.

Franklin Roosevelt is largely credited with the establishment of collective security II. Roosevelt's declining health at Yalta led him to accommodate the demands of Winston Churchill, Joseph Stalin, and Chiang Kaishek. Collective security II was a combination of Wilsonian internationalism and Monroevian sphere of influence (Steil 2018). Four key qualities define collective security II: (1) the geographical expansion to global membership, starting with the founding member states being primarily European and American to including Asian states in the 1950s to 1960s and African states in the 1960s to 1970s, and reaching close to 200 member states today; (2) membership in the Security Council reflects a Monroevian sphere of influence with power accorded to five permanent powers—the United States, Russia (former Soviet Union), the United Kingdom, France, and China; (3) the notion of the East-West confrontation and mutually assured destruction by long range intercontinental ballistic missiles, causing war-deaths to dramatically plummet; and (4) the idea of a web of economic interdependence, a tool kit of economic sanctions for states, and an unprecedented level of goods and services trade.

In 1989, the United States claimed victory in the Cold War and sought to reassert its primacy. On September 11, 2001, global terrorism struck places symbolic of US financial and military strength, and since then, global integration, particularly in financial sectors, has accelerated. These are the four key traits of this era of primacy: (1) The significant increase in globalization and digitalization, alongside the decrease in barriers of territorial borders, prompted increased migration; (2) the United States emerging as a unilateralist, and encountering the problems associated with being a hegemon exercising quick punitive external action; (3) the shift toward high-tech, high precision unmanned weaponry, accompanied by stalled momentum among nuclear states for nuclear disarmament and non-nuclear states considering the possibility of acquiring such nuclear status; and (4) the growing trend to engage in financial statecraft in the area of exchange rate manipulation and use of US financial institutions while decreasing use of economic sanctions for tradable products.

11.8 The Next Momentum of Political Transition: An Imminent Dialectic Momentum from Primacy to Global Governance?

Since 2008 and the ensuing world economic depression, the United States as hegemon has felt a mounting sense of frustration toward other states. During President Barack Obama's administration, the hegemon pursued a policy of "strategic patience" toward North Korea—that is, reluctance to engage in external military action. The current presidential administration under Donald Trump continues to feel this sense of frustration, albeit with a distinctly different tone than the preceding administration as Trump totes an "America first" policy, which is essentially a policy of protectionism, isolationism, and racism. To make an educated, informed guess on how long this primacy will endure, we look to the Mongol empire (1206–1291) to draw comparison to the American empire (1945–?). Given the entrenched structure of the US-led liberal world order, even an attempt at providing a basis for predicting the demise of US primacy on the Mongol hegemony may be an act of foolhardiness. Yet the point here is that some similarities do exist, illustrated, for example, through the gradual loosening of the once-solid structure and functioning of the US-led liberal world order in handling currency from dollar-gold convertibility to inconvertibility and the restriction of use of US dollars only through US banks under US-led UN economic sanctions. Four important variables to consider are as follows: (1) the size and extent of their global governance structures; (2) the use of scare tactics and aggressive threatening language toward other states as part of a psychological strategy to undermine other states' sense of ability (threatening wholesale elimination on mutually assured destruction); (3) the maintenance of strong long-distance communications; (4) the decision to not implement a single imperial currency policy (Mongols used military coupons for a significant portion of the thirteenth century, while the US chose not to tie the US dollar to gold in 1971 and further even to use currency trade since 1985 to make the US dollar be only to be undervalued vis-à-vis other major currencies). Based, in particular, on the length of use of military coupons by the Mongol empire and the unilateral decision by the United States to end dollar convertibility to gold, I speculate that US primacy will end by 2030 or 2050. (Cf. Immerwahl 2019).

Of course, any speculation of such a matter will more than likely fail. That said, when US hegemony ends, some predict a world without leadership. Other predictions include the continuation of a global governance structure that contains many of the features of the liberal world order post-2008 but takes on a new form through the process of restoration and consolidation of the selected features.

References

Axelrod, R. (1976). Decision for neoimperialism: the deliberations of the British Eastern Committee in 1918. In *Structure of decision: The cognitive maps of political elites* (pp. 77–95). Princeton: Princeton University Press.

Carroll, L. (2016). *Alice in wonderland collection: All four books*. London: Create Space Independent Publishing Platform.

Cooper, R. (2004). *The breaking of nations: Order and Chaos in the Twenty-first Century*. London: Grove Press. reprint edition.

Gilpin, R. (1981). *War and change in world politics*. Princeton: Princeton University Press.

Gourevitch, P. (1978). The second image reversed: The international sources of domestic politics. *International Organization, 32*(4), 881–912.

Hathaway, O., & Shapiro, S. (2016). *The internationalists: How a radical plan to outlaw war remade the world*. New York: Simon and Schuster.

Immerwahr, D. (2019). *How to hide an empire: A short history of the greater United States*. New York: Farrar, Straus and Giroux.

Inoguchi, T. (2010). World order debates in the twentieth century: Through the eyes of the two-level game and the second image (Reversed). *Chinese Journal of International Politics, 3*(2), 155–188.

Kaplan, M. (1957). *System and process in international politics*. New York: Wiley.

Kissinger, H. (2000). *A world restored*. London: Weidenfeld and Nicolson.

Lake, D. (1983). International economic structures and American foreign economic policy, 1887–1934. *World Politics, 35*(4), 517–543.

Lamy, P. (2005). Beikoku daitoryo sen go. (After the U. S. Presidential Election), *Mainichi shinbun*, November 20.

McNeill, W. (2001). *The Conservation of catastrophe*. Available from: https://www.nybooks.com/articles/2001/12/20/the-conservation-of-catastrophe/. Accessed 11 June 2018.

McNeill, W., & Kindleberger, C. (1989). Control and catastrophe in human Affairs. *Daedalus, 118*(1), 1–15.

Mill, J. S. (2007). *The history of British India*. New Delhi: Atlantic Publishers & Distributors.

Mimaki, S. (2016). *Senso Ihoka Undo no Jidai (The development of international political thought during the "Twenty Years" crisis in the United States)*. Nagoya: Nagoya University Press.

Moore, B. (1964). *Social origins of dictatorship and democracy: Lord and peasant in the making of the modern world*. Boston: Beacon Press.

Putnam, R. (1988). Diplomacy and domestic politics: The logic of two-level games. *International Organization, 42*(3), 427–460.

Scharre, P. (2018). *Army of none: Autonomous weapons and the future of war*. New York: W. W. Norton.

Sen, A. (1981). *Poverty and famines: An essay on entitlement and deprivation*. Oxford: Clarendon Press.
Steil, P. (2018). *The marshall plan: Dawn of the cold war*. New York: Simon and Schuster.
Tenner, E. (2004). Results tagged: Conversion of catastrophe. *The Atlantic Wire*, April 27
UNESCO. (1955). *UNESCO charter*. Paris: UNESCO.
Waltz, K. (1959). *Man, the State and war*. New York: Columbia University Press.

Chapter 12
Theory of Civilizational Clash

Abstract This chapter examines the politics of civilizational clash focusing on Samuel Huntington (The clash of civilizations and the remaking of world order. Simon and Schuster, New York, 1997). It has been given enormous attention after the Cold War once capitalist democracy prevailed over communist dictatorship. 'Democracy is the only game in town' has become a cliche and in turn civilizational clash has seemingly replaced democracy as the *zeigeist* of the post-Cold War global politics. Religiously flavored and adversarially toned, the theory of civilizational clash was propounded by Huntington. Collet and Inoguchi (Jpn J Polit Sci 13(Part 4):553–585, 2012) has tested its four hypotheses against AsiaBarometer Survey data and shown that overall they are not empirically and theoretically valid. Perhaps most importantly, the subtlety, complexity and the context-dependency of culture are not very well understood and skillfully handled as Foucault and Bagehot advise.

Samuel Huntington's thesis on the clash of civilizations has sparked widespread debate and discussion. We add to this conversation by examining his thesis using examples from Asia. The framework for this Chapter is taken from an article in the *Japanese Journal of Political Science*, which I jointly co-authored with Christian Collet (Collet and Inoguchi 2012). Let us start by discussing the state of world politics that led Huntington to propose such a thesis. The theory of civilizational clashes emerged after 1989 with the end of the Cold War. Some academics believed that the end of the East-West ideological confrontation meant resuming the balance of power as embraced by realists and neo-realists (Waltz 2000; Mowle and Sacko 2007). Yet others viewed the dissolution of the Soviet Union after years of ideological hostility as a victory for democracy, reflected in the popular saying, "Democracy is the only game in town" (Fukuyama 1992). Other academics and policy analysts believed that the United States had won the Cold War and accordingly, had become the dominant power in terms of might, wealth, and ideology (i.e., democracy) (Posen 2003). Against this intellectual milieu, Huntington argued that world politics would become a very fervent, adversarial form of "us" versus "them," but instead of contesting might and wealth, religious and cultural identities would form the dividing lines as religiously defined civilizations would push back again the cultural

T. Inoguchi, L. T. Q. Le, *The Development of Global Legislative Politics*,
Trust: Interdisciplinary Perspectives 3, https://doi.org/10.1007/978-981-32-9389-2_12

hegemony of the West (Huntington 1997). Henry A. Kissinger praised Huntington's thesis of civilizational politics as the most stimulating work to emerge after 1989. How Huntington's civilizational clash theory fits into the book's focus must be made clear. Fukuyama's and Huntington's theories came in amidst the possible resurrection of the capitalist vs communist adversary in the form of democratic and civilizational thrusts. The resurrection of adversarial battles in the Cold War such as capitalism vs communism, democracy versus dictatorship did appear to be a real possibility to some. That is liberal democracy versus illiberal democracy (Zakaria 1997, Cf. Mikami and Inoguchi 2010). The resurrection of adversarial battles in the Cold War period did seem to be a possibility of different adversarial battles to some others. This time, the adversarial battles are to be waged amongst eight civilizations, especially Islam versus the West. This book is an interjection in the ideological battle of democracy versus autocracy (George W.F. Bush, Jr. used this term on the occasion of the 50th anniversary of the victory of World War II at Liga, Latvia (Inoguchi 1998) and the battle of different gods if civilizations can be said to revolve around different gods. In Huntington's analysis, Islam versus the West seems to be one of those adversarial battles likely to unfold in the present and in the near future. In the sense of ideologically adversarial battles to be waged between liberal democracy versus illiberal democracy or between Islam and the West, the conventional Cold War framework remains very strong. Not only might and wealth, but ideological dimensional elements should also come into the equation of post-Cold War politics, or so these pundits-cum-strategists appear to have thought. After comparing and contrasting power transition theory and civilizational conflict theory, the latter seems to be a variant of the conventional Cold War framework with ideological content being replaced by civilizations. The core of Huntington's thesis is three fold: (1) religion's influence is increasing in contrast to might and wealth; (2) the world can be divided into eight major religious civilizations—Islam, Christianity, Judaism, Confucianism, Hinduism, Buddhism, Shintoism, and animism; and most critical (3) the Islamic civilization and Chinese civilization will increasingly become more assertive, both in their global communication and behavior.

12.1 Empirical Testing of Huntington's Civilization Clash Hypotheses with Data from the AsiaBarometer Survey

Collet and Inoguchi (2012) empirically tested Huntington's hypotheses using the AsiaBarometer Survey (Inoguchi and Fujii 2013).

Hypothesis 1 For each civilization, member states and their respective citizens will identify more strongly with the key state of that civilization than with citizens that reside in a different civilization.

Hypothesis 2 An increase in public religiosity among member states within a civilization is accompanied by an improvement in perception toward inside core state members and a deterioration of perception toward outside core state members.

Hypothesis 3 An increase in public nationalism among member states within a civilization is accompanied by an improvement in perception toward inside core state members and a deterioration of perception toward outside core state members.

Hypothesis 4 An increase in exposure to foreign cultures among member states within a civilization is accompanied by an improvement in perception toward inside core state members and a deterioration of perception toward outside core state members.

To illustrate our findings, we used more current events than those used by Huntington in his own work, following the end of the Cold War.

We provided the following recent example for Hypothesis 1. According to this hypothesis, states within the Sinic civilization—Vietnam, South Korea, Taiwan, and Japan—should be more open and sympathetic to China's Belt and Road Initiative than states outside this civilizational sphere, such as Pakistan, India, Bangladesh, and Sri Lanka.

Our findings indicated that Hypothesis 1 was empirically incorrect. The group of states within the civilization was more suspicious and skeptical of the overall plan than the latter group of states at least during the initial stages of China's plan. For the Sinic group of states, past geo-historical conflicts with China weigh heavy and create resistance toward this grand Chinese plan. China's aggressive and forceful assertions on sovereignty claims in the South China Sea, East China Sea, and Yellow Sea negatively influence the Sinic states' perception. In contrast, the latter group, though initially receptive to China's grand infrastructure scheme, have over time become more cautious and critical of the plan.

We provided the following recent examples for Hypothesis 2. According to this hypothesis, Indonesia, whose population is 95% Muslim, should be more sympathetic to the Iranians in the US decision to withdraw from the Iranian nuclear deal and Indonesian perceptions of the United States should also decrease.

Our findings indicated that Hypothesis 2 was, more or less, empirically collaborated.

We provided the following recent example for Hypothesis 3. According to this hypothesis, because Vietnam is an inside member state of the Sinic civilization, the Vietnamese should have increasing positive perceptions of China and equally deteriorating perceptions of the United States.

Our findings indicate that Hypothesis 3 was empirically incorrect. Vietnam is cautious in its approach to China and its perception of the United States is improving. Again, China's determination to establish territorial claims in the South China Sea in contested claims with Vietnam have negatively impacted Vietnamese opinion, irrespective of growing bilateral economic relations between the two states. In comparison, the relationship between Vietnam and the United States is now viewed as a "strategic partnership."

We provided the following recent example for Hypothesis 4: As the number of Australians studying Chinese language grows, Australians' perception of China improves and their perception of the United States deteriorates.

Our findings indicate that Hypothesis 4 is empirically incorrect. Chinese imports of Australian fossil fuels, coal and iron ore, makes Australia dependent on its Asian trade partner, but the absence of a solid alliance with the United States makes Australia feel insecure.

Before reviewing the test results, we will outline the research objectives of the AsiaBarometer Survey project, the data source for our empirical test of Huntington's hypotheses. Collet and Inoguchi (2012) empirically tested Huntington's hypothesis using the AsiaBarometer Survey (Inoguchi and Fujii 2013). The AsiaBarometer Survey is a quality-of-life-focused survey conducted via face-to-face interviews with 52,215 respondents in 29 Asian countries found in East Asia, Southeast Asia, South Asia, and Central Asia in addition to three Western countries—the United States, Australia, and the Russian Federation. The data pooled for our empirical testing occurred in four waves during 2005 and 2008. In 2005, the survey was carried out in Afghanistan, Bangladesh, Bhutan, India, the Maldives, Mongolia, Nepal, Pakistan, Sri Lanka, and the predominantly Islamic states of the former Soviet Union. In 2006, the survey included Japan, China, South Korea, Hong Kong, Singapore, Taiwan, and Vietnam. In 2007, the survey extended to Cambodia, Indonesia, Laos, Malaysia, the Philippines, and Thailand. In 2008, the survey again included China, India, and Japan but also looked to include Australia, Russia, and the United States. Overall, the aggregated data include eleven predominantly Islamic societies, seven Buddhist societies, five Sinic societies, four Western societies, two predominantly Hindu societies, one Orthodox society (Russia), and Japan—a region that represents a mixture of seven of Huntington's civilizations. For qualifications on the use of data from the AsiaBarometer Survey, see Collet and Inoguchi (2012).

The influence of core states and how the public of other states perceived it was tested with the question: "Do you think the following countries have a good influence or a bad influence on your country?" The dependent variable was core state influence and was tested in Collet and Inoguchi (2012). The core states were Iran, the United States, and China. The investigation sought to determine how Western-oriented and Islamic-oriented states in Asia perceive these core states and how the perception of influence compares. Of the three spheres of influence, Chinese influence is viewed most negatively by Mongolians and Japanese; public assessment by Americans and Taiwanese also view Chinese influence as "bad"; and neutral opinions are held by Russians and Australians. On how power of the three core states is viewed, Chinese power is regarded in more favorable terms in Islamic Asia than in states in the Sinic civilization category. South Korea and Vietnam view Chinese power as substantially negative or hold neutral opinions. Pakistan and Afghanistan belong to those who are most consistently positive toward Chinese influence. Iranian power is regarded most favorably by predominantly Islamic states in Asia, such as Tajikistan and Pakistan, while a more critical attitude is held in Kazakhstan and Uzbekistan. There is more variation in attitudes toward US influence than toward Chinese or Iranian influence. Among Asian states, Cambodia and the Philippines have the most favorable attitudes with regard to US influence, whereas Russians have the least favorable attitudes. Among Islamist Asian states, the general trend is

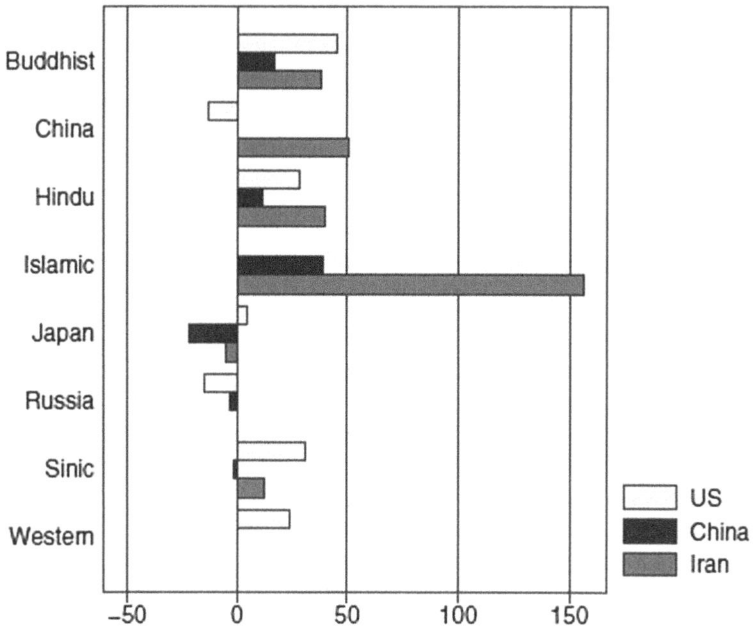

Fig. 12.1 Percent change in odds of seeing core states as a "good" influence, by civilization \ vis-à-vis the reference group (Islamic for the US, Western for China and Iran), with other factors held at their means

neutral with Malaysia and Indonesia as the exception, registering negative opinions toward US influence. The outlying negative views of these two states are offset by the positive attitude held in Afghanistan and Tajikistan. Chinese attitudes toward US influence register mostly "bad"; Australians and Japanese are more ambivalent; and Indians view US influence in generally good terms.

Other independent variables considered in relation to Hypotheses 2–4, include religiosity, nationalism, and foreign exposure. Apart from the following observations, for a summary of findings see Fig. 12.1 in Collet and Inoguchi (2012). We found two main categories of public religiosity and nationalism in Islamic Asia: the citizens of Indonesia, Malaysia, Bangladesh, and the Maldives show high degrees of religiosity and high nationalism, compared to Turkmenistan, Kazakhstan, Kyrgyzstan, and Tajikistan who register low religiosity and low nationalism. Two exceptions are Afghanistan that registers high religiosity and low nationalism and Pakistan that registers high religiosity and high nationalism. Of the respondents in Sinic states, China, Taiwan, Vietnam, and South Korea register low religiosity and high nationalism, and Japan stands out as the exception, indicating moderate religiosity and moderate nationalism. A number of states do not follow the usual patterns for Sinic and Islamic states: Australia, Mongolia, Hong Kong, Singapore, Bhutan, Nepal, Laos, and Cambodia. American respondents distinguished themselves from their Australian counterparts by being more nationalistic and religious, thereby appearing more similar to the respondents in globally engaged Buddhist states, such as Japan, South Korea, Taiwan, Hong Kong, Vietnam, and Thailand. Filipino respondents also display a strong sense of nationalism and faith, similar to other Southeast Asian Islamic citizens (Indonesians and Malaysians) and Indian citizens.

12.2 Results of the Huntington Model Empirically Tested by the AsiaBarometer Dataset

The dependent variable (core state influence), the three independent variables (religiosity, nationalism, and foreign exposure), and the four control variables (standard of living, education, gender, and age) form the model specification. The Reference Group is employed to determine the probability of core states being viewed as a positive influence. The Reference Group is identified in Huntington's terms as the strongest potential adversary (1997, p. 245), that is by civilization vis-à-vis the Reference Group (Islamic for the United States, Western for China and Iran). For China and the United States, the results are mixed, but for Iran the results are fairly positive according to Huntington's hypothesis (Collet and Inoguchi 2012, p. 566, Fig. 12.1).

$$+\beta_{4ij}\left(foreign\ exposure\right)+\beta_{5ij}\left(standard\ of\ living\right)+\beta_{6ij}\left(education\right)$$

$$+\beta_{7ij}\left(gender\right)+\beta_{8ij}\left(age\right)+\beta_{9ij}\left(nationalism*religiosity\right)$$

The citizens of Australia, the Philippines, and Hong Kong are deemed Westernized societies, and therefore, should, in theory, demonstrate more affinity for the United States than the reference group (Islam); however, they are overshadowed by Buddhist and Sinic states outside China, which are South Korea, Taiwan, Vietnam, Thailand, and Japan. On this continuum, Russian and Chinese societies are less likely than Islamic societies to consider the United States a "good" influence. When examining attitudes toward Chinese influence, Sinic and Western societies demonstrate no statistically significant difference in attitudes. Respondents in predominantly Islamic states register the highest probability for favorably viewing Chinese influence. Japanese citizens are the least likely to view Chinese influence as "good," even when compared to their Western counterparts. The findings clearly support Huntington's hypothesis: states within the Islamic civilization are 156% more likely to hold a better opinion (one standard deviation) of Iranian influence than those Westernized states in Asia. Of the other civilizations tested, Chinese, Hindu, and Buddhist citizens also generally view Iranian influence in more favorable terms than the contrast group. Sinic states, although less distinguishable in their response, still meet a standard level of significance (p 0.05). Again, the Japanese public indicates that they are less likely to see Iranian influence as favorably as the reference group.

Without going into detail, the research and analysis of Collet and Inoguchi (2012) indicate that Huntington's characterization of the public's role and their inclination to differentiate between "us" and "them" in geopolitical terms is overstated. In Huntington's analysis, civilizational identities impact the structuring of global affairs. The empirical testing offered above provides sufficient evidence that Huntington's framework must be approached with caution and skepticism. Citizens in the Asia Pacific region do not automatically identify more closely with the core states within their civilizational grouping, and, vice versa, they do not necessarily consider the core states of competing civilizations more negatively. Religion and foreign exposure may also not be significant contributing factors to how core states of outside civilizations are viewed in public opinion. If the civilizational paradigm is to be used in comparative politics and international relations, then Peter Katzenstein's middle-ground framework that casts them as "weakly institutionalized orders" is more empirically credible (Katzenstein 2010; Cf. Grant 2019 on Walter Bagehot's view of civilization). From these results, we argue that our framework of global quasi-legislative behavior and its typological framework are better suited to structuring global politics at the macro level.

12.3 Difficulties in Sustaining Premises of Huntingtonian Hypotheses

Until now, we have focused on testing Huntingtonian hypotheses with data from the AsiaBarometer Survey. In the ensuing section, we take the next step in examining the empirical difficulties encountered when analyzing the basic premises of the theory of civilizational politics with respect to Asia. The two basic premises are: (1) religiosity as a primordial identity is the principal explanatory variable, and (2) the pivotal role of core states in influencing other member states within a civilization.

Measuring religiosity is a difficult task. The year-end world survey carried out by WIN-Gallup International (The World Independent Network of Market Research and the Gallup International Association) has a demographic question on religiosity.

In 2011 the subject of the year-end survey carried out by WIN-Gallup International was Fukushima's triple disasters and in 2016 it was US Presidential Election. The common questionnaire is used with a dozen or so questions in over 40–50 countries of the world.

Respondents are to select one category that best suits them from the following choices:

Roman Catholic, Protestant, Russian or Eastern Orthodox, Other Christian, Hindu, Muslim, Jewish, Buddhist, Other, Atheist/agnostic (or Nothing), Refused/DNK/Na

East Asia is mostly secular. The regional breakdown for those who identify as atheist or agnostic is as follows: 62.2% in China, 73.1% in Japan, 37.7% in South Korea, and 79% in Hong Kong. In South Asia, although the predominant religion is either Hinduism or Islam, other faiths still have a strong following, including Sikhism, Christianity, and Buddhism. In Southeast Asia, secularism along with Islam, Buddhism, and Christianity coexist. Southeast Asia is an intersection of civilizations that contains concentrated pockets of both Sino and Indo civilizations. In evaluating and assessing the primordiality of religion according to Huntington's premise, it is important to note the following: (1) that East Asia has a high degree of secularism and that Central Asia also has fairly strong secular tendencies, although to a lesser degree, and (2) that the identification of core states can be problematic. In the case of China, it has one formal ally in North Korea, but other states within the Sinic civilization have a complicated relationship with China that range in tone from friendly to hostile. In the case of India, although two of its neighbors are Islamic (Pakistan and Bangladesh) and the South Asian region has close to half a billion Muslims—making it the largest concentration of Muslims in the world, only 10.6% of India's population is Muslim. In contrast, the region of Southeast Asia is a mixture of religions: Indonesia has the largest Muslim population in the world; Thailand and Myanmar identify as predominantly Buddhist; the Philippines is largely Christian; and Central Asia has no core state. Collet and Inoguchi (2012) list the core state for East Asia as China (excluding Japan); the core state for the Asia Pacific states of Japan, Taiwan, the Philippines, and Australia as the United States; and the core state for the Islamist states of Indonesia, Pakistan, Bangladesh, India, Sri Lanka, Malaysia as Iran, even though it is outside the regional area. Moreover, Islamic terrorism occurs throughout the world from South and Southeast Asia to Western countries, the Middle East, and Africa.

Huntingtonian premises appear to overemphasize the role of religiosity and core states. To be fair, Huntington's clash of civilizations thesis should be analyzed globally with global data. Huntington's civilizations paradigm was an attempt to understand the post-Cold War era, after the end of the East-West confrontation. At times, the ever-shifting geo-political world conditions enhance the plausibility of Huntingtonian premises. Consider the following events from 1989 until the present: (1) the collapse of the Soviet Union and the crumbling of certain Middle East states due to US unilateralism (Afghanistan and Syria); (2) the continued destructive power of unilateralism, this time by Russia in Crimea, the Ukraine, and Middle East; (3) the inaction and mixed response of the European Union on issues requiring principled decisions, such as refugees, the euro, Brexit, authoritarianism, and democratic populism; and (4) the US decision to pull out of the Iranian nuclear deal. Yet as long as the focus is on religiosity, civilizations, and core states' influence within "civilizations," the challenge to sustain a clash of civilization theory is significant.

12.4 Some Merits of Huntingtonian Thrust

Despite the conceptual shortcomings of Huntington's theory in terms of religion and core state, there are positive attributes to his framework that should be acknowledged. They are: (1) the growing role that religion and civilization play in the world, and (2) the intricate and sophisticated levels of political interactions throughout the world.

With regard to the former, a global phenomenon is the rise of religion in world politics since the end of the East-West confrontation in 1989 and the collapse of the Soviet Union in 1991 (Inoguchi 2007a, b). This phenomenon occurs as the world transitions from materialism or modernism to post-materialism or post-modernism (Inglehart 1997). The values and norms of materialism center on survival, whereas the values and norms of post-materialism center on social relations. The argument is that there is a hierarchy of needs and once survival needs are mostly met, then people's attention moves to social relations, such as leisure and sports (Inglehart and Welzel 2005). In a post-modern world, religion and taking time to attend faith services becomes part of the values and norms. Some research draws associations between pre-modernism, modernism, and post-modernism with geo-historical areas, such as Africa, Asia, and the Atlantic, respectively (Cooper 2004). However, such an understanding of world politics is difficult to confirm due to the turmoil and upheaval occurring in US and European politics. In the United States, evangelicalism is increasing (Putnam and Campbell 2012) and Donald Trump's mantra of "America first" is divisive. In Europe, the challenge is European populism that rejects the region's standardization of rules and regulations, the free flow of trade and services—that extended to the free movement of people, and the currency unification that commenced over two decades ago. In Inglehart and Welzel's world values map, the US position for two dimensions on the values map is similar to that of Sub-Saharan African. The two dimensions are secular vs. religious and open vs. protective. The overlap between the United States and the African region is more pronounced in the former dimension. European populism contests critical values of the EU, such as rule of law, free trade and market access, democracy, observance of international law and institutions, and equality of people—irrespective of gender, race, income, education, and religion. For several Asian countries, the impressive rise of income levels and gross national product (GNP), headed by China and India, does not fit with the shift from materialism to post-materialism. This is especially true in East and Southeast Asia, where the countries with the highest income and GNP reflect an equal emphasis on materialism and post-materialism. Countries' positions along the secular and protective dimensions combined with an ongoing concern for survival and security are readily apparent. The world is increasingly complicated and, for some, more chaotic when viewed along these lines.

With regard to the latter, just as critical to the complexity of our world are the levels on which global politics occurs and the units that ignite change. World politics is transitioning away from conventional international politics to unpredictable transnational politics. At one time, the standard levels of analysis required to clearly understand international relations were the individual, domestic society, and international system (Waltz 1959; Singer 1961; Evans et al. 1993; Gourevitch 1978). In this new century, especially since 2008, the world has been changing rapidly, substantially, and subtly (Sharma 2016; Bremmer 2013). Too many unknown knowns and unknown unknowns exist. The strength of Huntington's work is its prescient realization of the changing nature of world politics that is full of complexity and unpredictability. His weakness is his foresight and ability to persuade readers with a well-built argument, using materials of time and space most familiar to him. The take away here is that the new century is dramatic and fast paced. (For different approaches to civilizations, see Coker 2019, Debray 2019, Patterson 1992).

References

Bremmer, I. (2013). *Every nation for itself: Winners and losers in a G-zero world* (Reprint ed.). New York: Portfolio Penguin.

Coker, C. (2019). *The rise of the civilizational state*. Cambridge: Polity.

Collet, C., & Inoguchi, T. (2012). Is globalization undermining civilizational identities? A test of Huntington's core state assumptions among the publics of greater Asia and the Pacific. *Japanese Journal of Political Science, 13*(Part 4), 553–585.

Cooper, R. (2004). *The breaking of nations: Order and chaos in the twenty-first century* (Reprint ed.). London: Grove Press.

Debray, R. (2019). *Civilization: How we all became American*. London: Verso.

Evans, P., Jacobson, H., & Putnam, R. (Eds.). (1993). *Double-edged diplomacy: International bargaining and domestic politics*. Berkley: University of California Press.

Fukuyama, F. (1992). *The end of history and the last man*. London: Penguin.

Gourevitch, P. (1978, Autumn). The second image reversed: The international sources of domestic politics. *International Organization, 32*(4), 881–912.

Grant, J. (2019). *Bagehot: The life and times of the greatest Victorian*. New York: W. W. Norton.

Huntington, S. (1997). *The clash of civilizations and the remaking of world order*. New York: Simon and Schuster.

Inglehart, R. (1997). *Modernization and postmodernization: Cultural, economic, and political change in 43 societies*. Princeton: Princeton University Press.

Inglehart, R., & Welzel, C. (2005). *Modernization, cultural change, and democracy: The human development sequence*. Cambridge: Cambridge University Press.

Inoguchi, T. (1998). Japan's foreign policy under US unipolarity: Coping with uncertainty and swallowing some bitterness. *Asian Journal of Political Science, 6*(2), 1–20.

Inoguchi, T. (2007a). How to assess world war II in world history: One Japanese perspective. In D. K. W. Hock (Ed.), *Legacies of world war II in south and east Asia* (pp. 138–151). Singapore: Institute of South and East Asian Studies.

Inoguchi, T. (2007b, June 27–28). Religion, peace and international relations in Asia. *Meeting of Experts of the International Commission for Peace Research*, United Nations Educational, Scientific and Cultural Organization, pp. 19–23.

Inoguchi, T., & Fujii, S. (2013). *The quality of life in Asia: A comparison of quality of life in Asia*. Dordrecht: Springer.

Katzenstein, P. (2010). A world of plural and pluralist civilizations: Multiple actors, traditions, and practices. In P. Katzenstein (Ed.), *Civilizations in world politics: plural and pluralist perspectives* (pp. 1–40). London: Routledge.

Mikami, S., & Inoguchi, T. (2010). Diagnosing the micro foundation of democracy in Asia: Evidence from the AsiaBarometer survey, 2003–2008. In Y.-w. Chu & S.-l. Wong (Eds.), *East Asia's new democracies: Deepening, reversal, non-liberal alternatives* (pp. 246–292). London: Routledge.

Mowle, T., & Sacko, D. (2007). *The unipolar world: An unbalanced future*. New York: Palgrave Macmillan.

Patterson, O. (1992). *Freedom: Vol. 1: Freedom in the making of western culture* (Reprint ed.). New York: Basic Books.
Posen, B. (2003). *Restraint: A new foundation for U.S. grand strategy*. Ithaca: Cornell University Press.
Putnam, R., & Campbell, D. (2012). *American grace: How religion divides and unites us*. New York: Simon & Schuster.
Sharma, R. (2016). *The rise and fall of nations: Forces of change in the post-crisis world*. New York: W. W. Norton.
Singer, J. D. (1961). The level-of-analysis problem in international relations. *World Politics, 14*(1), 77–92.
Waltz, K. (1959). *Man, the state, and war: A theoretical analysis*. New York: Columbia University Press.
Waltz, K. (2000). *Theory of international politics*. New York: Waveland Press.
Zakaria, F. (1997). The rise of illiberal democracy. *Foreign Affairs, 76*(6), 22–47.

Chapter 13
Theory of Global Legislative Politics

Abstract The theory of global legislative politics claims a perspective revolution of a sort in international relations research. We argue that instead of focusing on sources of power like wealth, might and ideology, i.e., the trinity of the Cold War period, and instead of focusing on communication messages in international relations, we had better examine the interaction modes and attributes of communications in international relations. When digitalized globalization permeates each and every part of the earth, the distinction between the three levels of analysis, i.e., individual, domestic (national) and international, has ceased to function neatly. Everything is connected to everything else; connectivity functions closely with vulnerability; complexity contains unpredictability. The development of multilateral treaties has played a key role in shaping and sharing an unprecedented liberal world order under digitalized globalization with two conditions: decline of use of violence and growth of democracy.

This chapter articulates the theory of global legislative politics. To begin, we start with the following definition of politics—the need to get things done collectively and voluntarily on a global scale. This is an ordinary definition that involves three major elements, the first of which is encapsulated by the voluntary and diverse nature of the concept. Collectively is meant to include sovereign states, global citizens, transnational social movements, international organizations, and non-governmental organizations. In other words, global legislative politics cannot be subsumed by state-centric international relations as proclaimed by realism or neo-realism. Voluntarily means that participation is based on the accord decided by sovereign states. To join or not to join is up to sovereign states. Therefore, there is no world assembly where a fixed number of legislative members are selected or elected. Rather sovereign states decide on the basis of their calculation and aspiration to be a legislator or not, on a case-by-case basis. In other words, global legislative politics cannot be subsumed by institutions theorized and practiced in their domestic/national societies. On a global scale, it is meant to include all kinds of legislation. This includes not only an ordinary legislation as practiced in sovereign states but also a declaration of solidarity of those similarly minded across borders; a collective

T. Inoguchi, L. T. Q. Le, *The Development of Global Legislative Politics*,
Trust: Interdisciplinary Perspectives 3, https://doi.org/10.1007/978-981-32-9389-2_13

determination to reduce negative phenomena such as crime, poverty, discrimination by race, gender, and religion; and a collective action to restrain and/or punish violations of the prohibition against violence, of free and fair trade, and of the rule of law. In other words, global legislative politics cannot be subsumed by constructivism of sorts whereby norms, values, and memories of historical experiences on various social settings come to the fore.

The second major element of global legislative politics is that it includes such matters as settling on standards to uniform gauging (e.g., use of meters, health standards); guideline setting (e.g., poverty definition, working hours per week); crediting to inventors and innovators; respecting human dignity and rights; settling disputes without resorting to violence (peacekeeping operations, collective security, economic sanctions); sustaining global commons (e.g., climate change, ocean resources, outer space, water, and inhabitable space); easing communications and commerce (e.g., regulations on hacking, suing courts, economic sanctions). All these issues exist beyond the distinction between high politics and low politics and the distinction between sovereign states and global citizens. In other words, global legislative politics is transnational politics. In Kofi Annan's words, it deals with "problems without passports."

The third major element of global legislative politics is that this form of global governance tries to eliminate, to the extent possible, politics framed by the adversarial terms of "us" and "them." The primary task of global legislative politics is to get things done, leaving all the adversarial bilateral issues to international relations of power politics. In reformulating what otherwise would be adversarial bilateral politics to multilateral politics in which the "us" and "them' adversary and acrimony therebetween can be discouraged and possibly tamed. In other words, global legislative politics is a kind of non-violent participatory politics on a global scale.

War and peace used to be the juxtaposition of two alternatives confronting sovereign states that were forced to choose from in defense of the honor of sovereignty. During times of peace, bilateral agreements dominated multilateral agreements. Multilateral agreements used to be rare. However, already in the late nineteenth century, *A World Connecting 1870–1945* (Rosenberg 2012; Cf. Howard 2012) evidenced the gradual and steady increase of multilateral treaties, especially on peace settlements, tariffs, health, and migration. In 1945, when the United Nations was established, multilateral treaties and joint declarations began to cover such policy domains as intellectual property rights, the environment, and human rights (Iriye 2004; Le et al. 2014; Inoguchi and Le 2016; Inoguchi 2018).

The number of military deaths, separate from civilian deaths, during times of war in the last 80 or so years informs the transformation of the international system. During this 80 year span, we have experienced three distinct periods: the war period of 1938–1945, the Cold War period between 1945 and 1989, and the post-Cold War period since 1989 until the present. War-related deaths of those actively engaged in war per year are: 5 million for the war period, 100,000 for the Cold War period, and 10,000 for the post-Cold War period (Inoguchi 2015). These figures were calculated on the basis of war-related deaths (excluding civilians) per year as registered in the International Institute of Security Studies in 2017.

Yet the advent of the new millennium has heralded something new: transnationalism (Iriye 2004; McGrew and Held 2007; Davies 2014; Murphy 1994; Tallberg et al 2013; Vertovec 2009; Anderson 2002; Iwabuchi 2002). Some examples of transnationalism include: transnational terrorism of human beings and cyber communications; transnational social movements on gender and human rights; and transnational laws regulating investment, tax, and currency. In tandem with the enhancement of connections among different parts of the world, in terms of commodity, migration, currency and communication, the need to create transnational legislation to regulate the flow of such things has increased by leaps and bounds; such legislation is bound to take the form of a multilateral treaty.

Before developing the global legislative theory, we need to have a summary grasp of multilateral treaties focusing on (1) six policy domains (human rights, peace and disarmament, environment, intellectual property, trade, commerce and communications, labor, health and safety), as categorized in the United Nations depository; (2) year of deposit; (3) type of membership (type A: unpopular (currently not many members), type B: steady increase, type C: popular (not many at the start but at certain point membership rose), type D: popular (with very many from the start); (4) name of the ten geo-historico-cultural groups by Christian Welzel (2013) in a modified form ((a) Indic East: South Asia and Southeast Asia, (b) Islamic East: the Middle East and North Africa, (c) Latin America: All the Americas minus the United States and Canada, (d) New West: New settler societies like the US, Canada, Australia, and New Zealand, (e) Old West: West since the Roman Empire such as Italy, France, and Spain, (f) Orthodox East: Russia, Macedonia, Bulgaria, Ukraine, (g) Reformed West: West since the Reformation such as Germany, Sweden, Denmark, (h) Sinic East: China, Korea, Vietnam, Japan, Taiwan, (i) Sub-Saharan Africa: This needs no explanation, (j) Returned West: West since the end of the Cold War such as Poland, Czech Republic, Hungary, Latvia; and (5) number of Current Members as of 2014. (The full list of multilateral treaties 1945–2014 appears at Appendix 1.)

For a brief overview of the 120 analyzed multilateral treaties, 18 treaties are provided brief annotations: (1) policy domain, (2) treaty name, (3) type of membership, (4) number of current membership, as of 2014.

The different types are indicated below:

Type A: Extremely unpopular
Type B: Steady increase
Type C: Not very popular at the start but at a certain point, membership rose
Type D: Popular with a great many members from the start

Human Rights

T3: International Convention on the Elimination of All Forms of Racial Discrimination (1966)

Type C. The current number of members is 174. 66% are occupied by non-Western states.

T9: The Convention on the Elimination of All Forms of Discrimination against Women (1980)

Type D. It is one of the few conventions that enjoyed popularity from the start. There are currently 185 registered members.

T14: International Convention on the Protection of the Rights of All Migrant Workers and Members of their Families (1993)

Type A and has 46 registered members. States in Sinic East, Old West, Reformed West, New West, and Returned West are not members.

Peace and Disarmament

T24: Convention on Prohibition or Restrictions on the Use of Certain Conventional Weapons which may be Deemed to be Excessively Injurious or to Have Indiscriminate Effects, Geneva (1980)

Type C and has 115 registered members.

T31: Comprehensive Nuclear-Test Ban Treaty

Type D and has 184 registered members.

T44: International Convention for the Suppression of Acts of Nuclear Terrors (2005)

Type B and has 91 registered members.

Environment

T48: Convention concerning the Protection of the World Cultural and Natural Heritage (1973)

Type C and has 185 registered members. Almost all the countries of the Islamic East, Indic East, and Sinic East are members.

T53: UN Convention on the Law of Sea (1982)

Type C and has 160 registered members. China's rise has coincided with the increase in maritime disputes. Almost of all the states in the Islamic East, Indic East, and Sinic East are members.

T62: UN Framework Convention on Climate Change (1992)

Type D and has 191 registered members.

Intellectual Property

T72: Universal Copyright Convention (1955)

Type B and has 99 registered members.

T75: World Intellectual Property Organization (1970)

Type C and has 185 registered members.

T77: Patent Cooperation Treaty (1978)

Type C and has 146 registered members.

Trade, Commerce, and Communication

T86: International Monetary Fund (1945)

Type C and has 187 registered members.

T88: Convention on International Civil Aviation (1945)

Type B and has 169 registered members.

T89: International Standardization Organization (1947)

Type B and has 88 registered members.

Labor Standard and Relations

T101: Abolition of Forced Labor Convention (1957)

Type B and has 169 registered members.

T111: Occupational Safety and Health Convention (1981)
Type B and has 60 registered members.
T118: Worst Forms of Child Labor Convention (1999)
Type D and has 175 registered members.

The number of multilateral treaties has increased steadily since 1945; currently, there are more than 560 major multilateral treaties. The number of international organizations and their offshoots, which are fountains of multilateral treaties, amounts to more than 8000 (Hale et al. 2013; Hale and Held 2017). Yet international organizations and their offshoots have reached a saturation point (Hale et al. 2013; Hale and Held 2017). As if to symbolize the saturation of multilateral treaties, a number of actions designed to reduce the roles of multilateral treaties have recently been taken. Some recent examples of such multilateral setbacks are summarized below. Accordingly, it is the right moment for us to present a bigger picture of multilateral treaties in a theoretical context, in order to see the theory of global legislative politics in terms of its nature, structure, and function.

13.1 Contemporary Illustrations of Global Legislative Politics: From Saturation Gridlock to Exit from Multilateral Treaties and Reformation of Global Legislation

Of all the developments in global legislative politics, the most important are the saturation of international organizations and their offshoots, numbering some 8000 by 2016 (Hale and Held 2017, p. (4) and the gridlock (Hale et al. 2013) of global governance through multilateral treaties as evidenced by the following six events occurring in 2017–2019: (1) the British referendum on exiting from the European Union; (2) US withdrawal from, and possible future return to, the Paris climate change accord; (3) US withdrawal from the Trans-Pacific Partnership; (4) summit meeting between the United States and the Democratic People's Republic of Korea on the denuclearization of the Korean Peninsula and toward a Peace Treaty; (5) Chinese claim of maritime sovereignty in the South China Sea, contravening the International Court of Justice's judgment; and (6) US withdrawal from the Iran deal on nuclear development.

13.1.1 British Referendum on Exiting from the European Union

Within the historical context of Britain, the United Kingdom and the European continent are considered two separate and different entities; fog over the Dover Channel divides them, often making it physically impossible to even see the others' shore. Yet Britain, after being devastated in World War II and further deprived of vast colonies in the world, joined the European Community in 1973. The notion of such a community started with and grew from the Schengen Five (France, Italy, Belgium, West Germany, and the Netherlands). Britain's application to join was twice vetoed by France under President Charles de Gaulle in 1963 and in 1967. The Treaty of Maastricht, the constitutional basis of the European Union, signed in 1992, envisioned a common and unified currency. Britain opted not to adopt the Euro, the common currency, which metamorphosed from the deutsche mark, the strongest currency in Europe. Britain was not comfortable using the deutsche mark. However, Britain, being an otherwise complete European Union member, agreed through legislation to guarantee the free movement of goods, services, capital, and labor within the European market. Britain has received a vast number of member country immigrants who took up employment in England. Some argue that this influx deprived Britons of jobs, subsequently leading to growing discontentment with the European Union. After the Great Depression of 2008 and thereafter, discontentment magnified in the form of mushrooming political movements that supported the idea of Britain leaving the EU—that is, to exit from the most influential multilateral institution of the Continental Western Europe in the post-1945 liberal world order. Certain Britons were frustrated not only by the idea of immigrants taking their jobs but also by having to make recurring financial payments for the development of the southern and eastern EU members. Thus, Brexit seems to be "an elegy for that brief interregnum when the country had ceased to rule but was nonetheless dazzlingly cosmopolitan" (Taseer 2018). If the United States under President Donald Trump is caricatured by some as the "Turkmenistan on the Potomac," (Cohen 2017) the United Kingdom may be caricatured by others as the "Singapore on the Thames" (The Economist 2017). In sum, Brexit is a devastating blow to one of the most densely woven multilateral agreements in the world.

13.1.2 US Withdrawal from the Paris Climate Change Accord

As noted by scientists and pundits the world over, the world's climate has been changing on unprecedented levels and at unprecedented intensity since the new millennium. Yet the path toward reducing carbon dioxide emissions and investing in ways to prevent global warming from rising two degrees (celcius) above the levels of the Industrial Revolution in the late eighteenth century and the nineteenth century was contentious enough to prevent the 1997 Kyoto Protocol from moving forward. Two ideas helped break the Kyoto gridlock (1) reducing the target from 2 degrees to 1.5 degrees and (2) changing the universality of responsibility to nationally determined contributions for investment in mitigating carbon dioxide emissions. These changes prompted the United States under President Barack Obama and China under President Xi Jinping to be in agreement with the Paris climate accord. This support, from the two largest emitter states, was sufficient for the accord to become effective on November 8, 2016. Yet the newly-elected US President Donald Trump announced on June 1, 2017, that the United States would withdraw from the Paris accord and immediately cease implementing the accord and financial contributions. President Trump was elected largely by the fossil fuel industry and by discontented unemployed or less than fully employed whites in the Midwest and the Appalachians and by those who are climate change deniers and anti-abortion activists. The Paris climate change accord is one of the few multilateral treaties, in addition to the Treaty on the Prohibition of Nuclear Weapons, which was adopted by an overwhelming number of sovereign states. The former, however, is qualitatively different from the latter because the latter is not equipped with clauses to punish violators. Even so, all the nuclear weapons states and allies of the United States abstained, except for the Netherlands, which did not abstain from vote and opposed to the treaties. Now a question remains: what is likely to happen in its implementation? With the absence of the United States (accounting for 14.3% of global emissions in 2015), a free rider in the accord, China (accounting for 29.5% of global emissions in 2015) and the European Union (accounting for 9.6% of global emissions in 2015) must take on a leadership roles. India, Russia, and Japan must also do the same. China has been demonstrating its willingness to take on a leadership role by dramatically reducing carbon dioxide emissions in Beijing, a heavily polluted capital city where one could not live without a heavy-duty gasmask in the winter of 2017–2018.

13.1.3 Trans-Pacific Partnership Agreement

For years, the World Trade Organization has been plagued by gridlock in multilateral treaties, hampering the ability to further liberalize trade and investment multilaterally and universally. In contrast, a small country's initiative to liberalize and enhance trade, called the Trans-Pacific Strategic Economic Partnership Agreement, was signed in 2005. The original signatories were Singapore, Brunei, New Zealand, and Chile. Having witnessed the possibility of further liberalizing trade, the United States and many other states were interested in making a liberalizing and enforceable agreement in which more members would participate. This resulted in the Trans-Pacific Partnership Agreement being signed by 12 states on February 4, 2016. Signatories are, in addition to the original four, Australia, Peru, Vietnam, Malaysia, Mexico, Canada, Japan, and the United States. During the US presidential election campaign in 2016, Donald Trump expressed his disapproval of the Trans-Pacific Partnership (TPP) Agreement. After his election to the office of President, Trump announced the US withdrawal from the agreement on January 23, 2017. Those domains where the US disavows TPP clauses are related to investment, government procurement, intellectual property, environment, pharmaceuticals, and labor. As if to prevent the US-originated protectionist tide from overwhelming the liberalizing momentum of the Trans-Pacific Partnership Agreement, Japan ratified the TPP on January 20, 2017, while New Zealand did so on May 11, 2017. After further discussions and negotiations in 2017, the remaining 11 states developed the "Comprehensive and Progressive Agreement for Trans-Pacific Partnership" (CPTPP) in January 2018. Although the estimated benefits to signatories vary, those benefits will not be immediately significant; however, they will play an important role in vigorously counteracting protectionist tides. Some major trading states have already shown interest: South Korea, Indonesia, and China from the Pacific, and the United Kingdom, after Brexit, from Europe. The partial success of the so called TPP-11 derives from three principles: (1) liberalizing with enforceable clauses for many potential joiners; (2) starting with a small number of states while trying to be inclusive; (3) listening to major impediments of major trading powers by leaking those chapters of the 5600-page-long agreement (to which President Donald Trump commented that it is so long and complex that nobody would read it) that involve investment, government procurement, and environment in an effort to entice them to be joiners.

13.1.4 South China Sea Disputes

The complex South China Sea disputes involve many dimensions, including territorial, maritime navigation, maritime natural resources, and maritime security. The key treaty referred to in relation to South China Sea disputes is the United Nations Convention on the Law of Sea (UNCLOS). In the growing context of the North-South disparity in the third quarter of the last century, the UNCLOS instituted the Economic Exclusive Zone, a zone that does not exceed 200 nautical miles from the coast. This concept was added to the traditional practice of giving everyone freedom of navigation beyond three nautical miles off the coast. Additionally, the utilization of seabed resources was added as a new regulation. It is important to note that China is a party to the UNCLOS, whereas the United States is not. In 2010, China reportedly let it be known that the South China Sea is "an area of core interest" that is non-negotiable and is on par with Taiwan and Tibet on the national agenda. From the very beginning, territorial, economic, and security issues have been intricately involved in the South China Sea disputes. Brunei, China, Indonesia, Malaysia, the Philippines, Taiwan, and Vietnam all have territorial claims in one way or another. Most states in the Association of Southeast Asian Nations (ASEAN) claim fishing rights in the South China Sea. All the trading states, except China, claim freedom of navigation. Australia, India, and Japan have had disputes with China, one way or another, via some ASEAN states or in other areas. The United States claims the most traditional meaning of freedom of navigation, including intelligence operations carried out very close to the coast. It also bitterly opposes the creation of artificial islets and islands for territorial aggrandizement, economic activities, and military enhancement. China and the United States have been key actors in the South China Sea in that they often carry out military exercises, showcasing their strength to each other. China continues to construct huge island cities where military bases (including air fields and naval ports) are consolidated and naval and paramilitary boats are deployed, if necessary en mass, to stop other claimants' actions. The United States maintains a show of force and continues intelligence operations in and outside the South China Sea. China has been quite aggressive in appeasing

ASEAN states and Asian states along the One Belt and One Road initiative with economic assistance thereto. In particular, China is attentive to South Asian states such as Sri Lanka, Pakistan, and India; ASEAN states such as Malaysia, Thailand, Cambodia, and Laos; and South Pacific states such as Vanuatu, Micronesia, and Australia.

13.1.5 Iran Nuclear Deal

In 2015, Iran agreed to a long-term deal regarding its nuclear program with the permanent members of the United Nations Security Council, plus Germany. The Joint Comprehensive Plan of Action, covers uranium enrichment, the plutonium pathway, monitoring of covert activity, break-out time, and the lifting of sanctions. As nuclear weapon states in the West had suspected, Iran had been working hard toward nuclear development. Through this agreement, a compromise was struck to allow Iran to build nuclear power plants, while prohibiting its development of nuclear weapons in line with the Nuclear Non-Proliferation Treaty (NPT) and permitting the International Atomic Energy Agency to monitor nuclear matters in Iran. In regard to the NPT, emerging countries have expressed dissatisfaction with the NPT for two main reasons—first, because nuclear weapon states have not reduced their volume of nuclear weapons, and, second, because under the NPT guidelines, nuclear power plants are extremely difficult to build. The nuclear West, including the United States under President Obama, agreed to let Iran develop nuclear power plants in order to prevent Iran from increasing its influence in the Middle East and to keep Iran from becoming a nuclear weapon state that would pose a real menace to the European Union, Israel, and the United States. Since coming to power, President Donald Trump has withdrawn from the 2015 Iran deal; he decried the deal as contrary to the interests of the US and Israel, though others suspect that his aversion to the deal was partly due to the fact that the deal was made by his predecessor President Obama. Following the US withdrawal, the United States is imposing economic sanctions and extraordinary fines on any businesses and states that conduct business with Iran, acting as though the US federal government has become the government of a world republic.

13.1.6 Nuclear Weapons Prohibition Treaty

On July 7, 2017, the treaty to comprehensively prohibit nuclear weapons was passed with the goal of total elimination. To be effective, at least 50 signatures and ratifications are required. As of May 2018, only 11 states had ratified; those states are Austria, Cote d'Ivoire, Cuba, Guyana, the Vatican, Mexico, Palau, Palestine, Thailand, Venezuela, and Vietnam. For those states that are party to the treaty (i.e., ratified states), the treaty prohibits the development, testing, production, stockpiling, stationing, transfer, and use and threat of use of nuclear weapons. In addition, those states are prohibited from assisting or encouraging any of the prohibited activities. For nuclear armed states joining the treaty, it provides a time-bound framework for negotiations leading to the verified and irreversible elimination of their nuclear weapons program. None of the nuclear weapon states nor their allies participated in the voting process for this treaty. Of those who participated in the voting, the Netherlands opposed it and Singapore abstained. Overall, there were 69 states that did not vote, and 122 states that voted in favor of the treaty and 1 that voted against it (the Netherlands).

13.2 Key Characteristics of Global Legislative Politics in Comparison to Clash of Civilization Politics and Power Transition Politics

We categorized 120 multilateral treaties of the UN system into the following six categories of scope, as is defined by the United Nations Depository: peace and security; environment; labor, health and safety; trade, communications, and commerce; intellectual property; and human rights (See Appendix 2 for the entire list of these multilateral treaties). Across these categories are distinct features of global legislative politics. To highlight the distinctive differences of global legislative politics from clash of civilization politics and power transition politics, the comparisons are made based on the following key words:

Power Transition Politics → Vulnerability: power oppresses and prolongs potentials to implode and explode.

Civilizational Politics → Religion: binary adversarial relationship for the clash of civilization theory.

Global Legislative Politics → Agreement: collective acceleration of bonding aspiration and multilateral commitment of binding agreement constitutes global legislative politics.

Civilizational politics positions religion as the strongest guiding force of politics. Replacing might, wealth, and ideology, religion is becoming a strident force for determining international relations. It downgrades the power of democracy's sway after the Cold War, rejecting the idea that democracy is "the only game in town." Religion with a long history of survival and a sizable faithful population that is cemented by geography, history, and race constitute a core state of a civilization. There are eight such civilizations: Christianity, Islam, Hinduism, Buddhism, Judaism, Shintoism, Confucianism, and Animism (Huntington 1997).

Power transition politics ranks vulnerability as the most significant element of politics. Power oppresses and prolongs potentials to implode and explode. Power is enhanced by the clever use of population, technology, and social economic system whereby sovereign states acquire wealth and might most effectively in relation to others in order to become the hegemonic leader. In the process of accumulating power, states underestimates the degree of oppressed and prolonged potentials to implode and explode. Power and vulnerability are inherently tied to each other. Power transition takes place when global power mismanages the balance of power and mishandles marginalized have-nots' rebellious sentiments and actions.

Global legislative politics values aspiration and agreement over all else. When determining their actions, sovereign states examine both national citizens and other sovereign states. This political system is what Robert Putnam (1988) calls a two-level game. On the one hand, sovereign states oftentimes accommodate their citizens' preference while simultaneously pushing forward their own state preference in an amalgamated form. Thus, what we call *a bundle of global quasi-social contracts*, as distinguished from Rousseau's and Locke's social contracts, has to take into consideration three types of preferences: (1) citizens' preference in each national sovereign state; (2) each sovereign state's own preference as a key driver, (3) other sovereign states' preferences. To proceed from the first task of showing the significant correlation between citizens' preference in value orientation and sovereign states' preference, information about participation in multilateral treaties has to be presented. Multilateral treaties registered from the late nineteenth century till today (Rosenberg 2012, Iriye 2014) are mostly deposited in the United Nations Depository including those in the late nineteenth century and the former half of the twenty-first century. The World Values Survey data covers the steadily increasing population from some 10% to 90% between the 1970s and 2010s (Inglehart 2018, p.xvii). We have used the fifth wave data of World Values Survey conducted in 2005–2009. Due to the data availability, our test on the relationship between citizens' preference in value orientation and sovereign states' preference is limited to the sample of 93 states. However, this is not too much of limitation because these 93 states spread all around the globe, include the biggest economies and largest population from each world region (accounting for 90% of the world population) (Welzel 2013). The sample size is large enough to empirically test the correlation between citizens' preference in value orientation and sovereign states' preference.

After all, the original global social contract models, Rousseau's and Locke's are the products of roughly the years of 1789 and 1688 respectively. In the global social contract theory we treat Rousseau and Locke as if they were active circa in late seventeenth and late eighteenth centuries, i.e., in a pre-industrialization era let alone pre-globalization era. When we call our theory, global social contract theory, it is applied to the late nineteenth century when the interconnecting world was tangibly registered as such in the meticulously researched historical works by Rosenberg (2012) and Iriye (2014) onward till today. The interconnecting world in the form of multilateral treaties aimed at helping to resolve issues across and beyond states started earlier than the late nineteenth century. The late nineteenth century, World War I years, and its postwar years were heralding the new era of multilateral treaties. However, the steady deposits of multilateral treaties in international bodies were of phenomenal degree only in the dust of World War II, i.e., in the dawn of the United States-led liberal world order. Two key phenomena of globalization with a focus on global social contract are: a) liberalization and democratization with slogans at the American independence and the French Revolution, followed by

Woodrow Wilson's Fourteen Points and the League of Nations, the Crimea Summit, and the United Nations and b) digitalization *allegro ma non troppo* in the late twentieth and early twenty-first centuries, materializing instantaneous communications and transactions whereby mutual interdependence and vulnerability have become "normal". On the other, sovereign states play multilateral games with many other sovereign states through manipulation and maneuvering.

The inherent elements of multilateral treaties are: (1) the identification of problems; (2) drafting treaties by drafters; (3) mobilizing support by what will become founding members of sovereign states and associated specialized international organizations and transnational non-governmental organizations; and (4) the promulgation and ratification process. At each stage, diversity is immense. Multilateral treaties are not effective because, when a treaty's membership level is too low, its reach and impact is limited such that it cannot effectively construct global quasi-legislation.

As there is no world parliament where legislators are elected and vote for bills, the reasons why countries join or opt not to join multilateral treaties differs from country to country. This is why it is important to examine *global quasi-legislative behavior*—because each sovereign state has its own style of *global quasi-legislative behavior*. It is an increasing trend for multilateral treaties to deal with policy matters of global importance, such as free trade, climate change, terrorism, and nuclear nonproliferation. Therefore, it is necessary to analyze multilateral treaties within a framework for *global quasi-legislative behavior*.

These frameworks can also be viewed as *strategies*. Two types of *global quasi-legislative behavior* exist, (1) the strategy of enlarging and enhancing similarly minded countries without too many articles to bind members; (2) strategy of governing members' conduct through rigorously binding articles. The former is called the bonding strategy of compassion through solidarity, whereas the latter is called the mutual binding strategy of governance through effectiveness. Global legislative politics has much stronger elements of the former than national legislative politics. Multilateral legislative politics needs the kind of leadership that can promise and collect support for often uncertain legislative outcomes by emphasizing compassion and camaraderie. Oftentimes, multilateral agreements and arrangements contain the content of aspiration and agitation toward what self-claimed leaders think are their common goals. Such multilateral treaties resemble the kind of national constitutions that tend to be heavily influenced by the *zeitgeist* defining the prevailing spirit, heralding the advent of a new era. For example, we can see how the French Revolution impacted the constitutions of newly independent republics in Latin America; how the Fourteen Points of Woodrow Wilson and the League of Nations impacted the constitutions of newly independent states in Central and Eastern Europe; and how the United Nations Charter impacted the constitutions of newly independent states in Asia and Africa.

The latter type of multilateral treaty, which can be called an ordinary multilateral treaty, emphasizes the implementation of binding articles. It is important to note, however, that multilateral laws evolve first by declaring compassion toward common goals and then by governing on the basis of binding articles. For example, the

General Agreement on Tariffs and Trade evolved to become the World Trade Organization, and the UN Conference on Trade and Development evolved to become an UN organizational entity.

Closely associated with legislative strategy are *speed* and *angle. Speed* is important when drafting multilateral treaties, negotiating articles, promulgating multilateral treaties, ratifying them in parliament, and implementing them. Drafting tasks tend to be shouldered by specialists from all over the world and scientists in specialized international organizations and specialists, scientists, and pundits in countries that have accumulated experiences of global legislative politics since the nineteenth century, especially in Northwestern European states, i.e., the Reformed West in Northwestern Europe and the New West in North America and Oceania. Article negotiations tend to be carried out in places where drafting specialists are concentrated or to where they can conveniently travel. Northwestern Europe is frequently a choice location for negotiations, as it symbolizes the spirit of multilateral treaties. Treaty signing requires coordination among bureaucratic agencies at home. Some countries suffer from fissiparous tendencies of government while others do not. The former sometimes delay a quick signing, resulting in the loss of founding membership status. For example, Japan missed that chance when both the United States and China, both of which had long been hesitant to sign, suddenly reached an agreement on signing the Paris climate accord. Therefore, Japan who had led the G7 countries to issue the joint action on global environment at the annual G7 meeting in Hokkaido missed out on becoming a founding member of the Paris Accord. Ratification sometimes takes time; the United States is a noteworthy example of a country that regularly delays ratification or sometimes fails to ratify. The US often experiences poor executive-legislature relations, and thus, there have been many multilateral treaties that the US signed but did not ratify. The no less remarkable examples include International Covenant on Economic, Social and Cultural Rights (1966), Convention on the Elimination of All Forms of Discrimination against Women (1979), Convention on the Rights of the Child (1989), United Nations Convention on the Law of the Sea (1991), Convention on Biological Diversity (1992), Comprehensive Test Ban Treaty (1996), Kyoto Protocol (1997), Rome Statute of the International Criminal Court (1998), Convention on the Rights of Persons with Disabilities (2007), Convention on Cluster Munitions (2008), and Trans-Pacific Partnership (2016). Implementation often takes time. Though China ascended to the World Trade Organization, its required action items—trade liberalization and intellectual property rights—were stalled or implemented very slowly.

Angle matters because two broad orientations are not necessarily compatible with each other. Global common goods versus individual citizens' interests and rights often come up sharply and mutually contradictory of the other. Provisionally drafted or proposed global labor and health care standards may not easily be signed by some countries because they may be too restrictive, making implementation impossible. Similarly, people in some countries are poverty stricken, and some governments are perennially short of relevant personnel and financial resources to address the roots of poverty, making the protection of individual human dignity and rights inherently difficult.

The relationships between speed, angle and strategy in certain kinds of situations must be noted. When a multilateral treaty is of the type of aspirational bonding, whether it is human rights or peace, signing and ratifying can be carried on without punishment, because there are no such clauses of punishment. Rather, the aim is to join the commitment and chorus of aspiration and to enhance solidarity among like minded states. When a multilateral treaty is of the type of strict implementation with treaty clauses, leading to punishment, signing and ratifying are more carefully carried out or not carried out at all when the concerned policy domains are about labor and health or intellectual property right. Here the aim is to jointly achieve the higher level of health and labor standards or the respect and non-violation of intellectual property owners, set out by such a treaty.

13.3 Integrated Global Quasi-Legislative Mechanism

The subtitle of this book is *Rousseau and Locke Writ Global*. The subtitle explains that in this book both Rousseau's and Locke's mechanisms are articulated and then broadly integrated. Rousseau's mechanism is simple and straightforward; in Rousseau's mind, citizens' preferences are immediately and directly connected to the will of global citizens through the force of compassion. Therefore, the Rousseauesque mechanism works through empathy. In most of his other writings besides *The Social Contract*, reason and reasoning are predominant in giving his philosophical conclusion its crucial power. But only in *The Social Contract* does Rousseau resort to the force of compassion, which requires neither mediators nor megaphones. However, for his *Social Contract*'s theory to prevail, he constrains its geographical scope—for example, when discussing Corsica and Poland, he does not mention the key word, compassion. Judging from this omission, we may infer that the Rousseauesque world is confined to what may be called the Old West, that is, those European societies that have existed since the time of the Roman Empire. In other words, only in the advanced Europe of his time does compassion work (Fig. 13.1).

To determine that citizens' preferences about norms and values are major bases on which multilateral treaties are promulgated and ratified to make them reflect norms and values of global activities, we must find through empirical analysis a convergence and correlation between citizens' preferences about norms and values on the one hand and the willingness of many states to participate in multilateral treaties on the other. By so doing Rousseau's contention that compassion (about ideas and emotions) becomes instantaneously global is vindicated *as long as a covariance or correlation is of the positive figures, of certain magnitude*. Here the sovereign states' willingness is gauged by six instrumental variables that reflect the speed, the angle, and the strategy of sovereign states in joining multilateral treaties.

What about Locke's mechanism? Locke's mechanism is a set of often routinized legislation and sometimes unusual quasi-legislation at multiple levels, occurring in many places on a global scale. Globally, Locke's mechanism begins at subnational levels, such as non-governmental organizations, local social movements, and youth

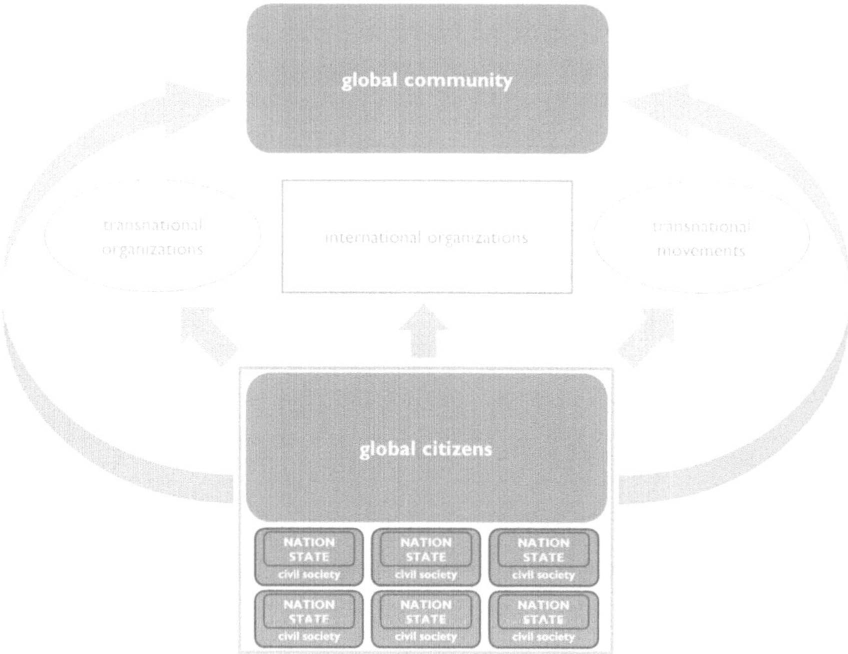

Fig. 13.1 Rousseauesque Global Citizens and Community through Instantaneous and Ubiquitous Digital Reach

business organizations; or at national levels, such as the national parliament and national labor union; or at regional levels, such as regional international organizations; or at transnational levels, such as transnational social movements, transnational terrorist groups, and transnational football associations. Coordinating different levels of legislation that cover each and every part of global society may be a difficult task (Fig 13.2).

To determine if the Lockean scheme of parliamentary representation is manifested in a global quasi-legislative arena, i.e., multilateral treaties, the diversity within the community in adhering to rules and norms in quasi-legislating multilateral treaties needs to be empirically verified. Again the six instrumental variables are used. The results are illustrated by the diverse locations of each and every society, and further by the diverse societies among Asian states.

In our framework, the Lockean legislative process is subsumed within sovereign states that take consider, more or less, the preferences observed at home and abroad with the two-level game of Putnam (1988) and the second-image reversed (Gourevitch 1978) concept. Since we empirically tested Huntingtonian hypotheses one to four, this simplification is very important. This simplification does not disregard the many legislative processes; instead, it takes into account such subnational, international, and transnational legislative processes with sovereign states acting on their behalf when they calculate and decide whether to join or not join multilateral treaties.

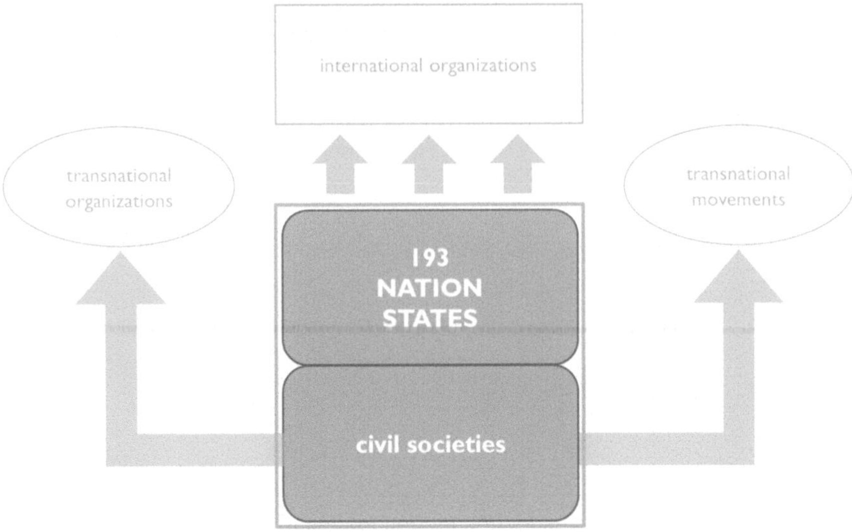

Fig. 13.2 Lockean Global Citizens and Community through Multi-layered Representation

13.4 Conclusion

Conceptually, joining or not joining multilateral treaties can be compared to a batter deciding to hit, miss, or pass balls from a pitcher. The US Major League has a machine to gauge the speed and angle of every ball coming from every pitcher for the past 50 matches. On the basis of machine-gauged data of balls, players, pitchers, catchers, coaches, and managers decide their action. Systematically and statistically knowing the speed, angle, and strategy of sovereign states' action on multilateral treaties is likely to enhance sovereign states' action in facing the choice of joining or not joining multilateral treaties. It will further improve our understanding of the 192 sovereign states' behavior in facing the decision of whether to join or not join multilateral treaties.

Albeit in a different context, but lamenting the lack of data when the world are facing the urgent need to have common rules and standards in the digitally globalized world, Tett (2019) argues for the urgent need to construct and consolidate all sorts of global data. It is in sync with the aim of writing this book encouraging such data consolidating efforts. Hidalgo (2016, p. x) argues, "What makes our planet special is not a singularity of matter or energy, but that it is a singularity of physical order, or information." "Our planet is to information what a black hole is to matter and what a star is to energy. Our planet is where information lives, grows, and hides in an otherwise mostly barren universe." Indeed it is not oil, for instance, that is considered to be one of the most important sources of power; it is information whose good grasp gives order, not disorder, to our planet.

Substantively, Asian states' *global quasi-legislative behavior* can be characterized as follows:

1. In comparison to Western states, especially those states belonging to the Reformed West, Asian states, whether it is the Sinic East, the Indic East, or the Islamic East, are passive to multilateral treaties. Those policy domains for which they are passive are human rights, labor, peace, intellectual property, and the environment.
2. Among the Islamic East, the Indic East, and the Sinic East, the last is most active in joining multilateral treaties.
3. Among 27 Asian states, large states in terms of population and GDP—those that can be categorized as abc and abC, Japan, China, and India—tend to be agile and globally oriented.
4. Those states with a centrifugal society and centripetal state, that is, those states belonging to aBC—Indonesia, Pakistan, the Philippines, Sri Lanka, and Thailand—are agile in judgment and action. They are concerned about individual interests, sectors, and rights within their society rather than global common goods. They are more interested in constraining all signatories rather than enlarging solidarity among those similarly aspiring.
5. Abc are cautious because they are vulnerable: ROK depends on the United States and US-led order with its hostile brother; Kazakhstan with its rich mineral resources has two large neighbors, China and Russia; Kyrgyzstan and Tajikistan are small states that must know which direction their neighbors and the world are moving to decide. Their angle is global and their strategy is appealing to those states similarly aspiring to reduce vulnerability.
6. ABc are cautious states because they have been victimized. Bangladesh gained independence from Pakistan, which almost suppressed it. Bhutan is on the border between India and China, both war-prone. Brunei, which is rich in mineral resources, is extremely rich and surrounded by Malaysia. Cambodia and Laos are sandwiched by Vietnam and Thailand, which are not only big but also bossy toward Cambodia and Laos. Singapore is very tiny and was victimized within the Malaysian Federation from which Singapore gained independence. Timor-Leste is very tiny and was victimized by Indonesia until it gained its independence after a long struggle. Turkmenistan is a sovereign state in Central Asia, bordered by Kazakhstan to the northwest, Uzbekistan to the north and east, Afghanistan to the southeast, Iran to the south and southwest, and the Caspian Sea. It is rich in oil and natural gas, with 85% of its land covered in desert. It is regarded as one of the most authoritarian states. Mongolia has been sandwiched by China and Russia for a long time. It took Vietnam a long time to enjoy its independence after being passed from Chinese rule to French rule, then to American force. ABc states are concerned about their individual interests, sectors, and rights rather than global common goods.
7. ABC are cautious states. They are inward looking because a centrifugal society and a centripetal state do not go well together. Ethnic and tribal strife and contestation, active or dormant, are the key elements of these societies. Uzbekistan,

which gained independence from the Soviet Union of Socialist Republics and from the monoculture of cotton, is concerned about individual interests, sectors, and rights rather than global common goods. It is careful in signing agreements, weighing its costs and benefits. In Malaysia, indigenous Malays and British-recruiting Chinese and Indians, compete for position, income, and education. More recently, Islam is becoming another point of contestation. The Maldives consist of some hundreds of islands inhabited by Indians, Arabs, Africans, etc. It is easy for external forces to intervene. Their concerns are predominantly about individual interests, sectors, and rights rather than global common goods. Their strategy is to keep promises to a minimum.

In sum, the typology of states, in terms of *global quasi-legislative behavior* makes enormous sense. The three criteria of this typology, speed, angle, and strategy, all help elucidate the characteristics of the state's internal and external preoccupations and their mode of handling issues. Inoguchi (1982, 2003) has already articulated the typology of the state, focusing on national security, internal and external. The typology of the state, focusing on participation in multilateral treaties has proved to be no less illuminating. These typologies increasingly reflect the sharp and deep penetration of globalizing and digitalizing technology and their impacts on states and societies as well as international relations and world politics.

References

Anderson, J. (Ed.). (2002). *Transnational democracy: Political spaces and border crossings*. London: Routledge.

Cohen, R. (2017, December 23–25). Wondering why, if this is America. *New York Times*.

Davies, T. (2014). *NGOs: A new history of transnational civil society*. New York: Oxford University Press.

Gourevitch, P. (1978). The second image reversed: The international sources of domestic politics. *International Organization, 32*(4), 881–912.

Hale, T., & Held, D. (2017). *Beyond gridlock*. Cambridge: Polity Press.

Hale, T., Held, D., & Young, K. (2013). *Gridlock: Why global cooperation is failing when we need it Most*. Cambridge: Polity Press.

Hidalgo, C. (2016). *Why information grows: The evolution of order, from atoms to economies*. New York: Penguin Books.

Howard, M. (2012). *Transnationalism in ancient and medieval societies: The role of cross-border trade and travels*. New York: McFarland.

Huntington, S. (1997). *The clash of civilizations and the remaking of world order*. New York: Simon and Schuster.

Inglehart, R. (2018). *Cultural evolution: People's motivations are changing, and reshaping the world*. New York: Cambridge University Press.

Inoguchi, T. (1982). *Kokusai Seiji Keizai no kozu (the framework of international political economy)*. Tokyo: Yuhikaku.

Inoguchi, T. (2003). Political security: Toward a broader conceptualization. *International Studies, 40*(2), 105–123.

Inoguchi, T. (2015). War occurrence, hyper-insecurity and multilateral institutions. *Japanese Journal of Political Science, 16*(3), 388–398.

Inoguchi, T. (Ed.). (2018). The Wilsonian moment: Japan 1912–1952. *Japanese Journal of Political Science, 19*(4), 565–621.
Inoguchi, T., & Le, L. T. Q. (2016). Toward modelling a global social contract: Jean-Jacques Rousseau and John Locke. *Japanese Journal of Political Science, 17*(3), 489–522.
International Institute of Security Studies. (2017). *Strategic survey 2017: The annual assessment of geopolitics*. London: Routledge.
Iriye, A. (2004). *Global community: The role of international organizations in the making of the contemporary world*. Oakland: University of California Press.
Iriye, A. (2014). *Global interdependence: The world after 1945*. Cambridge: Belknap Press of Harvard University Press.
Iwabuchi, K. (2002). *Recentering globalization: Popular culture and Japanese transnationalism*. Durham: Duke University Press.
Le, T. Q. L., Mikami, Y., & Inoguchi, T. (2014). Global leadership and international regime: Empirical testing of cooperation without hegemony paradigm on the basis of 120 multilateral conventions deposited to the United Nations system. *Japanese Journal of Political Science, 15*(4), 523–601.
McGrew, A., & Held, D. (2007). *Globalization theory: Approaches and controversies*. Cambridge: Polity.
Murphy, C. (1994). *International organization and industrial change: Global governance since 1850*. New York: Oxford University Press.
Putnam, R. (1988). Diplomacy and domestic politics: The logic of two-level games. *International Organization, 42*(3), 427–490.
Rosenberg, E. (Ed.). (2012). *A world connecting* (Vol. 1870–1945). Cambridge, Mass: Belknap Press of Harvard University Press.
Tallberg, J., Sommerer, T., Squatrito, T., & Jönsson, C. (2013). *The opening up of international organizations: Transnational access in global governance*. Cambridge: Cambridge University Press.
Taseer, A. (2018, June 22). How Britain lost its power of seduction. *The New York Times*.
Tett, G. (2019, April 17). Do we need an IMF to regulate the internet? *Financial Times*. (Nikkei Shimbun, April 29, 2019).
The Economist. (2017, July 13). *If Britain became 'Singapore-on-Thames': The British economy if the country crashes out of the European Union*. https://www.economist.com/the-world-if/2017/07/13/the-british-economy-if-the-country-crashes-out-of-the-european-union
Vertovec, S. (2009). *Transnationalism (key ideas)*. London: Routledge.
Welzel, C. (2013). *Freedom rising: Human empowerment and the quest for emancipation*. Cambridge: Cambridge University Press.

Conclusion

The global social contract is a concept that was first used in the West while experiencing modernism, whereby the state was considered an important political unit of the secular part of society and the individual was considered an important and indivisible component in which reason and rationalism constituted the basis of human judgment. On the basis of secularism and human reasoning, the social contract began to be considered as the fledgling democratic framework. It is not a coincidence that two great philosophers, Jean-Jacques Rousseau and John Locke, both penned *The Social Contract* and *Two Treaties of Government* as their definitive works on democracy, one direct democracy and the other representative democracy, respectively. Rousseau stressed the driving force of empathy and compassion, whereas Locke emphasized the driving force of human reasoning and pragmatism.

The number of states increased each time empires collapsed: Latin American state independence after the Napoleonic War, Central European state independence after World War I, and Asian and African state independence after World War II. After World War I, the League of Nations, and after World War II, the United Nations, were born; each registering a fledgling form of the world assembly. However, a fully powered world assembly was not born even today. The number of democracies increased as the once tight Cold War binding was reduced: first, Southern Europe and Latin America, followed by East and Southeast Asia, further followed by South and Central Asia, and finally followed by Africa and the Middle East. In a similar vein, a fully powered democratic world assembly has not been born either.

Nevertheless, the angel watching over human beings seems to smile more strongly as life has evolved over millions of years (Pinker 2012, 2018). Despite the unprecedented wartime killings during World War I and World War II, the world has experienced a steady decrease in wartime deaths for soldiers since 1945. Additionally, the number of democratic states reached a peak of 120 shortly after the end of the Cold War; although the force of democracy has receded over the ensuing quarter of a century.

T. Inoguchi, L. T. Q. Le, *The Development of Global Legislative Politics*,
Trust: Interdisciplinary Perspectives 3, https://doi.org/10.1007/978-981-32-9389-2

As if making up for the dominance of sovereign states over such a slightly less than fully powered world assembly, the tides of globalization and digitalization have contributed to the birth and development of fragmented global quasi-legislation in the form of multilateral treaties. This book has attacked the fragmented global quasi-legislation question head on for empirical analysis and synthesis. As Georg Simmel (1950) argues, interaction (Wechselwirkung) generates society (Vergesellschaftung). In the context of our study, sovereign states' joining or not joining multilateral treaties generates *a bundle of the global quasi-social contracts*, thus establishing the global society of a sort. One of the key questions has been whether such multilateral treaties reflect global citizens' preference for values and norms, and if so, to what extent. Thanks to the *World Values Survey* and the *Multilateral Treaties Survey*, this book has been able to answer the question fairly positively. Two problems remain to be tackled for this: (1) the alignment problem of data sources of global citizens' value orientation and sovereign states' treaty orientation and (2) the problem of adapting the two original ideas of social contract created at the pre-industrial revolution times to a bundle of *global quasi-social contracts* at the digitalized globalization times.

The *World Values Survey*, led by Ronald Inglehart (1997) and Christian Welzel (2013) and their associates, defines the concept of global citizens' preference on values and norms, such as freedom, democracy, wealth, health, empathy, love, friendship, morality, religiosity, and trust embraced worldwide. Whereas the *Multilateral Treaties Survey*, led by Lien Thi Quynh Le, Yoshiki Mikami, and Takashi Inoguchi (2014), Takashi Inoguchi and Lien Thi Quynh Le (2016), and Takashi Inoguchi (2018), focuses on the sovereign states' participation in multilateral treaties by their registered modes of, and attributes to, participation, such as the year of membership, the year when a treaty is deposited to the relevant international body, the number of current members of a treaty, the six policy domains of multilateral treaties, the difference between promulgation and ratification, and the world region to which each sovereign state belongs. The links between these two surveys have been examined via factor analysis with varimax rotation. More concretely, Welzel (2013), by factor analyzing data from the *World Values Survey* carried out in the 2000s, has developed two key dimensions: protective versus emancipative and sacred versus secular. In contrast, Inoguchi and Le (2016) have come up with three of their own key dimensions: agile versus cautious, global common good versus individual citizens' interests, and aspirational bonding versus mutual binding.

The links are thus multidimensional. The sacred versus secular dimension and the aspirational bonding versus mutual binding dimension are most strongly linked, with a correlation coefficient of .619. The agile versus cautious dimension is strongly linked to aspirational bonding versus mutual binding dimension with a correlation coefficient of −0.525. The protective versus emancipative dimension is fairly strongly linked to the dimension of aspirational bonding versus mutual binding with a correlation coefficient of 0.499. The sacred versus secular dimension is linked fairly moderately to global common good versus individual citizens' interests dimension with a correlation coefficient of −0.340; whether positive or negative, a sizable correlation evidences that citizens' preferences about value orientation and states' preference about treaty ratification are linked. This attested link seems to corroborate the longer secular trends toward human emancipation from bigotry and resort to non-violence, which modern philosophers like Rousseau and Locke and pacifist philosophers like Kant (Kant and Kleingeld 2006) and Gandhi (Gandhi and Fischer 2002) have portrayed in their writings. Some may say that this is beyond what one can do with empirical and statistical tests such as the ones conducted in this book since the data sources include the World Values Survey covering 105 countries from 1981 to 2014 containing 90% of the world population (Inglehart 2018, p. xvii) and the Multilateral Treaties Survey covering 193 sovereign states from 1945 to 2014 worldwide. Although we have used both the World Values Survey data and the Multilateral Treaties Survey data around the 20th and twenty-first centuries, these two time points are argued to be representative of the minds and actions of people as revealed in value orientation and treaty participation. One can also argue that. this can be observed in the longer human evolution from the birth of homo sapiens as portrayed by biologists, archeologists, anthropologists, psychologists and political scientists such as Diamond (2017), Harari (2018), Pinker (2012, 2018) and Inglehart (2018).

Thus, examining global links between citizens' preference about values and norms and states' participation in multilateral treaties has revealed fairly strong connections. In other words, it is not far-fetched to say that our initial hypothesis about the concept of *global quasi-legislation* seems to zero in to those global social contract ideas of Rousseau and Locke when we update and revise what social contract ideas to *a bundle of global quasi-social contracts* at the dawn of the twenty-first century.

To avoid any misunderstanding regarding the intent of writing this book, we briefly discuss the limitations of this study. We used the metaphors of Jean-Jacques Rousseau and John Locke to gain a better understanding of global politics in which the galloping tides of digitalized globalization have swayed human activities. Our initial hunch-cum-hypothesis was as follows: Since worldwide digitalized globalization has provided a whirlwind for slowly but steadily transforming the entire globe as one entity of a very loose yet complex kind, why do scholars continue treating global politics as if sovereign states have been the sole effective actors since at least the Westphalian Treaty of 1648? Why is a possible clash between the world number one and number two states given disproportionate attention? Why is a possible incompatibility among religions or civilizations exaggerated when the largest war-related death tolls of human beings are registered in the twentieth century, predominantly among Christians and Europeans? Glancing at post-Cold War discussions among scholars and journalists, pundits and politicians, and commentators and cynics, we believe that there is a need for more balance along with more precision.

Furthermore, our study has analyzed states' quasi-legislative behavior. Our three key dimensions have been agile versus cautious, global common good versus individual citizens' interests, and aspirational bonding versus mutual binding. To put these differently, we coin three different perspectives in states' *global quasi-legislative behavior* as *speed*, *angle* and *strategy*, respectively. With each of these three concepts rendered to binary variables, we have developed eight types of *global quasi-legislative behavior*: abc, abC, aBc, aBC, Abc, AbC, ABc, and ABC. Out of those sovereign states that fit one of the eight patterns, one state is singled out for illustration for each pattern. These states are: Brazil (agile, global, and aspirational), Iran (agile, national, and aspirational), Sweden (agile, global, and abiding), New Zealand (agile, national, and abiding), Slovakia (cautious, global, and abiding), South Korea (cautious, global, and aspirational), Nigeria (cautious, national, and aspirational), and Uzbekistan (cautious, national, and abiding). We have not provided detailed and deep analysis of each country's global quasi-legislative behavior. That task remains to be carried out in our next book.

Now, what should be the next step? What is the scope for further research? Once Rousseau and Locke writ global has been proven to be especially encouraging to the attempt of systematic and scientific kind like this book in an era of digitalized globalization, our next research agenda is to conduct an in-depth analysis of *global quasi-legislative behavior*. This is further conceptualized as sovereign states' external engagement or, more simply, foreign policy. When gauging a sovereign state's foreign policy, one is biased toward focusing on the so-called Cold War trinity of might, wealth, and ideology, which are crude indicators of power resources; moreover, it is evident that they were basic and most fundamental variables in the last century. However, with the world evolving in the new millennium, there is a need for more elaborate and polished indicators of sovereign states' external engagement. They must not be crude indicators of national attributes such as weapons and gross domestic product; rather, they must be elaborate indicators of attributes shared by some sovereign states in multilateral treaties; for example, the previously mentioned *global quasi-legislative behavior* of eight states.

One apparent question is the steady fracturing and fragmenting global politics most dramatically triggered by the United States' "transformative" foreign policy line under President Donald Trump. Our answer to the question is that the concept of *global quasi-legislative behavior*, as applied to the United States, is broadly effective in explaining this situation. Since our data set, the Multilateral Treaties Survey, covers the period between 1945 and 2014, we must extend our coverage further beyond 2014, including multilateral treaties that have been selected as more important, are less regionally narrow and least technical (such as the attached documents on institutions and procedures); these 510 treaties for our next study cover the period up to 2018. However, the United States' quasi-legislative behavior during the period when, according to Georgi Arbatov, it had no enemies, began manifesting what might be called the undisciplined (Bill Clinton), impulsive (George W. Bush, Jr.), or inactive (Barack Obama) behavior in three presidencies. In 1758, a Scottish philosopher, David Hume, eloquently described the mindset of the Trumpian policy line of America First:

> Having endeavoured to remove one species of ill-founded jealousy, which is so prevalent among commercial nations, it may not be amiss to mention another which seems equally groundless. Nothing is more usual, among states which have made some advances in commerce, than to look on the progress of their neighbours with a suspicious eye, to consider all trading states as their rivals, and to suppose that it is impossible for any of them to flourish, but at their expence. In opposition to this narrow and malignant opinion, I will venture to assert, that the encrease of riches and commerce in any one nation, instead of hurting, commonly promotes the riches

and commerce of all its neighbours; and that a state can scarcely carry its trade and industry very far, where all the surrounding states are buried in ignorance, sloth, and barbarism (Hume 1994).

After elucidating the broadly effective scheme of *a bundle of global quasi-social contracts* and *global quasi-legislative behavior*, our next agenda is to explore further beyond the eight types of global quasi-legislative behavior via multilateral treaties and develop an enriched theory of global legislative politics, compared to other schools of thought on global politics after the Cold War, in an era of digitalized globalization where things rapidly evolve in complex ways and the prospects for the future often remain uncertain and unpredictable, beyond the degree to which the habits of the past century allow.

In the first quarter of the new millennium, we are confronted by complex tides of social forces: climate changes, the decay of hegemonic stability, the decline of the principle of universal free trade, the rise of religiosity, and the ever-widening inequalities among classes and sectors, to name but a few. Yet it is very important to emphasize that because of the tides of globalization and digitalization permeating each and every part of the globe, we should be more keenly aware that in this densely connected world, one cannot be left alone in a disconnected world. As César Hidalgo (2016, Chap. 11) aptly says, "In Links We Trust." In this densely connected world the level of interdependence and vulnerability has increased alarmingly high with deep and sharp interpenetration between domestic forces and transnational forces kept simultaneously enlivened and enmeshed often against the facade of seeming normalcy and tumultuousness. Multilateral treaties as conceptualized as *a bundle of global quasi-social contracts* has become so heightened to play the positive role of building the entire globe in which one could aspire to live with hope and abide by safely and with mutual gains and minimum losses. Multilateral treaties participation conceptualized as global *quasi-legislative politics* are like a transparent world barometer. It is our hope that our work will trigger the innovation of developing it into the transparent world barometer (Cf. The Economist Intelligence Unit 2019) gauging the map of global health and weather (Cf. The Economist Intelligence Unit 2019 and Tett 2019).

References

Diamond, J. (2017). *Guns, germs, and steel: The fates of human societies*. New York: W. W. Norton.

Gandhi, M., & Fischer, L. (2002). *The essential Gandhi: An anthology of his writings on his life, work, and ideas*. New York: Vintage.

Harari, Y. N. (2018). *Sapiens: A brief history of humankind*. New York: Harper Perennial.

Hidalgo, C. (2016). *Why information grows: The evolution of order, from atoms to economies*. New York: Penguin Books.

Hume, D. (1994). Of the jealousy of trade. In K. Haakonssen (Ed.), *Hume: Political essays* (pp. 150–153). Cambridge: Cambridge University Press.

Inglehart, R. (1997). *Modernization and postmodernization: Cultural, economic, and political change in 43 societies*. Princeton: Princeton University Press.

Inglehart, R. (2018). *Cultural evolution: People's motivations are changing, and reshaping the world*. New York: Cambridge University Press.

Inoguchi, T. (2018). Theoretical underpinnings of global social contract. In W. Thompson (Ed.), *The encyclopedia of Oxford empirical international relations theory* (Vol. 4, pp. 223–240). Oxford: Oxford University Press.

Inoguchi, T., & Le, L. T. Q. (2016). Toward modelling a global social contract: Jean-Jacques Rousseau and John Locke. *Japanese Journal of Political Science, 17*(3), 489–522.

Kant, I., & Kleingeld, P. (2006). *Toward perpetual peace and other writings on politics, peace and history*. New Haven, Conn: Yale University Press.

Le, T. Q. L., Mikami, Y., & Inoguchi, T. (2014). Global leadership and international regime: Empirical testing of cooperation without hegemony paradigm on the basis of 120 multilateral conventions data deposited to the United Nations system. *Japanese Journal of Political Science, 15*(4), 523–601.

Pinker, S. (2012). *The better angles of our nature: Why violence has declined*. Reprinted edition. New York: Penguin Books.

Pinker, S. (2018). *Enlightenment now: The case for reason, science, humanism, and progress*. New York: Viking.

Simmel, G. (1950). *The sociology of Georg Simmel*, compiled and translated by Kurt Wolff, Glencoe, Illinois: Free Press.

Tett, G. (2019, April 17). Do we need an IMF to regulate the internet? *Financial Times*. (Nikkei Shimbun, April 29, 2019).

The Economist Intelligence Unit. (2019). *The transparent business barometer: Preparing for the end of easy data*. London: The Economist Intelligence Unit.

Welzel, C. (2013). *Freedom rising: Human empowerment and the quest for emancipation*. New York: Cambridge University Press.

Appendices

Appendix 1: The Welzel Category (2013) and the Modified/Extended Welzel Category or Inoguchi/Le Category

ID	Country name	Country code	Welzel category	Inoguchi/Le category	Ten regional groups
1	Afghanistan	AFG		Islamic East	Islamic East
2	Albania	ALB	Orthodox East		Orthodox East
3	Algeria	DZA	Islamic East		Islamic East
4	Andorra	ADO	Old West		Old West
5	Angola	AGO		Sub-Saharan Africa	Sub-Saharan Africa
6	Antigua and Barbuda	ATG		Latin America	Latin America
7	Argentina	ARG		Latin America	Latin America
8	Armenia	ARM		Orthodox East	Orthodox East
9	Australia	AUS	New West		New West
10	Austria	AUT	Old West		Old West
11	Azerbaijan	AZE	Orthodox East		Orthodox East
12	Bahamas	BHS		Latin America	Latin America
13	Bahrain	BHR		Islamic East	Islamic East
14	Bangladesh	BGD	Indic East		Indic East
15	Barbados	BRB		Latin America	Latin America
16	Belarus	BLR	Orthodox East		Orthodox East
17	Belgium	BEL	Old West		Old West
18	Belize	BLZ		Latin America	Latin America
19	Benin	BEN		Sub-Saharan Africa	Sub-Saharan Africa
20	Bhutan	BTN		Indic East	Indic East
21	Bolivia	BOL		Latin America	Latin America

(continued)

T. Inoguchi, L. T. Q. Le, *The Development of Global Legislative Politics*,
Trust: Interdisciplinary Perspectives 3, https://doi.org/10.1007/978-981-32-9389-2

ID	Country name	Country code	Welzel category	Inoguchi/Le category	Ten regional groups
22	Bosnia and Herzegovina	BIH	Orthodox East		Orthodox East
23	Botswana	BWA		Sub-Saharan Africa	Sub-Saharan Africa
24	Brazil	BRA	Latin America		Latin America
25	Brunei Darussalam	BRN		Indic East	Indic East
26	Bulgaria	BGR		Orthodox East	Orthodox East
27	Burkina Faso	BFA	Sub-Saharan Africa		Sub-Saharan Africa
28	Burundi	BDI		Sub-Saharan Africa	Sub-Saharan Africa
29	Cambodia	KHM		Indic East	Indic East
30	Cameroon	CMR		Sub-Saharan Africa	Sub-Saharan Africa
31	Cape Verde	CPV		Sub-Saharan Africa	Sub-Saharan Africa
32	Canada	CAN	New West		New West
33	Central African Republic	CAF		Sub-Saharan Africa	Sub-Saharan Africa
34	Chad	TCD		Sub-Saharan Africa	Sub-Saharan Africa
35	Chile	CHL	Latin America		Latin America
36	China	CHN	Sinic East		Sinic East
37	Colombia	COL	Latin America		Latin America
38	Comoros	COM		Sub-Saharan Africa	Sub-Saharan Africa
39	Congo	COG		Sub-Saharan Africa	Sub-Saharan Africa
40	Costa Rica	CRI	Latin America		Latin America
41	Cote d'Ivoire	CIV		Sub-Saharan Africa	Sub-Saharan Africa
42	Croatia	HRV	Returned West		Returned West
43	Cuba	CUB		Latin America	Latin America
44	Cyprus	CYP	Old West		Old West
45	Czech Republic	CZE	Returned West		Returned West
46	Democratic People's Republic of Korea	PRK		Sinic East	Sinic East
47	Democratic Republic of the Congo	ZAR		Sub-Saharan Africa	Sub-Saharan Africa
48	Denmark	DNK	Reformed West		Reformed West
49	Djibouti	DJI		Sub-Saharan Africa	Sub-Saharan Africa
50	Dominica	DMA		Latin America	Latin America
51	Dominican Republic	DOM		Latin America	Latin America
52	Ecuador	ECU		Latin America	Latin America

(continued)

ID	Country name	Country code	Welzel category	Inoguchi/Le category	Ten regional groups
53	Egypt	EGY	Islamic East		Islamic East
54	El Salvador	SLV	Latin America		Latin America
55	Equatorial Guinea	GNQ		Latin America	Latin America
56	Eritrea	ERI		Sub-Saharan Africa	Sub-Saharan Africa
57	Estonia	EST	Returned West		Returned West
58	Ethiopia	ETH		Sub-Saharan Africa	Sub-Saharan Africa
59	Fiji	FJI		New West	New West
60	Finland	FIN	Reformed West		Reformed West
61	France	FRA	Old West		Old West
62	Gabon	GAB		Sub-Saharan Africa	Sub-Saharan Africa
63	Gambia	GMB		Sub-Saharan Africa	Sub-Saharan Africa
64	Georgia	GEO	Orthodox East		Orthodox East
65	Germany	DEU	Reformed West		Reformed West
66	Ghana	GHA	Sub-Saharan Africa		Sub-Saharan Africa
67	Greece	GRC	Old West		Old West
68	Grenada	GRD		Latin America	Latin America
69	Guatemala	GTM	Latin America		Latin America
70	Guinea	GIN		Sub-Saharan Africa	Sub-Saharan Africa
71	Guinea-Bissau	GNB		Sub-Saharan Africa	Sub-Saharan Africa
72	Guyana	GUY		Latin America	Latin America
73	Haiti	HTI		Latin America	Latin America
74	Honduras	HND		Latin America	Latin America
75	Hungary	HUN	Returned West		Returned West
76	Iceland	ISL	Reformed West		Reformed West
77	India	IND	Indic East		Indic East
78	Indonesia	IDN	Indic East		Indic East
79	Iran	IRN	Islamic East		Islamic East
80	Iraq	IRQ	Islamic East		Islamic East
81	Ireland	IRL	Reformed West		Reformed West
82	Israel	ISR	Old West		Old West
83	Italy	ITA	Old West		Old West
84	Jamaica	JAM		Latin America	Latin America
85	Japan	JPN	Sinic East		Sinic East
86	Jordan	JOR	Islamic East		Islamic East

(continued)

ID	Country name	Country code	Welzel category	Inoguchi/Le category	Ten regional groups
87	Kazakhstan	KAZ		Orthodox East	Orthodox East
88	Kenya	KEN		Sub-Saharan Africa	Sub-Saharan Africa
89	Kiribati	KIR		New West	New West
90	Kuwait	KWT		Islamic East	Islamic East
91	Kyrgyzstan	KGZ	Orthodox East		Orthodox East
92	Lao People's Democratic Republic	LAO		Indic East	Indic East
93	Latvia	LVA	Returned West		Returned West
94	Lebanon	LBN		Islamic East	Islamic East
95	Lesotho	LSO		Sub-Saharan Africa	Sub-Saharan Africa
96	Liberia	LBR		Sub-Saharan Africa	Sub-Saharan Africa
97	Libyan Arab Jamahiriya	LBY		Islamic East	Islamic East
98	Liechtenstein	LIE		Old West	Old West
99	Lithuania	LTU	Returned West		Returned West
100	Luxembourg	LUX	Old West		Old West
101	Madagascar	MDG		Sub-Saharan Africa	Sub-Saharan Africa
102	Malawi	MWI		Sub-Saharan Africa	Sub-Saharan Africa
103	Malaysia	MYS	Indic East		Indic East
104	Maldives	MDV		Indic East	Indic East
105	Mali	MLI	Sub-Saharan Africa		Sub-Saharan Africa
106	Malta	MLT	Old West		Old West
107	Marshall Islands	MHL		New West	New West
108	Mauritania	MRT		Sub-Saharan Africa	Sub-Saharan Africa
109	Mauritius	MUS		Sub-Saharan Africa	Sub-Saharan Africa
110	Mexico	MEX	Latin America		Latin America
111	Monaco	MCO		Old West	Old West
112	Mongolia	MNG		Sinic East	Sinic East
113	Montenegro	MNE	Orthodox East		Orthodox East
114	Morocco	MAR	Islamic East		Islamic East
115	Mozambique	MOZ		Sub-Saharan Africa	Sub-Saharan Africa
116	Myanmar	MMR		Indic East	Indic East
117	Namibia	NAM		Sub-Saharan Africa	Sub-Saharan Africa
118	Nauru	NRU		New West	New West
119	Nepal	NPL		Indic East	Indic East

(continued)

ID	Country name	Country code	Welzel category	Inoguchi/Le category	Ten regional groups
120	Netherlands	NLD	Reformed West		Reformed West
121	New Zealand	NZL	New West		New West
122	Nicaragua	NIC		Latin America	Latin America
123	Niger	NER		Sub-Saharan Africa	Sub-Saharan Africa
124	Nigeria	NGA	Sub-Saharan Africa		Sub-Saharan Africa
125	Norway	NOR	Reformed West		Reformed West
126	Oman	OMN		Islamic East	Islamic East
127	Pakistan	PAK	Indic East		Indic East
128	Palau	PLW		New West	New West
129	Panama	PAN		Latin America	Latin America
130	Papua New Guinea	PNG		New West	New West
131	Paraguay	PRY		Latin America	Latin America
132	Peru	PER	Latin America		Latin America
133	Philippines	PHL	Indic East		Indic East
134	Poland	POL	Returned West		Returned West
135	Portugal	PRT	Old West		Old West
136	Qatar	QAT		Islamic East	Islamic East
137	Republic of Korea	KOR	Sinic East		Sinic East
138	Republic of Moldova	MDA	Orthodox East		Orthodox East
139	Romania	ROM	Orthodox East		Orthodox East
140	Russian Federation	RUS	Orthodox East		Orthodox East
141	Rwanda	RWA	Sub-Saharan Africa		Sub-Saharan Africa
142	Saint Kitts and Nevis	KNA		Latin America	Latin America
143	Saint Lucia	LCA		Latin America	Latin America
144	Saint Vincent and the Grenadines	VCT		Latin America	Latin America
145	Samoa	WSM		New West	New West
146	San Marino	SMR		Old West	Old West
147	Sao Tome and Principe	STP		Sub-Saharan Africa	Sub-Saharan Africa
148	Saudi Arabia	SAU	Islamic East		Islamic East
149	Senegal	SEN		Sub-Saharan Africa	Sub-Saharan Africa
150	Serbia	SRB	Orthodox East		Orthodox East
151	Seychelles	SYC		Sub-Saharan Africa	Sub-Saharan Africa
152	Sierra Leone	SLE		Sub-Saharan Africa	Sub-Saharan Africa
153	Singapore	SGP	Indic East		Indic East

(continued)

ID	Country name	Country code	Welzel category	Inoguchi/Le category	Ten regional groups
154	Slovakia	SVK	Returned West		Returned West
155	Slovenia	SVN	Returned West		Returned West
156	Solomon Islands	SLB		New West	New West
157	Somalia	SOM		Sub-Saharan Africa	Sub-Saharan Africa
158	South Africa	ZAF	Sub-Saharan Africa		Sub-Saharan Africa
159	South Sudan	SSD		Sub-Saharan Africa	Sub-Saharan Africa
160	Spain	ESP	Old West		Old West
161	Sri Lanka	LKA		Indic East	Indic East
162	Sudan	SDN		Sub-Saharan Africa	Sub-Saharan Africa
163	Suriname	SUR		Latin America	Latin America
164	Swaziland	SWZ		Sub-Saharan Africa	Sub-Saharan Africa
165	Sweden	SWE	Reformed West		Reformed West
166	Switzerland	CHE	Reformed West		Reformed West
167	Syrian Arab Republic	SYR		Islamic East	Islamic East
168	Tajikistan	TJK		Orthodox East	Orthodox East
169	Thailand	THA	Indic East		Indic East
170	The former Yugoslav Republic of Macedonia	MKD	Orthodox East		Orthodox East
171	Timor-Leste	TMP		Indic East	Indic East
172	Togo	TGO		Sub-Saharan Africa	Sub-Saharan Africa
173	Tonga	TON		New West	New West
174	Trinidad and Tobago	TTO		Latin America	Latin America
175	Tunisia	TUN		Islamic East	Islamic East
176	Turkey	TUR	Islamic East		Islamic East
177	Turkmenistan	TKM		Orthodox East	Orthodox East
178	Tuvalu	TUV		New West	New West
179	Uganda	UGA	Sub-Saharan Africa		Sub-Saharan Africa
180	Ukraine	UKR	Orthodox East		Orthodox East
181	United Arab Emirates	ARE		Islamic East	Islamic East
182	United Kingdom	GBR	Reformed West		Reformed West
183	United Republic of Tanzania	TZA	Sub-Saharan Africa		Sub-Saharan Africa
184	United States of America	USA	New West		New West
185	Uruguay	URY	Latin America		Latin America
186	Uzbekistan	UZB		Orthodox East	Orthodox East

(continued)

ID	Country name	Country code	Welzel category	Inoguchi/Le category	Ten regional groups
187	Vanuatu	VUT		New West	New West
188	Venezuela	VEN	Latin America		Latin America
189	Viet Nam	VNM	Sinic East		Sinic East
190	Yemen	YEM		Islamic East	Islamic East
191	Yugoslavia	YUG		Orthodox East	Orthodox East
192	Zambia	ZMB	Sub-Saharan Africa		Sub-Saharan Africa
193	Zimbabwe	ZWE	Sub-Saharan Africa		Sub-Saharan Africa

Appendix 2: A Brief Profile of 120 Treaties of UN Multilateral Treaties Survey

Of all the multilateral treaties deposited to the United Nations System, we have selected 120 treaties for our analysis. Some of the multilateral treaties have strong regional aspects, which is not appropriate for our analytical purpose because we are examining treaties with a reasonably strong global nature. These 120 treaties are categorized according to our framework. Each treaty is categorized in terms of policy domains, year of UN deposit, type of membership, number of current members, and belonging to Welzel's ten region categories.

(1) **Policy domains:** There are six policy domains as follows:

(a) Human rights
(b) Peace and disarmament
(c) Environment
(d) Intellectual property
(e) Trade, communications, and commerce
(f) Labor, health and safety

Policy domains are almost indefinite. Multilateral treaties deal with policy issues that arise across sovereign states. When it is widely recognized that multilateral agreement among sovereign states is the best way forward, then multilateral treaties are drafted and discussed in appropriate settings. International governmental organizations, international non-governmental organizations, transnational non-governmental movements and organizations, transnational organizations, and other entities are often involved in what we call global quasi-legislative processes. These processes are largely referred to as Lockean as their driving forces consist of reason and pragmatism. No less important are digital interactions among global citizens, movements, and organizations. These interactions are largely referred to as

Rousseauesque as their driving force is compassion, often transmitted through Freudian unconsciousness and neuro-scientific processes.

(2) **Year of UN deposit:** This needs no explanation.
(3) **Type of membership:**

  (a) Type A: Extremely unpopular (currently not many members)
  (b) Type B: Steady increase
  (c) Type C: Not very popular at the start but at a certain point, membership rose
  (d) Type D: Popular with a great many from the start

(4) **Name of the 10 geo-historico-cultural groups by Christian Welzel (2013) in a modified form:**

  (a) Indic East: South Asia and Southeast Asia
  (b) Islamic East: the Middle East and North Africa
  (c) Latin America: all the Americas minus the United States and Canada
  (d) New West: new settlers societies like the US, Canada, Australia, and New Zealand
  (e) Old West: West since the Roman Empire such as Italy, France, and Spain
  (f) Orthodox East: Russia, Macedonia, Bulgaria, and Ukraine
  (g) Reformed West: West since the Reformation such as Germany, Sweden, and Denmark
  (h) Sinic East: China, Korea, Vietnam, Japan, and Taiwan
  (i) Sub-Saharan Africa: Includes all the countries in Sub-Saharan Africa
  (j) Returned West: Post-Cold War West such as Poland, Czech Republic, Hungary, and Latvia

(5) **Number of Current Members as of 2014**

This appendix takes a glance at the profiles of 120 multilateral treaties in each domain by domain.

Human Rights

T1: Slavery Convention (1926)

It was deposited to the League of Nations, which preceded the United Nations, in 1945. The pattern of membership increase is Type B and steady from initially less than 40 in 1926 to 80 in 2014. Sub-Saharan Africa, Latin America, and the relatively developed regions in the West are key participants. Members of Sinic East and India East are relatively few.

T2: Convention on the Prevention and Punishment of the Crime of Genocide (1949)

In 1949, 40 odd members joined and, by 2014, 142 states joined. This is Type B. Sixty percent of members are from the non-West.

T3: International Convention on the Elimination of All Forms of Racial Discrimination (1966)

Type C (popular but did not have many participants at the start—then, at a certain point membership rose). The current number of members is 174, 60% of which are non-Western states.

T4: International Convention on Economic, Social and Cultural Rights (1968)

Type C. The current number of members is 160. The non-West occupies 63%.

T5: International Covenant on Covenant on Civil and Political Rights

Type C. The current number of members is 167. The non-West occupies 64%.

T6: Optional Protocol to the International Covenant on Civil and Political Rights (1968)

Type C and has 114 registered members. Compared to the main Covenant, those Islamic, Indic and Sinic East members shrank.

T7: Convention on the Non-Applicability of Statutory Limitations to War Crimes and Crimes against Humanity (1969)

Type B. Membership is small—currently with 54 members; however, there are steady increases in membership.

T8: International Convention on the Suppression and Punishment of the Crime of Apartheid (1974)

Type B. There are 108 registered members of which the non-West occupies 79%.

T9: Convention on the Elimination of All Forms of Discrimination against Women (1980)

Type D. It is one of the few conventions that enjoyed popularity from the start. There are 185 current registered members.

T10: Convention against Torture and Other Cruel, Inhuman or Degrading Treatment or Punishment (1986)

Type C and has 152 registered members.

T11: International Convention against Apartheid in Sports (1986)

Type B and has 60 registered members. Non-Western members including Orthodox East (like Russia and Bulgaria) occupy 76% of the membership. Many Western states are not members.

T12: Convention on the Rights of the Child (1990)

Type D and has 189 registered members. Few states opposed it.

T13: Second Optional Protocol to the International Covenant on Civil and Political Rights, aiming at the Abolition of the Death and Penal type (1990)

Type B and has 76 registered members. Those states in Islamic, Indic, and Sinic East shrank from the main body document.

T14: International Convention on the Protection of the Rights of All Migrant Workers and Members of their Families (1993)

Type A (very unpopular) and has 46 registered members. States in Sinic East, Old West, Reformed West, New West, and Returned West are not members.

T15: Convention on the Rights of Persons and Disabilities (2007)

Type D (very popular from the start) and has 128 registered members.

T16: International Convention for the Protection of all Persons from Enforced Disappearance (2007)

Type A (unpopular) and has 37 registered members. Many states in Indic East, Sinic East, Islamic East, Reformed West, New West, and Returned West are not members.

Peace and Disarmament

T18: Hague Convention on War on Land (1907)

Type A (unpopular) and has 36 registered members. Many states in Islamic East, Indic East, Sinic East. New West, Returned West, and Sub-Saharan Africa are not members. Latin America, Reformed West, and Old West tend to remain.

T19: Protocol for the Prohibition of the Use in War of Asphyxiating, Poisonous or Bacteriological Methods of Warfare (1926)

Type C and has 136 registered members.

T20: Partial Test Ban Treaty (1963)

Type D (very popular from the start) and has 126 registered members.

T21: State Parties to the Non-Proliferation Treaty (1968)

Type B (steady increase) and has 187 registered members.

T22: Biological Weapons Convention (1972)

Type B (steady increase) and has 163 registered members.

T23: International Atomic Energy Agency Safe Guard Agreement (1972)

Type C (popular) and has 181 registered members.

T24: Convention on Prohibition or Restrictions on the Use of Certain Conventional Weapons which may be Deemed to be Excessively Injurious or to Have Indiscriminate Effects, Geneva (1980)

Type C (popular) and has 115 registered members.

T25: Treaty of Tlatelolco (1967)

Type A (unpopular) and has 33 registered members.

T26: Treaty of Rarotonga (1985)

Type A (unpopular) and has 11 registered members.

T27: Bangkok Treaty (1996)

Type A (unpopular) and has 10 registered members. It narrowly covers Indic East and Sinic East.

T28: Pelindaba Treaty (1996)

Type A (unpopular) and has 36 registered members. It narrowly covers Sub-Saharan Africa.

T29: Treaty on a Nuclear Weapon Free Zone in Central Asia (2007)

Type A (unpopular) and has 5 registered members. It narrowly covered Central Asia.

T30: States Parties to the Chemical Weapons Convention (1993)

Type D (popular) and has 184 registered members.

T31: Comprehensive Nuclear-Test-Ban Treaty (1996)

Type D (popular) and has 154 registered members.

T32: Convention on the Prohibition of the Use, Stockpiling, production and Transfer of Anti-Personnel Mines and on their Destruction (1997 Mine Ban Treaty)

Type D (popular) and has 158 registered members.

T33: Convention on Offences and Certain Other Acts Committed on Board Aircraft (1963)

Type C (popular) and has 183 registered members.

T34: Convention for the Suppression pf Unlawful Seizure of Aircraft (1970)

Type C (popular) and has 183 registered members.

T35: Convention for the Suppression of Unlawful Acts against the Safety of Civil Aviation (1971)

Type C (popular) and has 185 registered members.

T36: Convention on the Prevention and Punishment of Crimes against Internationally Protected Persons, including Diplomatic Agents (1973)

Type C (popular) and has 173 registered members.

T37: International Convention against the Taking of Hostages (1979)

Type C (popular) and has 171 registered members.

T38: Protocol for the Suppression of Unlawful Acts of Violence at Airports Serving International Civil Aviation (1988)

Type C (popular) and has 158 registered members.

T39: Convention for the Suppression of Unlawful Acts against the Safety of Maritime Navigation (1988)

Type C (popular) and has 158 registered members.

T40: Protocol for the Suppression of Unlawful Acts against the Safety of Fixed Platforms Located on the Continental Shelf (1988)

Type C (popular) and has 148 registered members.

T41: Convention on the Marking of Plastic Explosives for the Purpose of Detection (1991)

Type C (popular) and has 147 registered members.

T42: International Convention for the Suppression of Terrorist Bombings (1997)

Type D (popular from the start) and has 165 registered members.

T43: International Convention for the Suppression of the Financing of Terrorism (1999)

Type D (popular from the start) and has 181 registered members.

T44: International Convention for the Suppression of Acts of Nuclear Terrors (2005)

Type B (steady increase) and has 91 registered members.

T45: Convention on Cybercrime (2001)

Type A (unpopular) and has 41 registered members.

Environment

T46: Food and Agriculture of the United Nations (1945)

Type B (steady increase) and has 188 registered members.

T47: International Convention for the Regulation of Whaling (1948)

Type C (popular, not many at the start but at a certain point membership rose) and has 86 registered members. Many of those in Islamic East, Sinic East, Indic East, and Orthodox East are not members.

T48: Convention concerning the Protection of the World Cultural and Natural Heritage (1973)

Type C and has 185 registered members. Nearly all of Islamic East, Indic East, and Sinic East are members.

T49: Convention on International Trade in Endangered Species of Wild Fauna and Flora (1974)

Type B (steady increase) and has 176 registered members. Nearly all of Islamic East, Indic East, and Sinic East are members.

T50: Convention on the Prevention of Marine Pollution by Dumping of Wastes and Other Matter (1975)

Type B (steady increase) and has 87 registered members.

T51: Ramsar Convention on Wetlands of International Importance especially as Waterfowl Habitat (1975)

Type C and has 164 registered members. Nearly all of Islamic East, Indic East, and Sinic East are members.

T52: Convention on Long-range Transboundary Air Pollution (1980)

Type A (unpopular) and has 50 registered members. Islamic East, Indic East and Sinic East are mostly non-members.

T53: UN Convention on the Law of Sea (1982)

Type C and has 160 registered members. China's rise has coincided with the increase in maritime disputes. Nearly all of Islamic East, Indic East, and Sinic East are members.

T54: Convention on the Conservation of Migratory Species of Wild Animals (1983)

Type B (steady increase) and has 115 registered members.

T55: Convention on Early Notification of a Nuclear Accident (1986)

Type B (steady increase) and has 113 registered members. Islamic East, Indic East, and Sinic East are supportive of this convention.

T56: The Vienna Convention for the Protection of the Ozone Layer (1985)

Type D (popular with very many from the start) and has 193 registered members. All of Islamic East, India East, and Sinic East are members.

T57: Convention on Assistance in the Case of a Nuclear Accident or Radiological Emergency (1987)

Type B (steady increase) and has 106 registered members. All of Islamic East, India East, and Sinic East are members.

T58: Convention on the Physical Protection of Nuclear Material: 1987

Type C (popular, not many at the start but at a certain point membership rose) and has 145 registered members.

T59: The Montreal Protocol on Substances that Deplete the Ozone Layer (1987

Type D (popular with very many from the start) and has 193 registered members.

T60: Basel Convention on the Control of Transboundary Movements of Hazardous Wastes and their Disposal (1989)

Type C (popular, not many at the start but at a certain point membership rose) and has 176 registered members.

T61: Convention for Bio-Diversity (1992)

Type D (popular with very many from the start) and has 189 registered members.

T62: UN Framework Convention on Climate Change (1992)

Type D (popular with very many from the start) and has 191 registered members.

T63: Convention on Nuclear Safety (1996)

Type B (steady increase) and has 74 registered members.

T64: Kyoto Protocol to the UN FCCC (1998)

Type D and has 188 registered members.

T65: Rotterdam Convention on the Prior Informed Consent Procedure for Certain Hazardous Chemicals and Pesticides (1998)

Type C and has 148 registered members.

T66: Joint Convention on the Safety of Spent Fuel Management and on the Safety of Radioactive Waste Management (2001)

Type B (steady increase) and has 67 registered members.

T67: Stockholm Convention on Persistent Organic Pollutants (2001)

Type D (popular with very many from the start) and has 175 registered members.

Intellectual Property

T68: Paris Convention for the Protection of Industrial Property (1884)

Type C and has 173 registered members.

T69: Berne Convention for the Protection of Literary and Artistic Works (1886)

Type C and has 164 registered members.

T70: Madrid Agreement concerning the International Registration of Marks (1891)

Type B (steady increase) and has 56 registered members.

T71: Hague Agreement Concerning the International Deposit of Industrial Designs (1925)

Type B (steady increase) and has 59 registered members.

T72: Universal Copyright Convention (1955)

Type B (steady increase) and has 99 registered members.

T73: Rome Convention for the Protection of Performers, Producers of Phonograms and Broadcasting Organizations (1964)

Type B (steady increase) and has 91 registered members.

T74: International Convention for the Protection of New Varieties of Plants (1968)

Type B (steady increase) and has 70 registered members.

T75: World Intellectual Property Organization (1970)

Type C and has 185 registered members.

T76: Convention for the Protection of Producers of Phonograms against Unauthorized Duplication of their Phonograms (1973)

Type B (steady increase) and has 75 registered members.

T77: Patent Cooperation Treaty (1978)

Type C and has 146 registered members.

T78: Trade Related Aspects of Intellectual Property Systems (1995)

Type D (popular with very many from the start) and has 135 registered members.

T79: Trademark Law Treaty (1994)

Type B and has 53 registered members.

T80: WIPO Performances and Phonograms Treaty (2002)

Type B and has 91 registered members.

T81: WIPO Copyright Treaty (2002)

Type B.

Trade, Commerce and Communication

T82: International Telecommunication Union (1866)

Type B (steady increase) and has 188 registered members.

T83: Convention de Metre (1875)

Type B (steady increase) and has 54 registered members. Islamic, Indic, and Sinic East members tend to be users of the metric system.

T84: Universal Postal Union (1875)

Type B (steady increase) and has 190 registered members.

T85: International Electrotechnical Commission (1906)

Type B (steady increase) and has 66 registered members.

T86: International Monetary F und (1945)

Type C and has 187 registered members.

T87: World Bank (International Bank for Reconstruction and Development) (1945)

Type C and has 181 registered members.

T88: Convention on International Civil Aviation (1945)

Type B and has 188 registered members.

T89: International Standardization Organization (1947)

Type B (steady increase) and has 88 registered members.

T90: International Maritime Organization (1948)

Type B (steady increase) and has 169 registered members.

T91: General Agreement on Tariffs and Trade (1948)

Type B (steady increase) and has 126 registered members.

T92: Technical Barriers to Trade (1995)

Type D and has 135 registered members.

T93: World Trade Organization (1995)

Type D and has 153 registered members.

Labor, Health and Safety

T94: World Lead (Painting) Convention (1921)

Type B (steady increase) and has 63 registered members.

T95: Forced Labor Convention (1930)

Type C and has 175 registered members.

T96: Underground Work (Women) Convention (1935)

Type B (steady increase) and has 70 registered members.

T97: Safety Provisions (Building) Convention (1937)

Type A and has 21 registered members.

T98: Freedom of Association and Protection of the Right to Organize Convention (1948)

Type B (steady increase) and has 151 registered members.

T99: Rights to Organize and Collective Bargaining Convention (1949)

Type B (steady increase) and has 161 registered members.

T100: Equal Remuneration Convention (1951)

Type B (steady increase) and has 169 registered members.

T101: Abolition of Forced Labor Convention (1957)

Type B (steady increase) and has 170 registered members.

T102: Discrimination Convention (1958)

Type B (steady increase) and has 170 registered members.

T103: Radiation Protection Convention (1960)

Type A and has 49 registered members.

T104: Guarding of Machinery Convention (1963)

Type B (steady increase) and has 52 registered members.

T105: Hygiene (Commerce and Offices) Convention (1964)

Type B (steady increase) and has 51 registered members.

T106: Maximum Weight Convention (1967)

Type A and has 29 registered members.

T107: Benzene Convention (1971)

Type A and has 38 registered members.

T108: Minimum Age Convention (1973)

Type C and has 163 registered members.

T109: Occupational Cancer Convention (1974)

Type A and has 39 registered members.

T110: Working Environment (Air Pollution Noise and Vibration) Convention (1977)

Type A and has 45 registered members.

T111: Occupational Safety and Health Convention (1981)

Tpe B (steady increase) and has 60 registered members.

T112: Occupational Health Services Convention (1985)

Type A and has 31 registered members.

T113: Asbestos Convention (1986)

Type A and has 31 registered members.

T114: Safety and Health in Construction Convention (1988)

Type A and has 24 registered members.

T115: Chemicals Convention (1990)

Type A and has 17 registered members.

T116: Prevention of Major Industrial Accidents Convention (1993)

Type A and has 17 registered members.

T117: Safety and Health in Mines Convention (1995)

Type A and has 26 registered members.

T118: Worst Forms of Child Labor Convention (1999)

Type D and has 175 registered members.

T119: Safety and Health in Agriculture Convention (2001)

Type A and has 15 registered members.

T120: Promotional Framework for Occupational Safety and Health Convention (2006)

Type A and has 24 registered members.

Appendix 3: Hexagonal Profiles of 193 Member States of United Nations Towards Multilateral Treaties

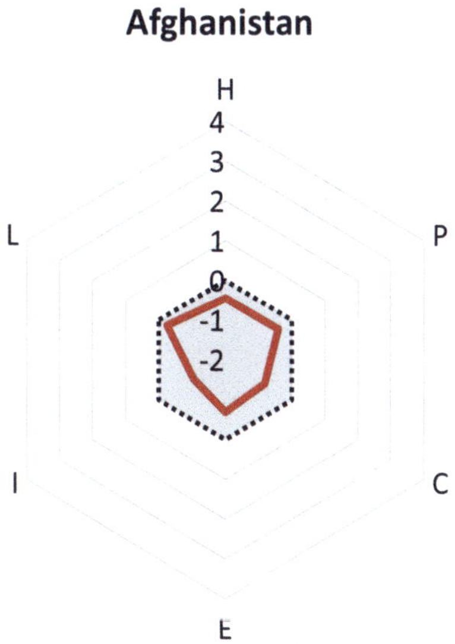

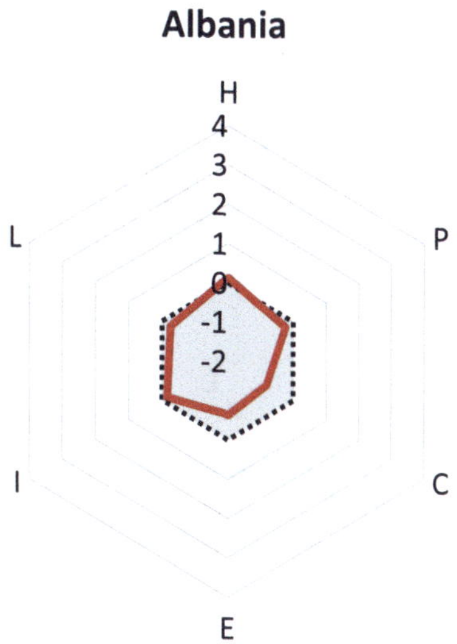

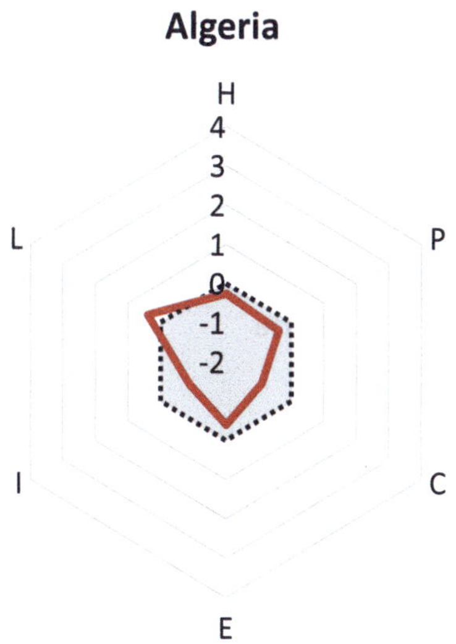

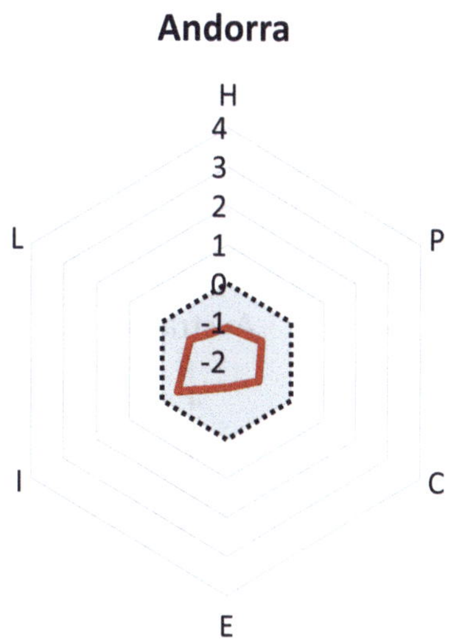

Angola

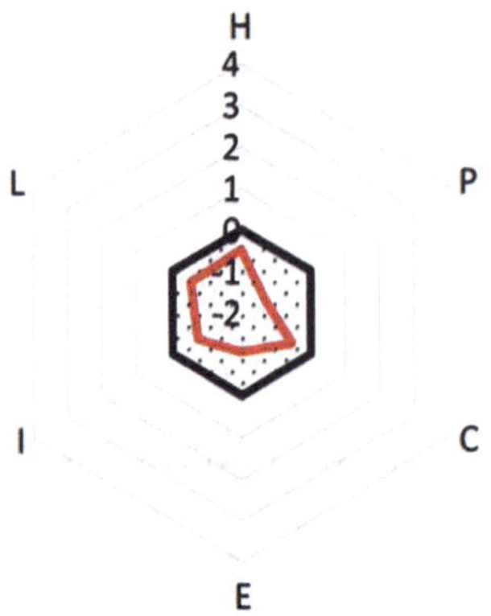

Antigua and Barbuda

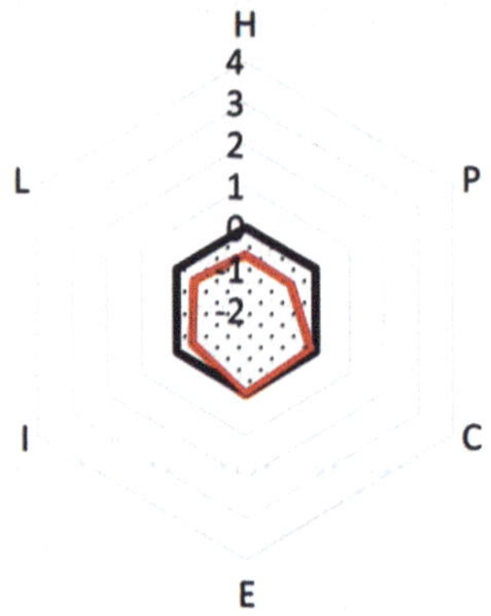

Argentina

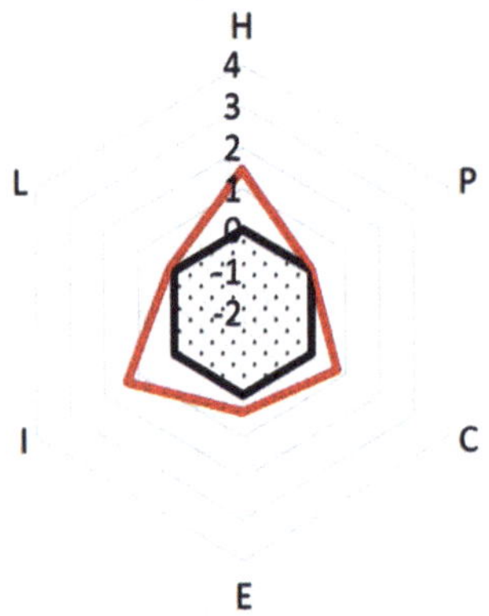

Armenia

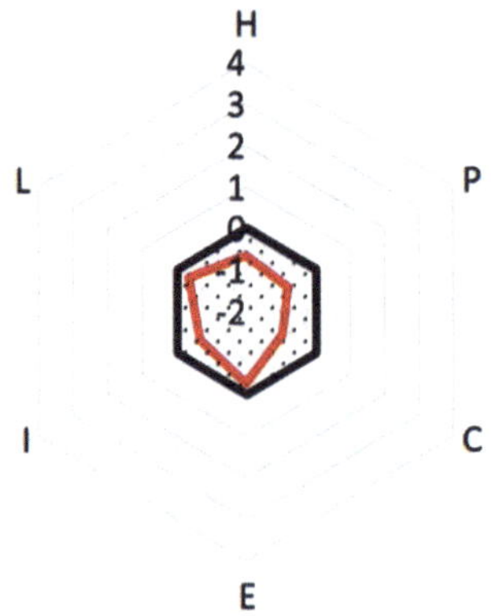

Australia

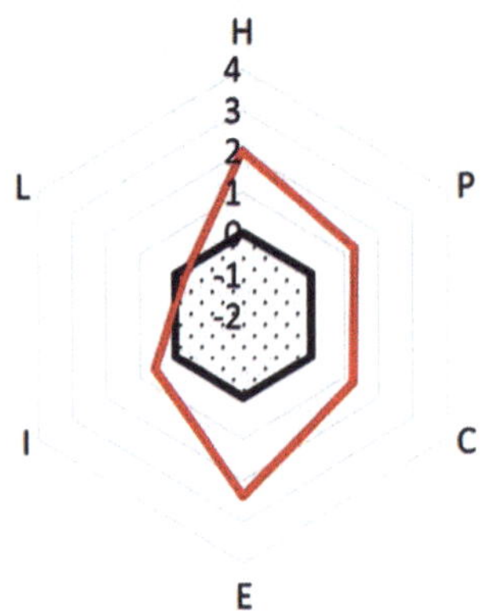

Austria

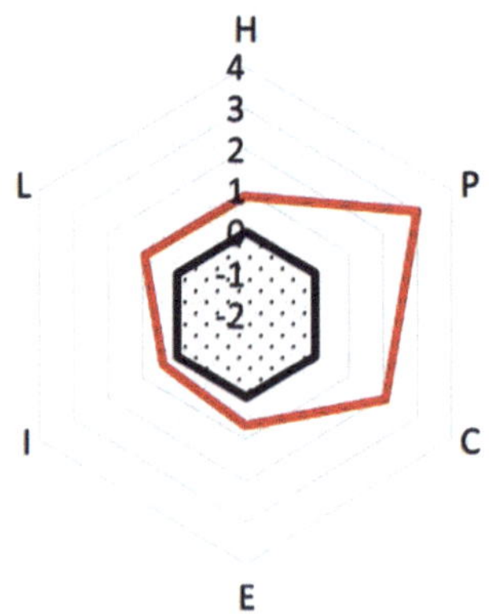

Azerbaijan

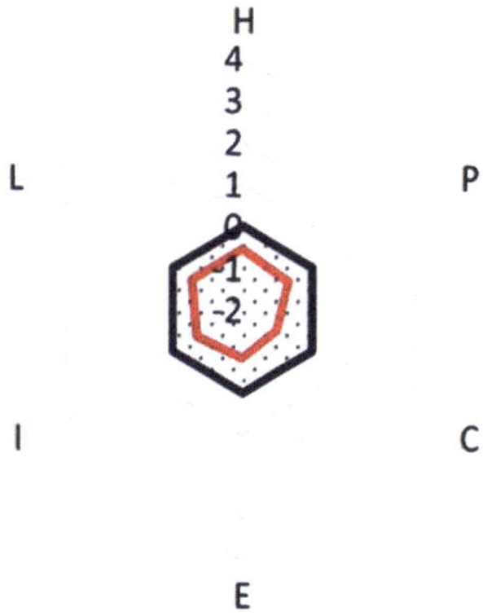

Bahamas

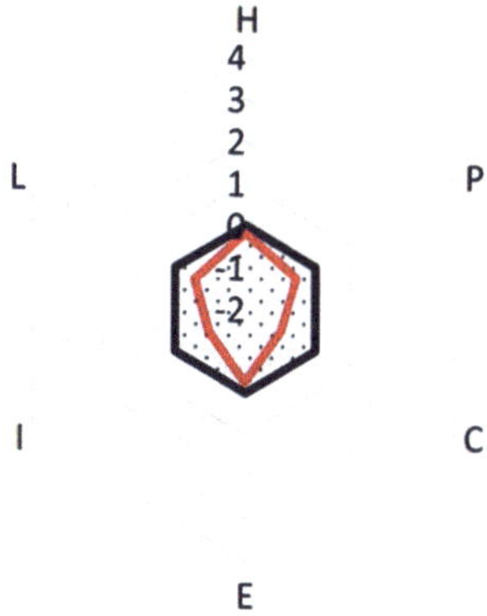

Bahrain

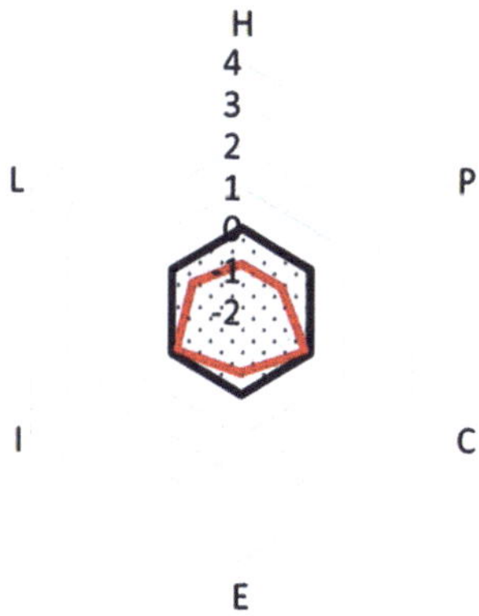

Bangladesh

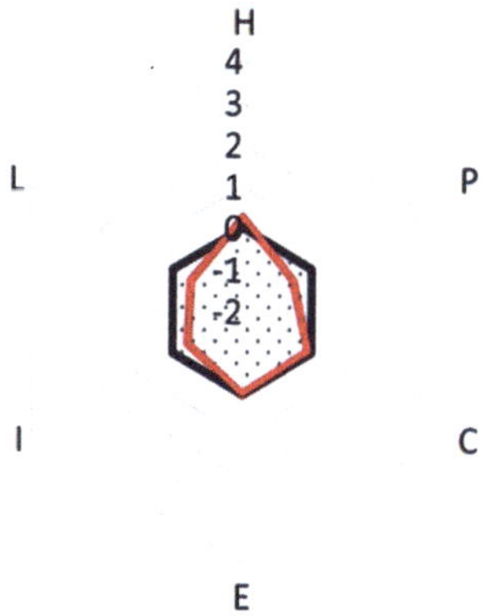

Barbados

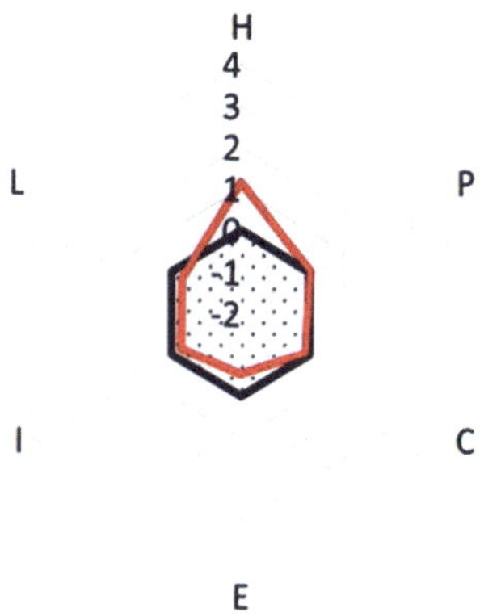

Belarus

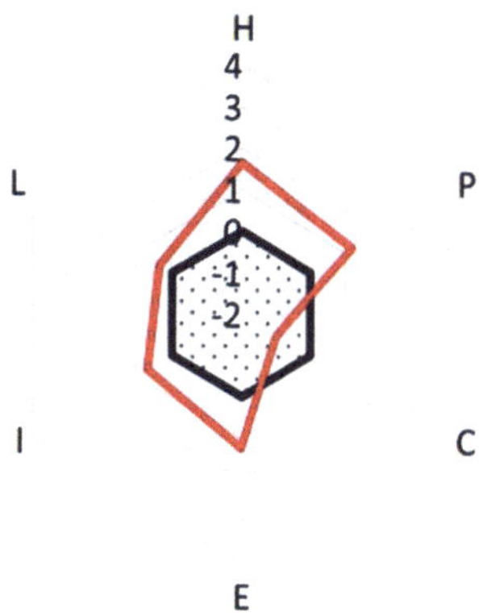

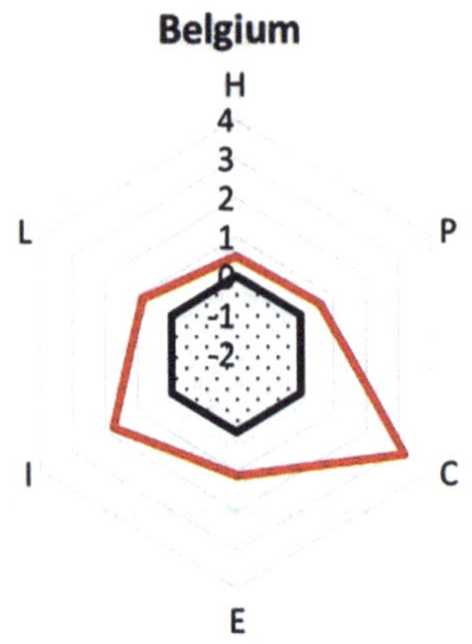
Belgium
H
4
3
2
1
0
-1
-2
P
C
E
I
L

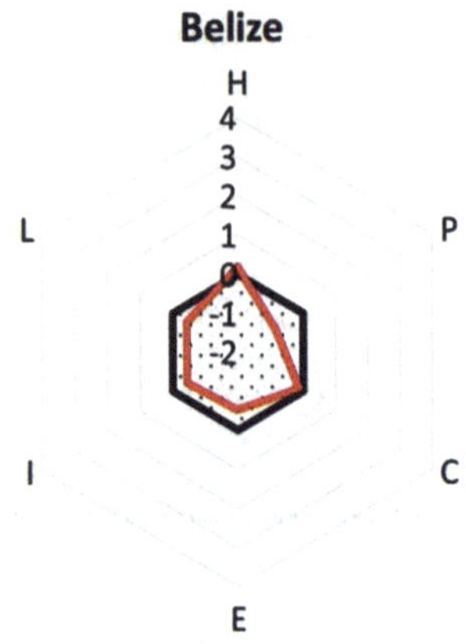
Belize
H
4
3
2
1
0
-1
-2
P
C
E
I
L

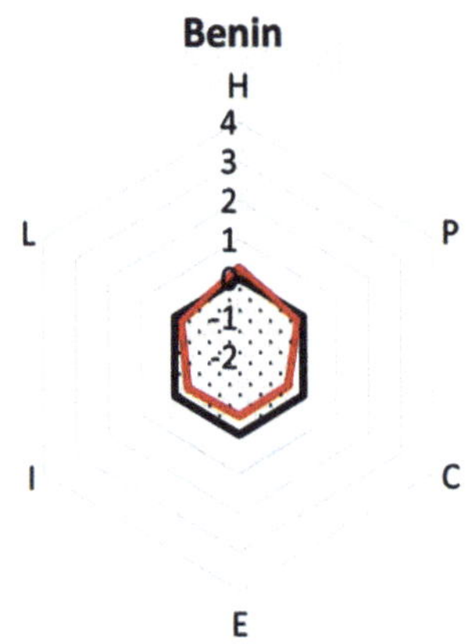
Benin
H
4
3
2
1
0
-1
-2
P
C
E
I
L

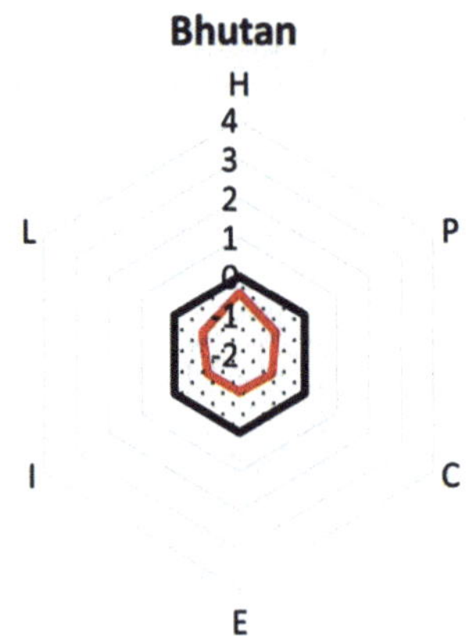
Bhutan
H
4
3
2
1
0
-1
-2
P
C
E
I
L

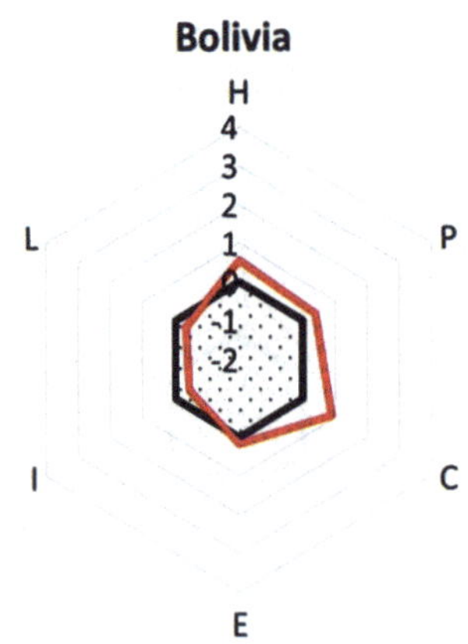
Bolivia
H
4
3
2
1
0
-1
-2
P
C
E
I
L

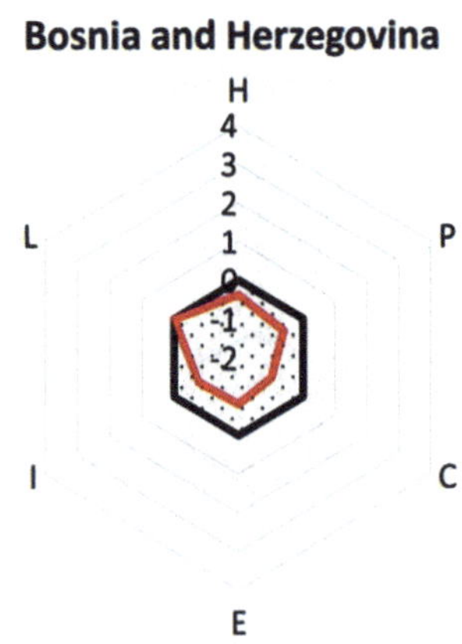
Bosnia and Herzegovina
H
4
3
2
1
0
-1
-2
P
C
E
I
L

Botswana

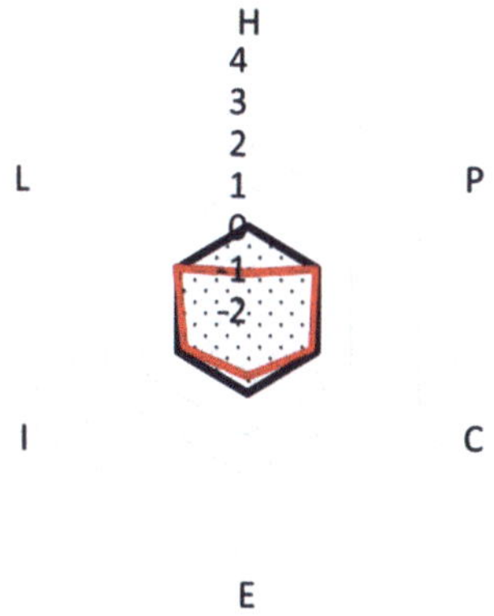

Brazil

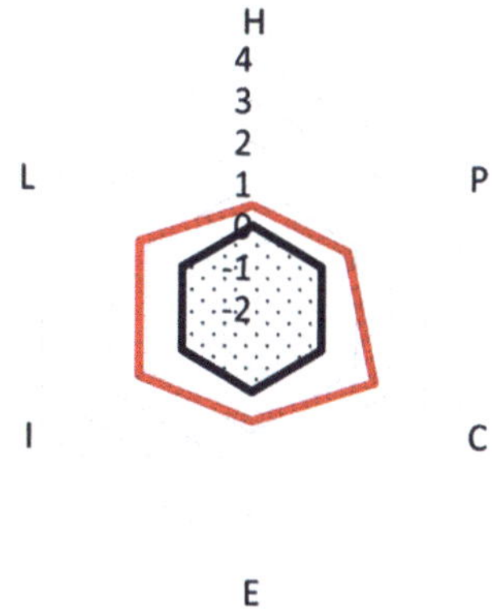

Brunei Darussalam

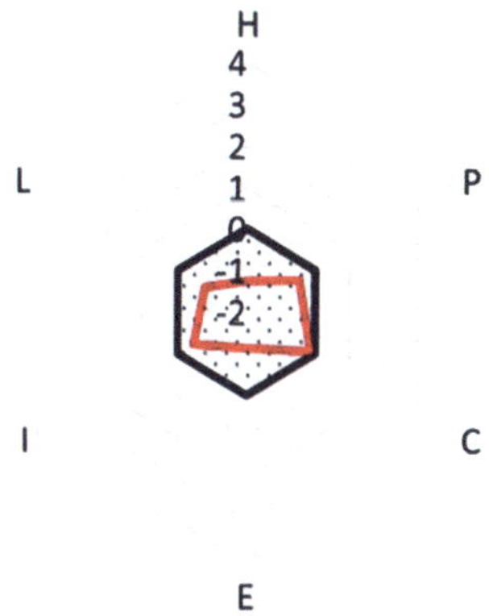

Bulgaria

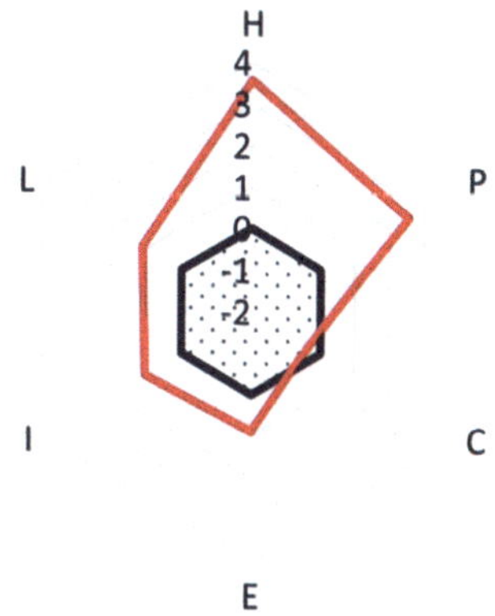

Burkina Faso

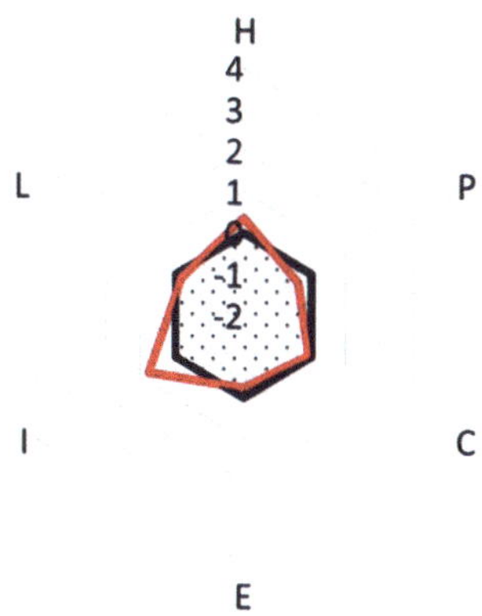

Burundi

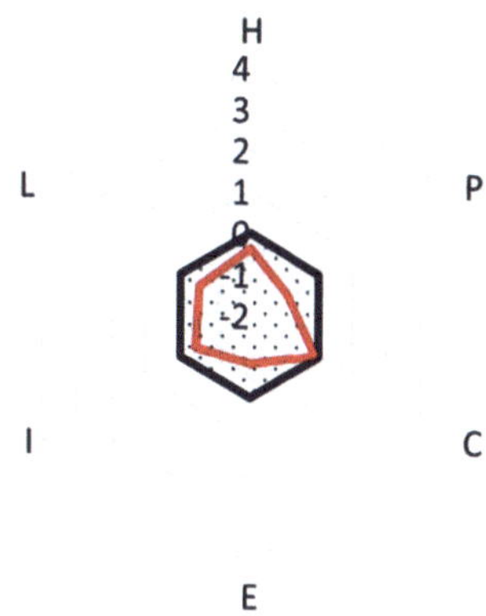

Cambodia

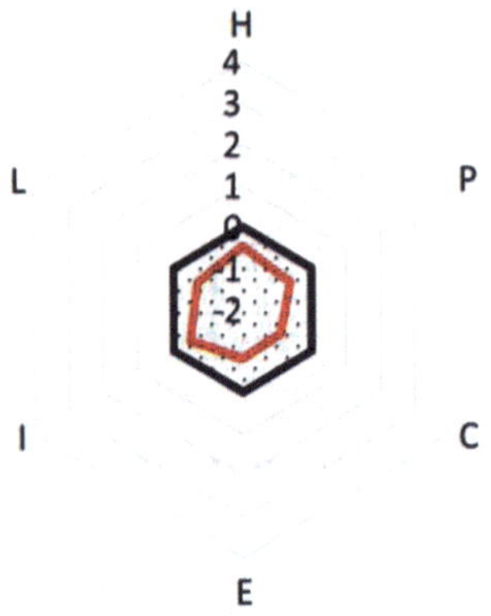

Cabo Verde

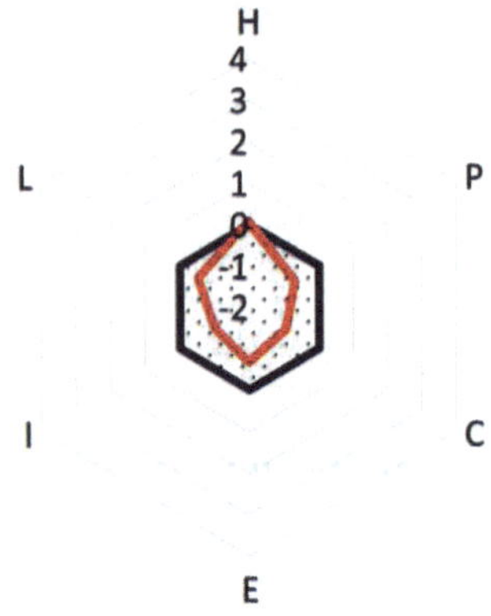

Cameroon

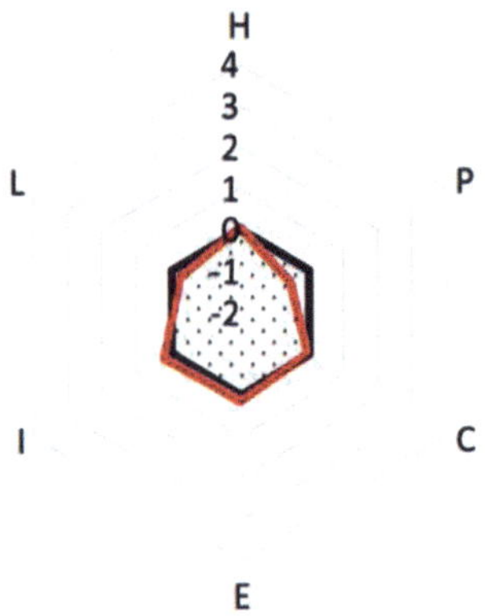

Canada

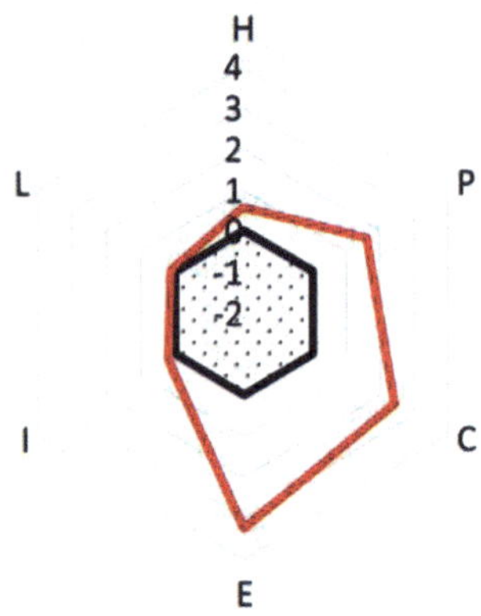

Central African Republic

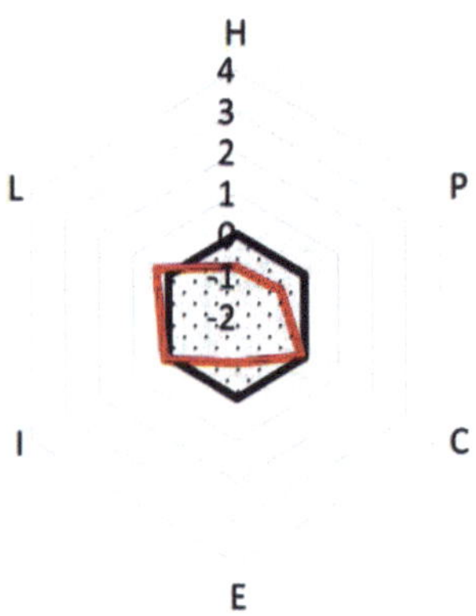

Chad

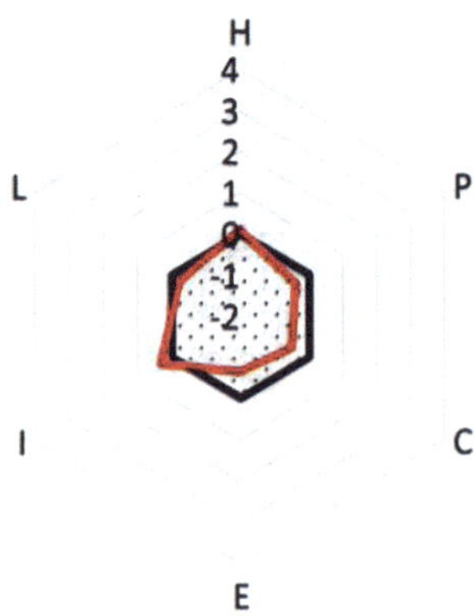

Chile

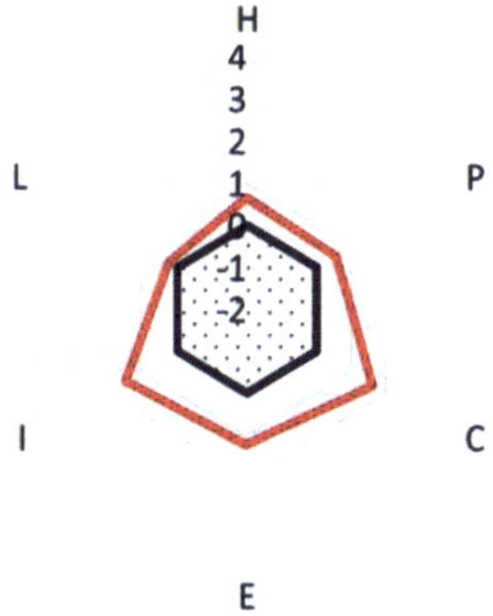

China

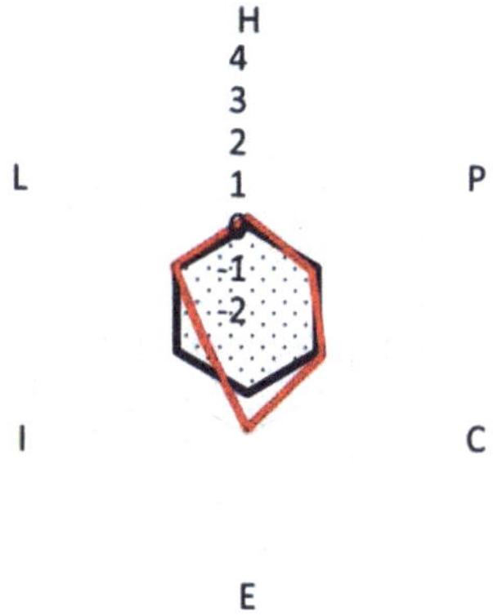

Colombia

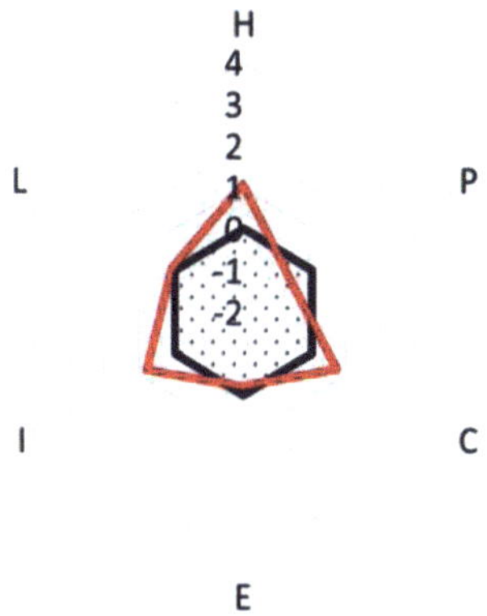

Comoros

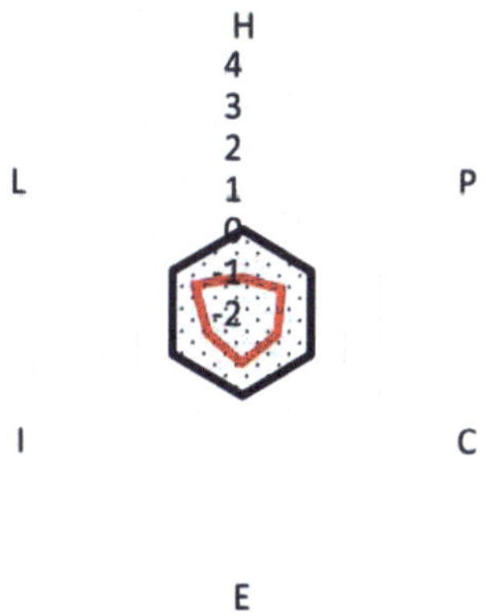

Congo

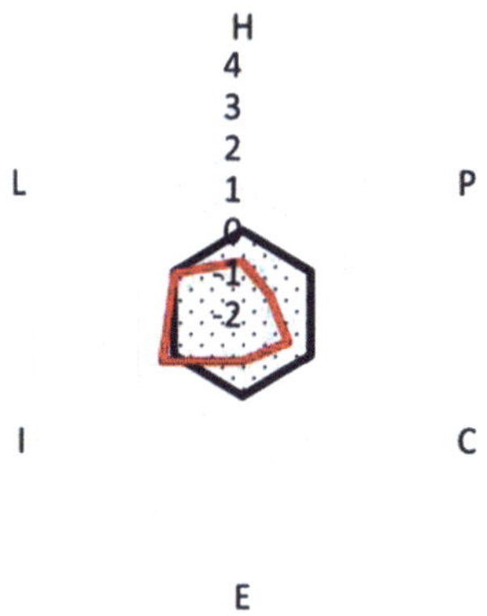

Costa Rica

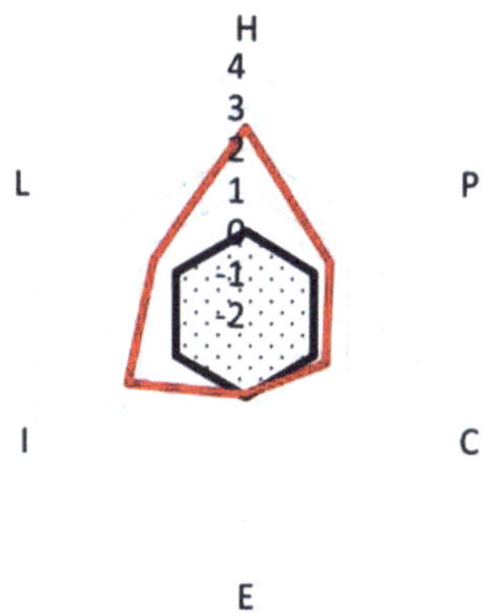

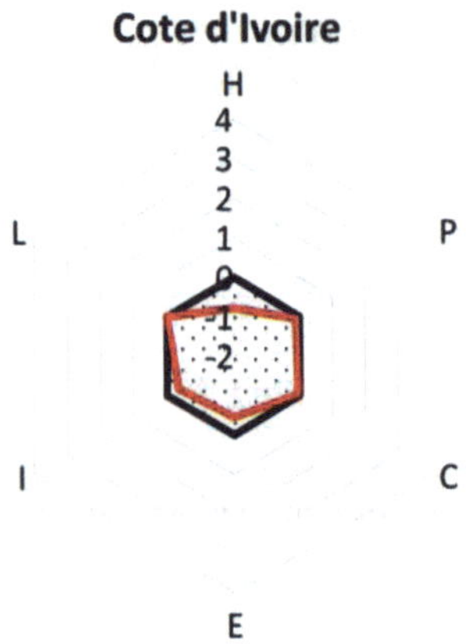
Cote d'Ivoire
H
4
3
2
1
0
-1
-2
P
C
E
I
L

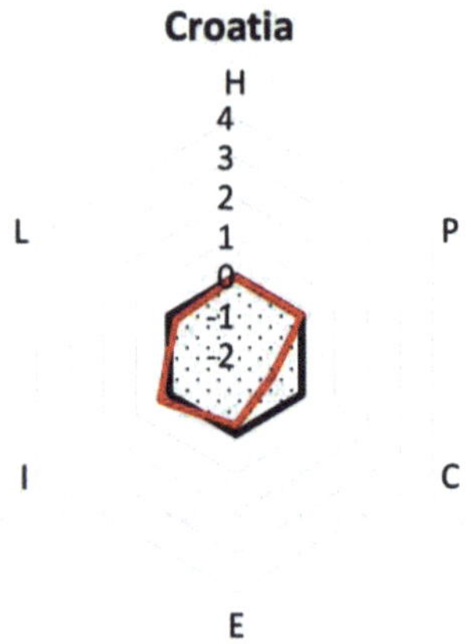
Croatia
H
4
3
2
1
0
-1
-2
P
C
E
I
L

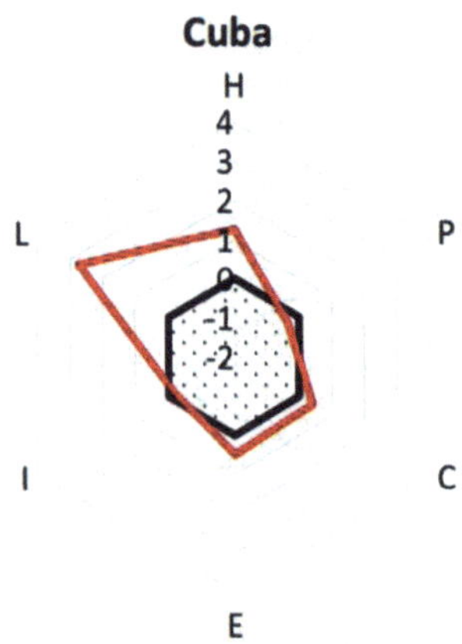
Cuba
H
4
3
2
1
0
-1
-2
P
C
E
I
L

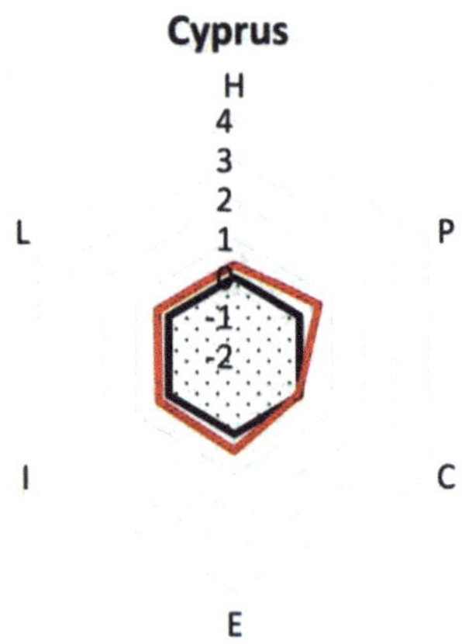
Cyprus
H
4
3
2
1
0
-1
-2
P
C
E
I
L

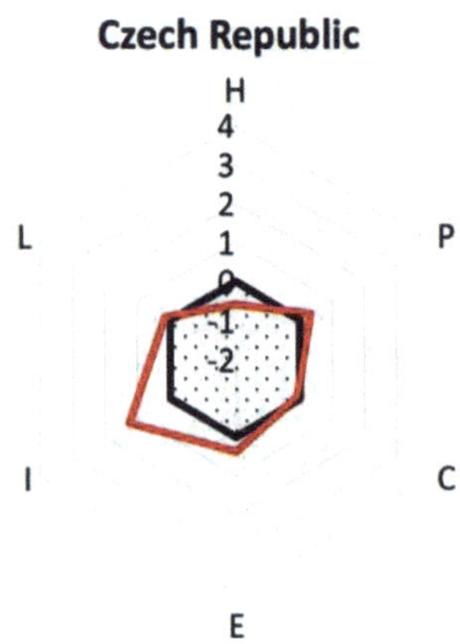
Czech Republic
H
4
3
2
1
0
-1
-2
P
C
E
I
L

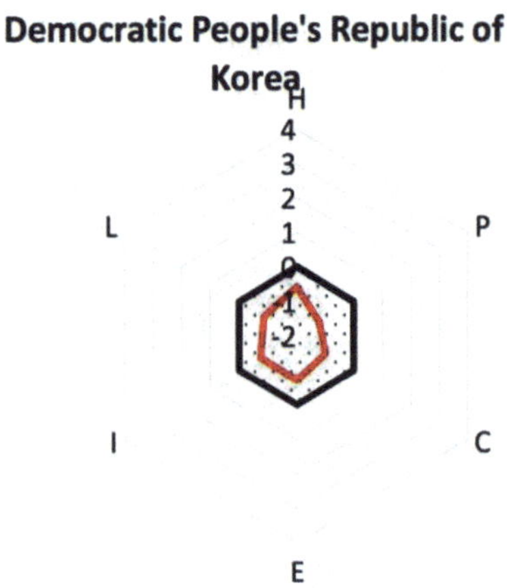
Democratic People's Republic of Korea
H
4
3
2
1
0
-1
-2
P
C
E
I
L

Democratic Republic of the Congo

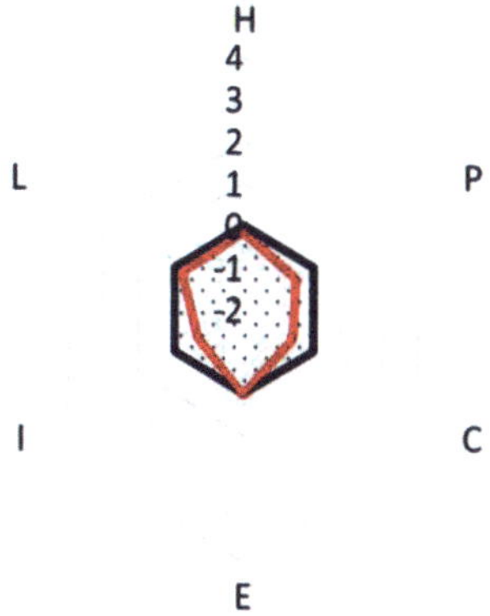

Denmark

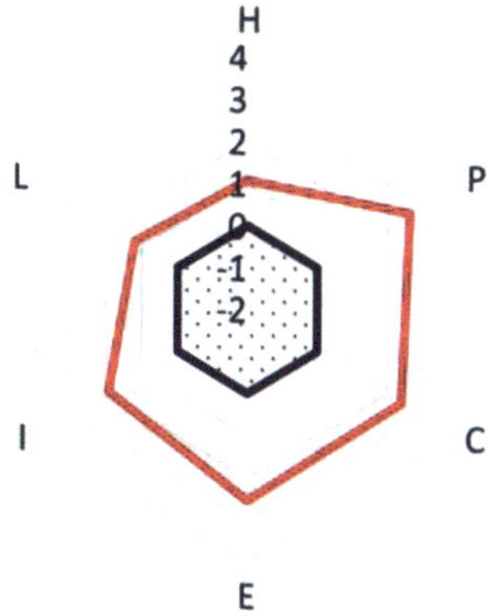

Djibouti

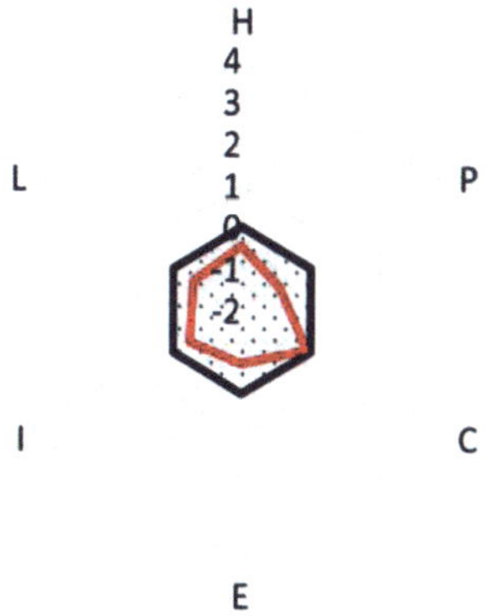

Dominica

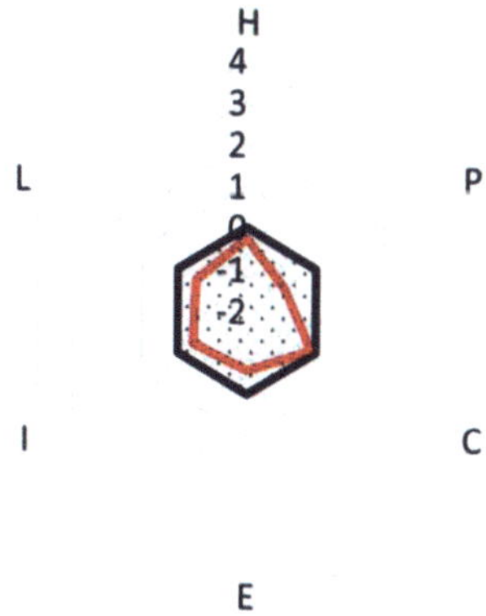

Dominican Republic

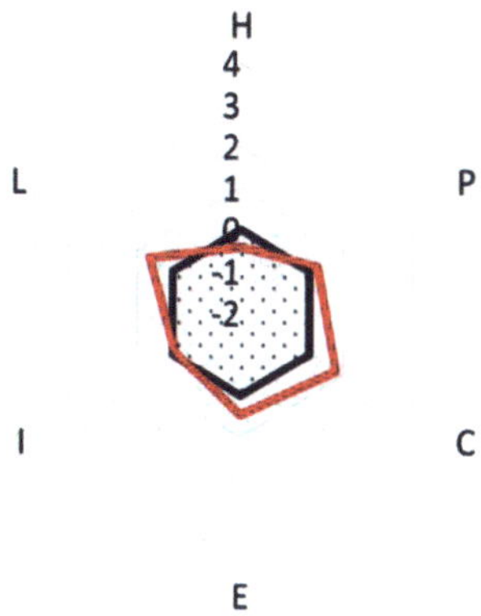

Ecuador

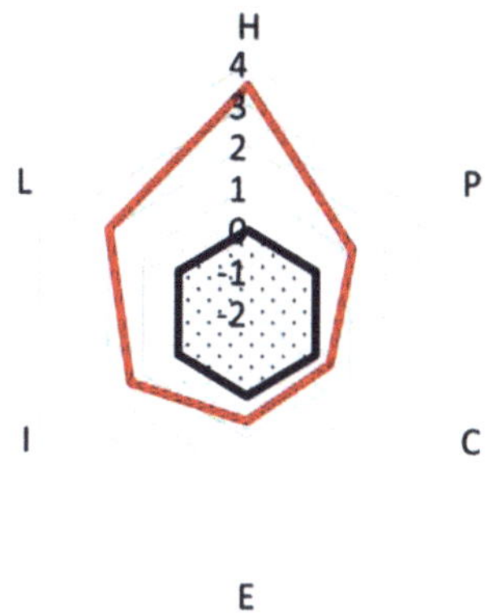

Egypt

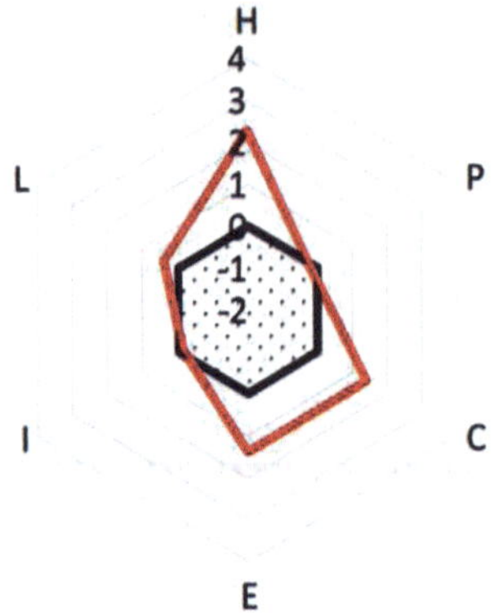

El Salvador

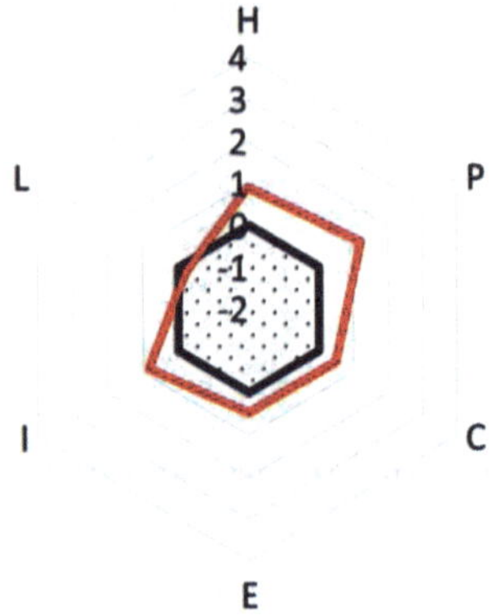

Equatorial Guinea

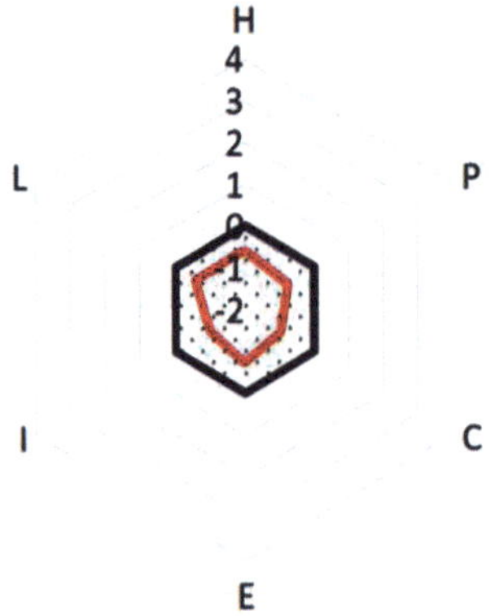

Eritrea

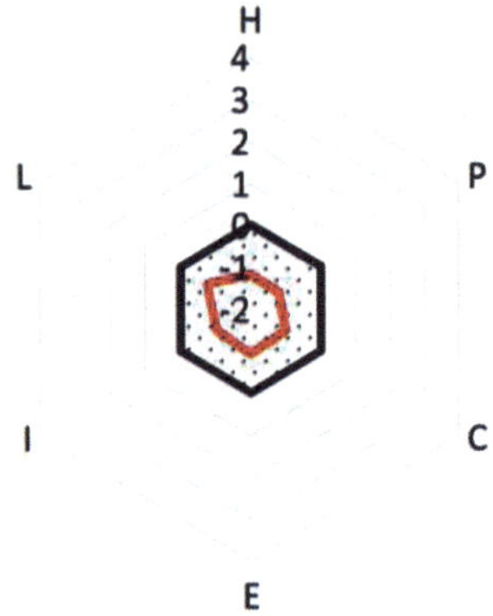

Estonia

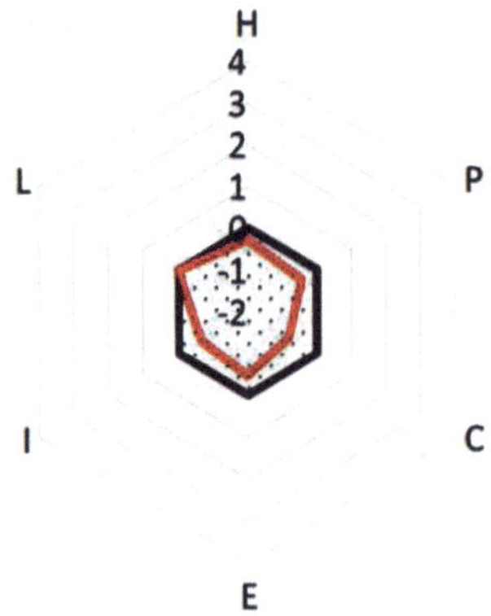

Ethiopia

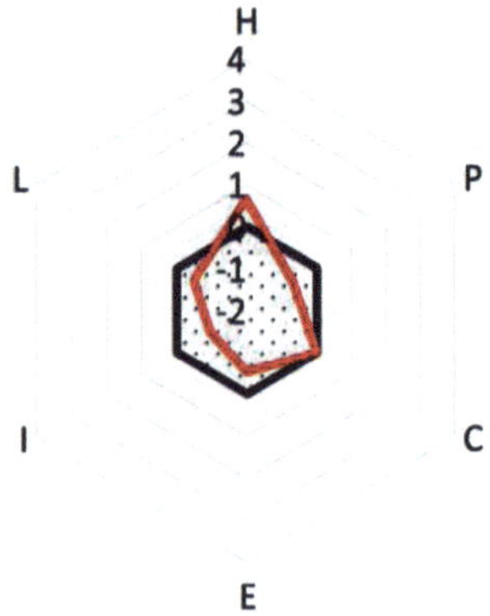

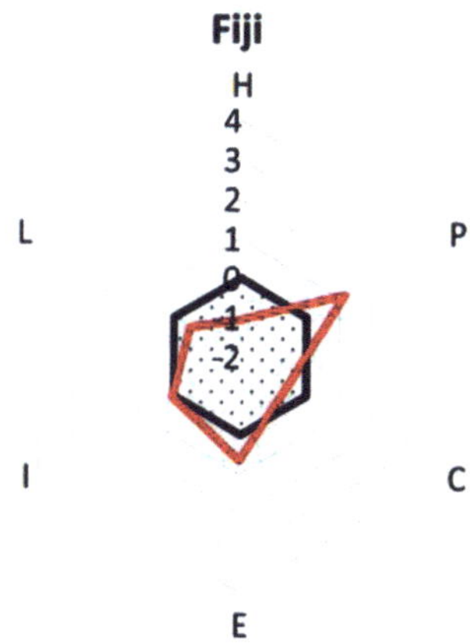
Fiji
H
4
3
2
1
0
-1
-2
L
P
I
C
E

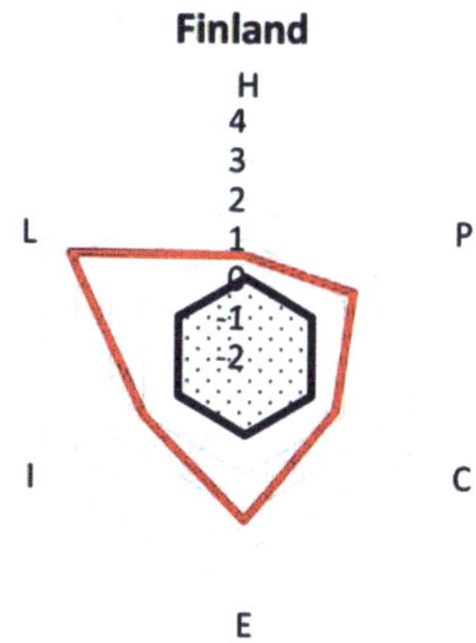
Finland
H
4
3
2
1
0
-1
-2
L
P
I
C
E

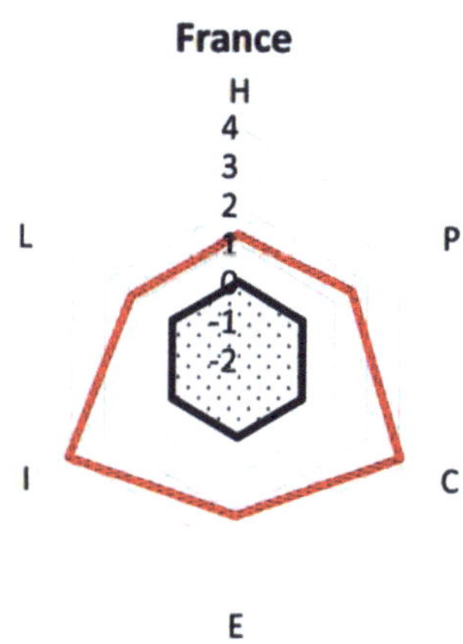
France
H
4
3
2
1
0
-1
-2
L
P
I
C
E

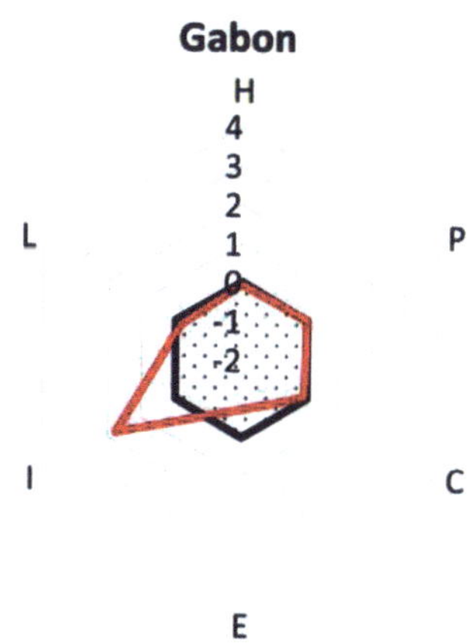
Gabon
H
4
3
2
1
0
-1
-2
L
P
I
C
E

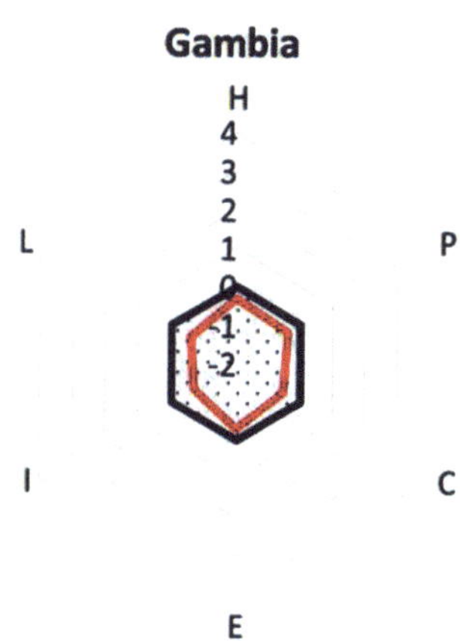
Gambia
H
4
3
2
1
0
-1
-2
L
P
I
C
E

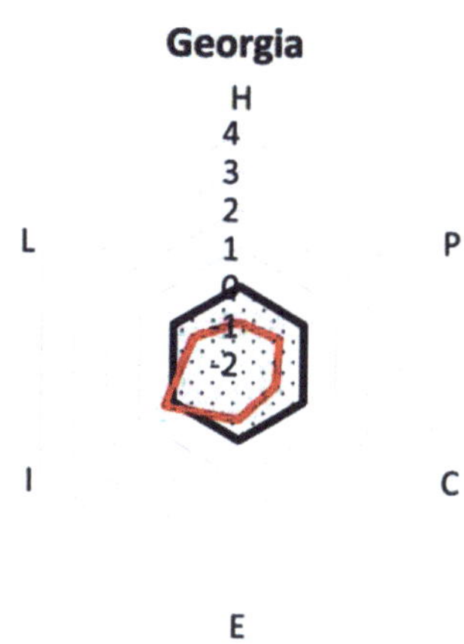
Georgia
H
4
3
2
1
0
-1
-2
L
P
I
C
E

Germany

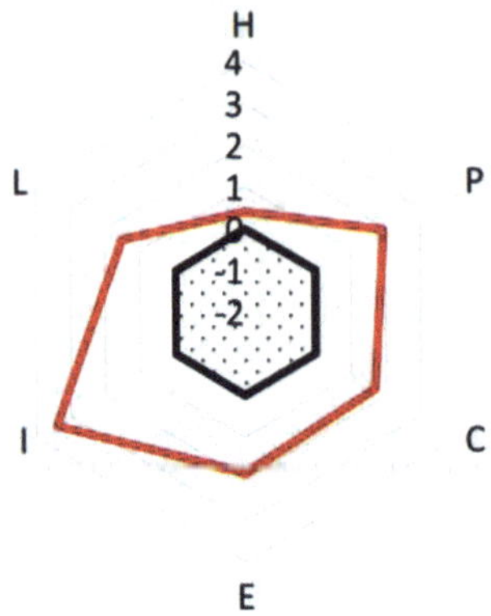

Ghana

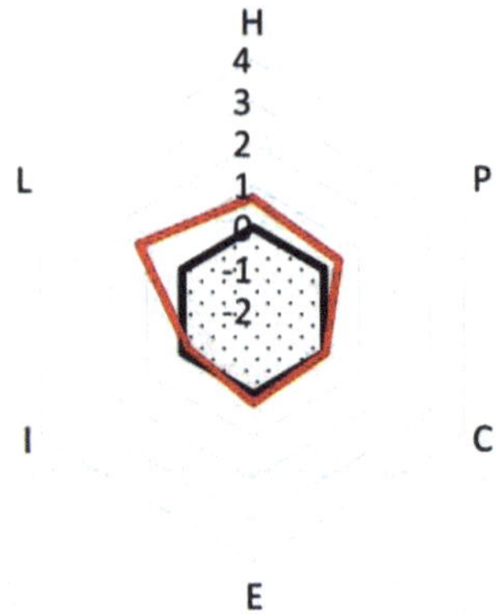

Greece

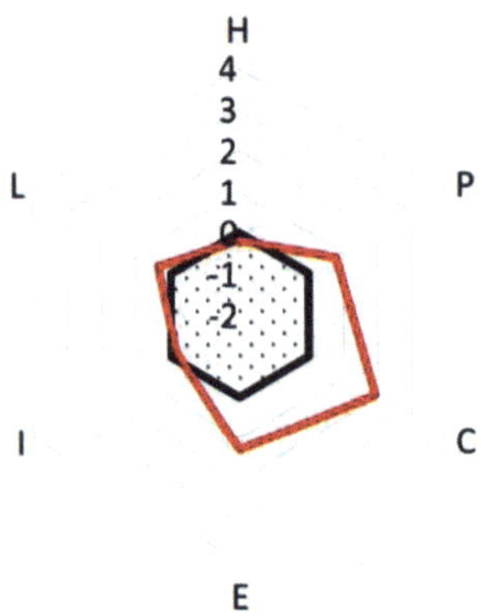

Grenada

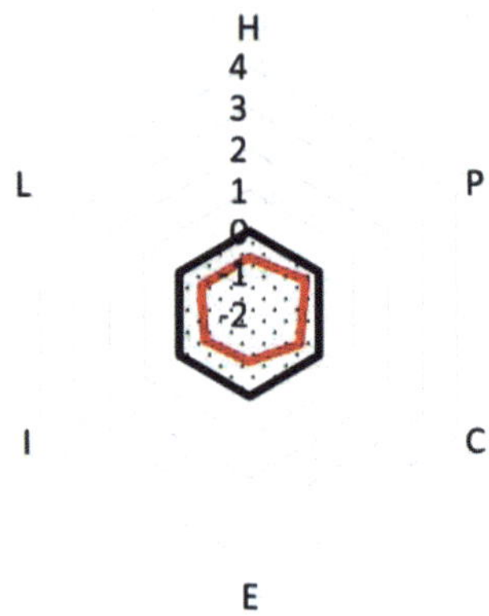

Guatemala

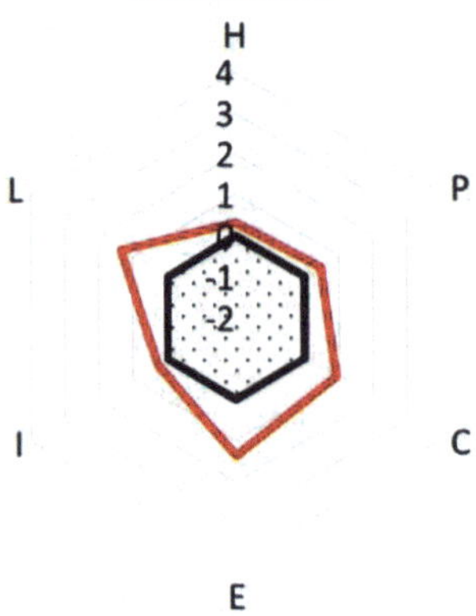

Guinea

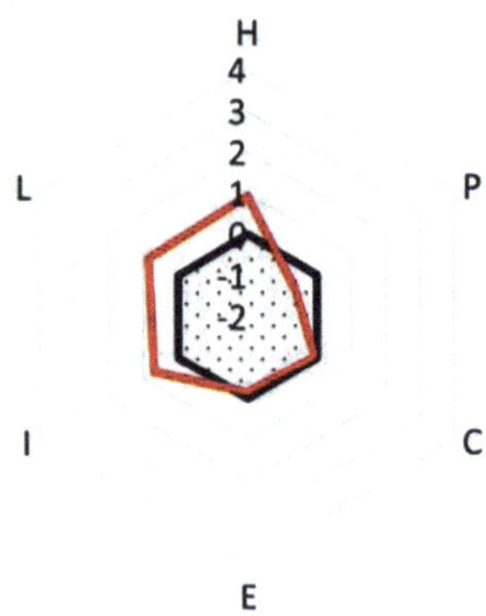

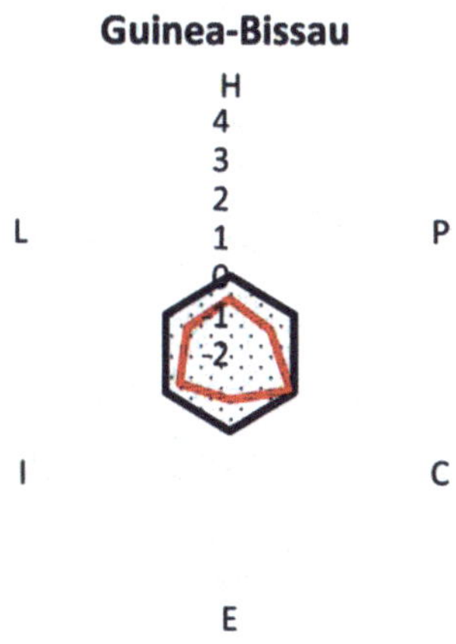
Guinea-Bissau
H
4
3
2
1
0
-1
-2
L
P
I
C
E

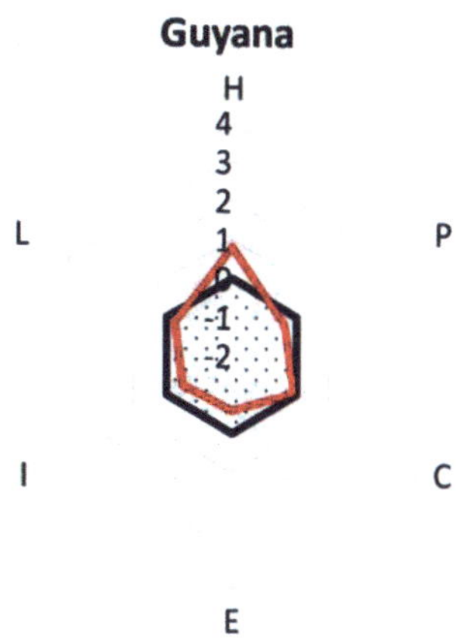
Guyana
H
4
3
2
1
0
-1
-2
L
P
I
C
E

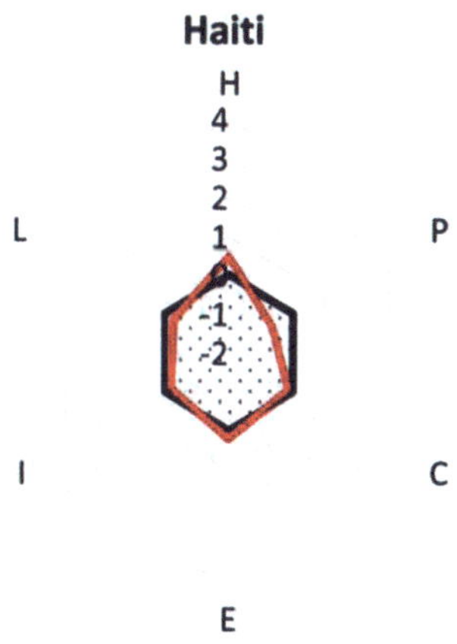
Haiti
H
4
3
2
1
0
-1
-2
L
P
I
C
E

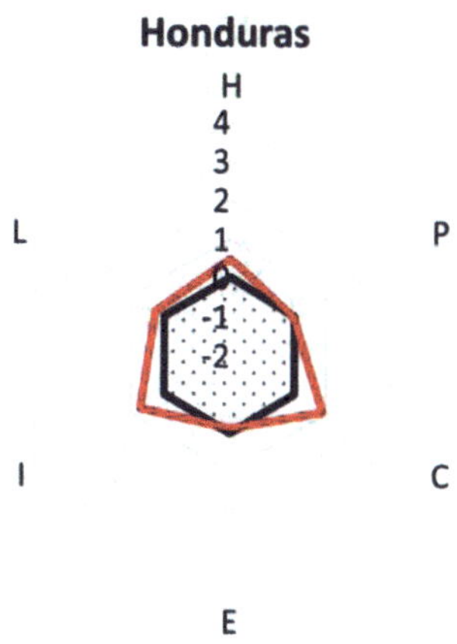
Honduras
H
4
3
2
1
0
-1
-2
L
P
I
C
E

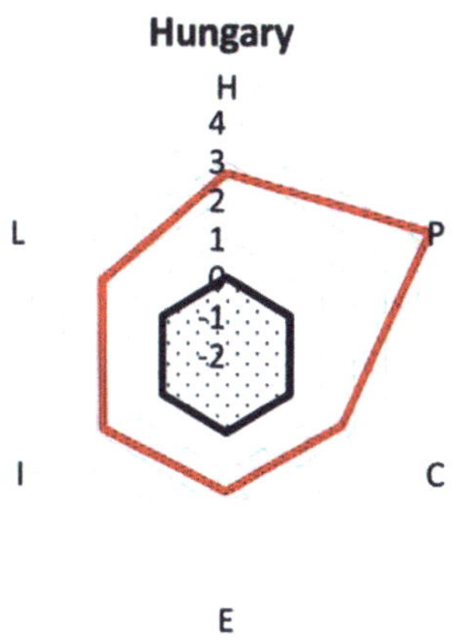
Hungary
H
4
3
2
1
0
-1
-2
L
P
I
C
E

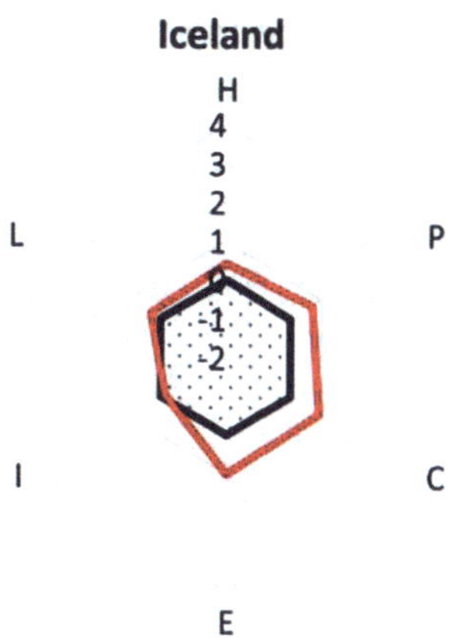
Iceland
H
4
3
2
1
0
-1
-2
L
P
I
C
E

India

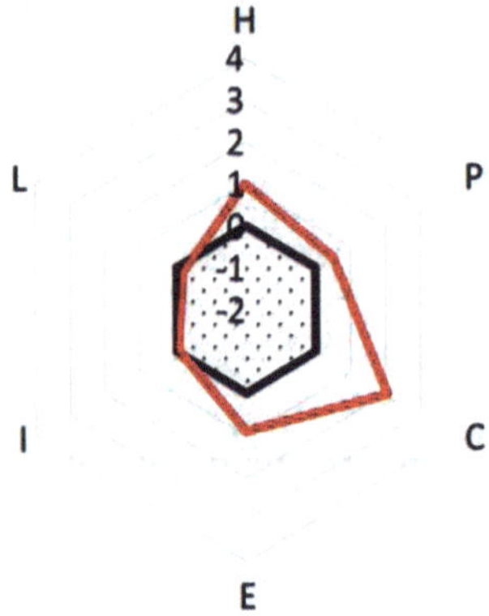

Indonesia

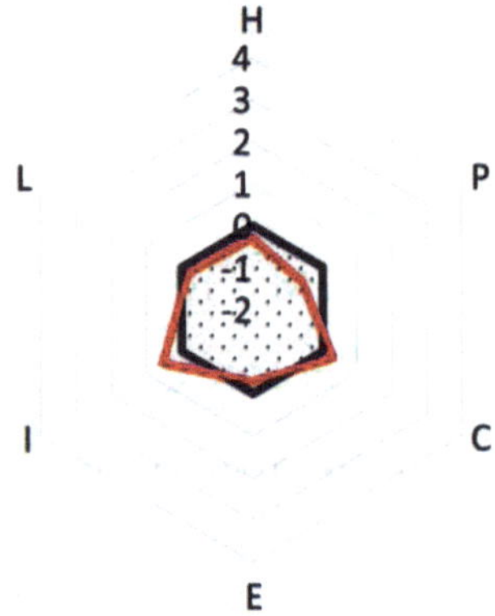

Iran

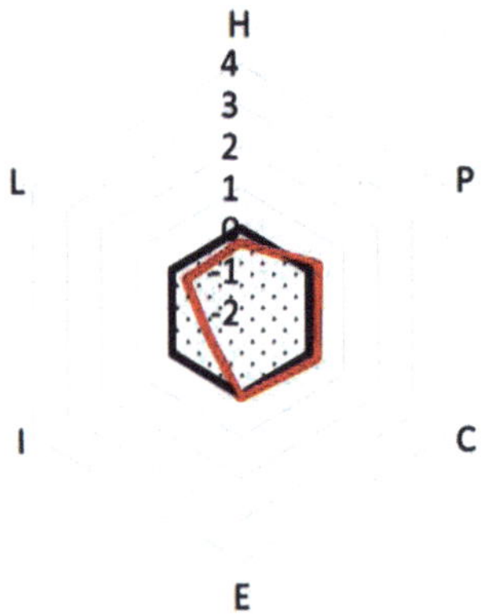

Iraq

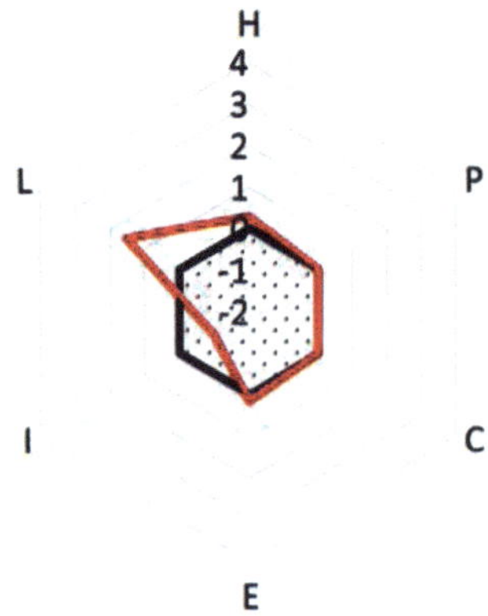

Ireland

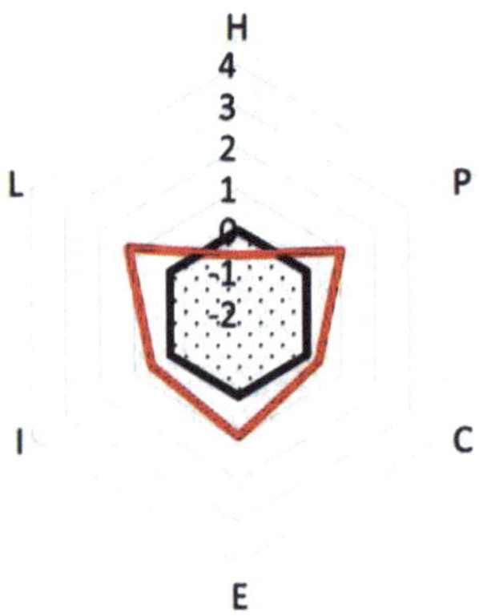

Israel

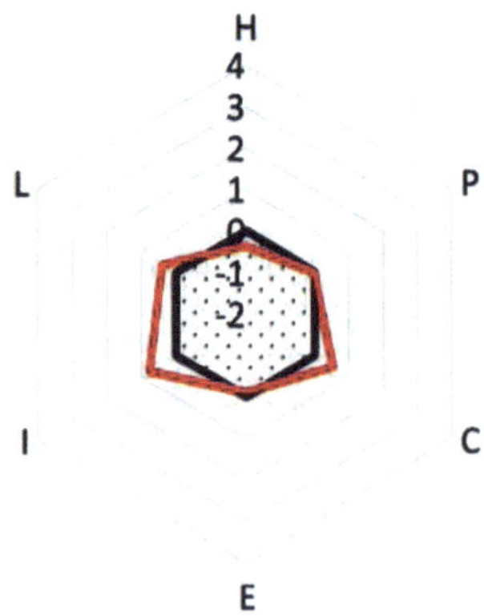

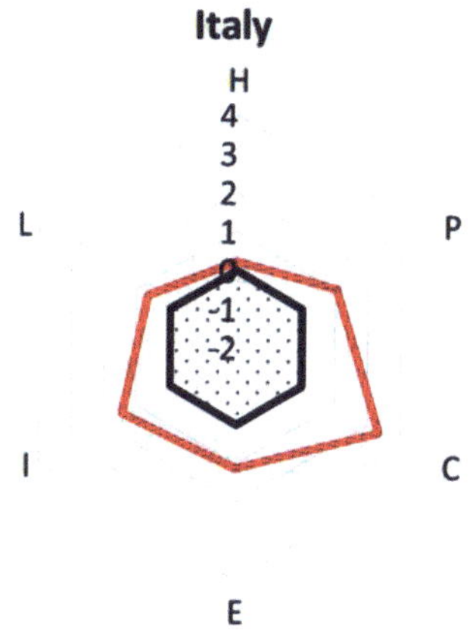
Italy
H
4
3
2
1
0
-1
-2
L
P
I
C
E

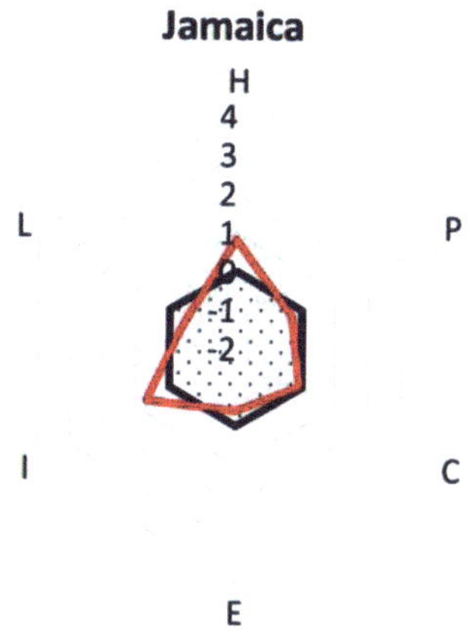
Jamaica
H
4
3
2
1
0
-1
-2
L
P
I
C
E

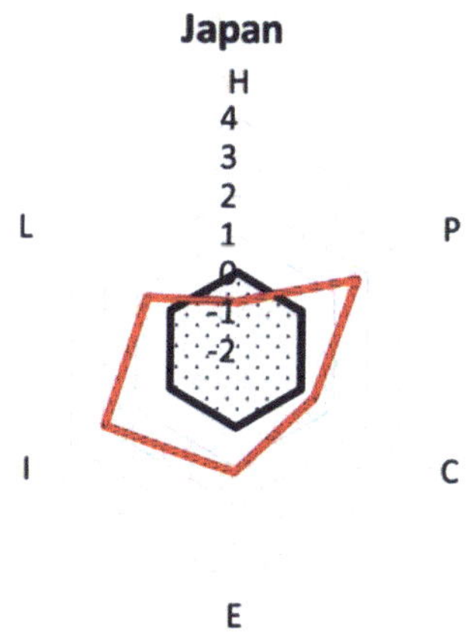
Japan
H
4
3
2
1
0
-1
-2
L
P
I
C
E

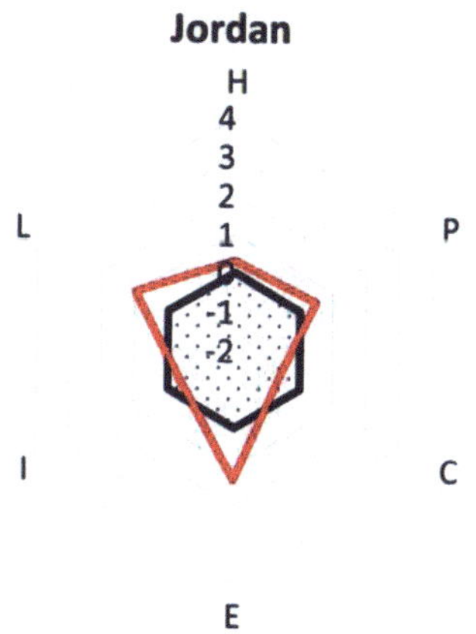
Jordan
H
4
3
2
1
0
-1
-2
L
P
I
C
E

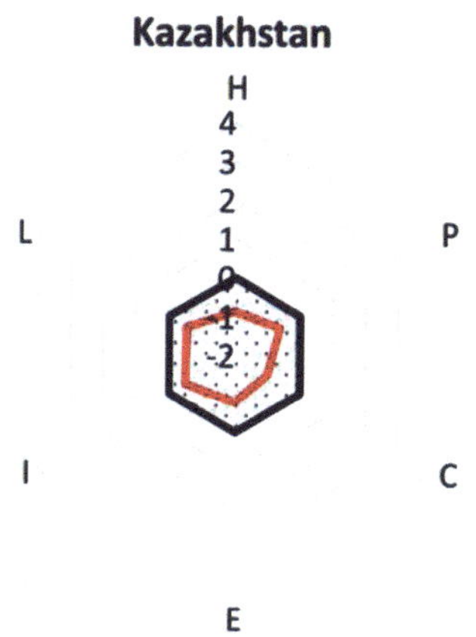
Kazakhstan
H
4
3
2
1
0
-1
-2
L
P
I
C
E

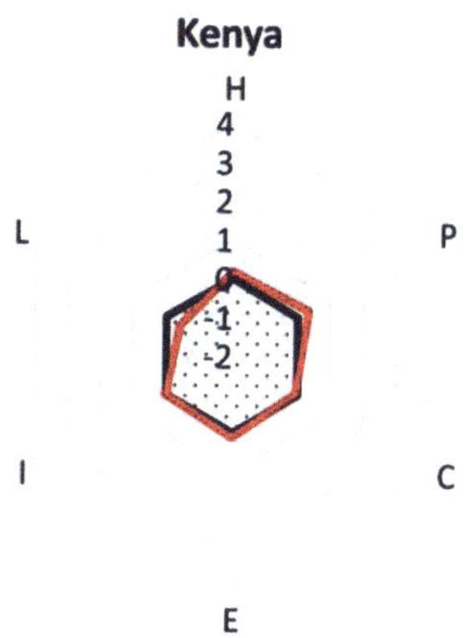
Kenya
H
4
3
2
1
0
-1
-2
L
P
I
C
E

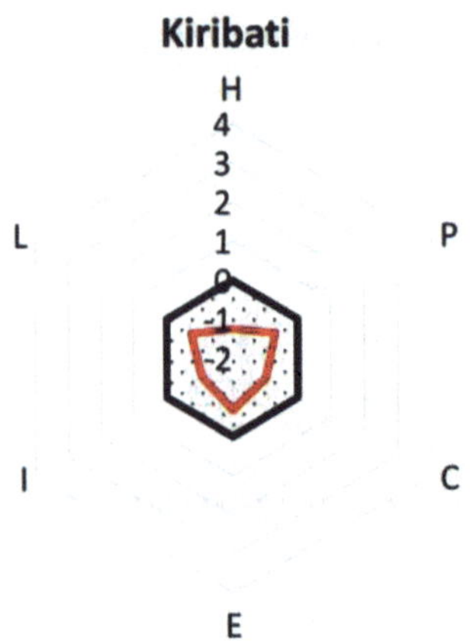
Kiribati
H
4
3
2
1
0
-1
-2
P
C
E
I
L

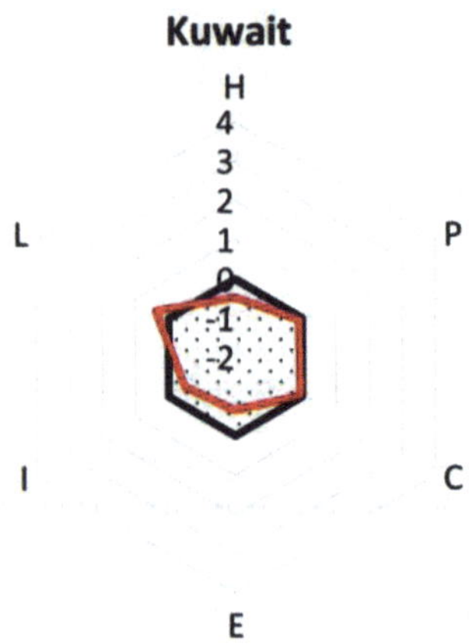
Kuwait
H
4
3
2
1
0
-1
-2
P
C
E
I
L

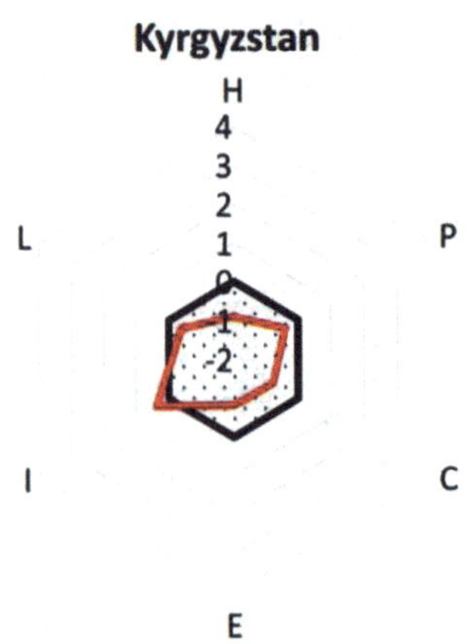
Kyrgyzstan
H
4
3
2
1
0
-1
-2
P
C
E
I
L

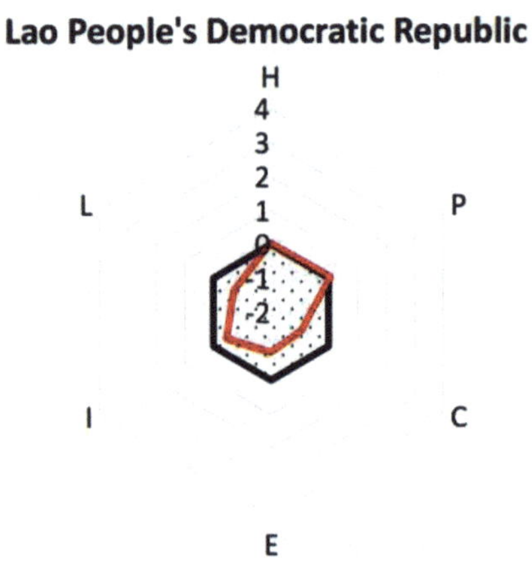
Lao People's Democratic Republic
H
4
3
2
1
0
-1
-2
P
C
E
I
L

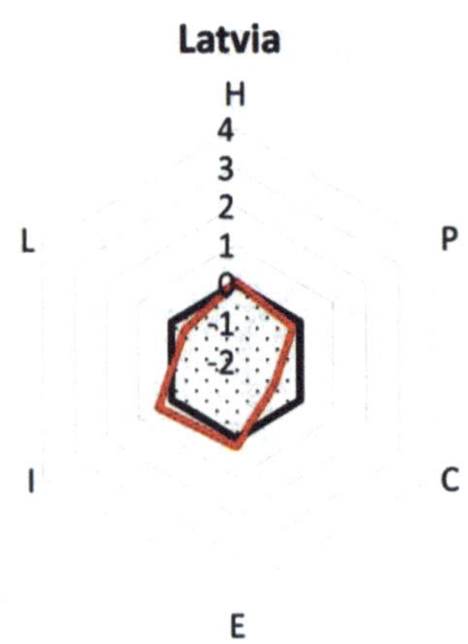
Latvia
H
4
3
2
1
0
-1
-2
P
C
E
I
L

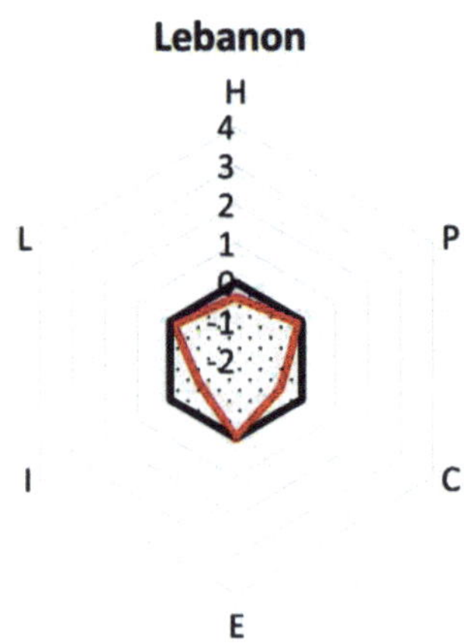
Lebanon
H
4
3
2
1
0
-1
-2
P
C
E
I
L

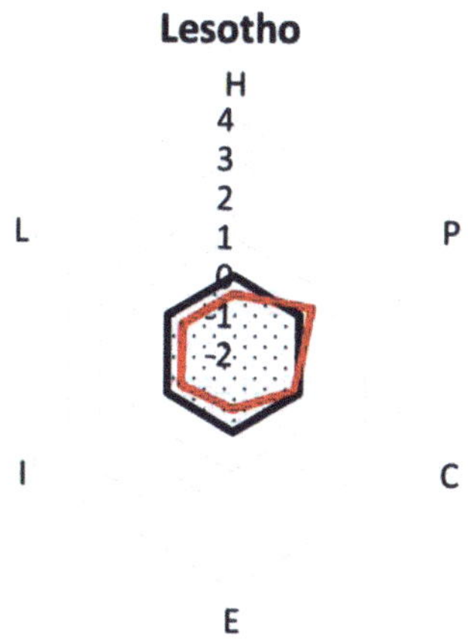
Lesotho
H
4
3
2
1
0
-1
-2
L
P
I
C
E

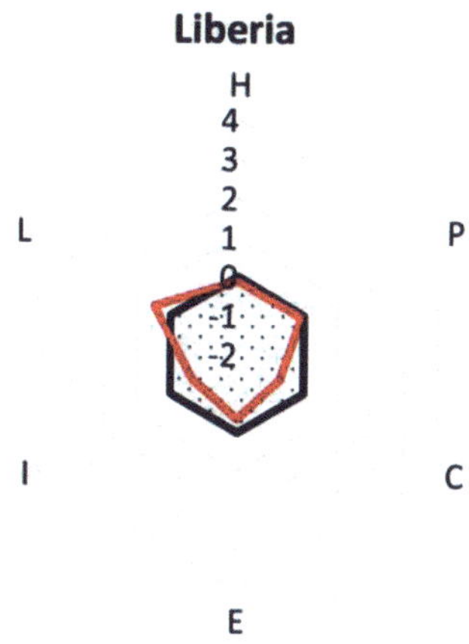
Liberia
H
4
3
2
1
0
-1
-2
L
P
I
C
E

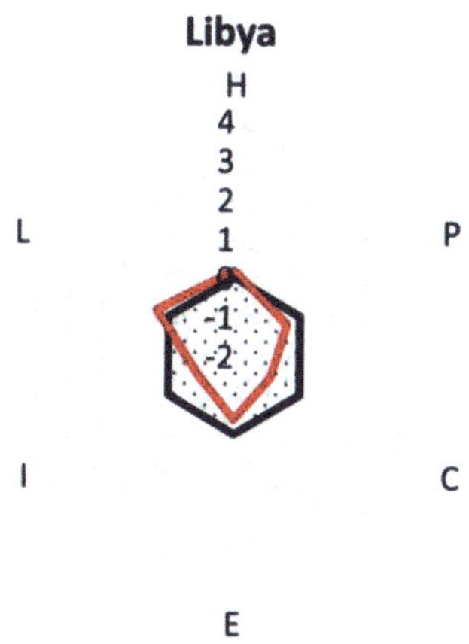
Libya
H
4
3
2
1
0
-1
-2
L
P
I
C
E

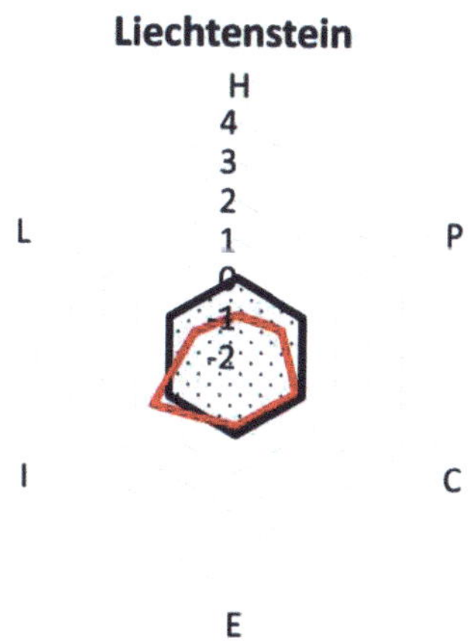
Liechtenstein
H
4
3
2
1
0
-1
-2
L
P
I
C
E

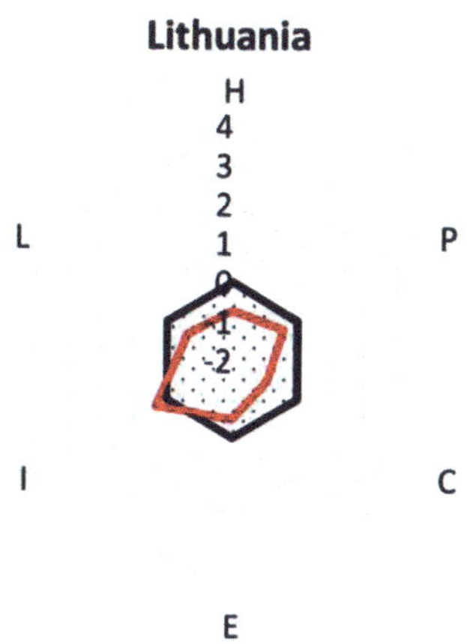
Lithuania
H
4
3
2
1
0
-1
-2
L
P
I
C
E

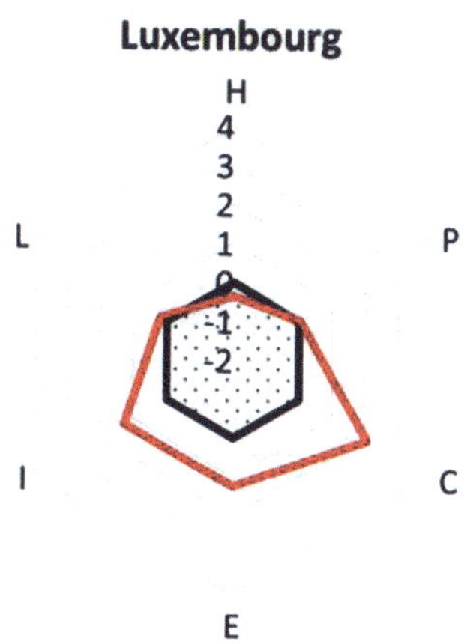
Luxembourg
H
4
3
2
1
0
-1
-2
L
P
I
C
E

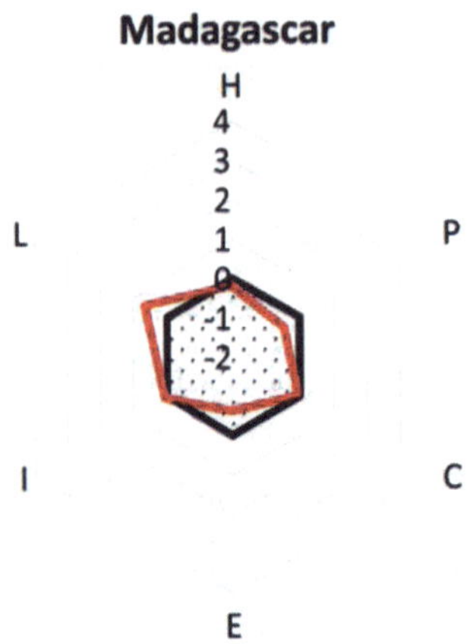
Madagascar
H
4
3
2
1
0
-1
-2
P
C
E
I
L

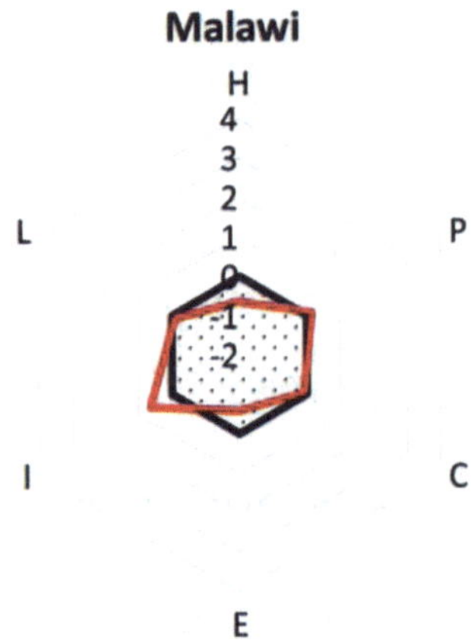
Malawi
H
4
3
2
1
0
-1
-2
P
C
E
I
L

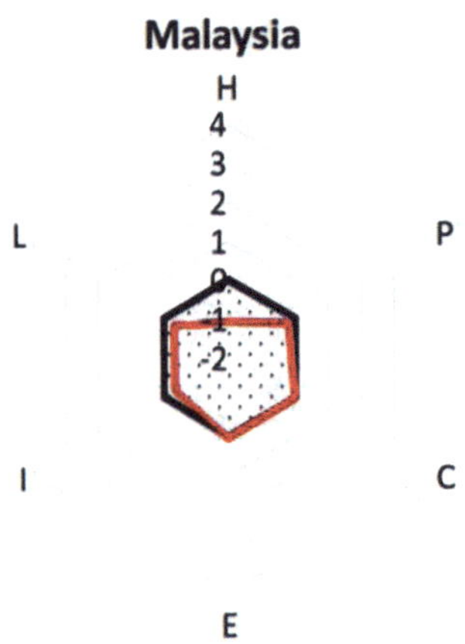
Malaysia
H
4
3
2
1
0
-1
-2
P
C
E
I
L

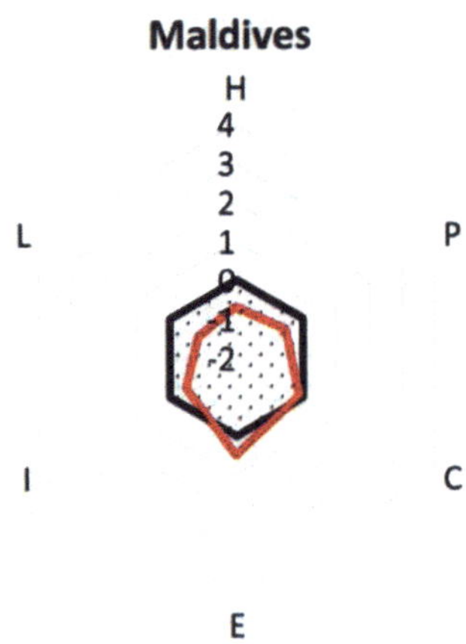
Maldives
H
4
3
2
1
0
-1
-2
P
C
E
I
L

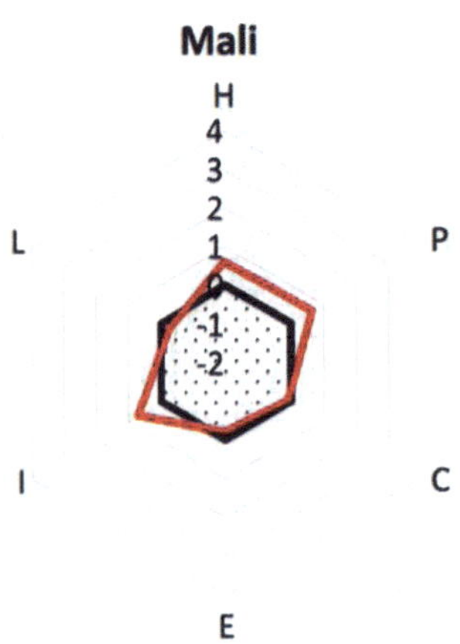
Mali
H
4
3
2
1
0
-1
-2
P
C
E
I
L

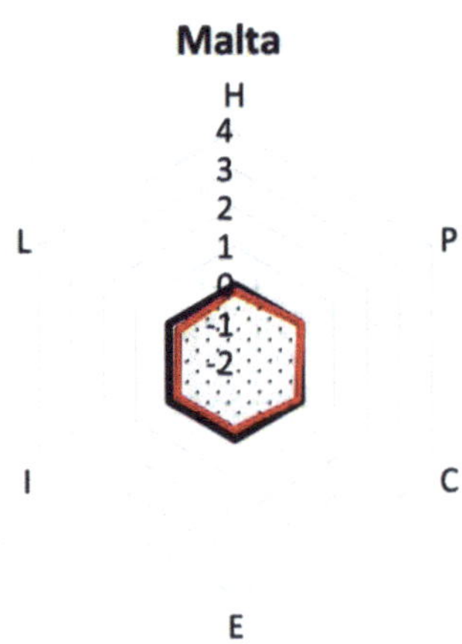
Malta
H
4
3
2
1
0
-1
-2
P
C
E
I
L

Marshall Islands

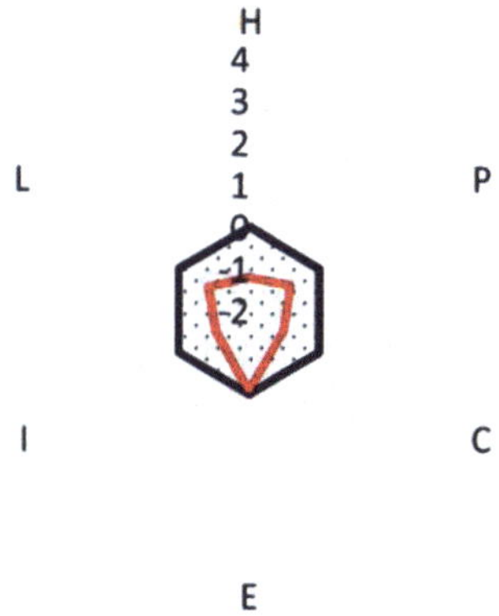

Mauritania

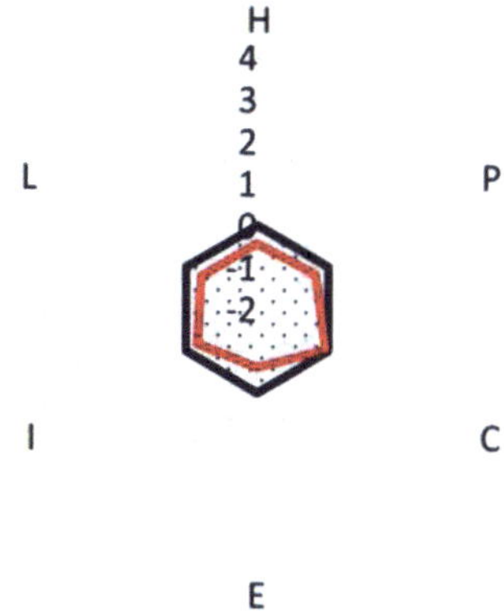

Mauritius

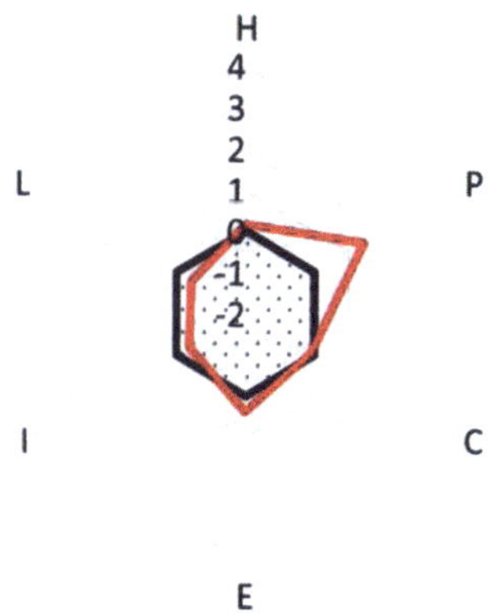

Mexico

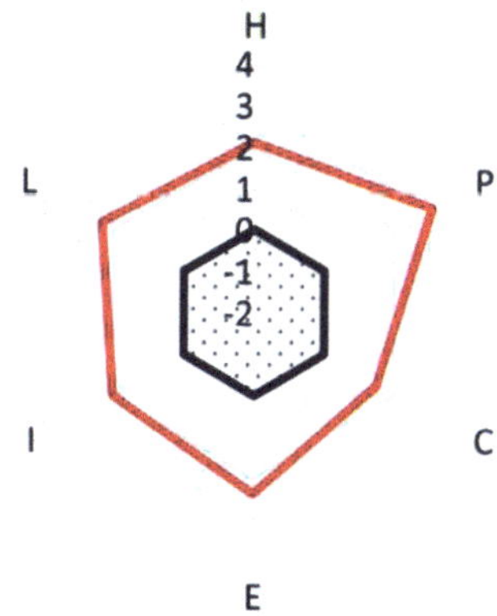

Micronesia

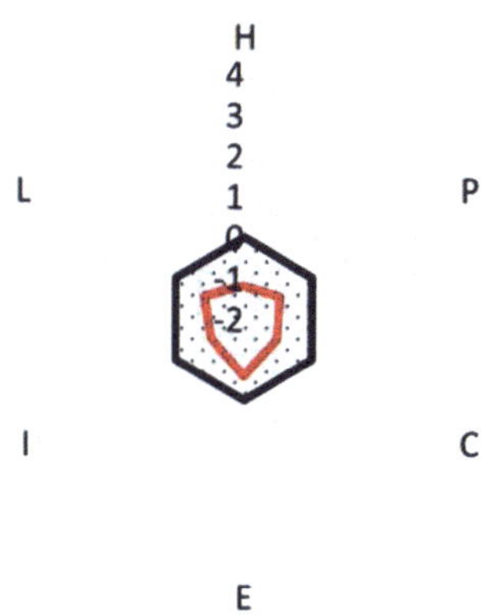

Monaco

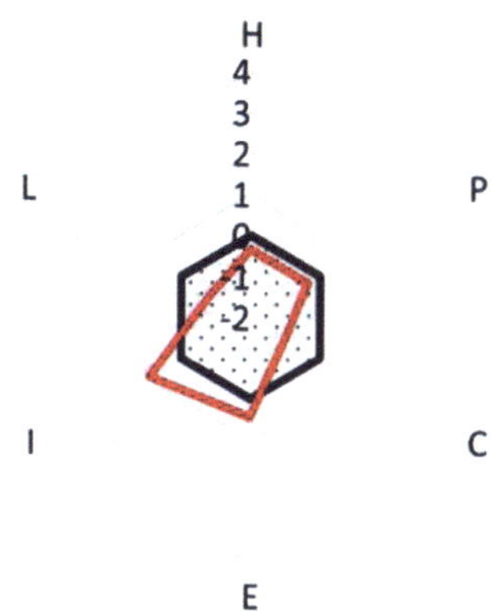

Mongolia

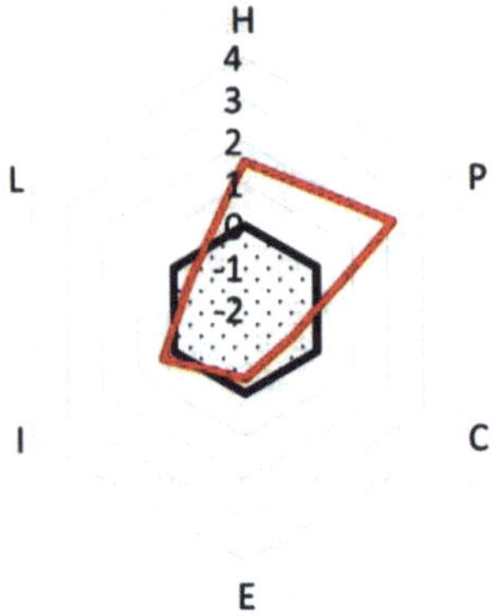

Montenegro

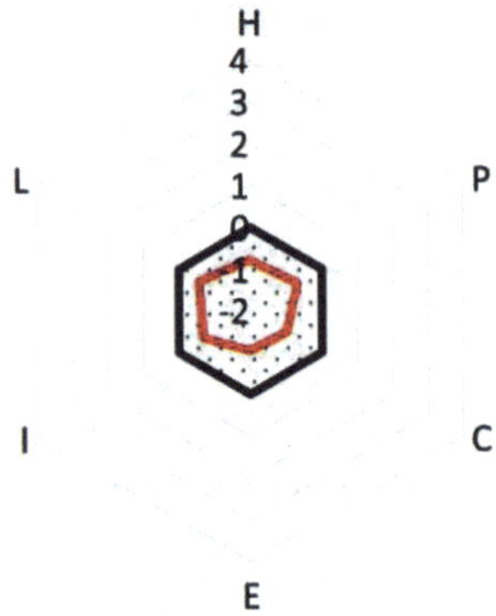

Morocco

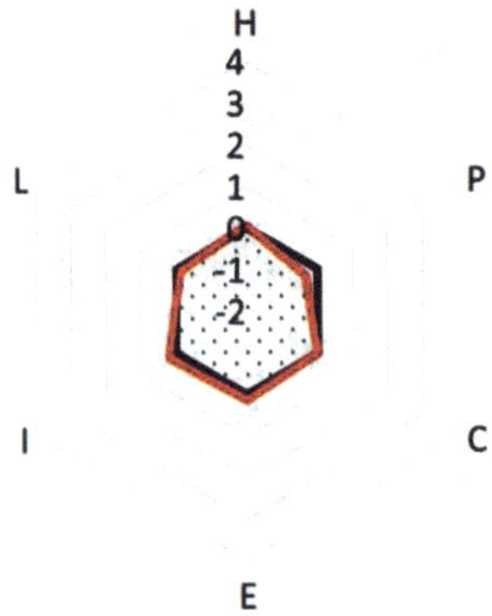

Mozambique

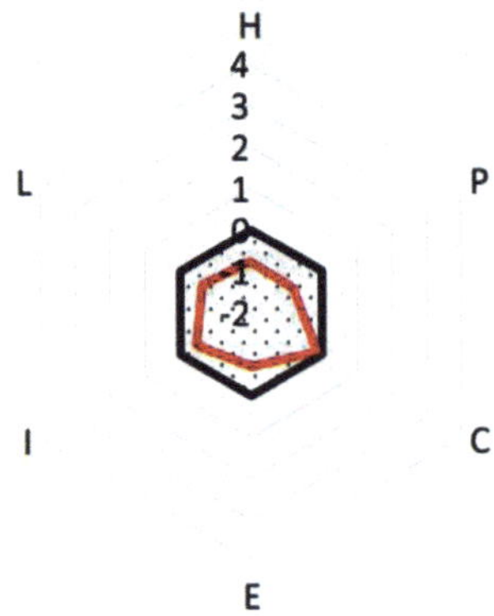

Myanmar

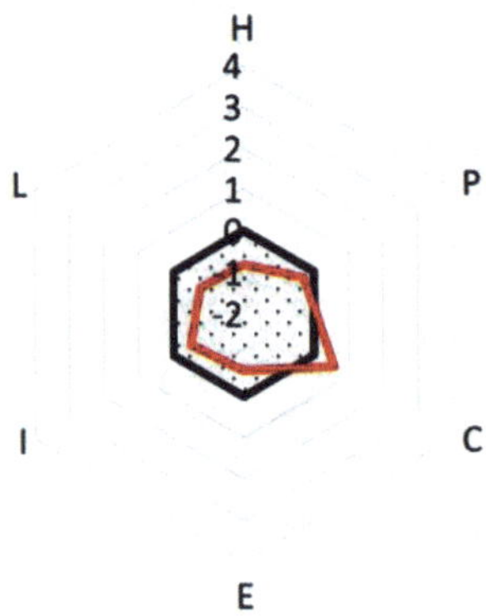

Namibia

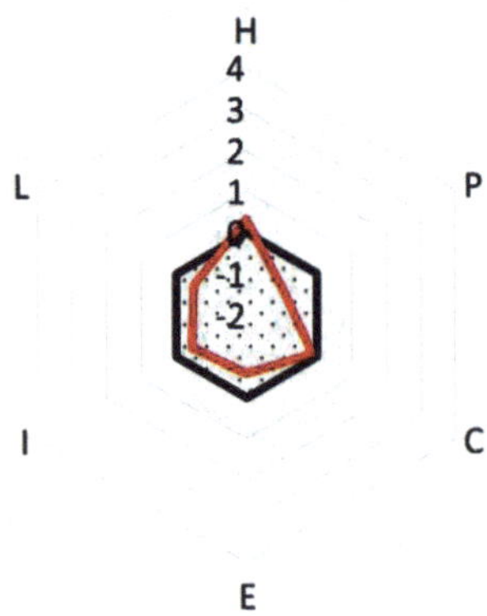

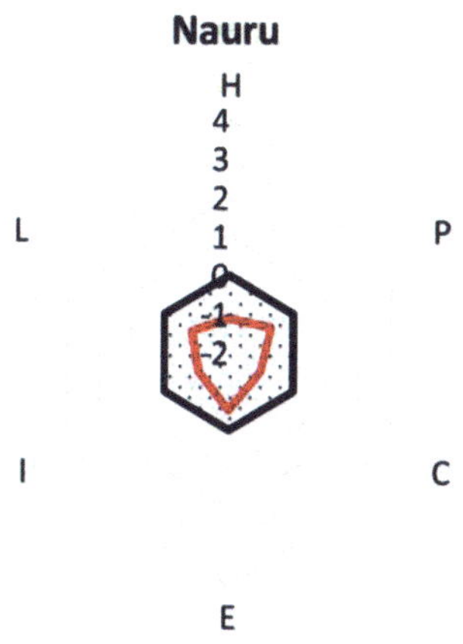
Nauru
H
4
3
2
1
0
-1
-2
L
P
I
C
E

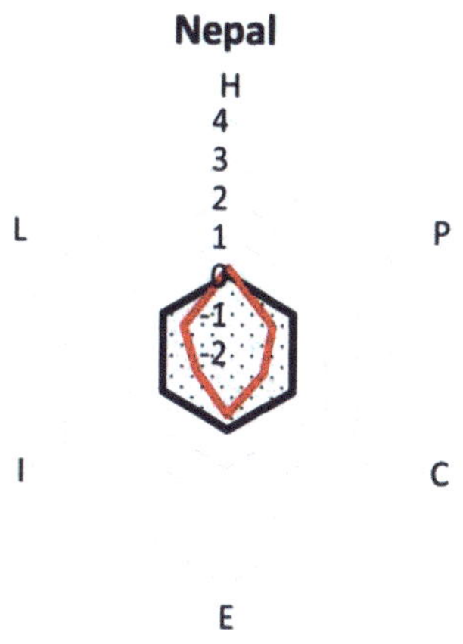
Nepal
H
4
3
2
1
0
-1
-2
L
P
I
C
E

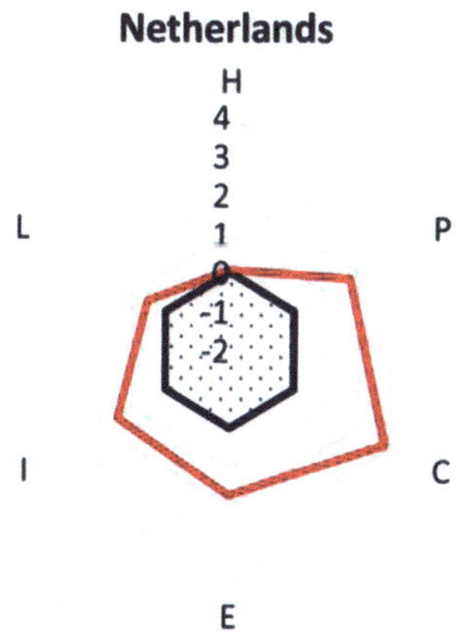
Netherlands
H
4
3
2
1
0
-1
-2
L
P
I
C
E

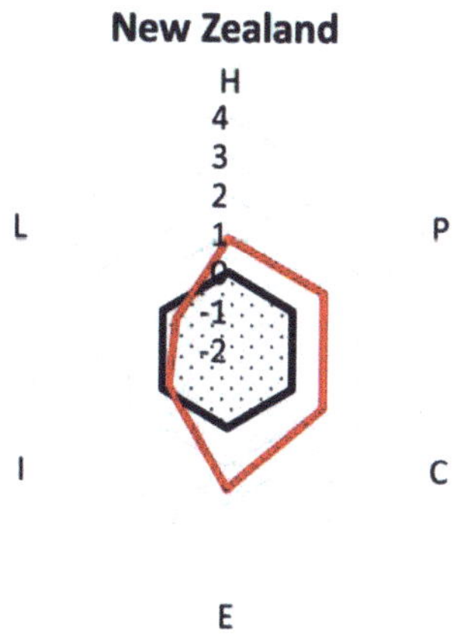
New Zealand
H
4
3
2
1
0
-1
-2
L
P
I
C
E

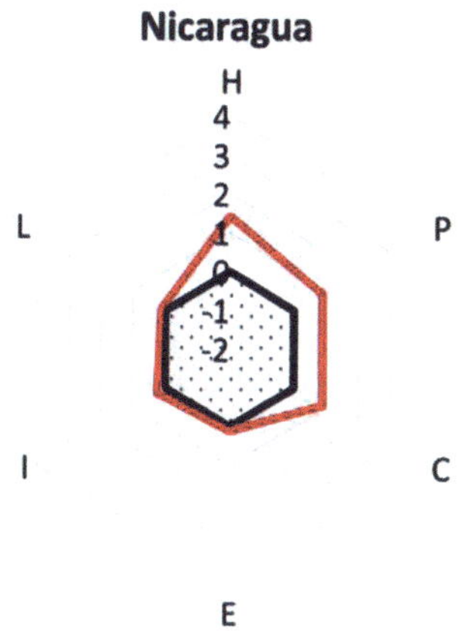
Nicaragua
H
4
3
2
1
0
-1
-2
L
P
I
C
E

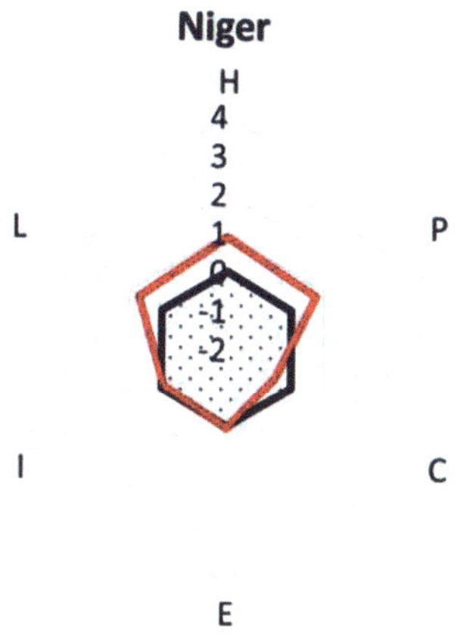
Niger
H
4
3
2
1
0
-1
-2
L
P
I
C
E

Nigeria

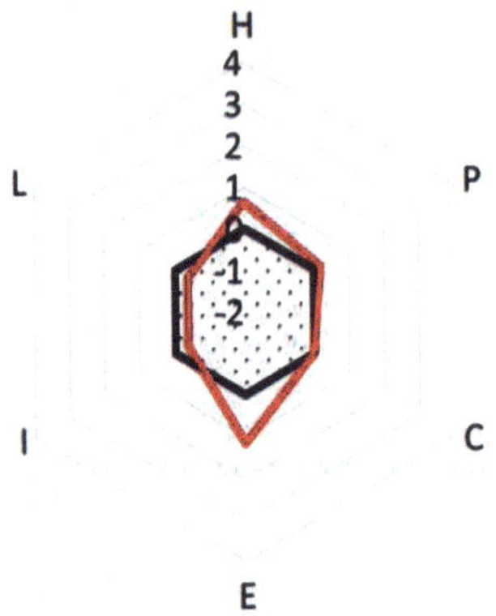

Norway

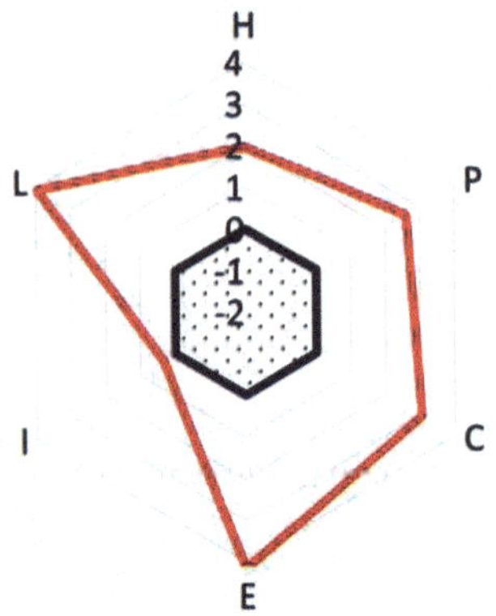

Oman

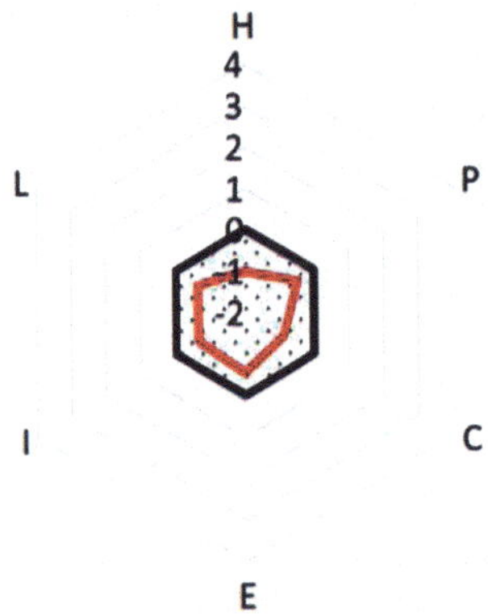

Pakistan

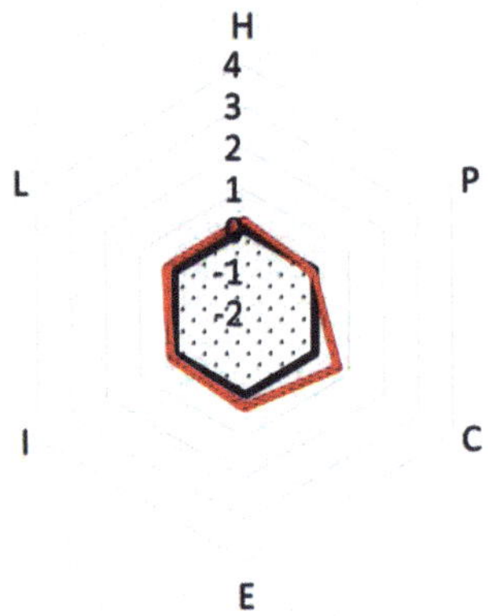

Palau

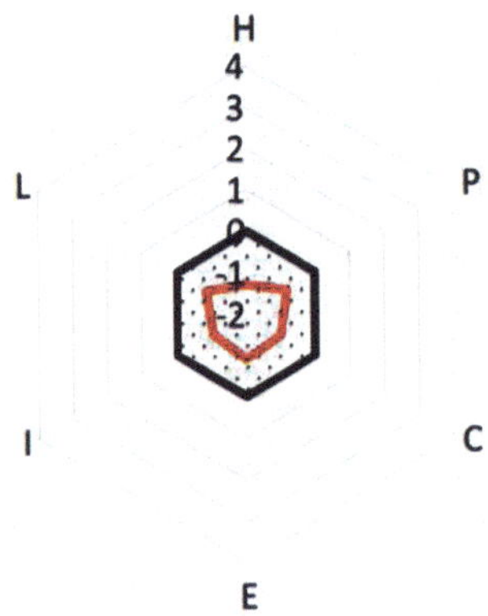

Panama

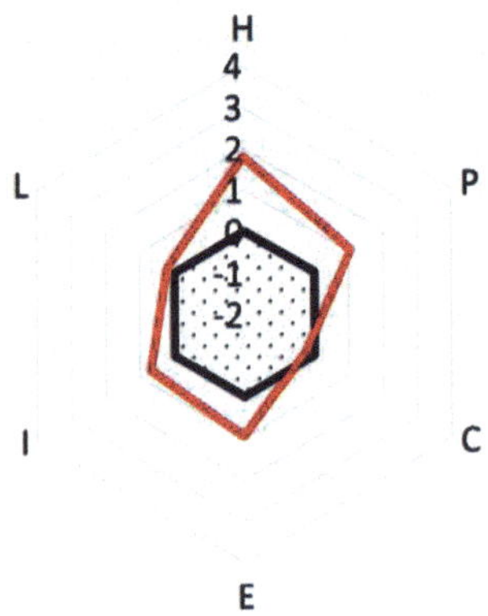

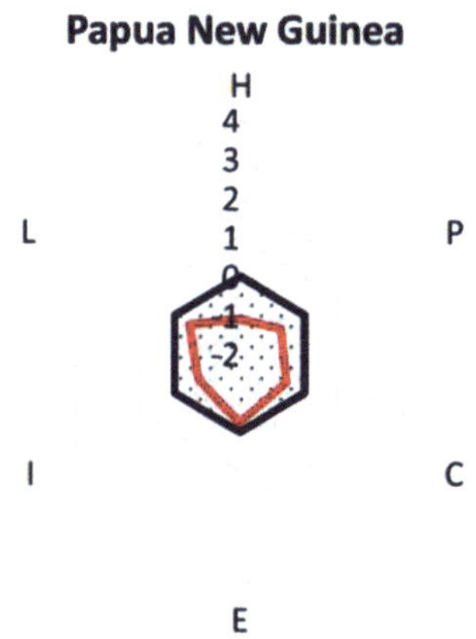
Papua New Guinea
H
4
3
2
1
0
-1
-2
P
C
E
I
L

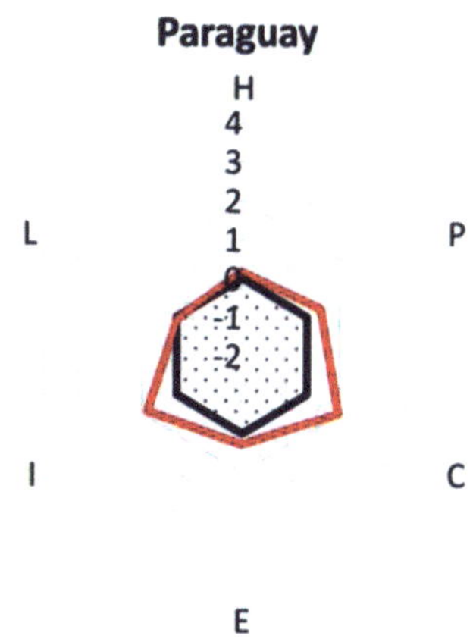
Paraguay
H
4
3
2
1
0
-1
-2
P
C
E
I
L

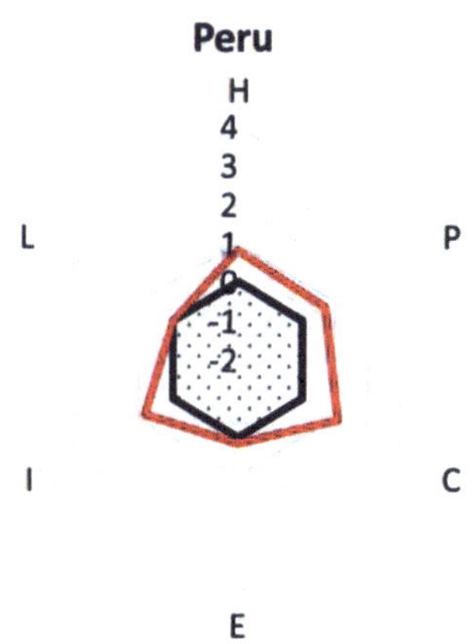
Peru
H
4
3
2
1
0
-1
-2
P
C
E
I
L

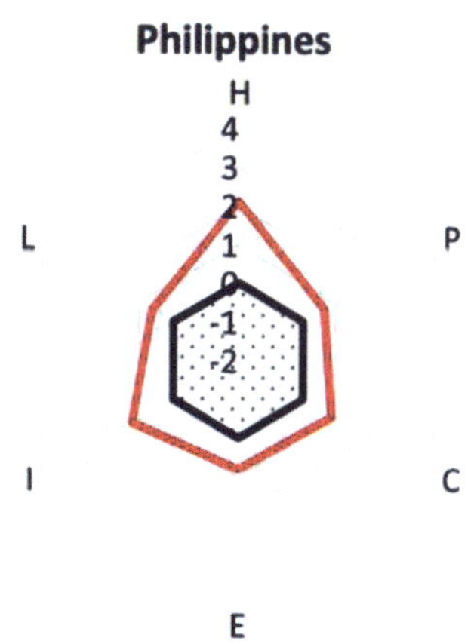
Philippines
H
4
3
2
1
0
-1
-2
P
C
E
I
L

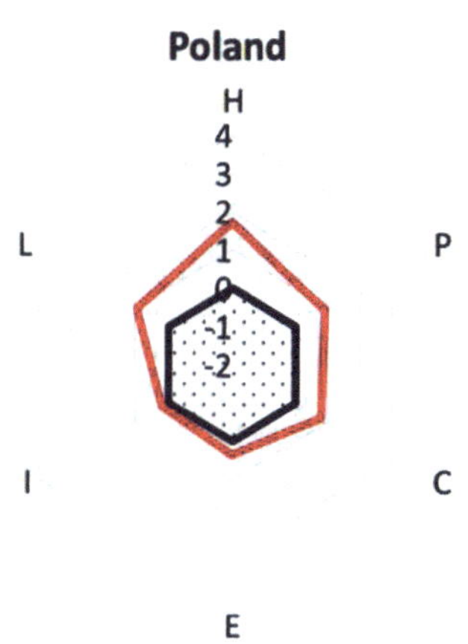
Poland
H
4
3
2
1
0
-1
-2
P
C
E
I
L

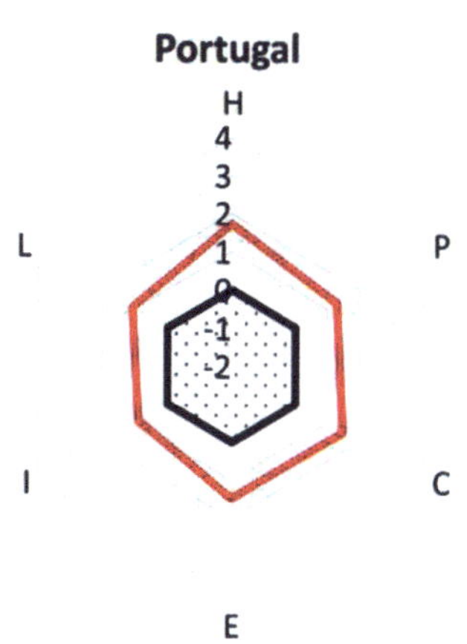
Portugal
H
4
3
2
1
0
-1
-2
P
C
E
I
L

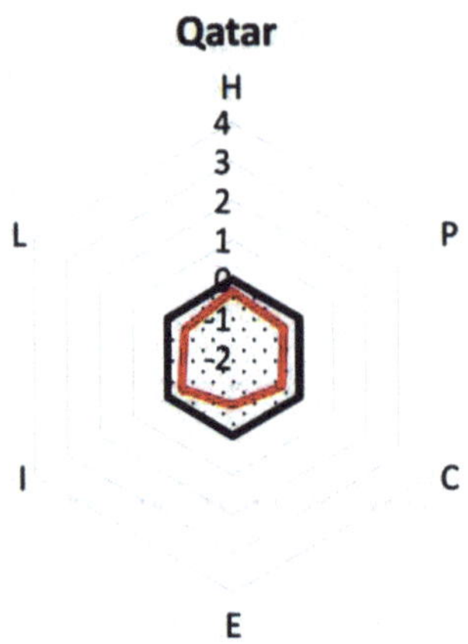
Qatar
H
4
3
2
1
0
-1
-2
P
C
E
I
L

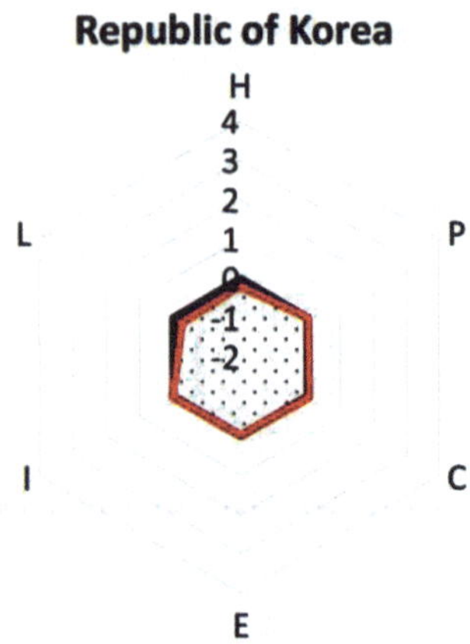
Republic of Korea
H
4
3
2
1
0
-1
-2
P
C
E
I
L

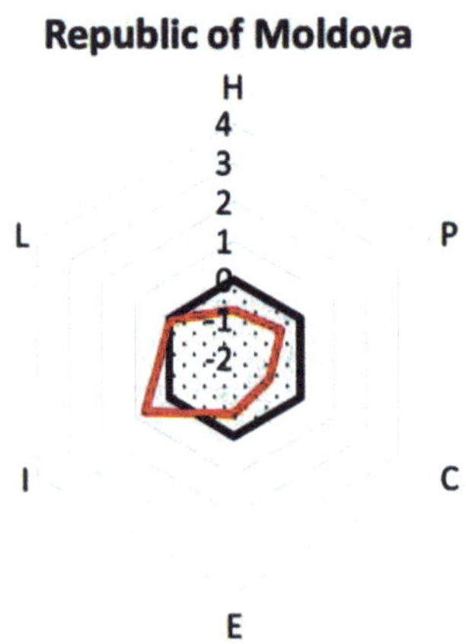
Republic of Moldova
H
4
3
2
1
0
-1
-2
P
C
E
I
L

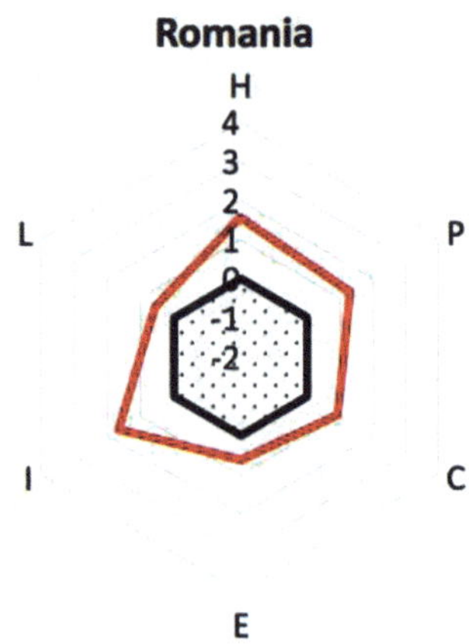
Romania
H
4
3
2
1
0
-1
-2
P
C
E
I
L

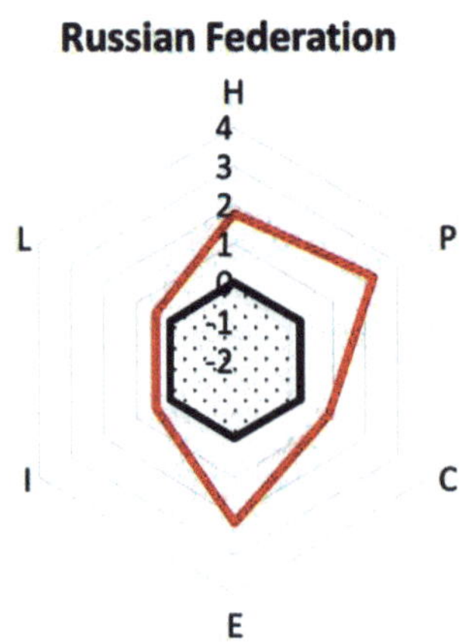
Russian Federation
H
4
3
2
1
0
-1
-2
P
C
E
I
L

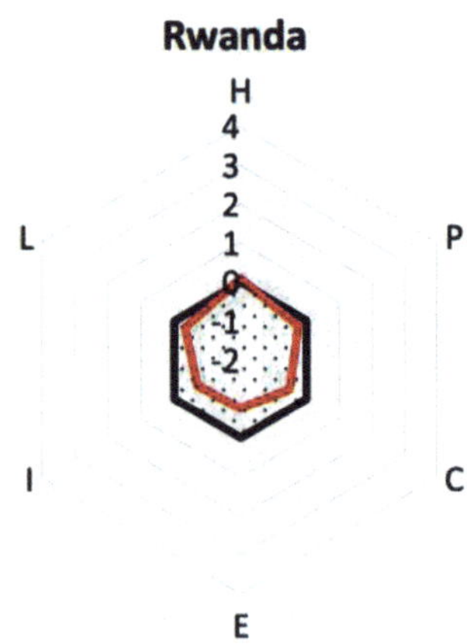
Rwanda
H
4
3
2
1
0
-1
-2
P
C
E
I
L

Saint Kitts and Nevis

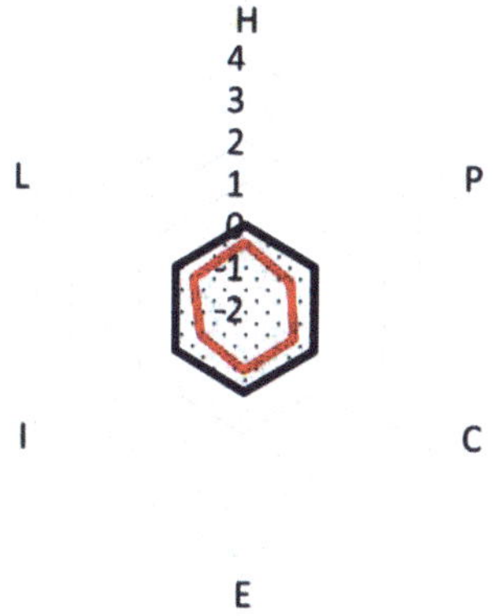

Saint Lucia

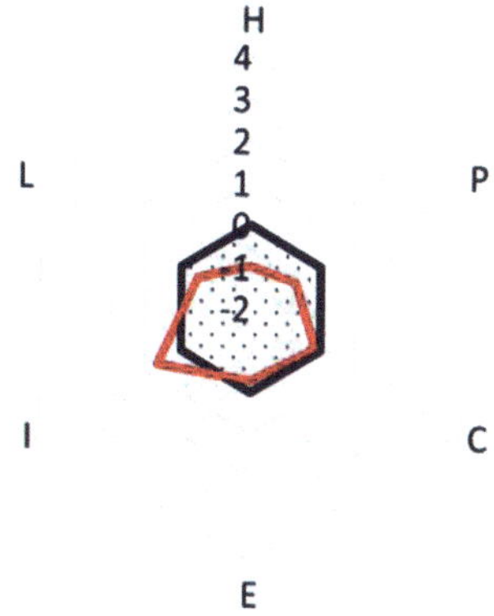

Saint Vincent and the Grenadines

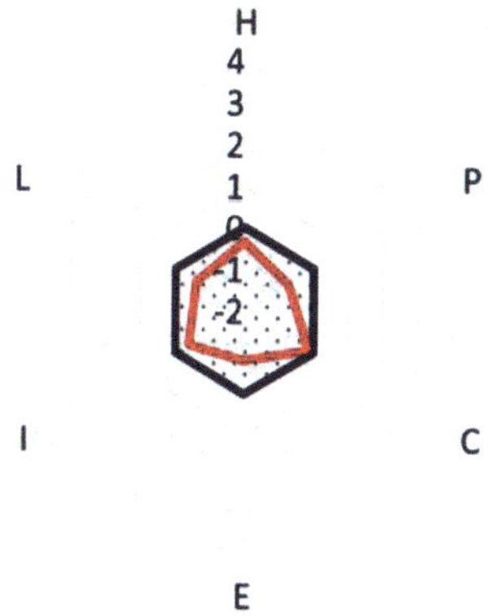

Samoa

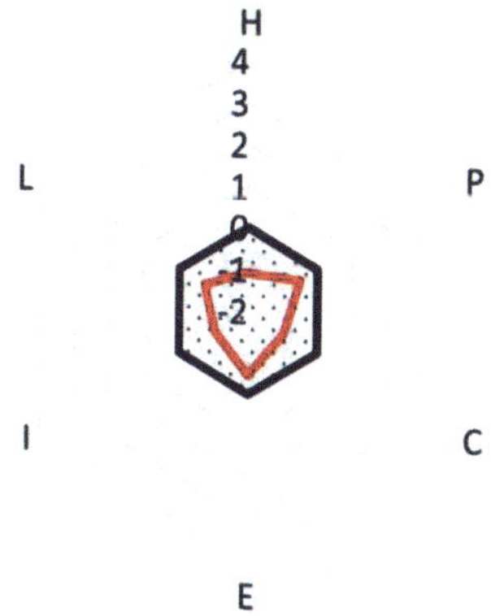

San Marino

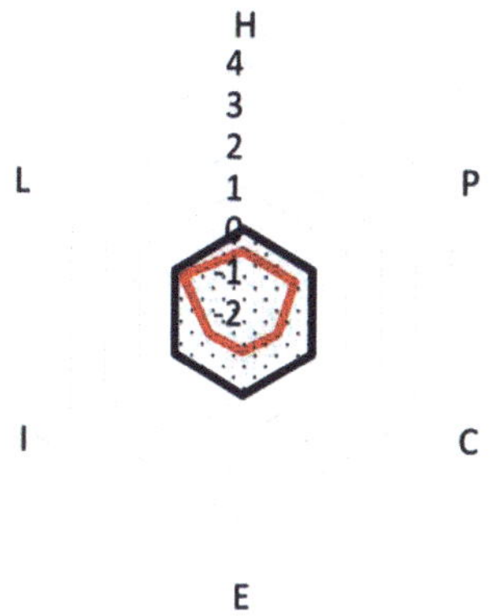

Sao Tome and Principe

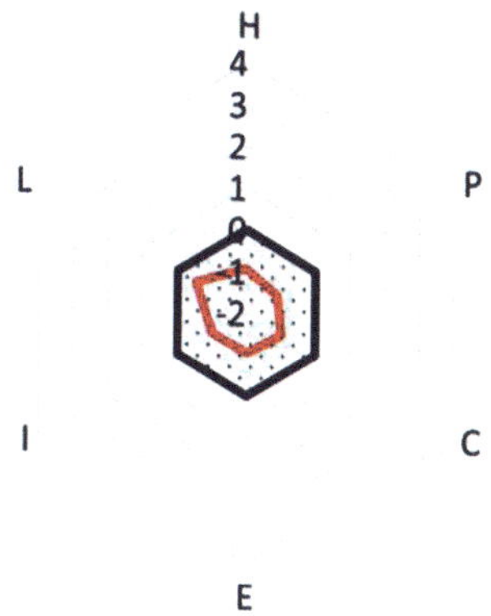

Saudi Arabia

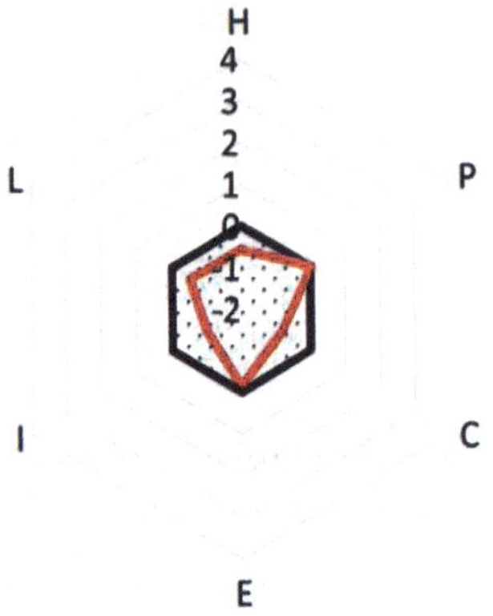

Senegal

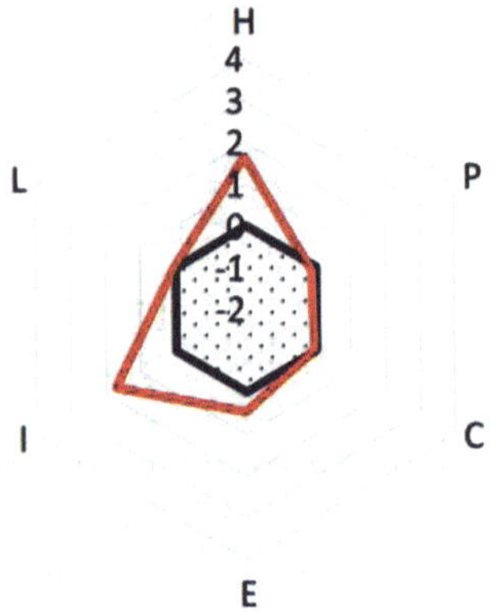

Serbia

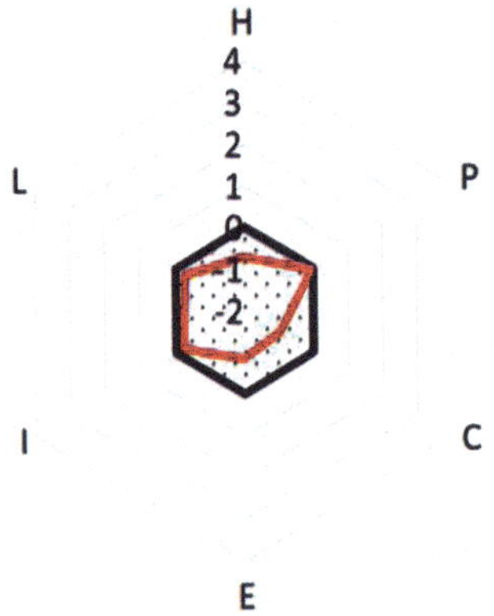

Seychelles

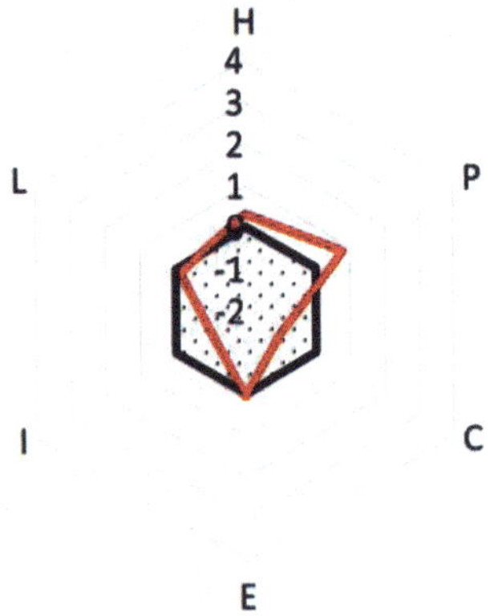

Sierra Leone

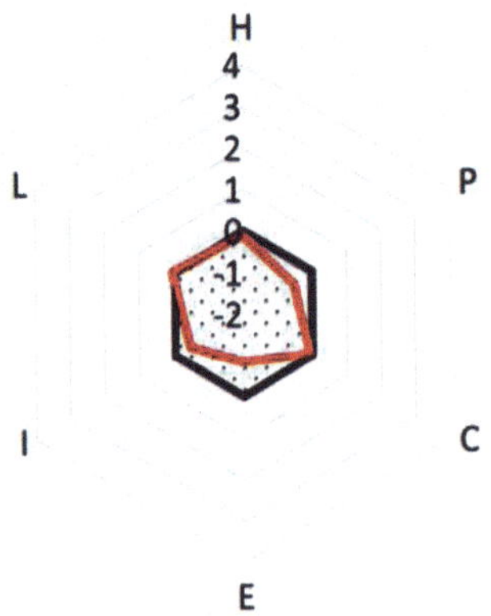

Singapore

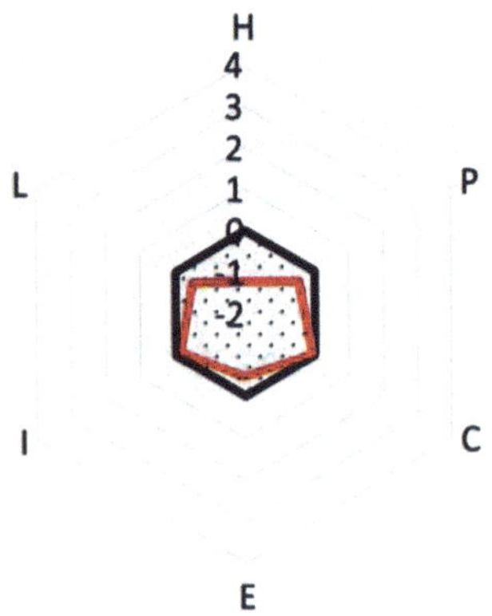

Slovakia

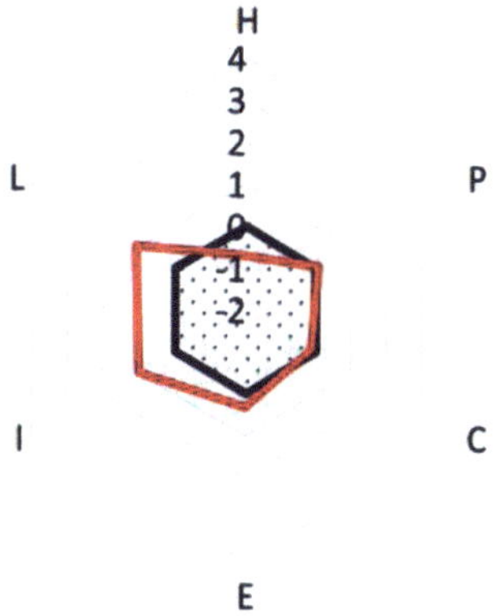

Slovenia

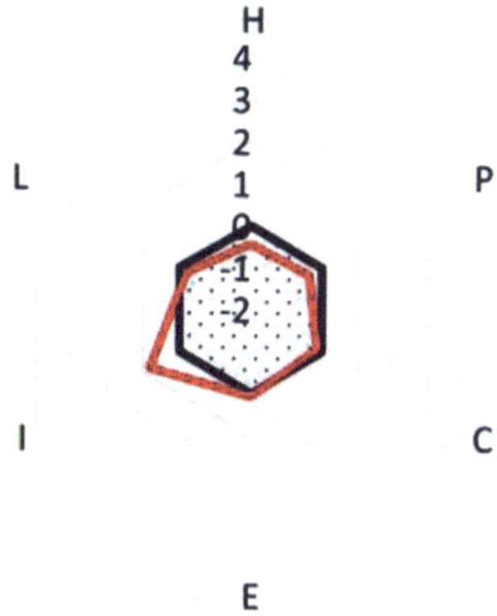

Solomon Islands

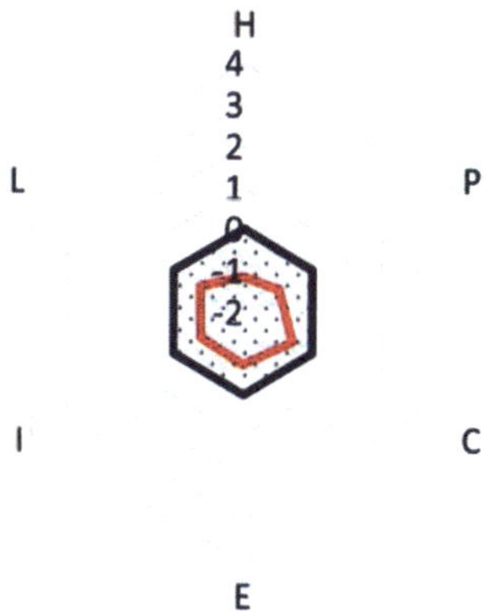

Somalia

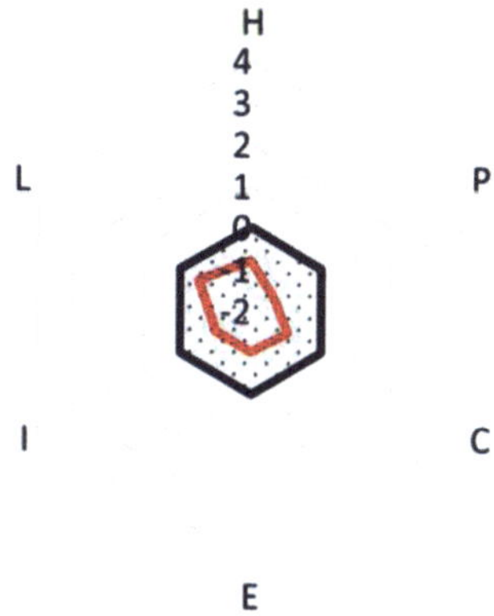

South Africa

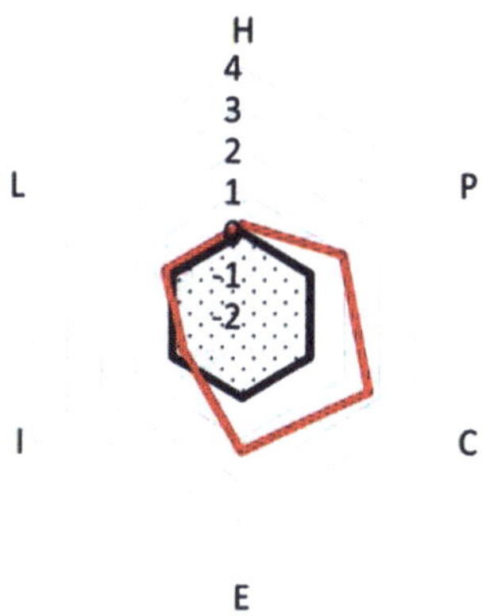

South Sudan

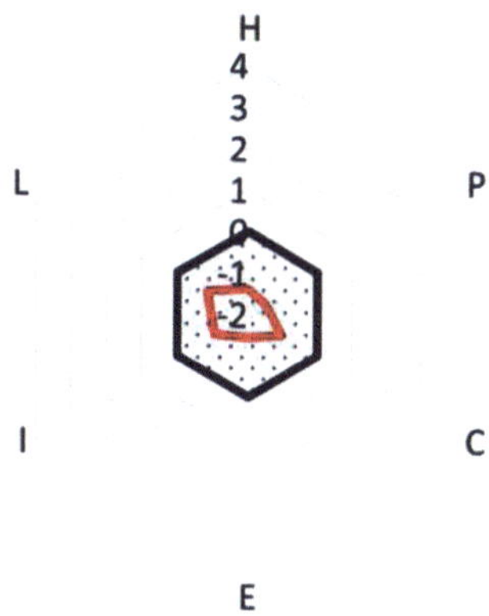

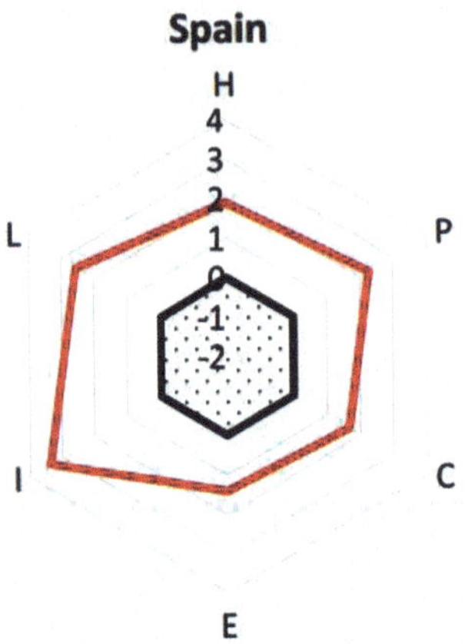
Spain
H
4
3
2
1
0
-1
-2
P
C
E
I
L

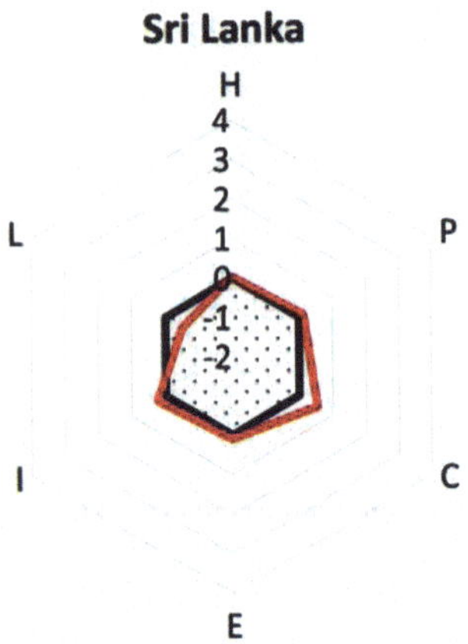
Sri Lanka
H
4
3
2
1
0
-1
-2
P
C
E
I
L

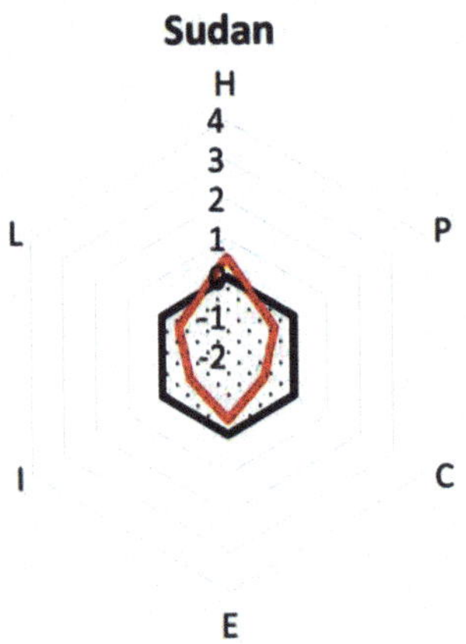
Sudan
H
4
3
2
1
0
-1
-2
P
C
E
I
L

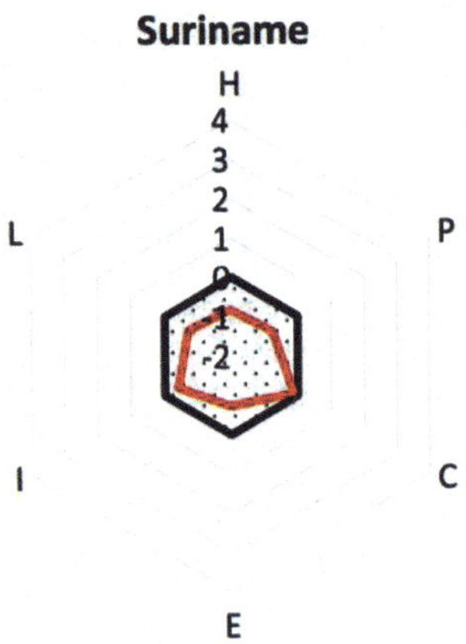
Suriname
H
4
3
2
1
0
-1
-2
P
C
E
I
L

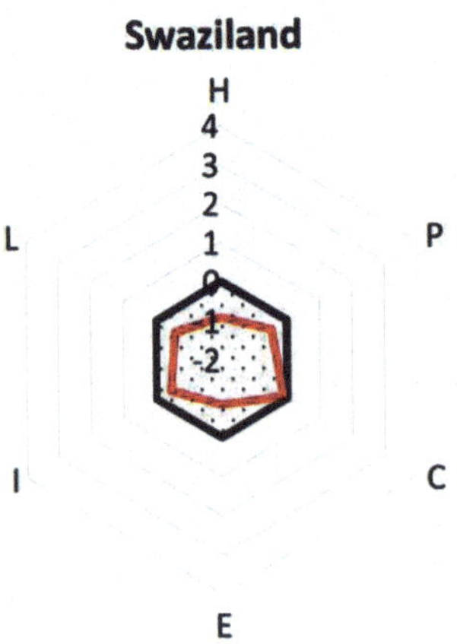
Swaziland
H
4
3
2
1
0
-1
-2
P
C
E
I
L

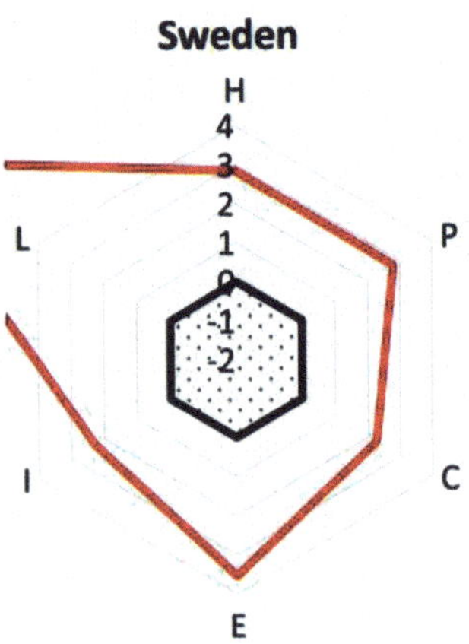
Sweden
H
4
3
2
1
0
-1
-2
P
C
E
I
L

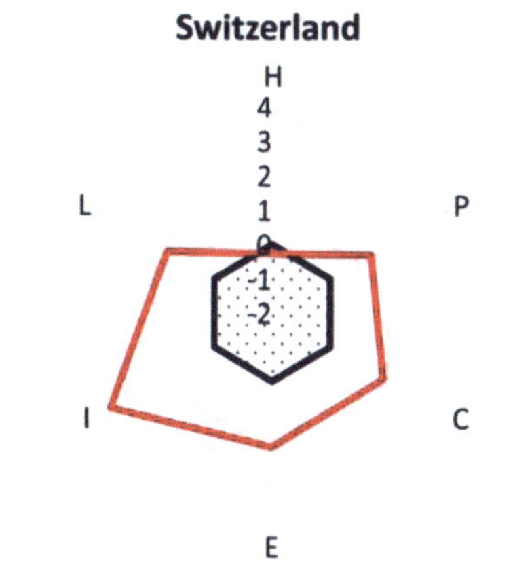
Switzerland
H
4
3
2
1
0
-1
-2
P
C
E
I
L

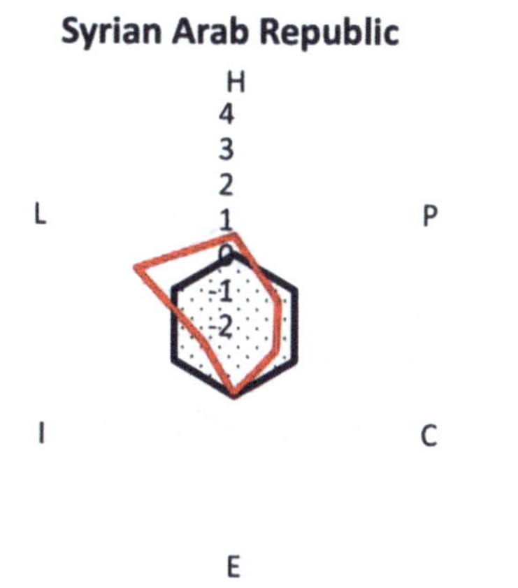
Syrian Arab Republic
H
4
3
2
1
0
-1
-2
P
C
E
I
L

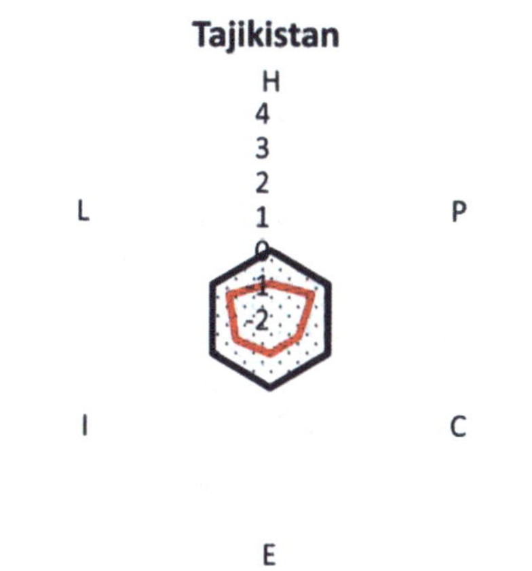
Tajikistan
H
4
3
2
1
0
-1
-2
P
C
E
I
L

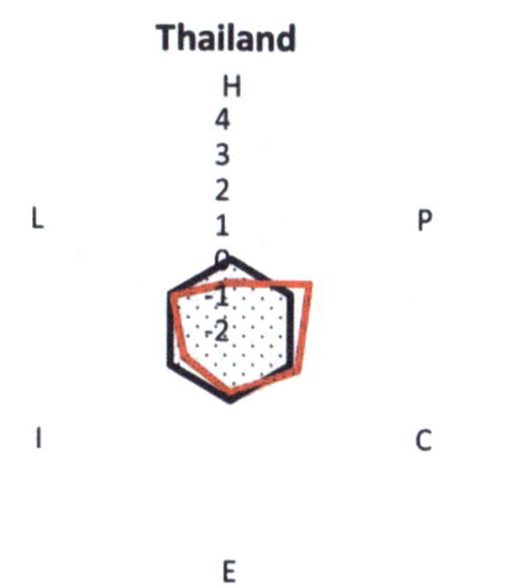
Thailand
H
4
3
2
1
0
-1
-2
P
C
E
I
L

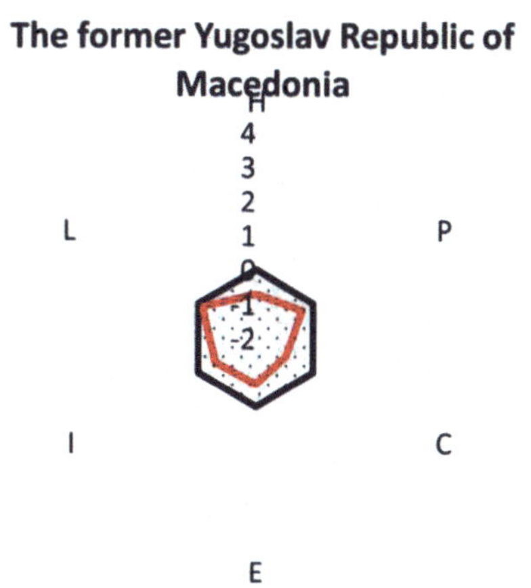
The former Yugoslav Republic of Macedonia
H
4
3
2
1
0
-1
-2
P
C
E
I
L

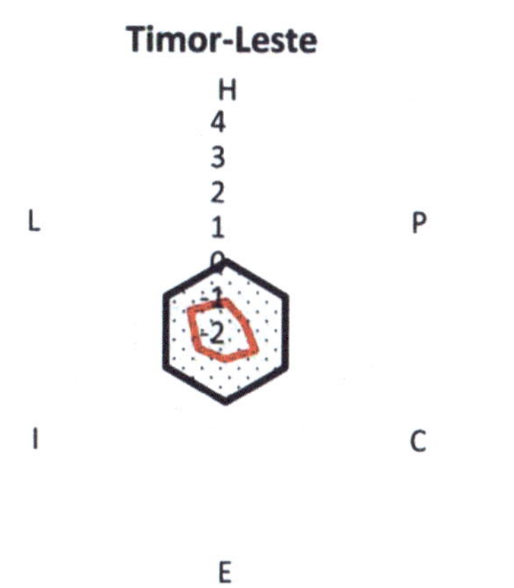
Timor-Leste
H
4
3
2
1
0
-1
-2
P
C
E
I
L

Togo

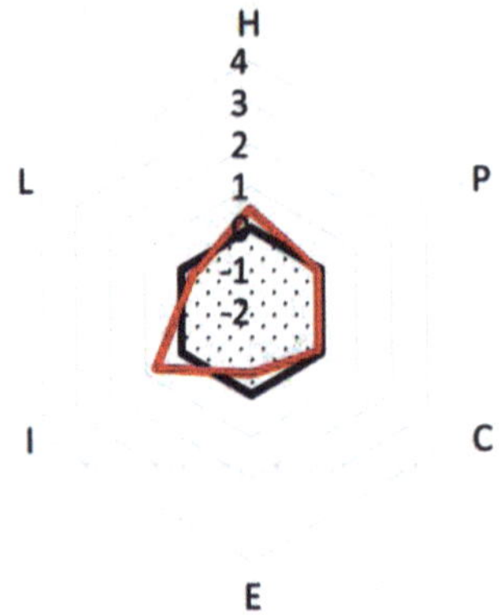

Tonga

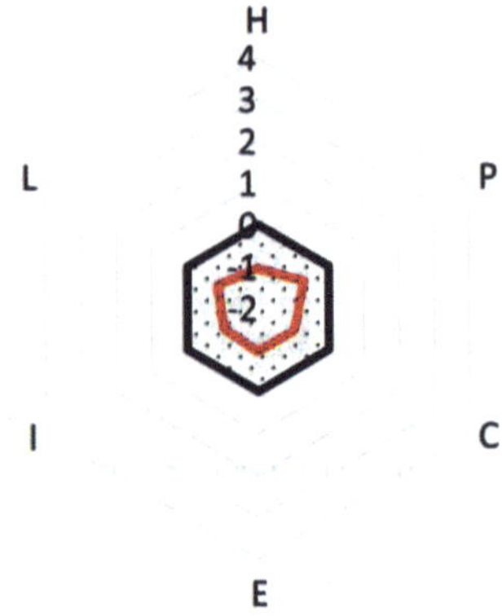

Trinidad and Tobago

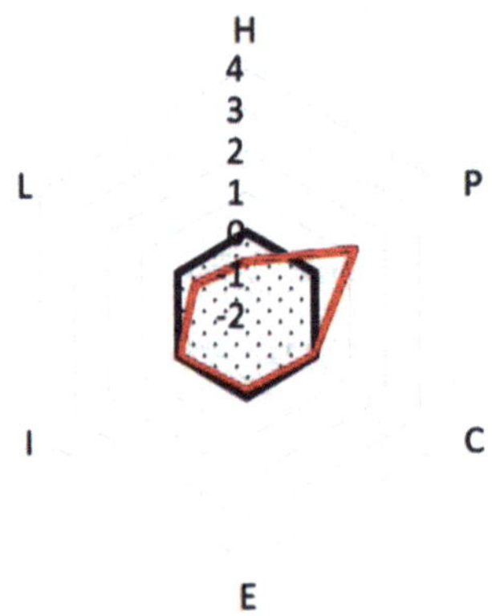

Tunisia

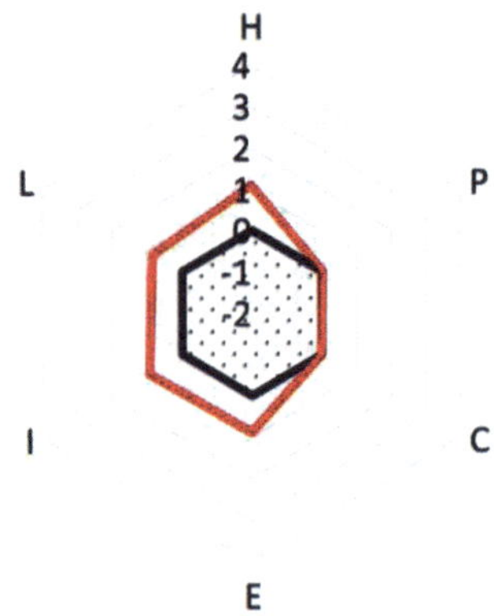

Turkey

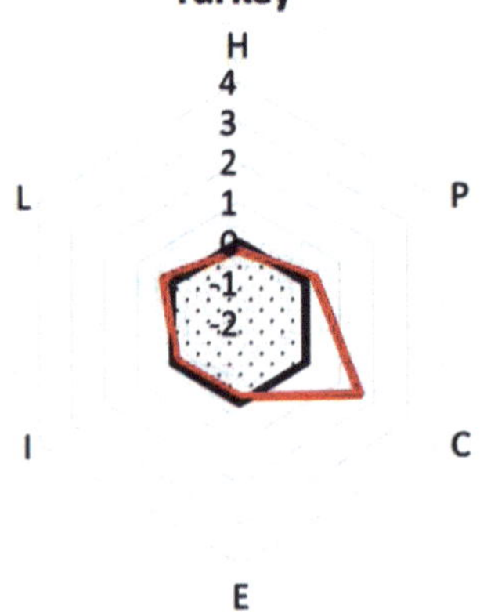

Turkmenistan

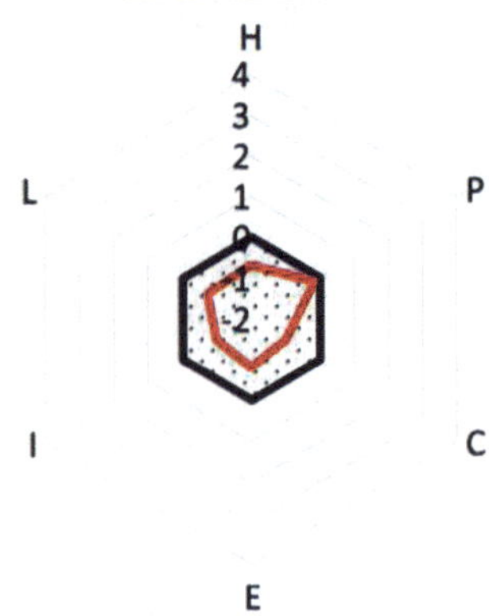

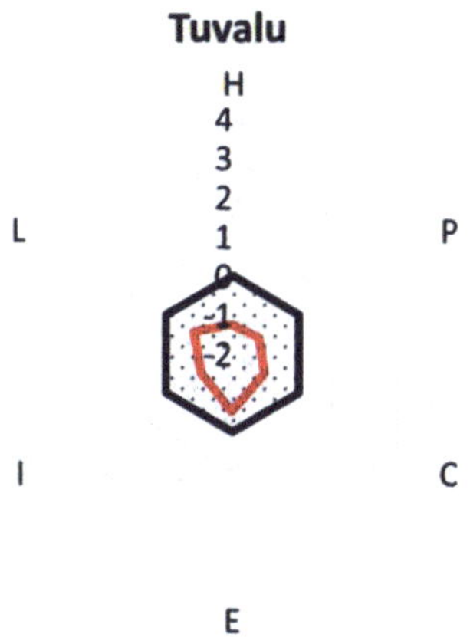
Tuvalu
H
4
3
2
1
0
-1
-2
L
P
I
C
E

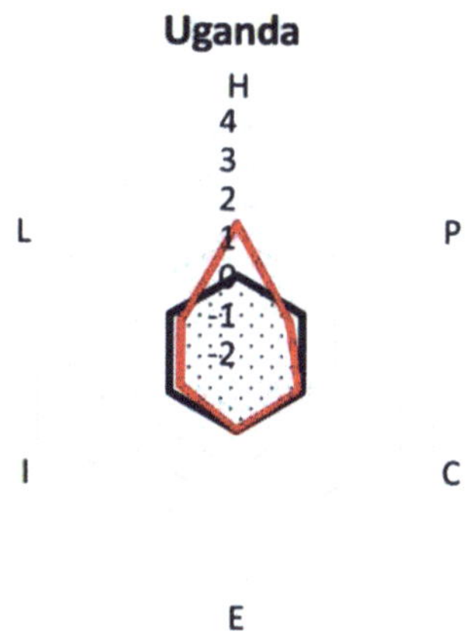
Uganda
H
4
3
2
1
0
-1
-2
L
P
I
C
E

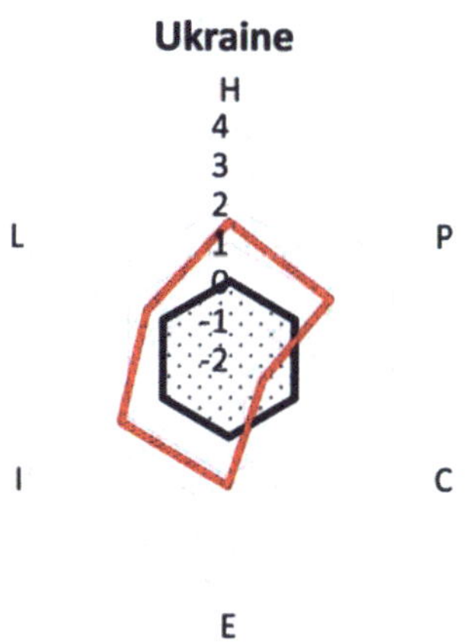
Ukraine
H
4
3
2
1
0
-1
-2
L
P
I
C
E

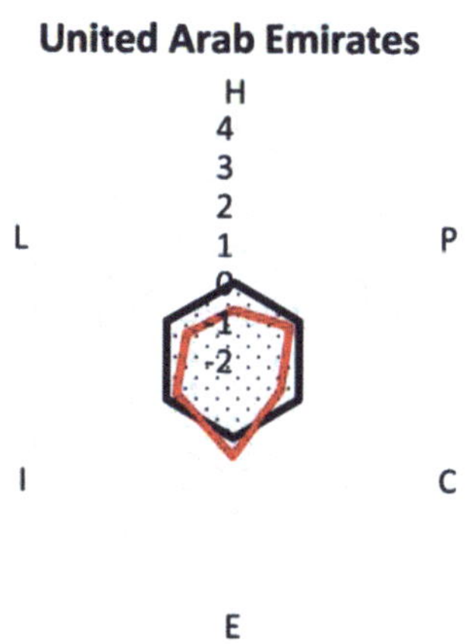
United Arab Emirates
H
4
3
2
1
0
-1
-2
L
P
I
C
E

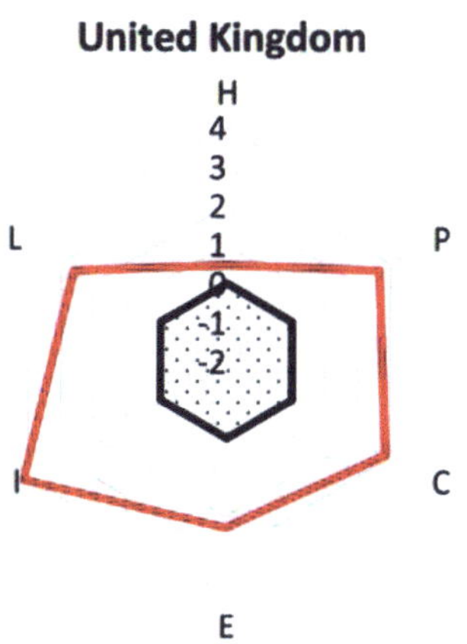
United Kingdom
H
4
3
2
1
0
-1
-2
L
P
I
C
E

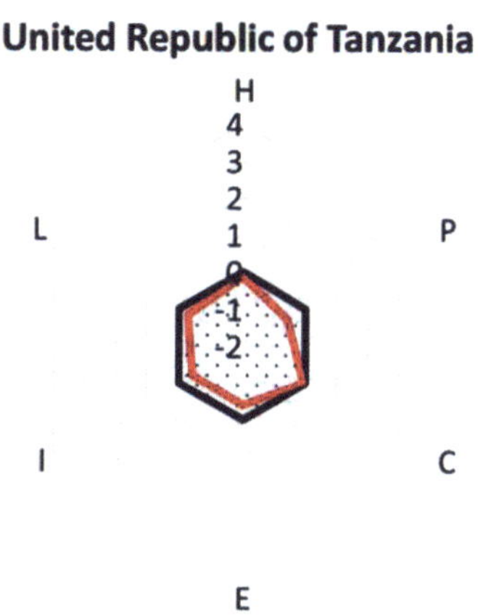
United Republic of Tanzania
H
4
3
2
1
0
-1
-2
L
P
I
C
E

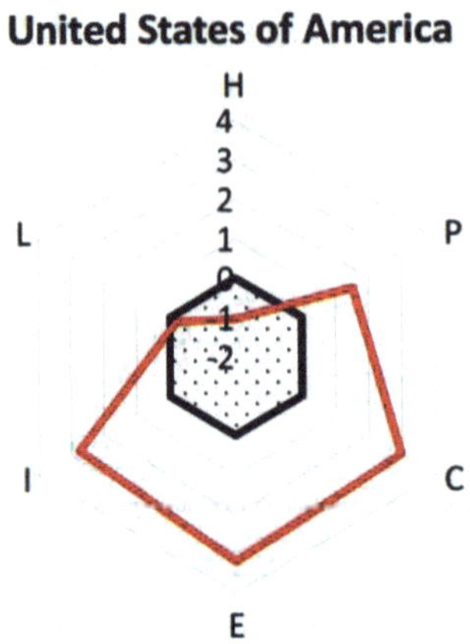
United States of America
H
4
3
2
1
0
-1
-2
P
C
E
I
L

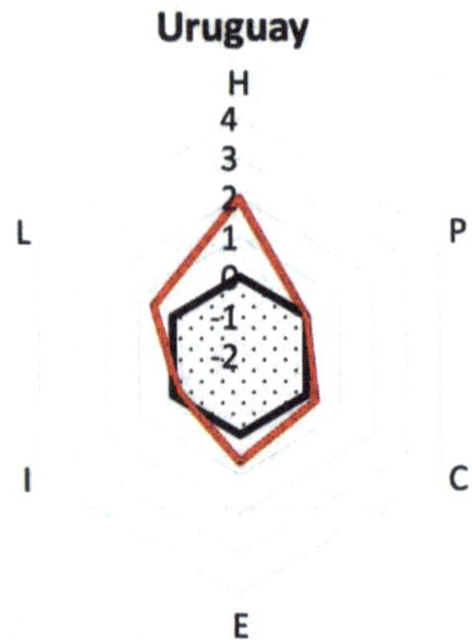
Uruguay
H
4
3
2
1
0
-1
-2
P
C
E
I
L

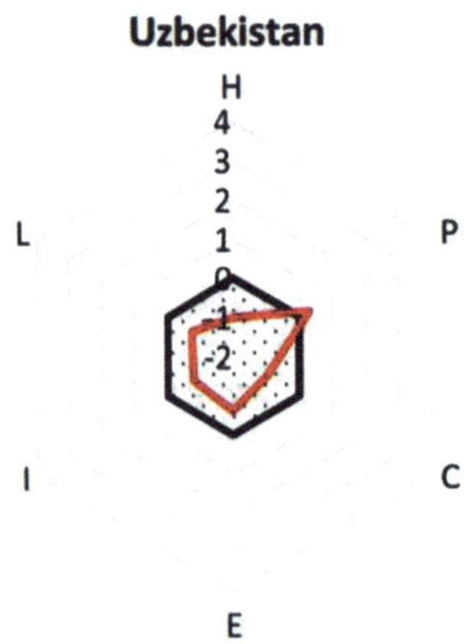
Uzbekistan
H
4
3
2
1
0
-1
-2
P
C
E
I
L

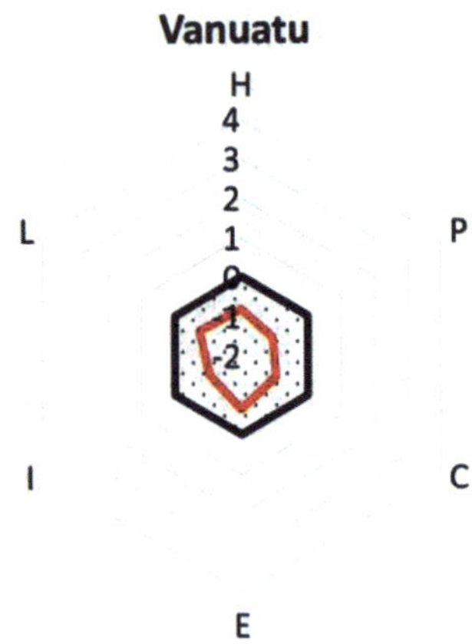
Vanuatu
H
4
3
2
1
0
-1
-2
P
C
E
I
L

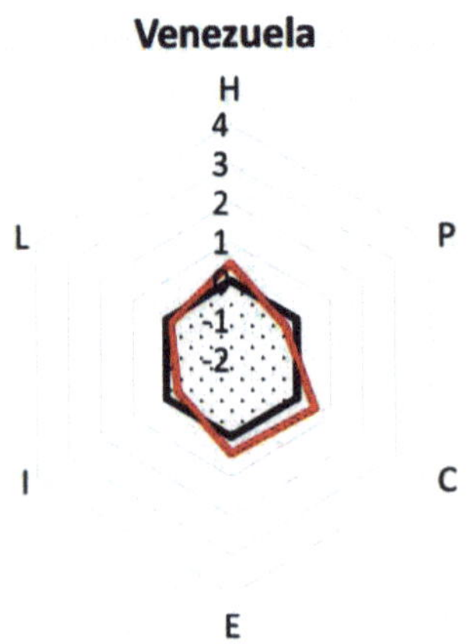
Venezuela
H
4
3
2
1
0
-1
-2
P
C
E
I
L

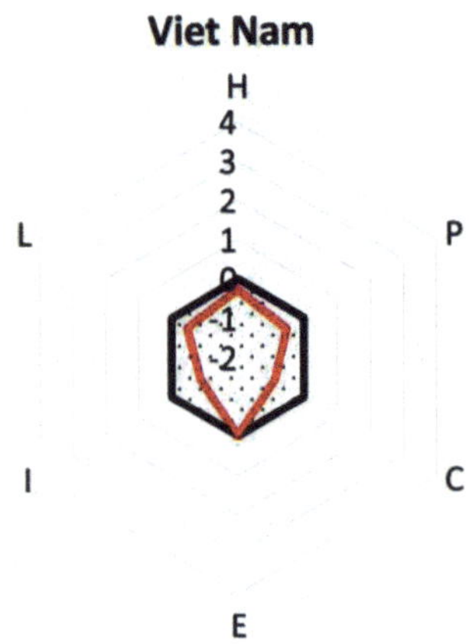
Viet Nam
H
4
3
2
1
0
-1
-2
P
C
E
I
L

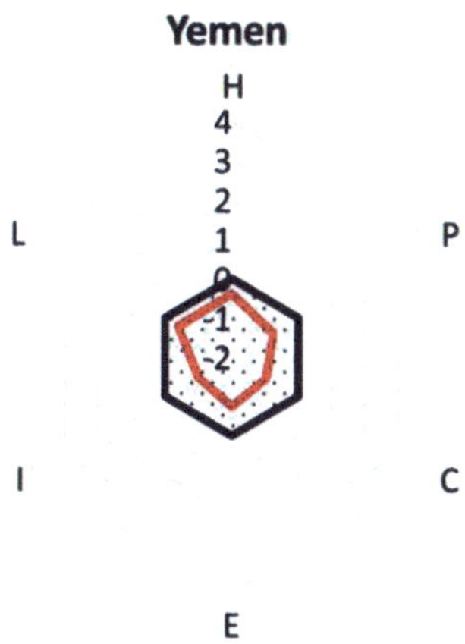
Yemen
H
4
3
2
1
0
-1
-2
L
P
I
C
E

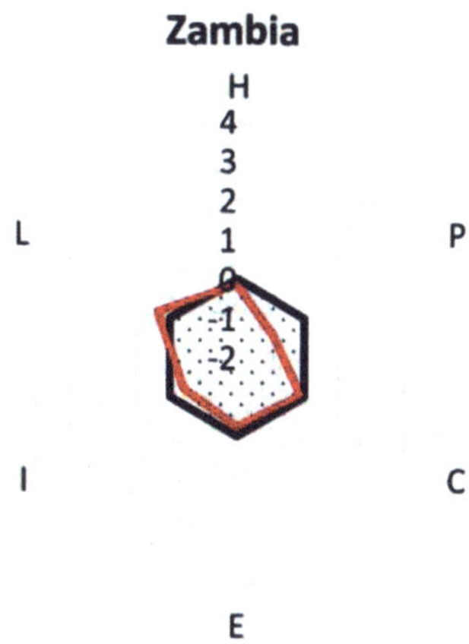
Zambia
H
4
3
2
1
0
-1
-2
L
P
I
C
E

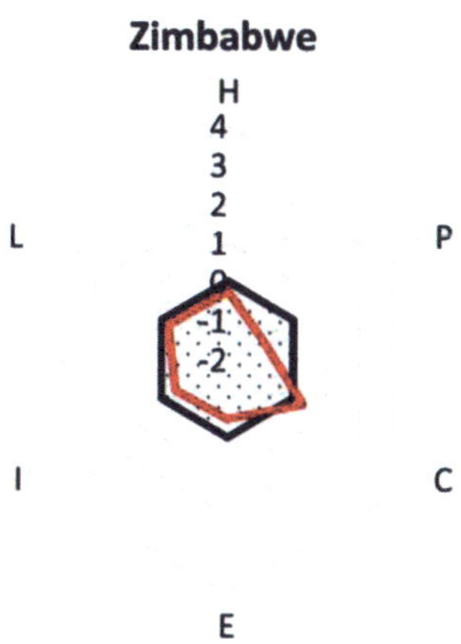
Zimbabwe
H
4
3
2
1
0
-1
-2
L
P
I
C
E

Appendix 4: States' Locations on Three Key Dimensions (Categorized by Regional Groups)

List of figures

	X axis	Y axis	For Region
1	Agile vs. cautious	Global commons vs. individual citizen's interests	Sub-Saharan Africa
2	Agile vs. cautious	Aspirational bonding vs. mutual binding	
3	Global commons vs. individual citizen's interests	Aspirational bonding vs. mutual binding	
4	Agile vs. cautious	Global commons vs. individual citizen's interests	Sinic East
5	Agile vs. cautious	Aspirational bonding vs. mutual binding	
6	Global commons vs. individual citizen's interests	Aspirational bonding vs. mutual binding	
7	Agile vs. cautious	Global commons vs. individual citizen's interests	Returned West
8	Agile vs. cautious	Aspirational bonding vs. mutual binding	
9	Global commons vs. individual citizen's interests	Aspirational bonding vs. mutual binding	
10	Agile vs. cautious	Global commons vs. individual citizen's interests	Reformed West
11	Agile vs. cautious	Aspirational bonding vs. mutual binding	
12	Global commons vs. individual citizen's interests	Aspirational bonding vs. mutual binding	
13	Agile vs. cautious	Global commons vs. individual citizen's interests	Orthodox East
14	Agile vs. cautious	Aspirational bonding vs. mutual binding	
15	Global commons vs. individual citizen's interests	Aspirational bonding vs. mutual binding	
16	Agile vs. cautious	Global commons vs. individual citizen's interests	Old West
17	Agile vs. cautious	Aspirational bonding vs. mutual binding	
18	Global commons vs. individual citizen's interests	Aspirational bonding vs. mutual binding	

(continued)

19	Agile vs. cautious	Global commons vs. individual citizen's interests	New West
20	Agile vs. cautious	Aspirational bonding vs. mutual binding	
21	Global commons vs. individual citizen's interests	Aspirational bonding vs. mutual binding	
22	Agile vs. cautious	Global commons vs. individual citizen's interests	Latin America
23	Agile vs. cautious	Aspirational bonding vs. mutual binding	
24	Global commons vs. individual citizen's interests	Aspirational bonding vs. mutual binding	
25	Agile vs. cautious	Global commons vs. individual citizen's interests	Islamic East
26	Agile vs. cautious	Aspirational bonding vs. mutual binding	
27	Global commons vs. individual citizen's interests	Aspirational bonding vs. mutual binding	
28	Agile vs. cautious	Global commons vs. individual citizen's interests	Indic East
29	Agile vs. cautious	Aspirational bonding vs. mutual binding	
30	Global commons vs. individual citizen's interests	Aspirational bonding vs. mutual binding	

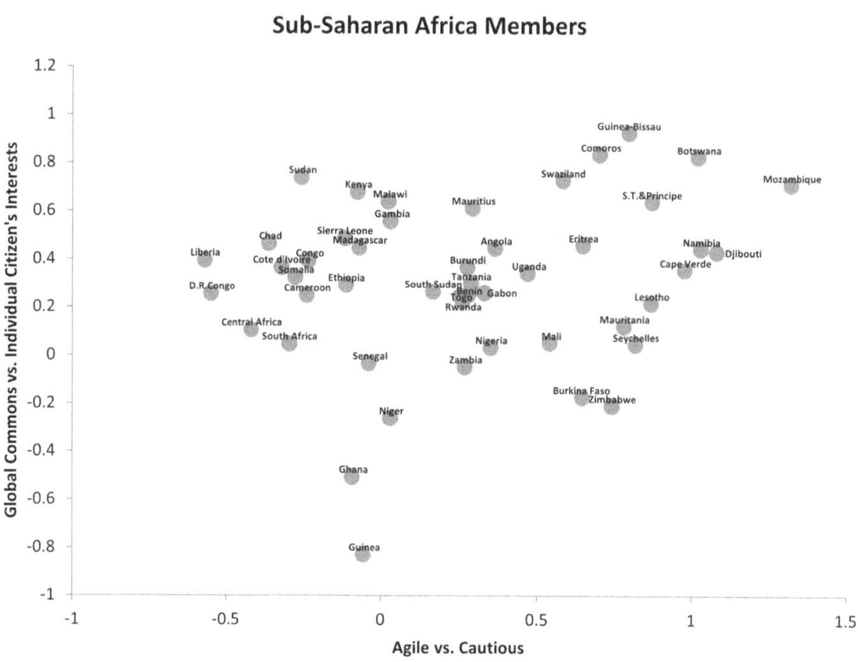

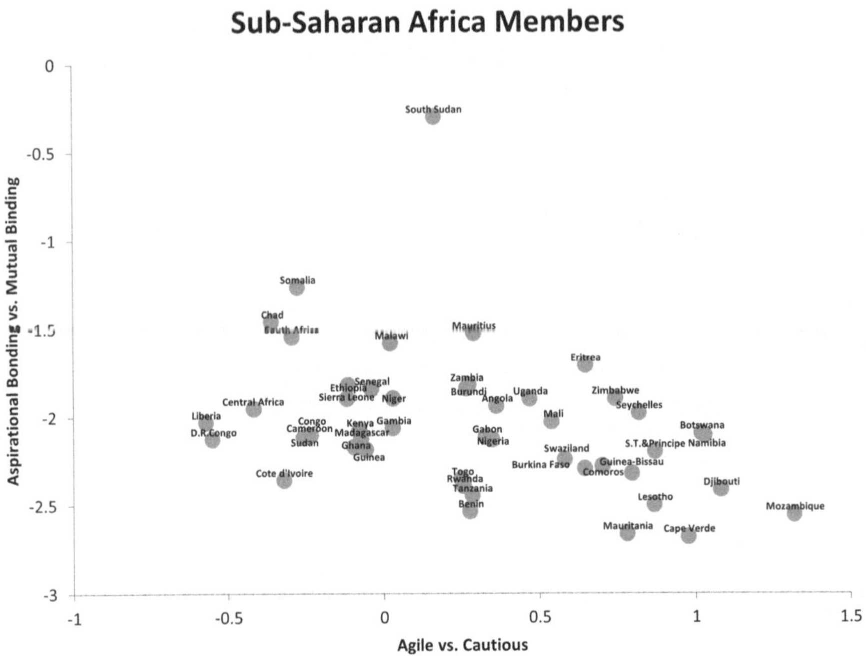
Sub-Saharan Africa Members
Aspirational Bonding vs. Mutual Binding
Agile vs. Cautious
South Sudan
Somalia
Chad
South Africa
Malawi
Mauritius
Eritrea
Zambia
Burundi
Angola
Uganda
Zimbabwe
Seychelles
Senegal
Ethiopia
Sierra Leone
Niger
Central Africa
Liberia
D.R.Congo
Congo
Cameroon
Sudan
Kenya
Gambia
Madagascar
Ghana
Guinea
Gabon
Nigeria
Mali
Botswana
S.T.&Principe
Namibia
Swaziland
Burkina Faso
Guinea-Bissau
Comoros
Cote d'Ivoire
Togo
Rwanda
Tanzania
Benin
Djibouti
Lesotho
Mozambique
Mauritania
Cape Verde

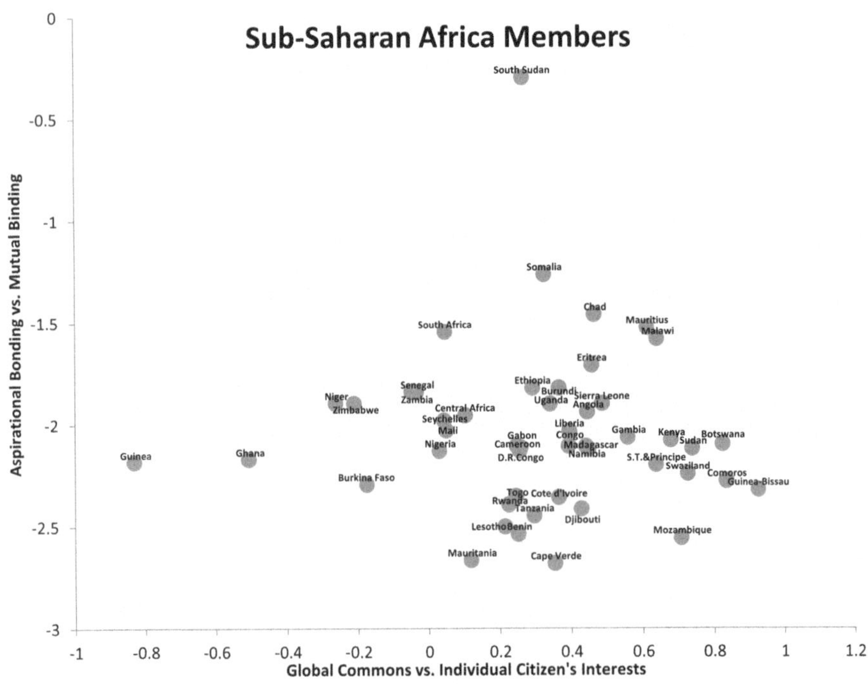
Sub-Saharan Africa Members
Aspirational Bonding vs. Mutual Binding
Global Commons vs. Individual Citizen's Interests
South Sudan
Somalia
Chad
South Africa
Mauritius
Malawi
Eritrea
Senegal
Zambia
Niger
Zimbabwe
Ethiopia
Burundi
Sierra Leone
Uganda
Angola
Central Africa
Seychelles
Mali
Liberia
Congo
Gabon
Cameroon
Gambia
Kenya
Sudan
Botswana
Nigeria
Madagascar
Namibia
D.R.Congo
Guinea
Ghana
S.T.&Principe
Swaziland
Comoros
Guinea-Bissau
Burkina Faso
Togo
Cote d'Ivoire
Rwanda
Tanzania
Djibouti
Lesotho
Benin
Mozambique
Mauritania
Cape Verde

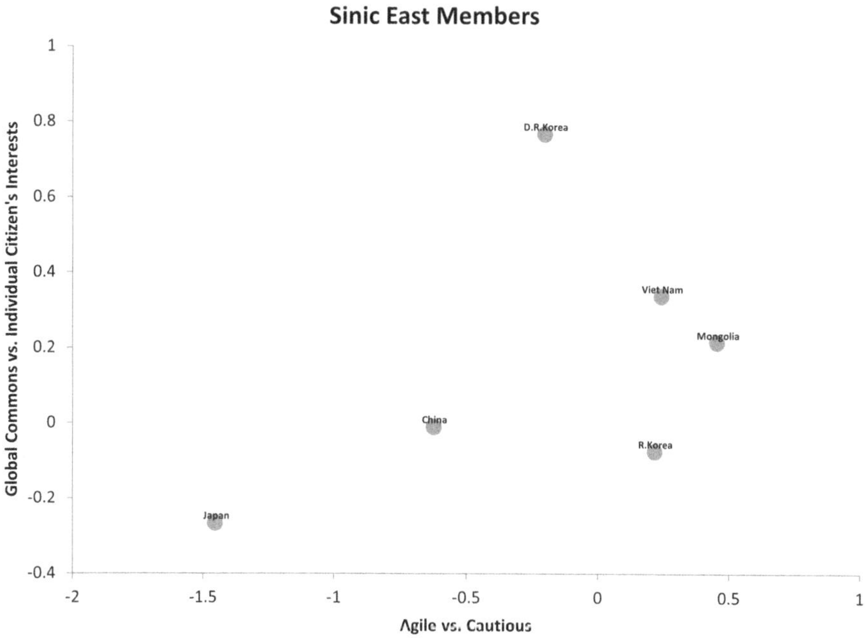
Sinic East Members
Global Commons vs. Individual Citizen's Interests
Agile vs. Cautious
D.R.Korea
Viet Nam
Mongolia
China
R.Korea
Japan
1
0.8
0.6
0.4
0.2
0
-0.2
-0.4
-2
-1.5
-1
-0.5
0
0.5
1

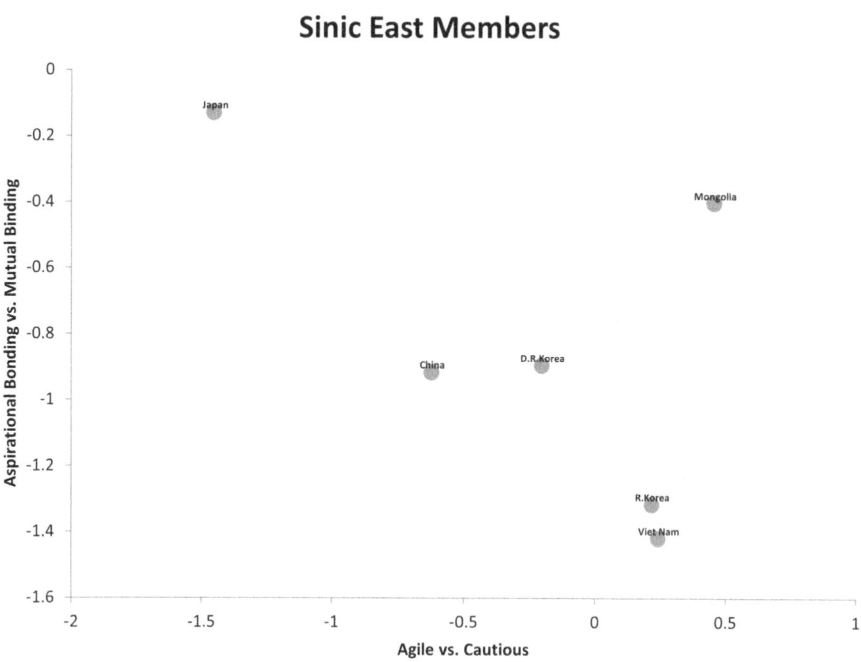
Sinic East Members
Aspirational Bonding vs. Mutual Binding
Agile vs. Cautious
Japan
Mongolia
China
D.R.Korea
R.Korea
Viet Nam
0
-0.2
-0.4
-0.6
-0.8
-1
-1.2
-1.4
-1.6
-2
-1.5
-1
-0.5
0
0.5
1

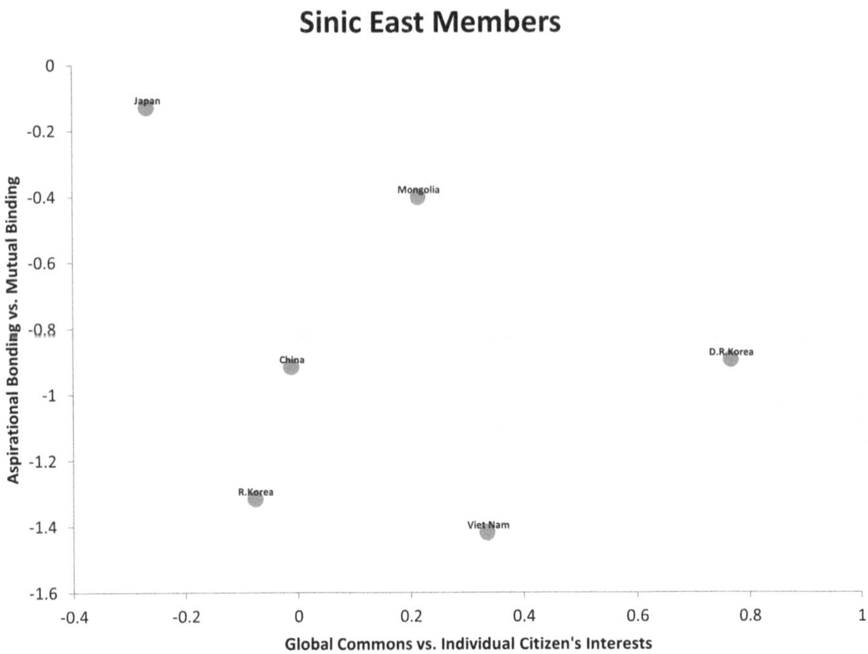
Sinic East Members
Aspirational Bonding vs. Mutual Binding
Global Commons vs. Individual Citizen's Interests
Japan
Mongolia
China
D.R.Korea
R.Korea
Viet Nam
0
-0.2
-0.4
-0.6
-0.8
-1
-1.2
-1.4
-1.6
-0.4
-0.2
0
0.2
0.4
0.6
0.8
1

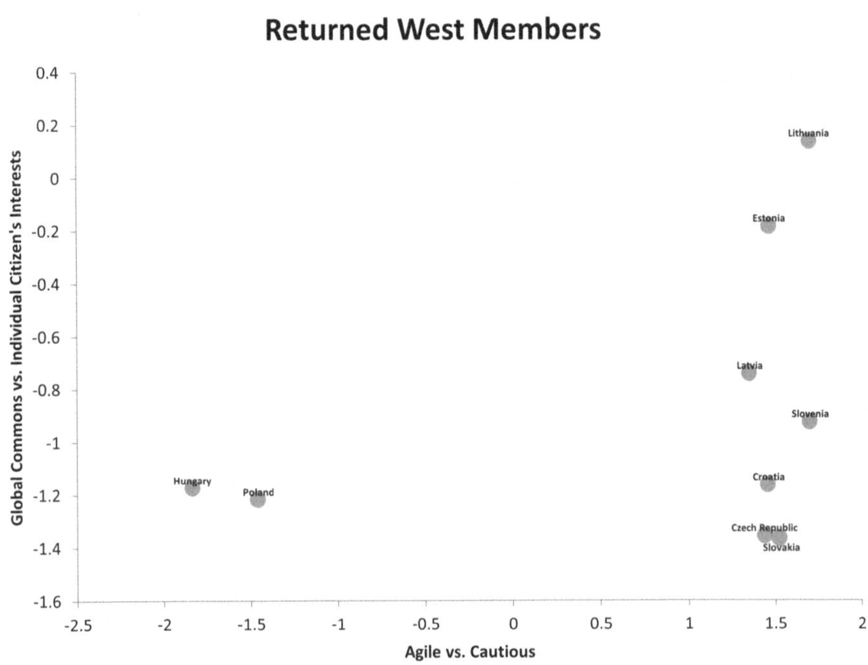
Returned West Members
Global Commons vs. Individual Citizen's Interests
Agile vs. Cautious
Lithuania
Estonia
Latvia
Slovenia
Croatia
Hungary
Poland
Czech Republic
Slovakia
0.4
0.2
0
-0.2
-0.4
-0.6
-0.8
-1
-1.2
-1.4
-1.6
-2.5
-2
-1.5
-1
-0.5
0
0.5
1
1.5
2

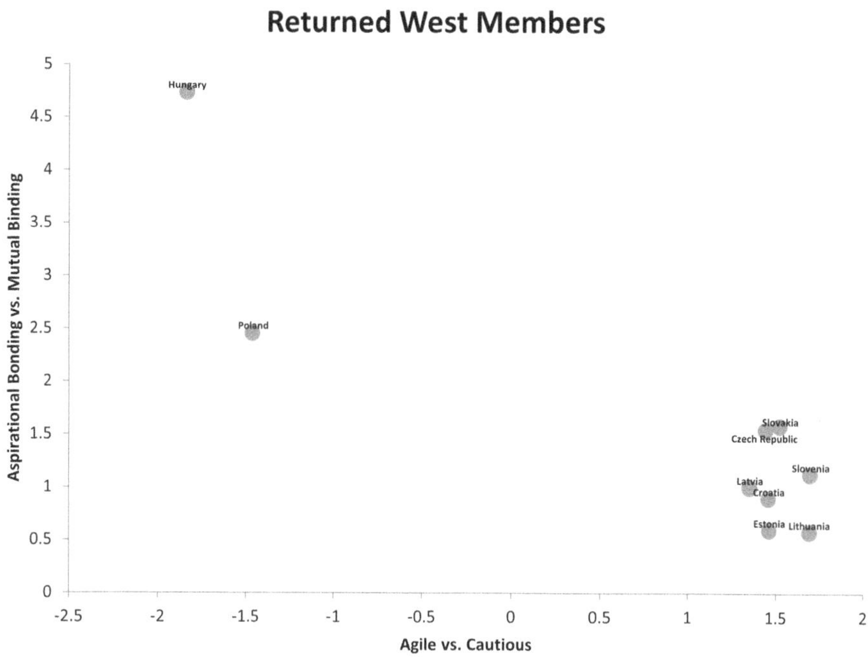
Returned West Members
Aspirational Bonding vs. Mutual Binding
Agile vs. Cautious
Hungary
Poland
Slovakia
Czech Republic
Slovenia
Latvia
Croatia
Estonia
Lithuania
5
4.5
4
3.5
3
2.5
2
1.5
1
0.5
0
-2.5
-2
-1.5
-1
-0.5
0
0.5
1
1.5
2

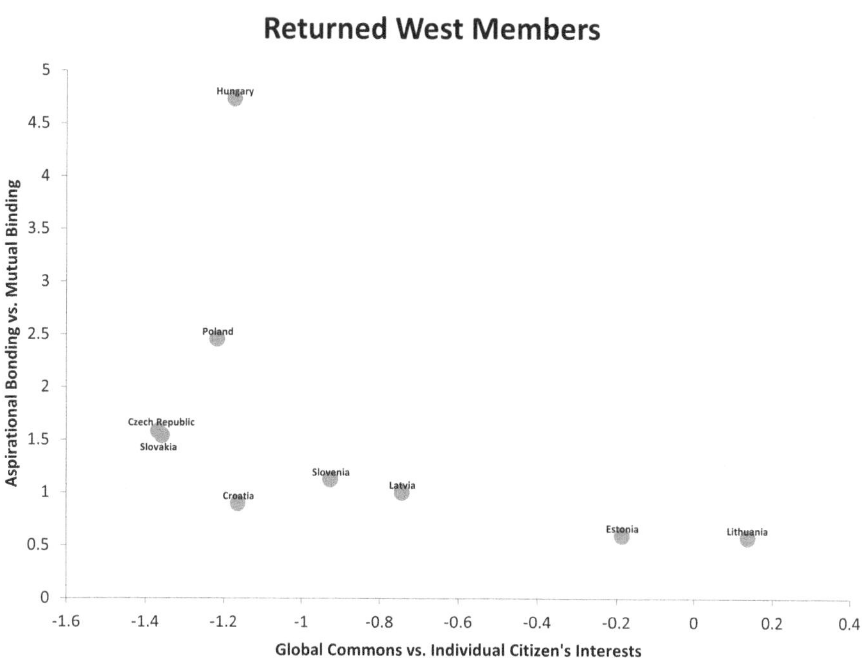
Returned West Members
Aspirational Bonding vs. Mutual Binding
Global Commons vs. Individual Citizen's Interests
Hungary
Poland
Czech Republic
Slovakia
Slovenia
Latvia
Croatia
Estonia
Lithuania
5
4.5
4
3.5
3
2.5
2
1.5
1
0.5
0
-1.6
-1.4
-1.2
-1
-0.8
-0.6
-0.4
-0.2
0
0.2
0.4

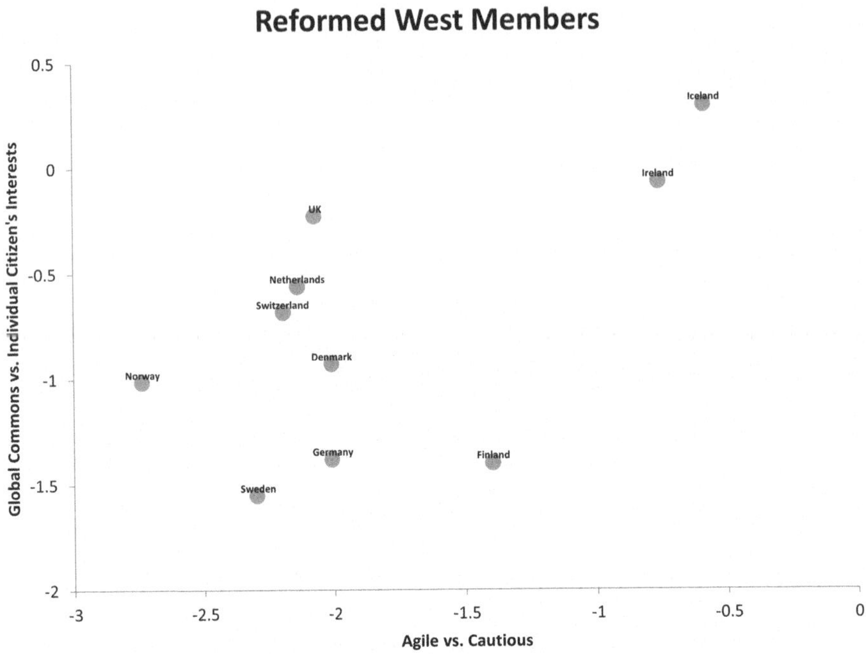
Reformed West Members
0.5
0
-0.5
-1
-1.5
-2
Global Commons vs. Individual Citizen's Interests
Iceland
Ireland
UK
Netherlands
Switzerland
Denmark
Norway
Germany
Finland
Sweden
-3
-2.5
-2
-1.5
-1
-0.5
0
Agile vs. Cautious

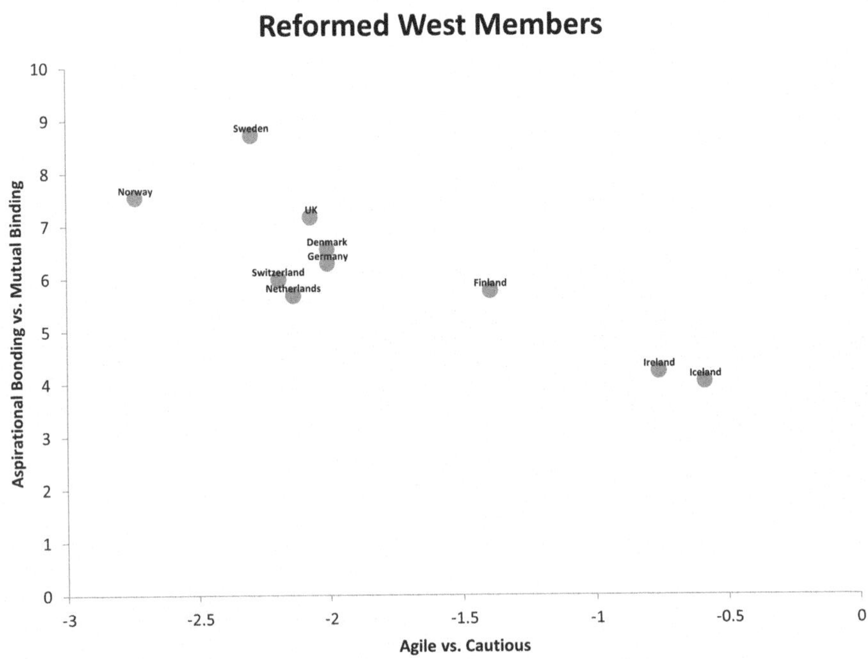
Reformed West Members
10
9
8
7
6
5
4
3
2
1
0
Aspirational Bonding vs. Mutual Binding
Sweden
Norway
UK
Denmark
Germany
Switzerland
Netherlands
Finland
Ireland
Iceland
-3
-2.5
-2
-1.5
-1
-0.5
0
Agile vs. Cautious

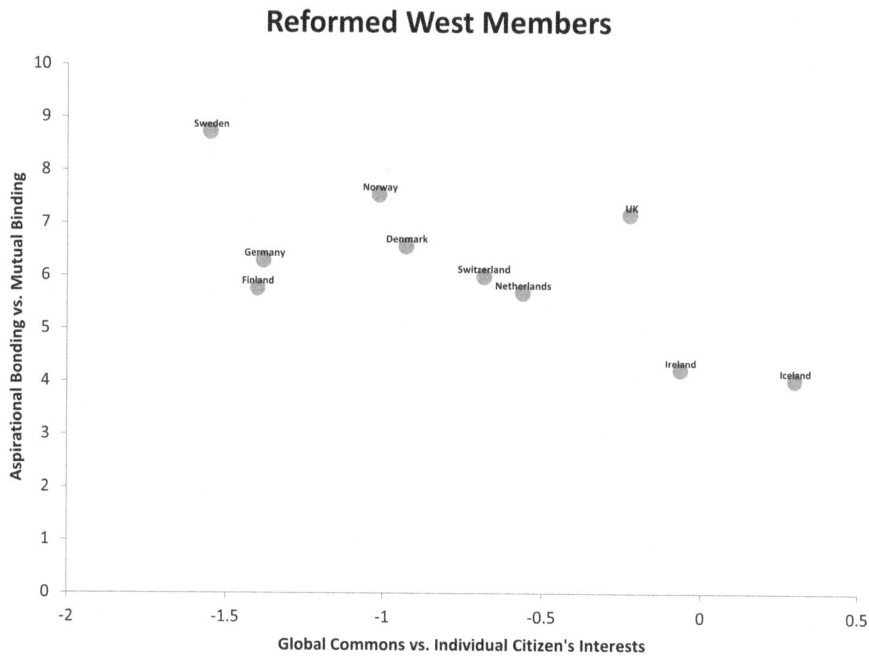
Reformed West Members
Aspirational Bonding vs. Mutual Binding
Global Commons vs. Individual Citizen's Interests
10
9
8
7
6
5
4
3
2
1
0
-2
-1.5
-1
-0.5
0
0.5
Sweden
Norway
UK
Denmark
Germany
Finland
Switzerland
Netherlands
Ireland
Iceland

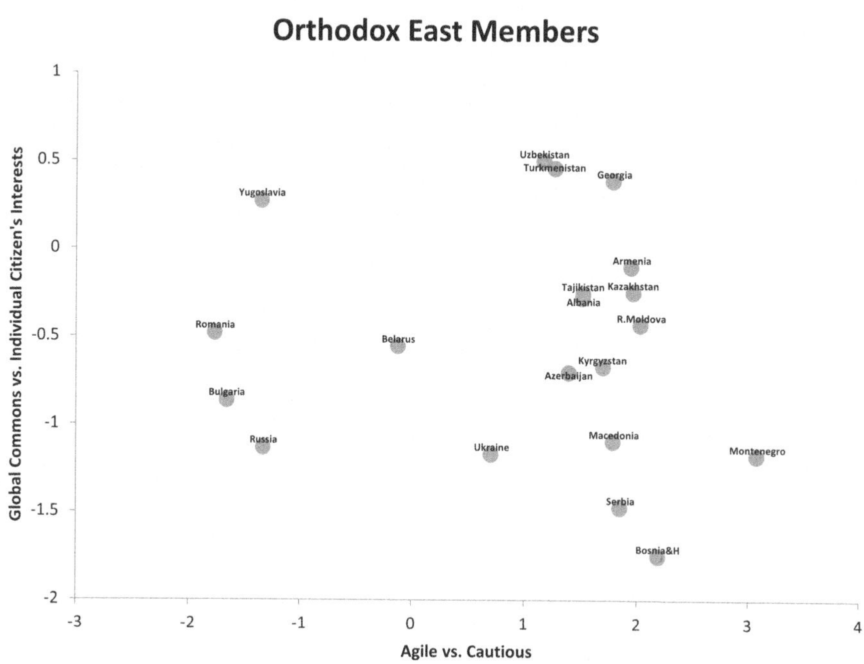
Orthodox East Members
Global Commons vs. Individual Citizen's Interests
Agile vs. Cautious
1
0.5
0
-0.5
-1
-1.5
-2
-3
-2
-1
0
1
2
3
4
Uzbekistan
Turkmenistan
Georgia
Yugoslavia
Armenia
Tajikistan
Kazakhstan
Albania
R.Moldova
Romania
Belarus
Kyrgyzstan
Azerbaijan
Bulgaria
Russia
Ukraine
Macedonia
Montenegro
Serbia
Bosnia&H

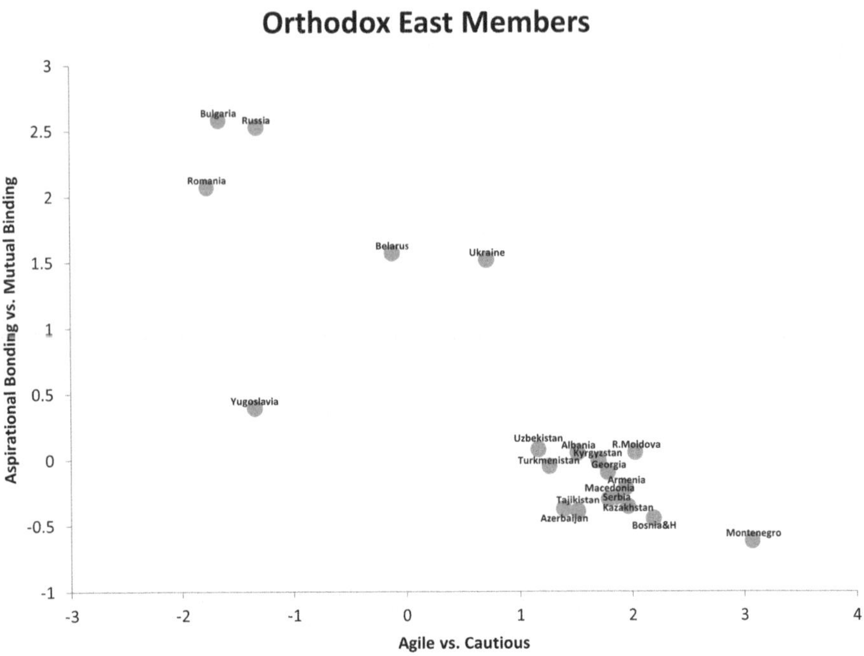
Orthodox East Members
Aspirational Bonding vs. Mutual Binding
Agile vs. Cautious
Bulgaria
Russia
Romania
Belarus
Ukraine
Yugoslavia
Uzbekistan
Albania
R.Moldova
Kyrgyzstan
Turkmenistan
Georgia
Armenia
Macedonia
Serbia
Tajikistan
Kazakhstan
Azerbaijan
Bosnia&H
Montenegro

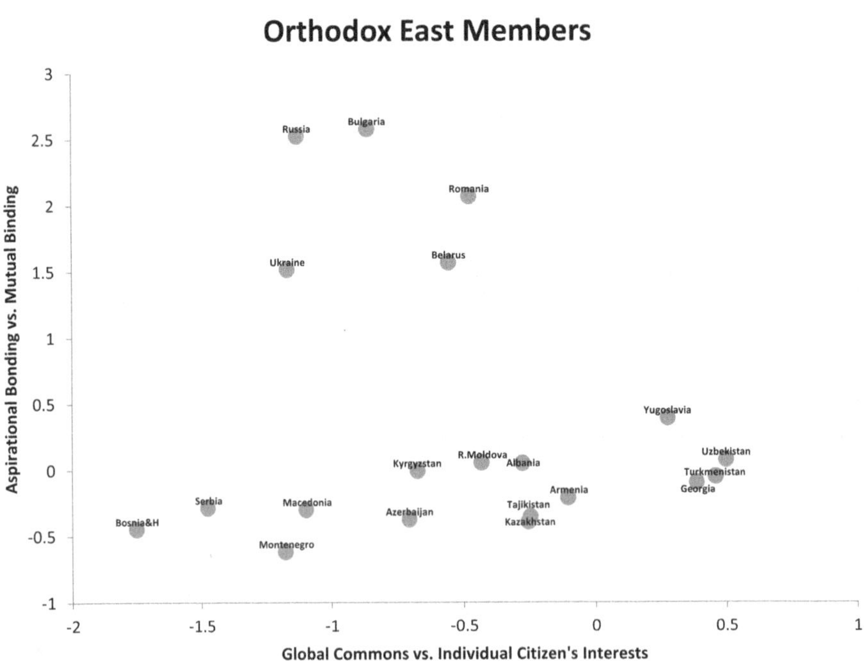
Orthodox East Members
Aspirational Bonding vs. Mutual Binding
Global Commons vs. Individual Citizen's Interests
Russia
Bulgaria
Romania
Ukraine
Belarus
Yugoslavia
Uzbekistan
Turkmenistan
Georgia
Kyrgyzstan
R.Moldova
Albania
Armenia
Serbia
Macedonia
Azerbaijan
Tajikistan
Kazakhstan
Bosnia&H
Montenegro

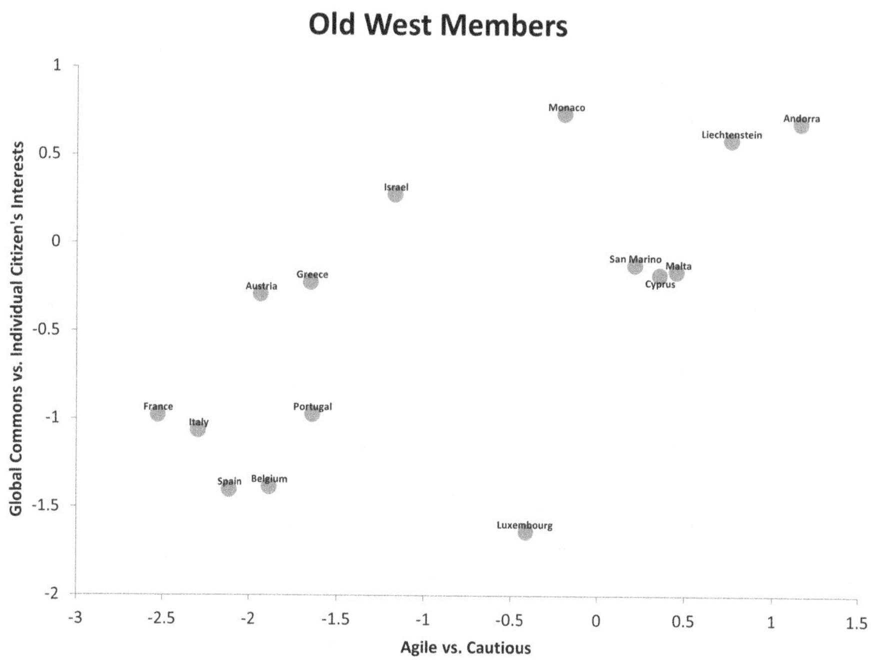
Old West Members
Global Commons vs. Individual Citizen's Interests
Agile vs. Cautious
Monaco
Andorra
Liechtenstein
Israel
San Marino
Malta
Cyprus
Greece
Austria
France
Italy
Portugal
Spain
Belgium
Luxembourg

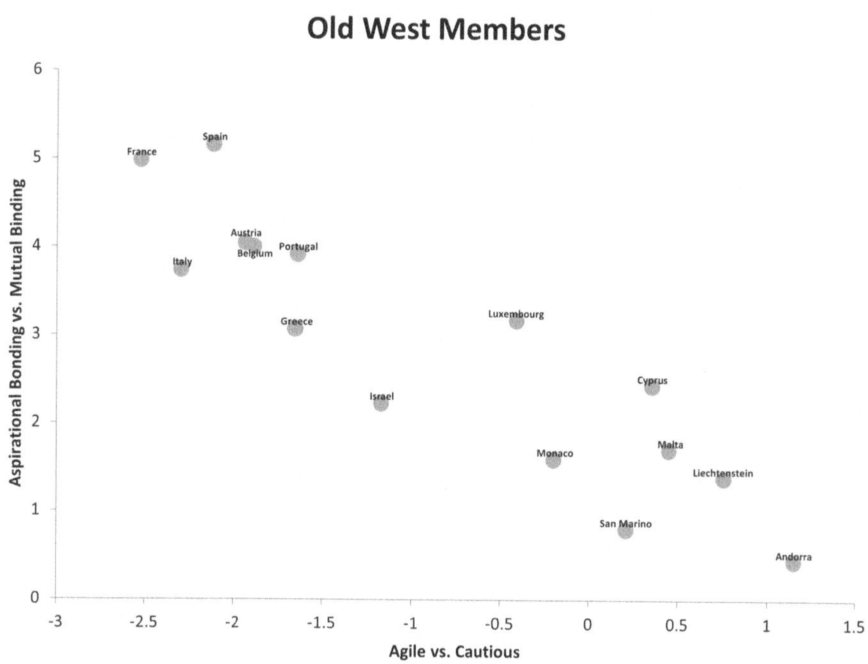
Old West Members
Aspirational Bonding vs. Mutual Binding
Agile vs. Cautious
Spain
France
Austria
Belgium
Portugal
Italy
Greece
Luxembourg
Cyprus
Israel
Malta
Monaco
Liechtenstein
San Marino
Andorra

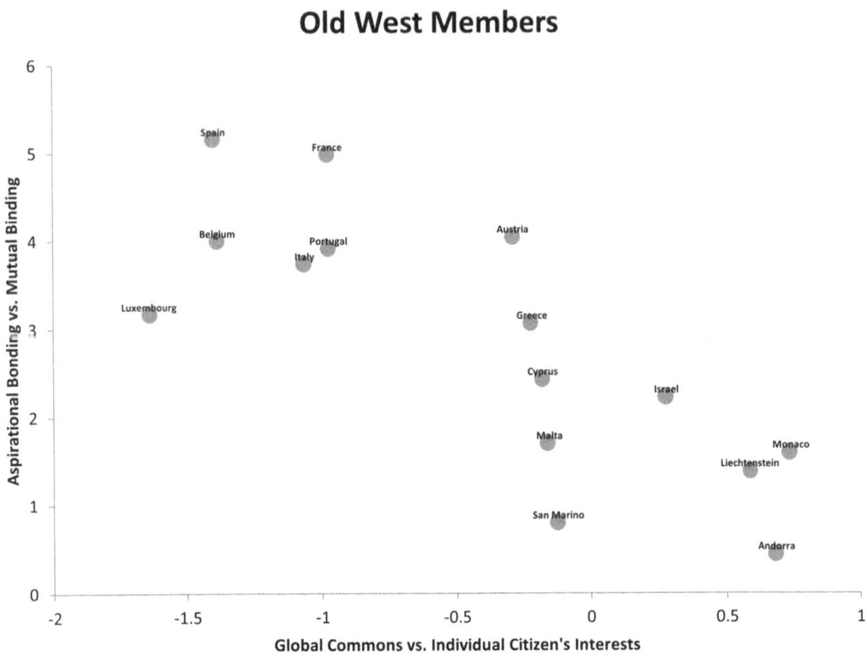
Old West Members
Aspirational Bonding vs. Mutual Binding
Global Commons vs. Individual Citizen's Interests
Spain
France
Belgium
Portugal
Italy
Austria
Luxembourg
Greece
Cyprus
Israel
Malta
Monaco
Liechtenstein
San Marino
Andorra
6
5
4
3
2
1
0
-2
-1.5
-1
-0.5
0
0.5
1

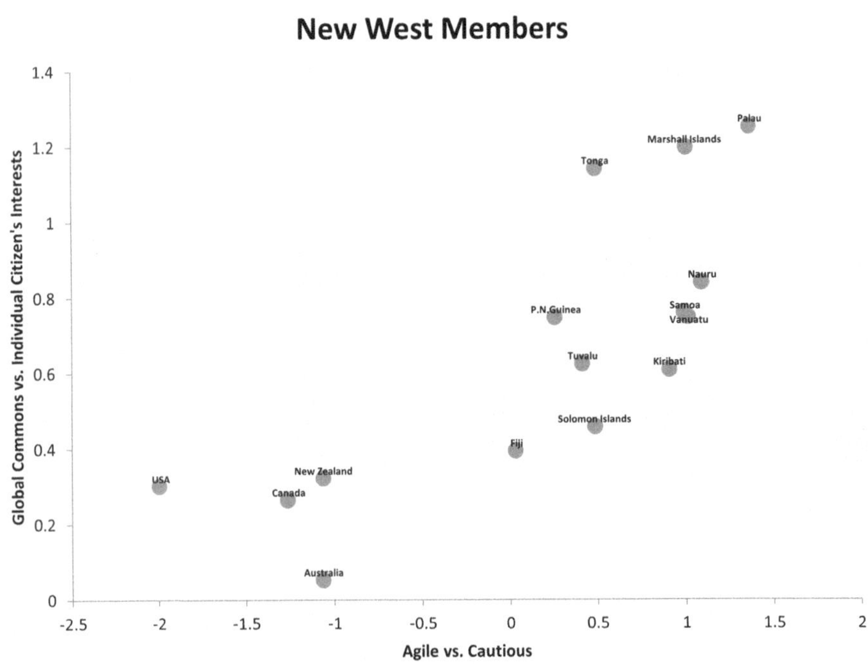
New West Members
Global Commons vs. Individual Citizen's Interests
Agile vs. Cautious
Palau
Marshall Islands
Tonga
Nauru
P.N.Guinea
Samoa
Vanuatu
Tuvalu
Kiribati
Solomon Islands
Fiji
USA
New Zealand
Canada
Australia
1.4
1.2
1
0.8
0.6
0.4
0.2
0
-2.5
-2
-1.5
-1
-0.5
0
0.5
1
1.5
2

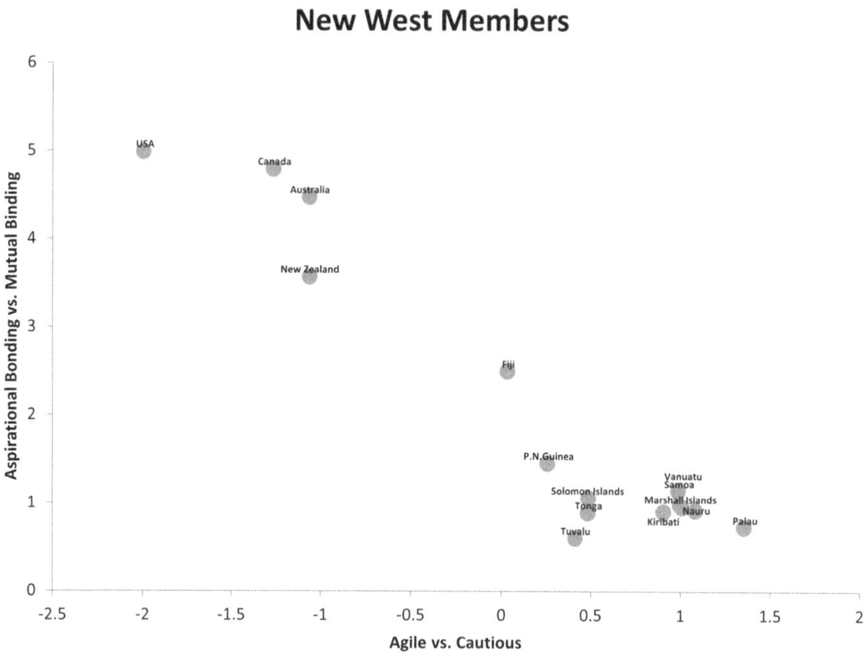
New West Members
Aspirational Bonding vs. Mutual Binding
Agile vs. Cautious
USA
Canada
Australia
New Zealand
Fiji
P.N.Guinea
Solomon Islands
Tonga
Tuvalu
Vanuatu
Samoa
Marshall Islands
Nauru
Kiribati
Palau
6
5
4
3
2
1
0
-2.5
-2
-1.5
-1
-0.5
0
0.5
1
1.5
2

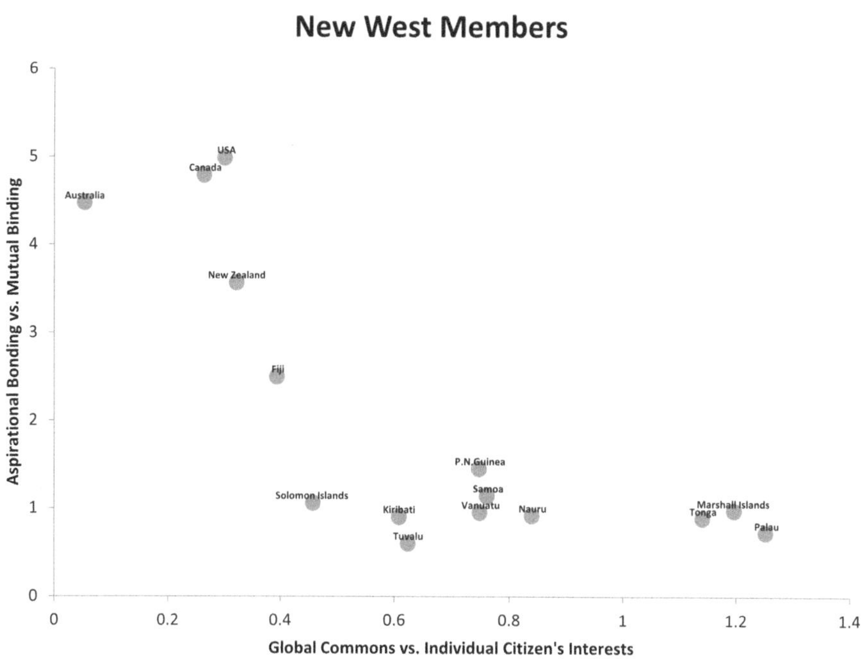
New West Members
Aspirational Bonding vs. Mutual Binding
Global Commons vs. Individual Citizen's Interests
USA
Canada
Australia
New Zealand
Fiji
P.N.Guinea
Solomon Islands
Samoa
Kiribati
Vanuatu
Nauru
Tuvalu
Marshall Islands
Tonga
Palau
6
5
4
3
2
1
0
0
0.2
0.4
0.6
0.8
1
1.2
1.4

Latin America Members

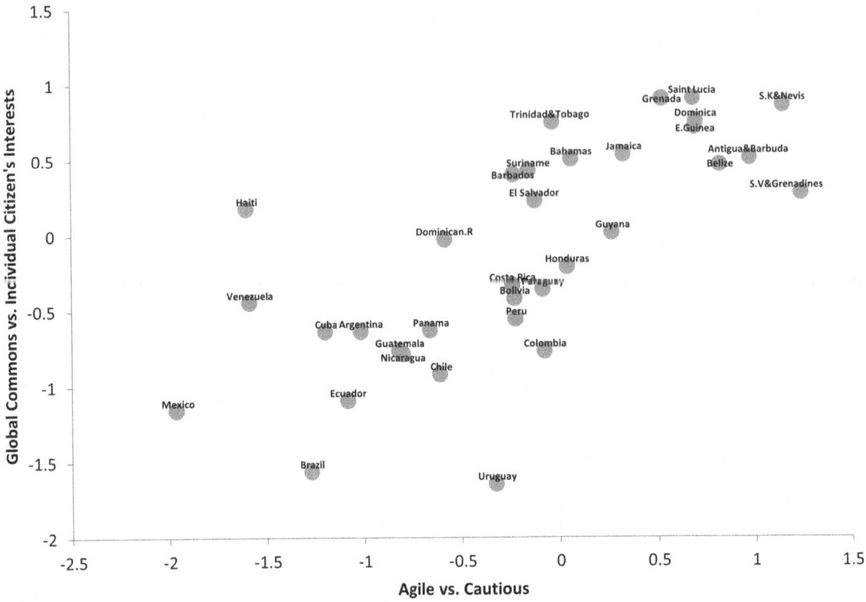

Latin America Members

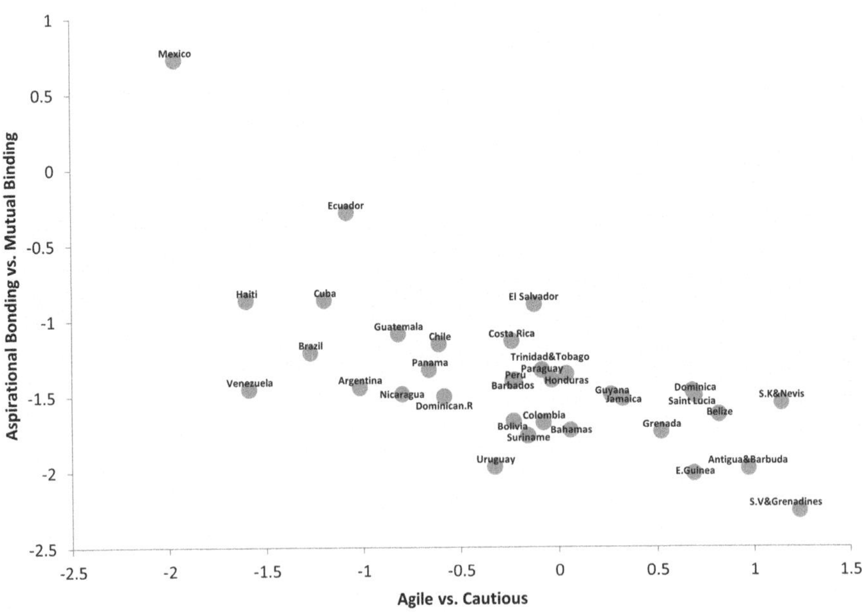

Latin America Members

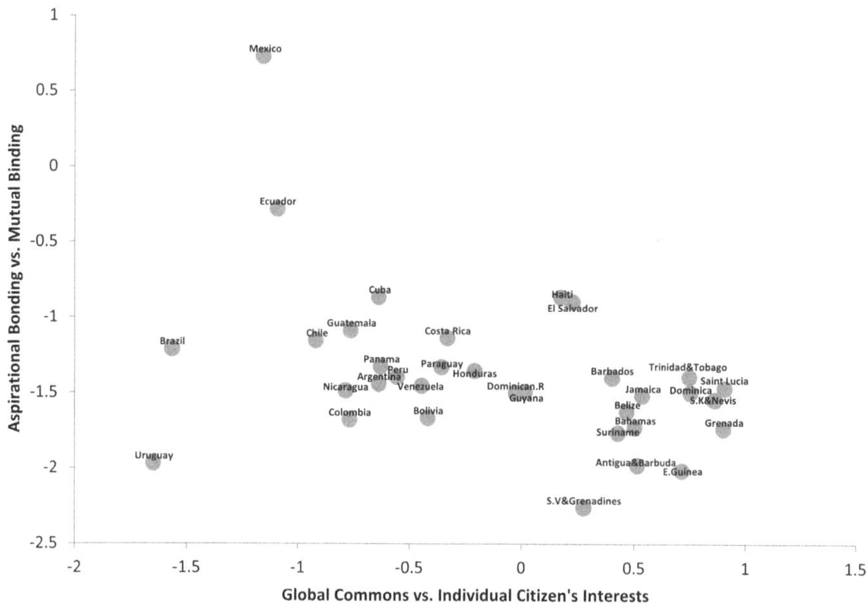

Islamic East Members

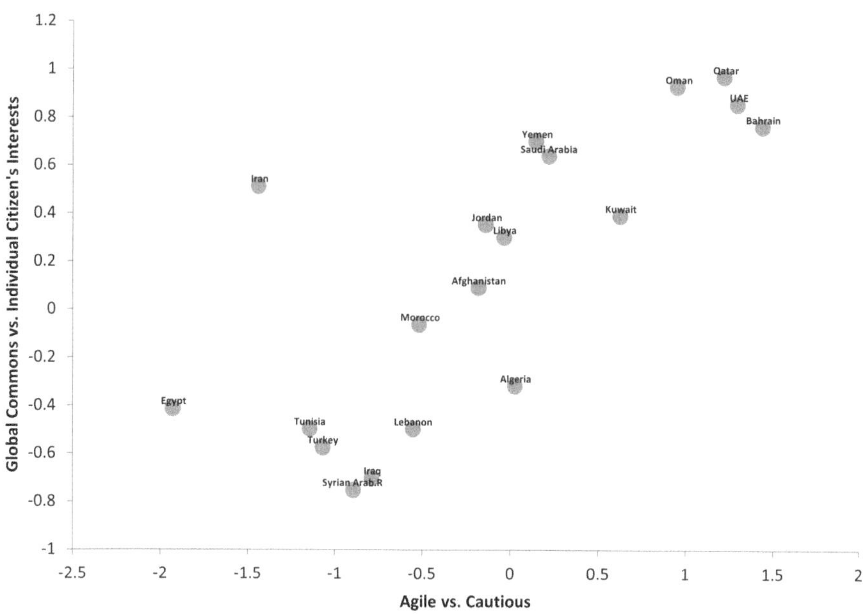

Islamic East Members

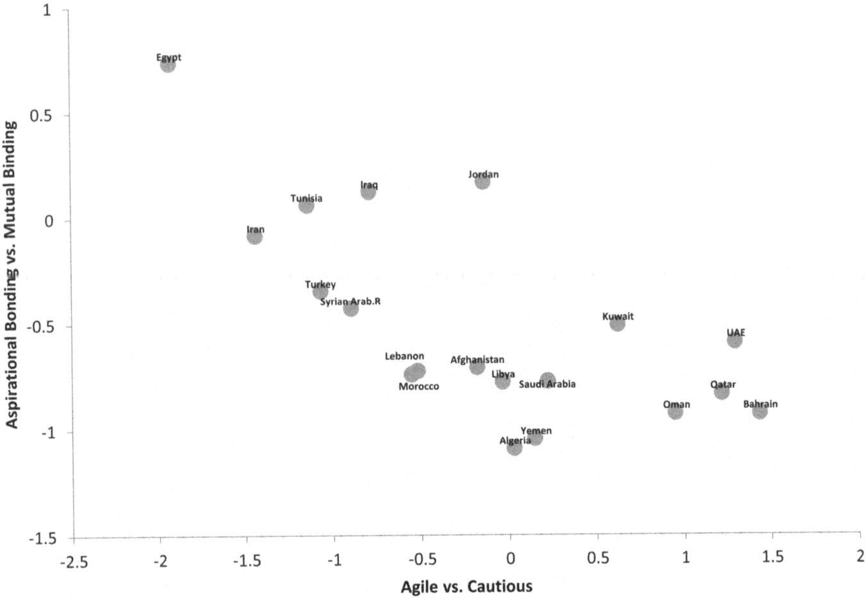

Islamic East Members

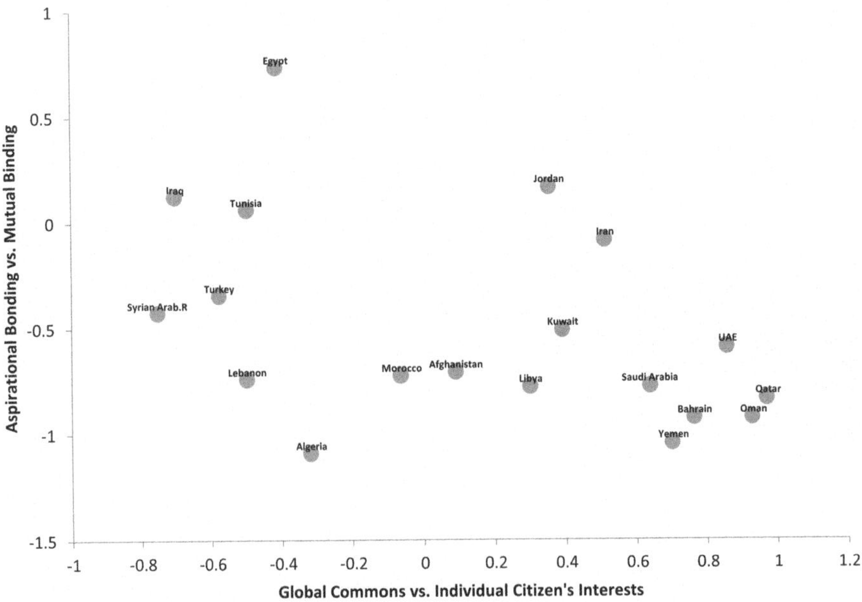

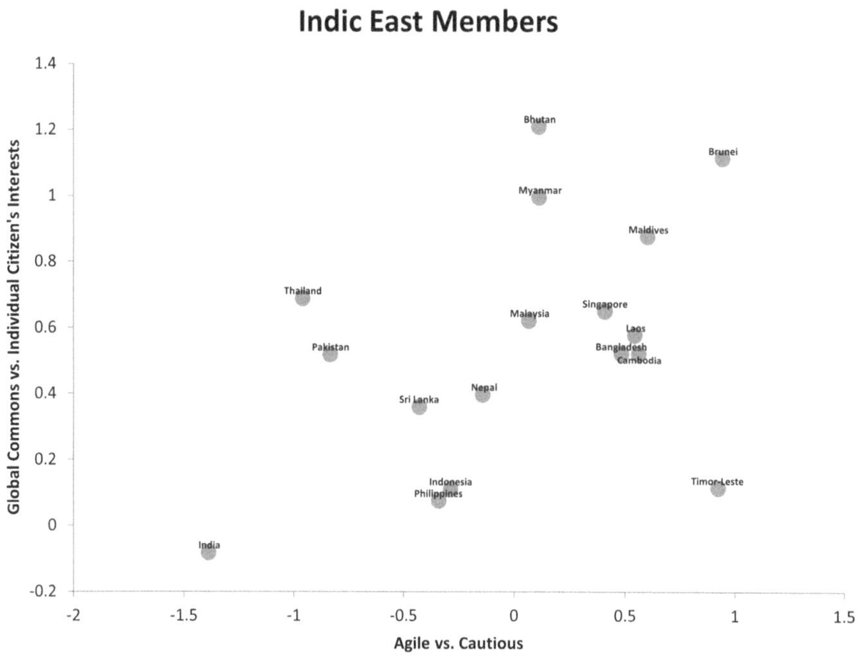
Indic East Members
Global Commons vs. Individual Citizen's Interests
Agile vs. Cautious
1.4
1.2
1
0.8
0.6
0.4
0.2
0
-0.2
-2
-1.5
-1
-0.5
0
0.5
1
1.5
Bhutan
Brunei
Myanmar
Maldives
Thailand
Singapore
Malaysia
Laos
Pakistan
Bangladesh
Cambodia
Nepal
Sri Lanka
Indonesia
Philippines
Timor-Leste
India

Indic East Members
Aspirational Bonding vs. Mutual Binding
Agile vs. Cautious
2
1.5
1
0.5
0
-0.5
-1
-2
-1.5
-1
-0.5
0
0.5
1
1.5
Philippines
India
Pakistan
Thailand
Sri Lanka
Myanmar
Maldives
Indonesia
Malaysia
Bangladesh
Brunei
Singapore
Nepal
Laos
Bhutan
Timor-Leste
Cambodia

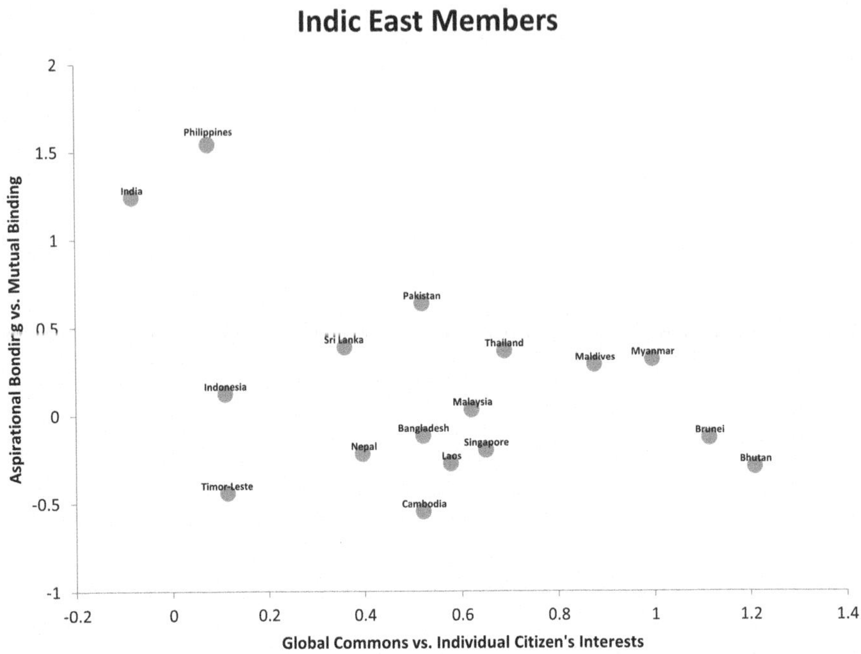
Indic East Members
Aspirational Bonding vs. Mutual Binding
Global Commons vs. Individual Citizen's Interests
2
1.5
1
0.5
0
-0.5
-1
-0.2
0
0.2
0.4
0.6
0.8
1
1.2
1.4
Philippines
India
Pakistan
Sri Lanka
Thailand
Maldives
Myanmar
Indonesia
Malaysia
Bangladesh
Brunei
Singapore
Nepal
Laos
Bhutan
Timor-Leste
Cambodia

Appendix 5: Categorization of States According to Eight Types of Global Quasi-Legislative Behavior

Regional group	Country name	Type
Indic East	Bangladesh	ABc
	Bhutan	ABc
	Brunei	ABc
	Cambodia	ABc
	India	abC
	Indonesia	aBC
	Laos	ABc
	Malaysia	ABC
	Maldives	ABC
	Myanmar	ABC
	Nepal	aBc
	Pakistan	aBC
	Philippines	aBC
	Singapore	ABc
	Sri Lanka	aBC
	Thailand	aBC
	Timor-Leste	ABc
Islamic East	Algeria	Abc
	Bahrain	ABc
	Egypt	abC
	Iran	aBc
	Iraq	abC
	Jordan	aBC
	Kuwait	ABc
	Lebanon	abc
	Libya	aBc
	Morocco	abc
	Oman	ABc
	Qatar	ABc
	Saudi Arabia	ABc
	Tunisia	abC
	Turkey	abc
	Afghanistan	aBc
	Syrian Arab.R	abc
	UAE	ABc
	Yemen	ABc
Latin America	Antigua&Barbuda	ABc
	Argentina	abc
	Bahamas	ABc

	Barbados	aBc
	Belize	ABc
	Bolivia	abc
	Brazil	abc
	Chile	abc
	Colombia	abc
	Costa Rica	abc
	Cuba	abc
	Dominica	ABc
	Dominican.R	abc
	Ecuador	abc
	El Salvador	aBc
	E.Guinea	ABc
	Grenada	ABc
	Guatemala	abc
	Guyana	ABc
	Haiti	aBc
	Honduras	Abc
	Jamaica	ABc
	Mexico	abC
	Nicaragua	abc
	Panama	abc
	Paraguay	abc
	Peru	abc
	S.K&Nevis	ABc
	Saint Lucia	ABc
	S.V&Grenadines	ABc
	Suriname	aBc
	Trinidad&Tobago	aBc
	Uruguay	abc
	Venezuela	abc
New West	Australia	aBC
	Canada	aBC
	Fiji	ABC
	Kiribati	ABC
	Marshall Islands	ABC
	Nauru	ABC
	New Zealand	aBC
	Palau	ABC
	P.N.Guinea	ABC
	Samoa	ABC
	Solomon Islands	ABC
	Tonga	ABC
	Tuvalu	ABC

	USA	aBC
	Vanuatu	ABC
Old West	Andorra	ABC
	Austria	abC
	Belgium	abC
	Cyprus	AbC
	France	abC
	Greece	abC
	Israel	aBC
	Italy	abC
	Liechtenstein	ABC
	Luxembourg	abC
	Malta	AbC
	Monaco	aBC
	Portugal	abC
	San Marino	AbC
	Spain	abC
Orthodox East	Albania	AbC
	Armenia	Abc
	Azerbaijan	Abc
	Belarus	abC
	Bosnia & Herzegovina	Abc
	Bulgaria	abC
	Georgia	ABc
	Kazakhstan	Abc
	Kyrgyzstan	Abc
	Montenegro	Abc
	R.Moldova	AbC
	Romania	abC
	Russia	abC
	Serbia	Abc
	Tajikistan	Abc
	Macedonia	Abc
	Turkmenistan	ABc
	Ukraine	AbC
	Uzbekistan	ABC
	Yugoslavia	aBC
Reformed West	Denmark	abC
	Finland	abC
	Germany	abC
	Iceland	aBC
	Ireland	abC
	Netherlands	abC
	Norway	abC

	Sweden	abC
	Switzerland	abC
	UK	abC
Returned West	Croatia	AbC
	Czech Republic	AbC
	Estonia	AbC
	Hungary	abC
	Latvia	AbC
	Lithuania	ABC
	Poland	abC
	Slovakia	AbC
	Slovenia	AbC
Sinic East	China	abc
	D. P. R. Korea	aBc
	Japan	abc
	Mongolia	ABc
	R. Korea	Abc
	Viet Nam	ABc
Sub-Saharan Africa	Angola	ABc
	Benin	ABc
	Botswana	ABc
	Burkina Faso	Abc
	Burundi	ABc
	Cameroon	aBc
	Cape Verde	ABc
	Central Africa	aBc
	Chad	aBc
	Comoros	ABc
	Congo	aBc
	Cote d'Ivoire	aBc
	D.R.Congo	aBc
	Djibouti	ABc
	Eritrea	ABc
	Ethiopia	aBc
	Gabon	ABc
	Gambia	ABc
	Ghana	abc
	Guinea	abc
	Guinea-Bissau	ABc
	Kenya	aBc
	Lesotho	ABc
	Liberia	aBc
	Madagascar	aBc
	Malawi	ABc

	Mali	ABc
	Mauritania	ABc
	Mauritius	ABc
	Mozambique	ABc
	Namibia	ABc
	Niger	Abc
	Nigeria	ABc
	Rwanda	ABc
	S.T.&Principe	ABc
	Senegal	abc
	Seychelles	ABc
	Sierra Leone	aBc
	Somalia	aBc
	South Africa	aBc
	South Sudan	ABc
	Sudan	aBc
	Swaziland	ABc
	Togo	ABc
	Uganda	ABc
	Tanzania	ABc
	Zambia	Abc
	Zimbabwe	Abc

Appendix 6: 193 Countries' Deviations from World Mean in Six Policy Domains (z-score of Treaty Participation Index)

The above table indicates the scores of 193 states and 10 regional groups in average in terms of participation in multilateral treaties by six policy domains. For each domain, to measure how many standard deviations above or below the world mean a country exercised, we have calculated the z-score for each state based on its treaty participation measurement. A positive z-score represents a country that has participated in multilateral treaties faster than the world mean, whereas a negative score represents a country that has participated in multilateral treaties slower than the world mean. This score is measured by normalizing the treaty participation index and is used to capture the comparative evaluation among countries. In this way, a z-score represents a country's relationship to the world mean; thus, it can illustrate whether a country is leading in participation in multilateral treaties or not on a given global issue. For instance, if Country A has the z-score of 1.0, in the normal distribution, we can infer that Country A achieved better than 68% of countries in the world and ranked roughly among the top 60 countries (32% × 200). Similarly, Country B with z-score of 2.0 means that Country B achieved better than 95% of the countries in the world and is among the top 10 countries worldwide. Using the same type of interpretation, if Country C achieves better than 99.7%, Country C with the z-score of 3.0 will be the best performer in the world. With that scaling of measurement, it can be interpreted that a country having the z-score in a given regime domain of 2.0 or higher is outstanding and leads the world in that domain.

Region	Country	Human rights	Peace and security	Trade, commerce, and communication	Environment	Intellectual property	labor
Indic East	Bangladesh	0.261	−0.518	−0.079	−0.017	−0.448	−0.528
	Bhutan	−0.427	−0.882	−0.993	−1.045	−1.025	−0.865
	Brunei Darussalam	−1.249	−0.467	−0.125	−1.149	−0.470	−0.796
	Cambodia	−0.439	−0.612	−0.881	−0.835	−0.492	−0.693
	India	1.018	0.504	2.047	0.897	−0.068	−0.193
	Indonesia	−0.279	−0.551	0.315	−0.344	0.526	−0.223
	Lao People's Democratic Republic	0.028	0.071	−0.934	−0.833	−0.469	−0.722
	Malaysia	−1.060	−0.215	0.008	0.054	−0.352	−0.332
	Maldives	−0.666	−0.523	−0.099	0.491	−0.503	−0.865
	Myanmar	−0.820	−0.307	0.578	−0.620	−0.501	−0.766
	Nepal	0.176	−0.625	−0.891	−0.383	−1.032	−0.622
	Pakistan	0.229	−0.054	0.678	0.276	0.106	0.215
	Philippines	2.129	0.846	0.896	0.618	1.221	0.620
	Singapore	−1.219	−0.454	−0.044	−0.469	−0.159	0.501
	Sri Lanka	0.029	0.109	0.552	0.111	0.227	−0.508
	Thailand	−0.657	0.605	0.265	−0.197	−0.458	−0.062
	Timor-Leste	−1.121	−1.389	−1.001	−1.233	−1.061	−0.791
	REGION AVERAGE	**−0.239**	**−0.263**	**0.017**	**−0.275**	**−0.292**	**−0.449**
Islamic East	Afghanistan	−0.432	−0.424	−0.829	−0.699	−1.046	−0.242
	Algeria	−0.262	−0.394	−0.908	−0.413	−0.888	0.406
	Bahrain	−0.853	−0.810	−0.102	−0.538	−0.140	−0.616
	Egypt	2.300	−0.159	1.399	1.422	−0.136	0.388
	Iran	−0.326	0.248	0.220	0.071	−1.032	−0.415
	Iraq	0.302	−0.006	−0.007	0.165	−0.977	1.523
	Jordan	0.307	0.480	−0.615	1.383	−0.402	0.980
	Kuwait	−0.462	−0.072	−0.037	−0.661	−0.499	0.384
	Lebanon	−0.370	−0.083	−0.628	−0.006	−0.882	−0.134
	Libyan Arab Jamahiriya	0.187	−0.394	−0.883	−0.370	−0.952	0.349
	Morocco	0.066	−0.331	−0.006	0.134	0.204	−0.105
	Oman	−1.001	−0.477	−0.892	−0.574	−0.673	−0.649
	Qatar	−0.306	−0.462	−0.529	−0.800	−0.415	−0.530
	Saudi Arabia	−0.550	0.037	−0.850	−0.158	−0.996	−0.523
	Syrian Arab Republic	0.533	−0.562	−0.612	−0.015	−0.982	1.239
	Tunisia	1.115	0.049	0.005	0.869	0.912	0.827
	Turkey	−0.177	0.323	1.588	−0.226	−0.148	0.246
	United Arab Emirates	−0.693	−0.271	−0.531	0.477	−0.317	−0.615
	Yemen	−0.368	−0.744	−0.949	−0.760	−0.998	−0.403
	REGION AVERAGE	**−0.052**	**−0.213**	**−0.272**	**−0.037**	**−0.546**	**0.111**

Latin America	Antigua and Barbuda	–0.636	–0.670	–0.118	0.003	–0.468	–0.520
	Argentina	1.485	0.044	0.759	0.372	1.347	0.129
	Bahamas	–0.172	–0.524	–0.967	–0.253	–0.956	–0.560
	Barbados	1.161	0.019	–0.082	–0.525	–0.290	–0.319
	Belize	0.197	–0.835	–0.119	–0.511	–0.441	–0.436
	Bolivia	0.560	0.372	0.882	0.174	–0.435	–0.324
	Brazil	0.485	0.799	1.532	0.658	1.232	1.232
	Chile	0.662	0.555	1.627	1.231	1.439	0.230
	Colombia	1.082	–0.569	0.735	–0.215	0.791	0.082
	Costa Rica	2.520	0.482	0.366	–0.054	1.367	0.630
	Cuba	1.270	–0.329	0.409	0.491	–0.182	2.757
	Dominica	–0.263	–0.891	–0.126	–0.589	–0.450	–0.526
	Dominican Republic	–0.406	0.226	0.782	0.461	–0.094	0.661
	Ecuador	3.494	1.056	0.424	0.604	1.370	2.010
	El Salvador	0.919	1.207	0.503	0.474	0.826	–0.221
	Equatorial Guinea	–0.573	–0.745	–0.959	–0.755	–1.009	–0.568
	Grenada	–0.633	–0.369	–0.543	–0.866	–0.735	–0.633
	Guatemala	0.321	0.501	0.906	1.339	0.293	1.350
	Guyana	0.812	–0.370	–0.079	–0.600	–0.486	–0.250
	Haiti	0.483	–0.651	–0.124	0.224	–0.196	–0.288
	Honduras	0.482	–0.025	0.883	–0.126	0.727	0.271
	Jamaica	0.828	–0.289	–0.047	–0.399	0.679	–0.498
	Mexico	2.121	3.058	1.512	2.381	2.006	2.333
	Nicaragua	1.433	0.864	0.888	0.111	0.255	0.125
	Panama	1.809	1.061	–0.225	0.955	0.685	0.211
	Paraguay	0.168	0.480	0.973	0.227	0.848	–0.045
	Peru	0.829	0.701	1.107	0.142	0.821	–0.022
	Saint Kitts and Nevis	–0.411	–0.685	–0.568	–0.537	–0.739	–0.513
	Saint Lucia	–0.973	–0.705	–0.126	–0.280	0.663	–0.490
	Saint Vincent and the Grenadines	–0.335	–0.731	–0.128	–0.808	–0.394	–0.603
	Suriname	–0.827	–0.762	–0.105	–0.727	–0.404	–0.704
	Trinidad and Tobago	–0.691	1.125	–0.039	–0.176	–0.042	–0.515
	Uruguay	1.985	–0.006	0.277	0.693	–0.183	0.568
	Venezuela	0.444	–0.356	0.538	0.450	–0.355	–0.133
	REGION AVERAGE	**0.577**	**0.089**	**0.316**	**0.105**	**0.220**	**0.130**

New West	Australia	2.011	1.307	1.256	2.384	0.582	–0.245
	Canada	0.585	1.639	2.438	3.254	0.198	0.106
	Fiji	–1.061	1.140	–0.531	0.663	0.033	–0.504
	Kiribati	–1.247	–0.707	–0.987	–0.672	–1.061	–0.740
	Marshall Islands	–1.196	–0.784	–0.994	–0.074	–1.061	–0.865
	Nauru	–1.102	–0.675	–1.011	–0.529	–1.061	–0.865
	New Zealand	0.886	0.945	0.953	1.611	–0.193	–0.414
	Palau	–1.272	–0.814	–1.002	–0.934	–1.061	–0.865
	Papua New Guinea	–1.093	–0.713	–0.534	–0.229	–0.744	–0.469
	Samoa	–1.081	–0.500	–0.956	–0.455	–1.037	–0.740
	Solomon Islands	–1.154	–0.935	–0.545	–0.728	–0.789	–0.769
	Tonga	–1.028	–0.675	–0.953	–0.989	–1.034	–0.865
	Tuvalu	–1.241	–1.174	–1.006	–0.517	–1.061	–0.865
	United States of America	–1.033	1.599	2.958	3.136	2.755	–0.203
	Vanuatu	–0.823	–1.064	–0.957	–0.638	–1.044	–0.740
	REGION AVERAGE	**–0.657**	**–0.094**	**–0.125**	**0.352**	**–0.438**	**–0.603**
Old West	Andorra	–1.126	–0.936	–1.023	–1.349	–0.474	–0.865
	Austria	0.878	2.984	2.089	0.642	0.386	0.934
	Belgium	0.510	0.594	3.162	1.112	1.761	0.866
	Cyprus	0.336	0.596	-0.035	0.413	0.293	0.339
	France	1.244	1.520	3.034	2.040	3.084	1.223
	Greece	–0.196	0.777	1.917	1.277	–0.163	0.370
	Israel	–0.360	–0.010	0.555	–0.113	0.762	0.383
	Italy	0.227	1.058	2.351	1.123	1.436	0.664
	Liechtenstein	–0.942	–0.585	–0.162	–0.261	0.475	–0.757
	Luxembourg	–0.346	0.063	2.082	1.237	1.300	0.207
	Malta	–0.143	0.009	–0.070	–0.243	–0.259	–0.293
	Monaco	–0.334	–0.331	–0.996	0.438	0.898	–0.865
	Portugal	1.733	1.309	1.495	1.478	0.869	1.071
	San Marino	–0.522	–0.524	–0.985	–1.069	–1.001	–0.234
	Spain	1.902	2.248	1.657	1.413	3.372	2.554
	REGION AVERAGE	**0.191**	**0.585**	**1.005**	**0.543**	**0.849**	**0.373**

Orthodox East	Albania	0.141	-0.247	-0.823	-0.649	-0.158	-0.245
	Armenia	-0.642	-0.773	-0.944	-0.299	-0.675	-0.356
	Azerbaijan	-0.542	-0.653	-0.991	-0.849	-0.710	-0.563
	Belarus	1.660	1.205	-0.982	1.245	0.682	0.348
	Bosnia and Herzegovina	-0.374	-0.590	-0.978	-0.828	-0.761	-0.008
	Bulgaria	3.573	2.491	-0.356	0.917	1.043	1.123
	Georgia	-0.928	-0.721	-0.849	-0.532	0.222	-0.633
	Kazakhstan	-0.870	-0.586	-0.980	-0.795	-0.509	-0.560
	Kyrgyzstan	-0.904	-0.429	-0.787	-0.814	0.372	-0.391
	Montenegro	-0.770	-0.664	-0.979	-1.060	-0.701	-0.572
	Republic of Moldova	-0.772	-0.571	-0.931	-0.586	0.737	-0.039
	Romania	1.576	1.306	0.939	0.616	1.669	0.568
	Russian Federation	1.766	2.201	0.841	2.230	0.442	0.446
	Serbia	-0.699	-0.033	-0.980	-0.887	-0.220	-0.272
	Tajikistan	-0.967	-0.527	-1.001	-1.020	-0.814	-0.571
	The former Yugoslav Republic of Macedonia	-0.704	-0.369	-0.943	-0.683	-0.603	-0.148
	Turkmenistan	-0.670	-0.142	-0.991	-0.846	-0.992	-0.737
	Ukraine	1.537	1.071	-0.942	1.276	1.239	0.464
	Uzbekistan	-1.013	0.296	-0.991	-0.630	-0.792	-0.732
	Yugoslavia	-1.167	-0.968	-0.446	-0.945	-0.913	-0.326
	REGION AVERAGE	**-0.038**	**0.065**	**-0.706**	**-0.257**	**-0.072**	**-0.160**
Reformed West	Denmark	1.085	2.615	2.415	2.567	1.947	1.220
	Finland	0.562	1.270	0.759	2.177	1.011	3.217
	Germany	0.411	1.914	1.683	1.879	3.415	1.520
	Iceland	0.424	0.683	0.902	1.028	-0.130	0.299
	Ireland	-0.579	1.012	0.342	0.964	0.524	1.170
	Netherlands	0.067	1.709	2.814	1.745	1.470	0.552
	Norway	1.983	2.624	3.048	4.178	0.319	3.940
	Sweden	2.850	3.130	2.253	3.183	2.288	8.243
	Switzerland	-0.259	1.410	1.833	1.907	3.534	1.593
	United Kingdom	0.478	2.629	2.849	2.304	4.132	2.608
	REGION AVERAGE	**0.702**	**1.900**	**1.890**	**2.193**	**1.851**	**2.436**
Returned West	Croatia	-0.016	0.019	-0.902	-0.221	0.265	-0.191
	Czech Republic	-0.585	0.324	-0.092	0.366	1.260	0.159
	Estonia	-0.256	-0.428	-0.815	-0.490	-0.662	0.016
	Hungary	2.697	4.262	1.610	1.557	1.811	1.849
	Latvia	0.054	-0.216	-0.815	0.205	0.400	-0.397
	Lithuania	-0.725	-0.404	-0.925	-0.508	0.327	-0.640
	Poland	1.735	0.880	0.797	0.374	0.174	0.956
	Slovakia	-0.696	0.095	-0.106	0.304	0.989	1.063
	Slovenia	-0.422	-0.323	-0.114	0.050	0.796	-0.215
	REGION AVERAGE	**0.198**	**0.467**	**-0.151**	**0.182**	**0.595**	**0.289**

Sinic East	China	0.194	–0.095	0.160	0.830	–0.726	0.049
	Democratic People's Republic of Korea	–0.569	–1.201	–0.976	–0.707	–0.747	–0.865
	Japan	–0.762	1.680	0.434	1.149	1.966	0.691
	Mongolia	1.517	2.106	–0.691	–0.334	0.322	–0.485
	Republic of Korea	–0.190	0.055	0.059	–0.047	0.021	–0.254
	Viet Nam	–0.270	–0.520	–0.882	0.005	–0.882	–0.476
	REGION AVERAGE	**–0.013**	**0.337**	**–0.316**	**0.149**	**–0.008**	**–0.223**
Sub-Saharan Africa	Angola	–0.450	–1.318	–0.544	–1.068	–0.733	–0.532
	Benin	0.274	–0.191	–0.488	–0.476	–0.405	–0.200
	Botswana	–1.103	–0.011	–0.104	–0.426	–0.191	0.036
	Burkina Faso	0.367	–0.389	–0.076	–0.246	0.772	–0.166
	Burundi	0.368	0.931	0.085	0.824	0.444	0.542
	Cameroon	0.062	–0.525	–0.042	0.126	0.202	–0.256
	Cape Verde	0.099	–0.676	–0.942	–0.692	–1.020	–0.535
	Central African Republic	–0.775	–0.685	–0.074	–0.888	0.098	0.331
	Chad	0.114	–0.390	–0.502	–0.645	0.309	–0.246
	Comoros	–1.150	–0.835	–0.981	–0.803	–1.017	–0.644
	Congo	–0.745	–1.157	–0.629	–0.839	0.310	–0.046
	Cote d'Ivoire	–0.775	–0.104	–0.040	–0.455	–0.349	0.014
	Democratic Republic of the Congo	–0.154	–0.503	–0.586	0.027	–0.668	–0.216
	Djibouti	–0.450	–0.876	–0.113	–0.744	–0.492	–0.589
	Eritrea	–1.157	–1.176	–0.987	–0.948	–1.041	–0.780
	Ethiopia	0.670	–0.671	0.013	–0.533	–0.982	–0.509
	Gabon	–0.059	0.024	–0.061	–0.728	1.764	–0.187
	Gambia	–0.298	–0.383	–0.512	–0.288	–0.703	–0.600
	Ghana	0.704	0.422	0.028	0.201	–0.174	1.221
	Guinea	0.932	–0.626	–0.066	–0.155	0.687	0.851
	Guinea-Bissau	–0.584	–0.728	–0.110	–0.827	–0.452	–0.677
	Kenya	0.183	0.342	–0.044	0.116	0.000	–0.435
	Lesotho	–0.458	0.364	–0.112	–0.604	–0.420	–0.454
	Liberia	–0.118	–0.061	–0.716	–0.355	–0.686	0.490
	Madagascar	–0.173	–0.457	–0.045	–0.651	0.065	0.650
	Malawi	–0.621	0.162	–0.074	–0.597	0.628	–0.107
	Mali	0.619	0.641	–0.090	–0.219	0.706	–0.252
	Mauritania	–0.419	–0.348	–0.046	–0.620	–0.337	–0.429
	Mauritius	0.167	1.382	–0.079	0.399	–0.391	–0.447
	Mozambique	–0.765	–0.799	–0.115	–0.725	–0.465	–0.634
	Namibia	0.328	–0.898	–0.127	–0.604	–0.452	–0.510
	Niger	0.887	0.750	–0.501	0.045	–0.086	0.707
	Nigeria	0.661	0.183	–0.016	1.158	–0.380	–0.366
	Rwanda	0.089	–0.239	–0.509	–0.772	–0.704	–0.328
	Sao Tome and Principe	–0.929	–1.109	–0.977	–1.053	–1.013	–0.531

	Senegal	1.654	−0.120	−0.037	0.463	1.703	0.034
	Seychelles	0.327	0.794	−0.975	0.044	−1.017	−0.143
	Sierra Leone	−0.092	−0.547	−0.052	−0.854	−0.449	0.061
	Somalia	−0.788	−1.348	−0.942	−1.019	−1.019	−0.538
	South Africa	0.204	0.927	1.708	1.331	−0.327	0.192
	South Sudan	−1.378	−1.481	−1.018	−1.450	−1.061	−0.865
	Sudan	0.518	−0.571	−0.907	−0.388	−0.859	−0.512
	Swaziland	−0.915	−0.464	−0.115	−0.863	−0.443	−0.587
	Togo	0.464	−0.067	−0.066	−0.522	0.712	−0.308
	Uganda	1.340	−0.371	−0.072	−0.008	−0.346	−0.350
	United Republic of Tanzania	−0.125	−0.553	−0.041	−0.411	−0.443	−0.305
	Zambia	−0.144	−0.929	−0.097	−0.225	−0.416	0.362
	Zimbabwe	−0.247	−0.951	0.306	−0.471	−0.434	−0.212
	REGION AVERAGE	**−0.095**	**−0.364**	**−0.264**	**−0.418**	**−0.260**	**−0.210**

Index

T. Inoguchi, L. T. Q. Le, *The Development of Global Legislative Politics*, Trust: Interdisciplinary Perspectives 3, https://doi.org/10.1007/978-981-32-9389-2